Preparing to Teach in Secondary Schools

Preparing to Teach in Secondary Schools

A student teacher's guide to professional issues in secondary education

Fourth edition

Edited by Ian Abbott, Prue Huddleston and David Middlewood

 Open University Press

Open University Press
McGraw-Hill Education
8th Floor, 338 Euston Road
London
England
NW1 3BH

and Two Penn Plaza, New York, NY 10121-2289, USA

First published 2019

Commissioning Editor: Hannah Kenner
Development Editor: Tom Payne
Editorial Assistant: Karen Harris
Content Product Manager: Ali Davis

A catalogue record of this book is available from the British Library

ISBN-13: 9780335227129
ISBN-10: 0335227120
eISBN: 9780335228515

Library of Congress Cataloging-in-Publication Data
CIP data applied for

Typeset by Transforma Pvt. Ltd., Chennai, India

Contents

Figures and tables

Figures

Tables

Notes on contributors

Ian Abbott is an associate professor at the University of Warwick's Centre for Education Studies. He was formerly the Director of the Centre and before that led the Institute of Education at Warwick. Prior to higher education, he worked in schools and colleges in senior leadership roles for a number of years. He has extensive experience of initial teacher education and has worked with various external organizations, including Teach First and Teaching Leaders. He has published widely on education policy and reform, teacher education, and leadership and staff development in schools and colleges.

Isobel Ashmead is a senior teacher at a secondary school. She has had responsibility for assessment and curriculum matters in five schools over the last twenty years. She has worked in a wide variety of schools, including those facing challenging circumstances to schools in leafy suburbs. Isobel gained her MA from the University of Sussex, researching the education of girls and female choices of work. She is currently studying for her PhD at the University of Warwick, researching how head teachers get difficult messages across to their staff in times of change.

Fay Baldry taught mathematics in secondary comprehensive schools for over fifteen years before moving to posts in higher education. She is now a lecturer in education at the University of Leicester, where she is currently the subject leader for the PGCE in Secondary Mathematics and the course leader for SCITT PGCE programmes. Her research interests include exploring how teachers adapt their classroom activities for different groups of students and how this shapes the mathematics made available to learners. She also has a keen interest in the role of Lesson Study within initial teacher education, in particular the complexities involved in obtaining and analysing data through classroom observation.

Cheryl Cane began her career as an English, drama and performing arts specialist in secondary and further education. She also held a number of pastoral roles that inspired her interest in pupils-as-researchers, leading her to explore pastoral issues through pupil-led research projects. She progressed into school leadership gaining her NPQH whilst in post as Director of Arts at Avon Valley School and Performing Arts College. She moved into teacher education in 2005, working with the Warwick Institute of Education, and later became the course leader for the English and Drama PGCE. She is currently a senior teaching fellow at the University of Warwick, leading the MA in Drama and Theatre Education.

Jean Conteh has worked in multilingual contexts throughout her career, first as a primary teacher and teacher educator in different countries and then as an academic at the University of York from 2003 and Leeds University where, from 2007, she took up a senior lectureship and was in charge of PGCE Primary English. She has a particular interest in the roles of language and culture in the processes of learning, and has published many books, chapters and articles about these issues, including *The Multilingual Turn in Languages Education* (Multilingual Matters, 2014). Jean has been involved in many projects relating to researching EAL in teacher education and development.

Ruth Dann is an associate professor at University College London (UCL), Institute of Education. Previously a teacher, she has worked at both Keele University and Manchester Metropolitan University. Ruth has led initial teacher education, and worked closely with teachers at all stages of their careers. She researches and publishes in the field of assessment, particularly formative assessment. She is also involved in initiatives that promote research as relevant and accessible to teachers. For over ten years, Ruth has been chair of governors of an outstanding school. Her current work, in the Department of Curriculum, Pedagogy and Assessment at UCL, involves her in MA teaching and research supervision.

Brian Everest was deputy head of a large special school for over thirty years, including periods of being acting head. He led and managed change and developments, some of which were directly linked to statutory requirements. He was responsible for the annual review processes, in which he worked closely with the local authority as well as other stakeholders. Brian preferred to be a teaching deputy head so that he could experience the effects of many of the changes he himself had put in place in the same way his colleagues did, something he felt helped him keep his feet firmly on the ground.

Judith Everington is an associate professor at the University of Warwick's Centre for Education Studies. She has worked with beginning and experienced teachers for twenty-five years as a teacher educator, MA course leader and PhD supervisor. She is a member of the Warwick Religions and Education Research Unit and was co-director of the Warwick RE Project and the Warwick Life History RE Teachers Project. She is the author of several pupils' textbooks and teachers' handbooks and has written extensively about her research on teachers and teacher development.

Victoria Elliott is an associate professor of English and literacy education at the University of Oxford, where she teaches on the PGCE and works with teachers undertaking the MSc in Learning and Teaching. Her research is in the area of curriculum and assessment; working mainly in the area of secondary English, she has a particular interest in literature in the curriculum. Her recent research is on the representation of women authors and protagonists in set texts in the UK. Before becoming a PGCE tutor and education researcher, she worked in state schools in Yorkshire.

Paul Elliott is a professor and director of Graduate Studies in the School of Education and Professional Learning at Trent University, Ontario. He formerly coordinated the Secondary Science PGCE course at the Institute of Education at the University of Warwick. Before becoming involved in teacher education, he worked for several years at a comprehensive school in Wiltshire. His research interests are wide-ranging, including the interface between science and literacy and the development of biodiversity education. In recent years, he has been leading a movement advocating for better teacher education in environmental and sustainability education.

John Gordon is a senior lecturer at the University of East Anglia in Norwich. His research interests include English education, literary response, teachers' subject expertise, arts-based research methods and narrative inquiry. In 2017, he led the project, *Literature's Lasting Impression*, investigating reading in class and its lifelong impact on learners. He has published two monographs, *A Pedagogy of Poetry* (IOE Press, 2014) and *Teaching English in Secondary Schools* (Sage, 2015), as well as articles for international journals, including *The Curriculum Journal, English in Education* and *Educational Research* (NFER). His doctoral thesis considered learning around poetry and how children respond to poetry that they hear.

Sean Hayes is head of Children's Services Performance and Data for Hounslow Council, having worked previously in three other London councils and the Cabinet Office. A significant educational interest is the provision of high-quality performance data analysis for schools. His research interests relate to educational attainment and the intersection of social class, race and gender. He is a member of the British Educational Research Association (BERA), holding the Local Authority research portfolio, and is currently BERA treasurer. He has been writing and presenting educational research papers for over twenty years and is a governor at a secondary school in London.

Mick Hammond is an associate professor at the Centre for Education Studies at the University of Warwick. He has extensive experience of researching the use of new technology in teaching and learning and has published widely for both practice and academic audiences. His research has covered the teaching of ICT as a subject, the professional development of teachers using ICT, and the potential of online community for supporting teachers and students. He has worked in schools, led initial teacher education courses, and worked with teachers on action research and other continuing professional development projects. He has a special interest in research methods and methodologies for evaluating organizational change.

Judith Hanks started teaching in 1987 and has worked as a language teacher, teacher educator and lecturer in China, Italy, Singapore and the UK. She is now an assistant professor at the School of Education at the University of Leeds. She has been working with colleagues from Brazil, China and Japan to develop a framework of principles for practitioner research for language teachers and learners. This culminated in *The Developing Language Learner: An Introduction to Exploratory Practice* (with Dick Allwright; Palgrave Macmillan, 2009) and her most recent book, *Exploratory Practice in Language Teaching: Puzzling About Principles and Practices* (Palgrave Macmillan, 2017). Judith's research interests lie in the areas of practitioner research, teacher education, professional development and intercultural issues in language education.

Prue Huddleston is an emeritus professor and former director of the Centre for Education and Industry at the University of Warwick. Her research interests include vocational education and training, vocational qualifications, and work-related learning. She has published widely on vocational learning and applied pedagogy. Before joining the university, she was a teacher and manager within the further education sector and worked on community and outreach programmes. She is a member of AQA's Research Committee, OCR's Qualifications Committee, and City & Guilds' Quality and Standards Committee. She is an editorial board member of the *Journal of Vocational Education and Training*.

Jenni Ingram began her career as a mathematics teacher in Coventry comprehensive schools. She now leads the Mathematics PGCE course at the University of Oxford where she is an associate professor of mathematics education. Jenni teaches on the Mathematics PGCE course and the MSc Learning and Teaching. The main area of her research has been in exploring classroom interactions and the development of students' mathematical language. She also has a keen interest in issues of social justice and equity within teacher education.

Steve James is a senior leader in a state secondary school. He teaches German and politics and worked as a middle leader. He led school-based teacher training in his subject before moving to senior leadership in 2011, with a focus on training and appraisals. Steve progressed to his current SLT role in 2016, where he is a safeguarding lead and manages all pastoral work within the school. He has done much training in areas of safeguarding, including the recent emphasis on radicalization and online safety. He is also a safeguarding governor for his local primary school.

David Lambert is a professor of geography education at UCL's Institute of Education. He is a former secondary school teacher and teacher educator and, from 2001 to 2010, was chief executive of the Geographical Association. His overarching concern has been to advance understanding of the goals and purposes of geography in schools and the significance of geographical thinking for young people. Significant publications include *Teaching Geography 11–18: A Conceptual Approach*, co-written with John Morgan (Open University Press, 2010), and *Debates in Geography Education*, co-edited with Mark Jones (2nd edition; Routledge, 2017). He led the EU-funded GeoCapabilites project (www.geocapabilites.org) from 2013 to 2017, which explores the notion of powerful knowledge in school geography related to his 2014 publication with Michael Young, *Knowledge and the Future School* (Bloomsbury, 2014).

Kate Mawson is a senior teaching fellow at the University of Warwick's Centre for Teacher Education. Kate has fourteen years' secondary school teaching experience, leaving secondary teaching as an assistant head teacher. She specializes in biology, has been a lead teacher for science and has recently been awarded Chartered Science Teacher status. During her career, Kate has been continually involved in teacher education, through ITE, GTTP, Teach First, NQT and School Direct mentoring. She has published works on developing trainee teacher reflective practice, improving literacy in secondary science as well as writing articles for wider professional development and education management.

David Middlewood is a part-time research fellow at University of Warwick's Centre for Educational Studies, having worked previously at two other English universities. Prior to that, he worked in schools for many years, including being principal of a secondary comprehensive for nine years. David has published more than twenty books on a variety of education topics, including curriculum, staff leadership and management, teacher professionalism, practitioner research, dissertation writing and succession planning. His research projects have included works on leadership teams, Pupil Premium, student voice, support staff and school collaboration. David has taught and researched in various countries, including Greece, Seychelles, South Africa and New Zealand, and he has been a visiting professor in the last two.

Daniel Muijs is head of research at Ofsted and a visiting professor at the University of Southampton. Previously, he worked at the University of Southampton as Professor of Education. Daniel is an expert in educational effectiveness and quantitative research methods, and has published widely in the fields of school and teacher effectiveness. He is co-editor of the journal *School Effectiveness and School Improvement*, and member of the Executive Council of the European Association for Research on Learning and Instruction.

Faith Muir is a former senior lecturer (Teach First) at Canterbury Christ Church University, tutoring ITE students in London schools. She has also supervised candidates preparing MA dissertations at the Centre for Education Studies at the University of Warwick, where she is studying for a PhD. Previously, as regional director with the Centre for Education and Industry at Warwick, and as former head of music, TVEI (technical and vocational education initiative) coordinator and EBP (Education Business Partnership) manager, she gained substantial experience of working with government departments, professional organizations, businesses, schools, colleges and universities. Her research interests include 14–19 curriculum/qualification reform and enactment, particularly regarding the EPQ (Extended Project Qualification).

Andrea Pitt taught mathematics for many years in Warwickshire and the West Midlands, including several years as head of mathematics. She now works in teacher education, specifically the Teaching Advanced Mathematics course at the University of Warwick and as a tutor on the PGCE course at the University of Leicester. Her research interests include the professional development of mathematics teachers and social justice issues in school mathematics.

Lynn Reynolds taught secondary science for a number of years before moving to the University of Warwick, where she worked across the secondary PGCE and MA in Educational Studies. She moved to the University of Birmingham as a lecturer in science education and has now returned to the classroom.

Robert Sharples has worked with multilingual young people in the UK, Canada and Australia. He is a teaching fellow at the University of Edinburgh's Moray House School of Education, where he teaches on MA and MSc programmes in language education. Robert's research examines the impact of global mobility on education and language learning, with a particular focus on EAL learners and young migrants. He is the editor of the *EAL Journal*.

Kate Shilvock is a former associate professor at the Institute of Education at the University of Warwick, where she was course leader for the secondary PGCE in English with Drama and led the core professional studies course. A former head of English in Warwickshire, she has substantial experience of teaching in secondary schools across the country.

Sarah Younie is a professor of education at De Montfort University and a visiting senior research fellow at the University of Bedfordshire. She has been involved in international research on educational technologies and teaching for twenty-five years, including the EU-funded projects, 'European Schoolnet Multimedia', 'Schoolscape of the Future' and 'Web@classroom'. Sarah has been chair of the Association for IT in Teacher Education and gathered evidence for the Parliamentary Select Committee Inquiry into Education. Sarah has presented research papers at international conferences, produced articles on ICT and education, and recently published a co-authored book with Marilyn Leask, *Teaching with Technologies: The Essential Guide* (Open University Press, 2013).

Acronyms and abbreviations

AfL	Assessment for learning
A8	Attainment 8
AL	Advanced Level
AS-Level	Advanced Subsidiary Level
AOC	Association of Colleges
AQA	Assessment and Qualifications Alliance
ARG	Assessment Reform Group
ASD	Autistic spectrum disorder
ASP	Analyse School Performance
BESD	Behavioural, emotional and social difficulties
BICS	Basic interpersonal communication skills
BTEC	Business and Technology Education Council diploma
CAF	Common assessment framework
CALP	Cognitive academic language proficiency
CAMHS	Child and Adolescent Mental Health Services
CASE	Cognitive Acceleration in Science Education
CAT	Cognitive ability test
CBI	Confederation of British Industry
CEO	Chief executive officer
CIP	Cognitive information processing
CLA	Children looked after
CPD	Continuous professional development
CSE	Certificate of Secondary Education
CUP	Common underlying proficiency
CUREE	Centre for the Use of Research & Evidence in Education
CYPU	Children and Young People's Unit
DARTS	Directed activities for reading and thinking
D&T	Design and technology
DBIS	Department for Business Innovation and Skills
DCSF	Department for Children, Schools and Families
DES	Department for Education and Science
DfE	Department for Education

DfEE	Department for Education and Employment
DfES	Department for Education and Skills
DoH	Department of Health
EAL	English as an additional language
EBD	Emotional and behavioural difficulties
EBI	Even Better If
EBacc	English Baccalaureate
ECM	Every Child Matters
EFA	Education Funding Agency
EHA	Early Help Assessment
ERA	Education Reform Act
ESFA	Education and Skills Funding Agency
FBVs	Fundamental British values
FE	Further education
FFT	Fischer Family Trust
FSM	Free school meals
GCSE	General Certificate of Secondary Education
GLHs	Guided learning hours
HI	Hearing impairment
HLTA	Higher level teaching assistant
ICT	Information and communications technology
IEP	Individual Education Plan
IET	Institution of Engineering and Technology
ILP	Individual Learning Plan
IQ	Intelligence quotient
ITE	Initial teacher education
ITT	Initial teacher training
IWB	Interactive whiteboard
KS	Key Stage
LAC	Literacy across the curriculum
LGBT	Lesbian, gay, bisexual or transgender
MAGT	More able, gifted and talented
MASH	Multi-agency safeguarding hub
MAT	Multi-Academy Trust
MI	Multiple intelligences
MiDYIS	Middle years information system
MIS	Management information system
MLD	Moderate learning difficulty
MSI	Multi-sensory impairment
NC	National Curriculum
NHS	National Health Service
NNS	National Numeracy Strategy
NQT	Newly qualified teacher
OECD	Organization for Economic and Cultural Development
OCR	Oxford Cambridge and RSA Examination
OSR	Occupational Stress Ratings
Ofqual	Office of Qualifications and Examinations Regulation

Ofsted	Office for Standards in Education
PD	Physical disability
PE	Physical education
P8	Progress 8
PGCE	Postgraduate Certificate in Education
PISA	Programme for International Student Assessment
PMLD	Profound and multiple learning difficulties
PPG	Pupil Premium Grant
PSE	Personal and social education
PSHE	Personal, social and health education
PSHEE	Personal, social, health and economic education
PTA	Parent–Teacher Association
QCA	Qualifications and Curriculum Authority
QTS	Qualified teacher status
RAISE	Reporting and Analysis for Improvement through Schools' Self-evaluation
RE	Religious education
RPA	Raising of the participation age
RSA	Royal Society of Arts
SCAA	Schools and Curriculum Assessment Authority
SEAL	Social and emotional aspects of learning
SEN	Special educational needs
SENCo	Special educational needs coordinator
SEND	Special educational needs and disability
SENDCo	Special educational needs and disabilities coordinator
SLCN	Speech, language and communication needs
SLD	Severe learning difficulty
SMCD	Spiritual, moral and cultural development
SMSC	Spiritual, moral, social and cultural
SORTT	Support, Outcome, Resource, Task and Team
SoW	Scheme of work
SpLD	Specific learning difficulties
STEM	Science, technology, engineering and maths
TA	Teaching assistant
TPaCK	Technological, pedagogical and content knowledge
TQT	Total qualification time
UPN	Unique Pupil Number
UTC	University Technical College
VI	Visual impairment
VLE	Virtual learning environment
WWW	What Went Well
ZPD	Zone of proximal development

Introduction

Ian Abbott, Prue Huddleston and David Middlewood

Content and organization

This book has been written for those individuals preparing to teach in secondary schools. It is intended to complement your subject studies by covering a range of core professional topics with which all teachers need to be familiar, irrespective of their subject specialism. The teaching profession is at a point of considerable transformation: national policies designed to make initial training and continuing professional development increasingly school-based; shifting relationships with para-professionals and other adults in the classroom; new ways of relating to other children's services; fresh opportunities and threats created by technological advances; novel approaches to teaching in the light of brain-based research; changes to the curriculum and methods of assessment; new thinking on teachers' professionalism and teacher leadership; data-rich approaches to managing school and pupil performance; reductions to funding; and issues surrounding teacher recruitment and retention. The origins of some of these developments are to be found in academic research. The impetus for others is policy initiative at government level – part of an ongoing drive to raise standards of education nationally. Taken together, these developments have greatly expanded the core curriculum for initial teacher training. Their implications for those about to enter the profession – the opportunities and challenges they present – are an important feature of this book.

The book is divided into four parts:

- **Part 1:** Becoming a Teacher
- **Part 2:** Core Professional Competences
- **Part 3:** Secondary Schools and the Curriculum
- **Part 4:** Making schools work for all: *Every Child Matters*, Safeguarding and the Inclusion Agenda

Those new to teaching may be most familiar with teaching as a classroom activity. The three chapters in **Part 1** seek to broaden your perspective, placing teaching in its wider professional context and drawing attention to issues and challenges that student teachers will face. Chapter 1 addresses your most immediate challenge – that of learning to teach! It draws on research into teachers' early professional development to elucidate this process.

Chapter 2 widens the context by exploring the legal and professional framework for teaching, and professional values and practice. Chapter 3 looks beyond your period of initial training to highlight the range of opportunities, issues and challenges that new teachers will encounter as they embark on their early professional development. A key theme in Part 1 is the importance of regarding initial teacher training not as an end in itself, but as the opening phase in a teacher's ongoing professional development.

Having set the scene in Part 1, the nine chapters in **Part 2** adopt a classroom focus. They examine some of the core professional competences – the knowledge, skills and understanding – that newly qualified teachers need to acquire. Chapter 4 opens by exploring the fundamental question of how learning takes place. The remaining chapters consider how different aspects of teaching, such as planning and differentiation, can be used to support learning.

In **Part 3**, the focus shifts to the secondary school curriculum. The opening chapter, 'What should we teach? Understanding the secondary curriculum' (Chapter 13), provides a conceptual framework for the following chapters by discussing some of the basic concepts of curriculum thinking. The remaining chapters consider government initiatives across all three Key Stages of the secondary curriculum (ages 11–19). Ways in which schools provide for pupils' spiritual, moral and cultural development are also explored (Chapter 14).

Part 4 concludes the book by considering major components of recent government policy and the inclusion agenda, under the heading 'Making Schools Work for All'. As well as examining some of the more enduring aspects of the inclusion agenda such as provision for pupils with special educational needs (Chapter 21), closing the attainment gap (Chapter 24) and pastoral care (Chapter 25), this section discusses some of the latest national initiatives, including provision for the introduction of new types of state secondary schools (Chapter 26).

It is natural to adopt a narrow focus centred on oneself when learning to teach. However, education is not divorced from its broader social and political contexts, and the impacts of social change and political reforms make themselves powerfully felt in schools. This is especially true at the time of writing of this book, 2017–2018. Thus, it is important to recognize the likely impact of these factors on your work as a teacher. In 1960, the then-minister of education, Sir David Eccles, described the curriculum as a 'secret garden' (Hansard, 1960). The notion of the curriculum, or indeed most other aspects of education, as the preserve of educationalists has long since faded in policy circles. Indeed, change seems to be a constant feature of education and many elements of the education system are currently subject to major reform. Throughout the book, you will find references to proposed changes. In some cases, the nature of the reform has already been determined; in others, the changes are still the subject of consultation, making the future uncertain. In all cases, the longer-term impact of this overhaul of the system remains to be seen. By the time you read this book, evidence of the impact will be accumulating, enabling you to judge whether intended consequences are materializing.

Ways of using this book

This book can be read in more than one way. It is possible to read it in its entirety, for instance as an introductory text at the start of your training. However, it is really intended for repeated reference throughout a course of study. To this end, each chapter is a self-contained entity, focusing on a specific topic and designed to be read as and when appropriate. For instance, you may read the chapter on 'Planning for Learning' (Chapter 5) when you first attempt to construct lesson plans, whereas you may consult the chapter on 'Using Assessment Data to Support Pupil Achievement' (Chapter 10) as part of your preparation for a written assignment on this topic. Chapters are cross-referenced to related material elsewhere in the text to help you to pursue specific interests.

This book is intended primarily for postgraduate students who are preparing to teach in secondary schools. It assumes an educated but non-expert audience. Therefore, imparting basic factual information about topics with which readers may be unfamiliar is an important feature of the book. However, this text was not designed simply to be read to gain information. Reading is meant to be an *active* rather than a *passive* process, so readers are invited to engage with the text and respond to it. Various stylistic features are designed to encourage you to do this. For instance, each chapter opens with a set of objectives to be achieved by the end of the chapter. Where we hope to challenge you to think about complex, sensitive or contentious issues, we may ask questions or provide case studies for consideration. Where we want to help you to further your knowledge or skills, we may set tasks or direct you to websites, as well as making recommendations for further reading. Practical examples are used throughout to make abstract or unfamiliar ideas concrete and meaningful. Where appropriate, chapters provide a brief historical context or an outline of government policy to help make sense of a subject.

The text contains a mix of tasks, case studies and scenarios designed to help you to address issues that are raised and the practical application of ideas. Occasionally, chapters open with a question or a task, requiring you to engage directly with a topic from the outset. The majority of tasks are designed to be self-contained, enabling you to complete them there and then, without the need for additional resources. For instance, if a task requires you to analyse pupil performance data, a suitable example will be provided for that purpose. You are, of course, welcome to use your own materials if you have some to hand, but being able to complete a task will not depend on this in most instances. Some of the tasks do, however, require internet access and several are school-based.

A note on terminology

Like all other professional activities, education has its own 'shorthand', which can appear as jargon to those to whom it is unfamiliar. Terms that have a specialized meaning in education, separate from their everyday use, are explained at their first mention. Education also has its fair share of acronyms for the uninitiated to become acquainted with! When a commonly used acronym is introduced, it is spelt out in full on the first occasion it is used in each chapter, with the abbreviation used thereafter. Acronyms and abbreviations are also listed at the front of the book.

Many schools refer to their pupils as students. Trainee teachers are also sometimes described as students. To avoid confusing the two, we use the term 'student' to denote only those who are learning to teach. The young people who student teachers will teach are described as 'pupils' or 'children'.

The aim of this book is to promote a reflective approach to initial training among its readers. We hope you find it a useful aid to your early professional development and the beginning of your teaching career.

PART 1
Becoming a Teacher

1

Learning to be a teacher

David Middlewood

1.1 Introduction

As you begin your teacher training, you have already taken one of the most significant decisions of your life – you have decided that you want to become a professional teacher! This chapter, like others in Part 1, sets out things you may want to consider and may find useful about the training and years ahead as a teacher. The thing that you will be mainly focused on, of course, is *teaching* and most of your time will be spent doing that. But, being a teacher involves much more than teaching in the classroom because, as we will explore in this chapter, as a teacher you are a member of the teaching profession.

By the end of this chapter, you should:

- be aware of what is required of you as a teacher and how your training will help in this;
- begin to consider your approach to professional development.

1.2 The personal challenge

Teaching is both a very challenging profession and an extremely rewarding one. At times, it will be tough, but it can also bring the greatest satisfaction and be all the more satisfying *because* it is challenging. One thing to remember is that there is no single set model of the kind of person that is a teacher. Although there are certain key skills and competencies that need to be mastered, an effective teacher can, as a person, be anyone from a whole range of personalities – as any staffroom will quickly show. Teaching is a job in which the kind of person you are plays a huge part in the way you do the job, which is why the best teachers are said to 'put themselves into' it. Self-knowledge therefore is crucial to your development as a teacher and is vital to self-development, something that you will focus on in your training year.

What are some of the things that you need to know about yourself? Questions such as these are worth reflecting on:

- What values are important to me? (the moral challenge)
- Am I an effective learner? (the learning challenge)
- Do I know enough? (the cognitive/intellectual challenge)

- What do other people – adults and pupils – think of me? (the confidence challenge)
- How do I cope when problems occur? (the resilience challenge)

And there are practical concerns as well, such as:

- What are the biggest challenges I will face?
- Will I get enough support when I need it?

And, no doubt, many others.

Because teaching is something into which the person puts their whole sense of themselves, it is important to be prepared to reassess the attitudes, feelings, beliefs, assumptions and prejudices that we all hold about ourselves and the job we plan to do. Everyone has been to school and had a schooling experience that has influenced them in a variety of ways and helped to shape their thinking about teaching and learning.

1.2.1 The moral dimension

Task 1.1

Carefully read each of the following statements made by people entering their year of training to be a teacher. What do you think each one says about the person's approach to teaching and which one(s) are closest to your own (if any)?

A. 'I think good teaching is ultimately about acquiring a set of particular skills that enable you to do a good job for the pupils who are your responsibility. Obviously, you need to update your skills regularly.'
B. 'I see myself as a member of a profession that is committed to education, which is a basic human right. Everything else is subordinate to that.'
C. 'My job will be to enable young people to learn, so that they leave school ready to go on learning in adult life, and hopefully for all their life.'
D. 'Basically, whether we like it or not, teachers today are civil servants, paid by the government, and it is our job to carry out national policies whatever we think of them.'
E. 'I want to be a teacher to help children and young people develop and grow into decent and responsible adults who can help to create a better society. It may sound idealistic but what else is education for?'

It is interesting to think about what kind of teacher a person who holds each of these views might be, both in the classroom and in the profession at large.

1.2.2 The learning dimension

Understanding how to learn from experience and accepting that different people learn in different ways is important to you and your understanding of others. According to Honey (1988), learning from experience involves four stages:

1. *Having the experience*: some people are reactive, letting the experience come to them; some are proactive, deliberately seeking out an experience.
2. *Reviewing the experience*: this is basically looking back over the experience, not being judgemental but learning from it.
3. *Concluding from the experience*: drawing sound conclusions, not jumping to them!
4. *Planning the next steps*: turning some of the conclusions into a programme for future action.

There has been a great deal of research into learning styles. One of the best known pieces is Honey and Mumford's (1989) categorization of learners into four types. These are:

- Activist
- Reflector
- Theorist
- Pragmatist.

You can find out about the self-analysis exercises through the Honey and Mumford Learning Styles Questionnaire, but Table 1.1 provides a simplified guide.

Of course, human beings are more complex than such a simplification would suggest, and most people tend to use at least two of these styles much more than the other two. This is important because each learning style has its own drawbacks if practised solely as the one way of learning. For example, activists can sometimes take unnecessary risks and can rush into things, whereas reflectors can be slow to reach decisions, and are often not assertive enough. Theorists can be restricted in their lateral thinking, and distrustful of any subjective feelings, whereas pragmatists tend to be impatient with any kind of what they see as 'waffle', and can ignore the implications for people in their focus on getting things done.

I am someone who:	This means that I tend towards:
<ul><li>enjoys surprises and the unknown;</li><li>believes that the best ideas tend to come from gut feelings;</li><li>is a better talker than listener; and</li><li>tends to live for the present rather than the future.</li></ul>	The activist style of learning. You are happy to experiment and are optimistic about trying out new things
<ul><li>is mostly careful and methodical;</li><li>is a good listener; and</li><li>does not tend to jump to conclusions.</li></ul>	The reflector learner
<ul><li>is a logical thinker;</li><li>is rational; and</li><li>is good at asking questions.</li></ul>	The theorist learner
<ul><li>focuses on technique;</li><li>is practical and realistic; and</li><li>likes to test things out.</li></ul>	The pragmatist learner

Table 1.1 Honey and Mumford learner types

It is a good idea to try to modify your own learning approach as you gain experience: not only do you increase your own learning awareness, but you gain insight into other people's learning. Jones (2005) warns against going to extremes in expanding your learning approaches and suggests moving from your 'comfort' zone to a 'stretch' zone (where you test your ability to improve in one area) but to avoid the 'panic' zone, where you find yourself in situations way beyond your capability.

During your training year, it is a good idea (and you may be asked to do this) to keep a record or write an account of situations or problems that you have encountered. You can then write down the conclusions you reached in reviewing the situation. These conclusions then become your learning points and can form the basis of what you may do next time. This reviewing is fundamental because, if you merely solve the immediate problem by adjusting, you are in effect firefighting, rather than developing strategies – which, as a professional, is what you need to do.

1.2.3 The cognitive/intellectual dimension

'A sound knowledge and understanding of the subject you are planning to teach is a prerequisite for teaching it competently and confidently' (Brooks, 2012: 9). Although you will correctly spend much time developing and consolidating your subject knowledge, you will need to know how to make this knowledge meaningful and interesting for secondary school-age pupils. You may be fired with enthusiasm for certain topics, having studied them in-depth for three years as part of a degree course, but your pupils have not, and you need to consider what they will find difficult and whether there are any common misconceptions of which you should be aware. Other aspects of your knowledge are referred to in Chapter 2.

1.2.4 The confidence dimension

Pupils in the classroom need to feel secure, that things are under control, in order for them to focus on their learning. Feeling insecure is a huge threat to effective learning. This is equally true of teaching! One of a beginner teacher's biggest worries is whether they can manage pupil behaviour in the classroom. Macrae and Quintrell (2001: 153) suggest that whether a teacher actually feels confident or not is immaterial: 'if they appear in control they may be halfway there'. It is therefore important to present an image of being confidently in charge, not by pretending but by knowing about boundaries regarding what is and is not acceptable. This takes some time and can be learned through your experiences in training.

1.2.5 The resilience dimension

Resilience, along with resourcefulness and reflection, can be described as one of the 'three Rs' of schooling today (Brooks, 2012), compared with the traditional ones of Reading, writing and arithmetic. Resilience is the ability not to be deterred by setbacks, which are inevitable, but to learn from them. Some of these setbacks will be caused by the teacher's own mistakes and some will just happen through bad luck, bad timing, a colleague's error, a school policy fault, and so on. Such setbacks can occur at any stage of a teaching career, such as rejection of a job application, but the key component of this kind of resilience is not the ability to absorb the setback and 'bounce back', but to learn how to avoid letting it happen again, if at all possible. It is the quality that the teacher is trying to encourage in pupil learners, thus stressing once more how important it is for teachers to be learners!

1.3 Developing as a learner

As well as understanding about yourself as a learner (referred to earlier), it is important that you have an idea about how skills can be acquired as you gain experience. Dubin (1964) developed a model, regularly adapted by others, which suggests there are four basic stages that we all move through as we learn new skills:

1. The first is the 'unconscious incompetent', where we do not know something, but we do not know we are ignorant!
2. The second is that of the 'conscious incompetent'. This is a critical stage where we are the most conducive to learning, because we are aware that we do not know certain things and therefore are in a position to want to do something about it.
3. The third stage is when we begin to try out the new skills we have acquired and, as we use them, we do so self-consciously and carefully, making sure we are getting it right. This is the stage that many will reach during training in school practice, where we are doing things correctly and are consciously feeling our way with them.
4. The fourth stage is of the 'unconscious competent', where we are doing things using those skills almost instinctively, without thinking very much about it in advance. Much of what we do in our lives eventually becomes like this in the areas in which we have become proficient. However, there are some dangers here because at some point we can just assume we are doing something well and may not notice when we are not. Fortunately, in teaching, if a teacher of many years' experience is almost on autopilot and is in danger of assuming what worked last time will automatically work next time, a new set of pupils will make them very aware when it does not!

Learning to drive is an apt analogy. Most people start knowing they have it all to learn (consciously incompetent). As they progress, they learn the various techniques, but are very conscious of what they are doing, up to and including the driving test (consciously competent). Having passed the test, most drivers operate on autopilot when they get into their cars, driving without thinking about techniques (unconsciously competent). However, accident research shows over 70% of drivers are not as good as they think they are and many tell the police they were doing nothing wrong (unconsciously incompetent!).

Thus, if we can become aware of our strengths and weaknesses in learning, we are more able to develop strategies for our development as we progress through a career.

Task 1.2

Make a note of any skills that you think you have that you do not have to think about when you use them (unconsciously competent). Which ones do you think will be useful to you as a teacher?

Now make a list of those skills that you know you need to develop because you feel you are not very good in that area (consciously incompetent). How do you hope to improve there? What help will you need?

1.4 Developing as a teacher

As in any profession, you will pass through various stages in your development. You may already have ambitions to rise to a particular post or level, or you may be preparing to take everything one step at a time. In either case, it is likely that you may pass through the teaching career phases shown in Table 1.2.

At this stage, you are of course likely to be focused on Phase A only, and even this can be seen to be divided into its own discrete phases, such as the following (based on Furlong and Maynard, 1995):

1. Starting as more idealistic. Having a personal educational philosophy, which you perhaps try to apply.
2. Facing reality in the classroom. You may find that educational philosophy challenged by the need to fit in with school routines, so personal professional 'survival' becomes the main aim.
3. You face the difficulties encountered and begin to find what seems to work for you.
4. Having reached a certain level of competence and confidence, you establish routines that use these because they provide security.
5. The most successful teachers recognize the need to move beyond this and are probably entering Phase B.

Of course, each trainee and each teacher is a unique person, so none of these phases are in any way fixed, and it is certainly not possible to ascribe periods of time to any one phase that fits teachers in general. What is helpful about such models is that, when an individual is encountering difficulties for example, they are able to see that they are in a similar position to the many others who have moved though such phases and effectively progressed.

Phase	Features
A. Initiation	Discovering ability to manage classrooms, finding out what works and establishing your own persona as a teacher
B. Consolidation	Taking on more responsibility, especially at subject level, developing increasing confidence and becoming more flexible in approaches to teaching
C. Autonomous	Possibly taking on responsibilities across the school, developing management and leadership skills and your ability to mentor others, and looking for other opportunities
D. Plateau	Deciding to remain and further consolidate at this level or aspire to wider responsibilities through promotion
E. Easing down	A winding down and settling as ready for exit, considering part-time employment or looking at activities beyond teaching

Table 1.2 Phases of a career

1.5 Approaching professional development

As classroom teaching is such a complex and dynamic job, with its multidimensional perspectives and unpredictability, it has been likened to having to 'keep all the plates spinning at the same time'. A commitment to continuous professional learning is imperative to be able to manage the inevitable changes that occur in education, in school society and its expectations, and of course in adolescents and young people. This is commonly called continuous professional development, or CPD. This is not only important for yourself but for the whole profession – and some would argue for education itself. Fullan (2001: 41) said that 'teacher development and school development go hand in hand; you cannot have one without the other'.

There will be various key people to help you in this, especially in training and your early years, such as mentors, tutors and more experienced colleagues. The best people are those who will try to give you the right balance of support and challenge. They will be those who do not solve problems for you but who help you learn to tackle them yourself. Such people tend to encourage you to:

* look for alternatives rather than for a quick fix;
* learn from your mistakes;
* take responsibility;
* ask you for your ideas about solutions first.

Let us now consider some of the ways in which teachers can develop professionally.

1.5.1 Reflection

The notion of the 'reflective practitioner' is an important one because, as already mentioned, being able to reflect on one's own – and perhaps others' – practice and draw out any points or conclusions from this reflection is at the heart of effective learning. It is not true to say that you always need a quiet space and time to engage in real reflection – teaching is often too hectic for that! More important is the determination to reflect and the ability to do so. As you gain more confidence and establish personal routines, you may find yourself becoming more adept at reflecting while you work; for example, you improve something you do in class simply by considering carefully why something did not work quite as you wanted and deciding to change it, even later in the same lesson. For example, a trainee teacher might come to realize during a lesson that, 'Perhaps I am going at this the wrong way and that is why they are not responding. I need to phrase this differently next time.'

Of course, quiet reflection is essential at times, away from the hurly-burly of the classroom or school, and sometimes before or after a discussion with a mentor, tutor or colleague. Without reflection, there is a risk of seeming to cast about trying one thing after another until you hit on what appears to be the right one! Reflection involves asking oneself *why* something went wrong and looking at that cause so that it can be addressed, not merely the surface outcome.

Some educationalists and philosophers go so far as to say that, without reflection, there can be no change. This is because reflective practice implies the ability to conceptualize, analyse, establish causal relationships and draw conclusions (Bowring-Carr and West-Burnham, 1997). It is certainly true of individuals, including teachers.

1.5.2 Reading and study

Reading continues to play a part in the development of many teachers as they progress through their careers. Some subjects, of course, require a good deal more reading than others, and all trainees and teachers are different from one another. Some cannot manage without having some reading at hand; others have been known to say they are glad they do not have to do so much reading now they are qualified! However, in supporting the reflective practitioner, reading can provide new ideas and perspectives, as well as new information. Indeed, in a fast-changing world, new things come along very quickly and regularly, and it is essential to try to keep up with as much as possible. There are several different types of reading literature and, because we are different, we will find some types more naturally interesting to us than others:

- Obviously, every secondary teacher will have to read *official* literature, especially at school level such as syllabuses, departmental handbooks, school policy statements, and so on. At national level, the literature setting out examination requirements, Ofsted requirements and some government papers often needs to be consulted.
- Then there is what is known as *normative* literature. In any bookshop, you can find books offering apparently easy solutions to issues at work. For example, books on successful meetings or how to control children are plentiful. Such books are usually written by people using their own experience, and often in a world different from your own in education. While such books often sell well and may contain a useful practical tip for a trainee, they need to be treated with great caution – for obvious reasons.
- Some literature concerns itself with setting out theories or models as a way of offering insights into issues, and these prove fascinating and often helpful to those who like to think deeply about issues. Thus, if you become very interested in the way children learn (as discussed in Chapter 4), you may want to explore this through such reading.
- Another category of valuable literature for trainees and teachers is research-based literature. Such literature is helpful because you can see the evidence that was collected, which may have led to a theory being formed.
- And, of course, particularly if you embark on a course of further study to gain a Master's degree for example, there are various books devoted to the notions of research methods.

I have referred to books, but the reading of articles in relevant journals is hugely important and usually less expensive! Journals in education abound, whether practitioner journals including subject-specific ones or those published by teacher unions and professional associations. Most schools subscribe to various journals and these can prove a valuable source of reading to trainee teachers and, indeed, teachers at any stage in their career.

It would be remiss of me to end a section on reading without referring to the value to many people of simply reading for pleasure. This can include fictional literature, and it is always interesting to hear so many trainee teachers say how much they loved reading 'school stories' when they were younger!

1.5.3 Conducting in-house inquiries

A powerful approach to professional development is that of making it needs-led. The more specifically any programme of training or development can be targeted at an individual's personal professional needs, the more effective it is likely to be. This is because we, as individuals, identify most strongly with training when we perceive it as being most relevant to us personally. Sometimes these needs can be seen as relevant to a whole school, and that therefore includes us as individuals; sometimes it might be a focus on a subject department's needs that have been identified as relevant to all departmental members. For example, a school priority and/or a departmental priority may be mentioned as part of the coming year's plan, in which case it is logical to have at least some training focused on that priority. Nevertheless, perhaps especially in the early years of teaching, the identification of one's development needs and the provision of training or development to meet those needs, on an individual or departmental level, can be of the upmost help in progression as a teacher. Let us now look at this in more detail.

Some secondary schools are well-advanced in terms of being what is often known as a 'research-based' or 'research-led' community, where staff members regularly carry out structured in-school inquiries to improve their own practice. However, many are not so advanced, and the practice may not be well established. It does take confidence but the impact on personal professional practice can be considerable, and it is possible for the practice to spread through a department or even a school, when it is seen to be both powerful and non-threatening.

When one reflects on discussions about the quality of teachers and teaching through the whole of the twentieth century, it is odd to note that the views of those persons most directly affected by that teaching seem almost never to be taken into account – I refer, of course, to the pupils. If anyone can offer thoughts and guidance to a teacher on possible ways of improving lessons, it is surely those who are 'on the receiving end' of those lessons! The proviso is that those thoughts and guidance must be gathered in a structured and objective way. So as not to produce simply reactive and emotional responses to a teacher's work, this way or method needs to be that of proper research. The growth in importance of pupil or student 'voice' is described in Chapter 3 as one of the issues of which new teachers need to be aware. School-based – or probably class-based – research is a logical extension of this, and one that is of the greatest importance to the pupils. Middlewood and Abbott (2015: 26–27), in their extensive research into the area of in-school inquiry, highlight the key principles that should be set out at the beginning:

- Participation should be entirely voluntary.
- Confidentiality must be respected: all data collected can only be used with the permission of those providing it.
- Privacy should be respected, and anonymity preserved in any ensuing reports arising from the research.
- Sensitivity needs to be shown: some things are too personal to be investigated.
- Any in-house rules (as well as normal legal ones) about the holding of data must be followed.

The process for in-house practitioner inquiry follows these steps:

- Choosing the topic
- Deciding on the method(s)

- Collecting the data
- Analysing that data
- Drawing conclusions
- Making recommendations
- Checking validity and noting limitations and presenting a report.

A few points need to be made here before examining possibilities. The topic should be relatively realistic and practical, probably focusing on small changes. The research design and the methods involved should also be relatively simple and carefully (1) agreed with all those involved and (2) piloted before actual use in the project. It is also useful to do a little preliminary reading on the chosen topic.

Case Study 1.1

Claire was a science teacher in her first year of teaching in a relatively new academy in the East Midlands. She encountered few behaviour problems in her classes but, although her Year 10 class seemed reasonably motivated when in class, she became worried that the homework from them (in a pre-examination year) was poor in content, poorly presented and regularly not completed. When she raised this with the class, the stock reactions were that it was 'boring', 'not worth doing' and 'didn't count in the exam'.

Case Study 1.2

Graham was a mature student in his first year of teaching history in a secondary school in a London borough. While he received satisfactory reports from his mentor and head of department, Graham felt he was not getting his pupils interested in the subject and began to see himself over the years becoming a 'boring routine teacher' (to use his own words), which was not what he had left his previous career for in his thirties to become a history teacher, a subject about which he had always been passionate.

COMMENTARY: Both Claire and Graham were willing to consider using some form of in-class inquiry to help them improve the situation, adopting the views and ideas of some of their pupils. What advice would you give as to what form such an inquiry might take? Consider some of the following points:

- What should be the focus of the inquiry? (Ask yourself carefully, 'What am I trying to find out?')
- Which pupils should be involved?
- How many pupils should be involved?

- How should the pupils be chosen?
- What research method(s) should be used – and why?
- How will you avoid 'leading questions' and remain objective?

Without relating the whole of the two stories, we can note that both inquiries included a rigorous interview with the respective teacher, where the first question was:

'What do *you* see as the point of homework/history?'

Such questions forced Claire and Graham back to the fundamental purpose of what they were doing, a sound basis for reflection on their practice. When summary reports of all the data collected had been completed, they were given to Claire and Graham. The teacher then has to reflect on issues such as:

'Do I have to change a lot or a little?'
'How does this affect me as a person?'
'Can I actually do what is being suggested?'

While difficulties may initially be encountered, and no small amount of confidence and even courage required to carry out a first in-house pupil-led inquiry of this kind, evidence shows it can be immensely rewarding for the teacher and thus the pupils.

1.6 Conclusion

Becoming a teacher means having membership of two communities. One is as a member of school staff, where you become a part of a subject group, become involved in decision-making and are expected to collaborate with colleagues. As a member of the teaching profession itself, you have a duty to try to continue to develop and improve, and this may involve relationships with colleagues from schools other than the one at which you work on a daily basis. As noted here and Chapters 2 and 3 will show, you will need to adapt as you progress and in your efforts to help pupils from all kinds of contexts and with a wide range of attitudes, ranging from excited motivation to initial indifference. The professional teacher remains the key to positive educational change and improvement, as ultimately no policies can succeed without them. By committing yourself to continuous development and being prepared to go on learning – including from any mistakes that you make – you will take responsibility for such positive improvement.

Recommendations for further reading

Middlewood, D. and Abbott, I. (2015) *Improving Professional Learning through In-House Inquiry.* London: Bloomsbury.

2

The professional framework and professional values and practice

Ian Abbott

2.1 Introduction

When you become a teacher, you do not just take up a new job, you acquire professional responsibilities and therefore need to understand the professional framework within which teachers work. There are two interlocking elements to this:

- the legal requirements and responsibilities laid on you as a teacher by the state; and
- the ethical responsibilities to uphold and exemplify certain professional values.

When preparing to become a teacher, you need to find out about these legal and professional requirements, and consider how your personal values fit with the common values espoused by the profession.

This chapter is divided into three sections: professional values and practice; teachers' legal responsibilities; and the role of school governors. These areas are inextricably linked to each other and form the statutory framework within which you will work in school.

By the end of the chapter, you should:

- understand the ways the legislative framework in which you work is evolving;
- know the duty of care that teachers have;
- understand the developing roles and responsibilities of governors and how these might affect your early professional life.

2.2 Professional values and practice

Values underpin everything that a school does: the teaching of the formal curriculum and the messages implicit in the hidden curriculum (see Chapter 13); provision for teaching and learning and extra-curricular activities; and the kind of relationships that are formed between individuals. Nothing in schools, therefore, is value-free. However, teachers and schools cannot afford to leave unexamined questions about what values underlie their practices and how widely those values are espoused by the school community.

New teachers face some difficult issues in relation to values. The first is to do with understanding the values that underpin teachers' and schools' responsibilities in the light of current legislative and policy frameworks. The second is to do with understanding how those values relate to the values of individual schools, formally expressed or informally understood. The third is to do with examining the relationship between these elements and your own values and developing strategies to resolve tensions and difficulties.

This chapter does not have any pretensions to explore general issues in the philosophy of education or to engage in an exploration of moral education (see Chapter 14 for an exploration of these). What it does do is to encourage you to consider how your own values relate to those espoused by the profession. The meaning of values has also been debated in many arenas: here it is used in the sense of the definition in the *Oxford English Dictionary*: 'one's judgement of what is valuable or important in life'. In this case, we mean what is important and valuable in the teaching profession. In considering this, we cannot detach ourselves from schools and pupils.

It is unwise to embark on the profession of teaching without having reflected on the question, 'What is the purpose of a school?' In answering it, you will progress in answering the lifelong question, 'What are my values as a teacher?'

Task 2.1

Make a note of what you consider to be the three most important purposes of secondary schools in the UK today. In each case, identify one or two values that are implied by that purpose.

Because the values that you demonstrate in your actions are visible to pupils, there is a strong link between the values you espouse as a teacher and the values that you promote to pupils. You do not exist in a vacuum, nor do the professional values you hold. For example, the Education Reform Act 1988 requires schools to provide a curriculum that pays attention to 'the spiritual, moral and cultural . . . development of pupils at school and in society [so that they may be prepared for the] opportunities, responsibilities and experiences of adult life' (ERA, 1988: 1[2]a, b). Another example of broader issues is the expectation that schools will promote fundamental British values such as the rule of law, individual liberty, mutual respect, and tolerance of alternative faiths and beliefs (see Chapter 14). Schools and teachers are also expected to play an active role in the anti-radicalization agenda (see Chapter 20).

How will you as a teacher develop a coherent approach to professional values when the values of pupils, parents, employers and the wider community may or may not match the codified statements of the statutory bodies' approach to professional values? The Teachers' Standards (DfE, 2011a: 14) contain guidance on personal and professional conduct (see Box 2.1).

You will also already know that values are inherent in choices and may be clear-cut in some situations but conflicting in others. One way of understanding your own values is to consider how you would react in situations in which different values make conflicting demands.

Box 2.1: The Teachers' Standards, Part Two: Personal and Professional Conduct

A teacher is expected to demonstrate consistently high standards of personal and professional conduct. The following statements define the behaviour and attitudes which set the required standard for conduct throughout a teacher's career.

- Teachers uphold public trust in the profession and maintain high standards of ethics and behaviour, within and outside school, by:
  - treating pupils with dignity, building relationships rooted in mutual respect, and at all times observing proper boundaries appropriate to a teacher's professional position;
  - having regard for the need to safeguard pupils' well-being in accordance with statutory provisions;
  - showing tolerance of and respect for the rights of others
  - not undermining fundamental British values, including democracy, the rule of law, individual liberty and mutual respect, and tolerance of those with different faiths and beliefs; and
  - ensuring that personal beliefs are not expressed in ways which exploit pupils' vulnerability or might lead them to break the law.
- Teachers must have proper and professional regard for the ethos, policies and practices of the school in which they teach, and maintain high standards in their own attendance and punctuality.
- Teachers must have an understanding of, and always act within, the statutory frameworks which set out their professional duties and responsibilities.

Task 2.2

Consider each of the following scenarios and think about how you would respond in each. What are the values that might drive you to act in a particular way?

Scenario 1
Your patience and tolerance have been tested for some months by a child in a challenging Year 9 class that you teach. His behaviour has been linked to a very dislocated home life and he is a fairly recent arrival in the locality. The special educational needs coordinator (SENCo) has established an Individual Behaviour Plan, but you know that an external assessment of his needs will not take place soon. His behaviour continues to be so disruptive to the class that parents of other children have complained that their children's education is being adversely affected by his presence in your class.

Scenario 2
In a tutorial, one of the Year 9 girls in your tutor group tells you that she is planning to leave school at the end of Year 12 because her parents think that further education is not appropriate for girls.

Scenario 3

One pupil in your Year 11 tutor group asks to speak to you in private and complains to you that the class is, as she puts it, being bullied by another teacher. She says that they have been intimidated into staying at lunchtimes and after school to work on their coursework assignments, and that some pupils have been 'forced' to choose the subject for A-Level.

Scenario 4

Three Year 9 pupils have just been admitted to the school having recently arrived in the country as asylum seekers. Their education in their home country has been severely disrupted by conflict for many years and these pupils, as well as speaking very little English, are barely literate in their first language. For them to make any progress, they need a teacher to work exclusively with them full time. The funding received by the school to support these pupils does not cover this expense.

Scenario 5

You are working as a support teacher in a colleague's mixed-ability class. Part of your role is to support differentiation in the lesson and you spend time with the highest and lowest attainers in the group. At the end of the lesson, the class teacher asks you to spend more time in the next lesson with a particular boy who is one of the highest attainers in the class because 'after all, he's the one who will be contributing most to my pension in a few years' time'.

Depending on your view of the purpose of schools, you may have professional values additional to those identified in the Standards and you will certainly place more emphasis on some than on others. You will want to work in schools that generally have values that match your own. How will you know? Nothing in a school is *value-free*. You can get some sense of a school's collective values by reading what they say about themselves – the school's aims as laid out in their prospectus, for example. But you will also want to look, for example, at how resources are allocated, how decisions are made, how pupils and staff are valued and rewarded, and how pupils and staff relate to each other outside lessons.

So, when you work in a school you will want to achieve a match. Student teachers often express a desire to work in a 'good school'. But how do you define a good school? You may want to work in a faith school or a selective school. You may want to work in a comprehensive school with strong expertise in special educational needs (SEN). You will want to work in a school where the teaching methods, content and organization most fit your own professional views about achieving your aims (why are you becoming a teacher?). Your aims will be the result of your values. While you might want to work in a school where the way you dress, speak and relate to pupils inside and outside the classroom matches the values of that school, this is not always possible.

Schools, by their nature, are places where individuals' exploration, development and expression of their own values need to be tested against, and tempered by, their membership of a structured community – and this is as true of the teachers as it is of the pupils. Becoming a teacher may mean setting aside some of your personal values in favour of those of the community. How will you react if the school does things that conflict with your values? Even if you were to see yourself as just an employee, nothing you do or say as a teacher is value-free.

So, the last question is: What is not for sale in your professional life? If you were to be, in Tim Brighouse's exhortation (quoted in Shaw, 2003), 'lovingly disobedient', on what matters would you be prepared to disobey 'lovingly'?

2.3 Teachers' legal responsibilities

There is a great deal of legislation relating to teachers' work that is constantly changing. There were more Acts of Parliament between 1990 and 2017 than in the previous fifty years. Legislation reflects changing government policy. The autonomous nature of schools, their need to compete in a quasi-market and the new statutory framework are all reflected in the legislation. The Teachers' Standards (DfE, 2011a), which came into effect in September 2012, apply to all members of the teaching profession. If you are completing a Postgraduate Certificate in Education (PGCE) programme, you will be assessed against the Standards that are consistent with the level that can be reasonably expected at that stage of your training. Once you have completed your training and induction, other Standards will be used to assess performance.

With such a vast amount of legislation affecting your work as a teacher, you cannot be expected to know all the details of the laws that apply to you. There are areas that you need to know about, there are areas that you need to have an overview of, and there are areas where you will need to know where to get some advice from. What this section does is to explain the types of documents related to legal requirements that are published by the government, to outline the main areas of legislation that affect teachers specifically and to discuss some of the issues involved in the interpretation of the law.

First, you need to understand the difference between primary legislation, secondary legislation, guidance (or circulars), codes of practice and case law:

- *Primary legislation* comprises Acts of Parliament.
- *Secondary legislation* includes regulations, statutory instruments and orders made by the Secretary of State under powers invested in him or her by primary legislation. The Education Reform Act 1988, for example, gave the Secretary of State no less than 200 powers to make statutory regulations and orders.
- *Departmental guidance and circulars* come from the Department for Education (DfE). Up to 2001, the name for these documents was 'circulars' and they were numbered and dated. For example, Circular 4/98, which set out arrangements for teacher training, was the fourth circular issued by the Department for Education and Employment, now the Department for Education, in 1998. This numbering system was dropped by the Department in 2002. These circulars, now called guidance, give advice on the meaning and implementation of specific Acts. They do not have the force of law and occasionally the courts find that the Department has given incorrect advice on an Act.
- *Codes of practice* are also issued for guidance. Although they do not have the force of law, codes of practice are similar to the Highway Code in that, while breach of a code is not in itself an offence, it may be used as evidence of negligence in a civil action; for example, if good practice advice in a code on a health and safety issue has been ignored and there has been an accident. The Secretary of State often has a duty to consult

widely with the appropriate bodies such as local authorities and the teachers' professional associations before promulgating a code of practice.

- *Common law* is the body of interpretations of the law through cases in the courts, which provide a precedent for future cases.

In most areas, the primary and secondary legislation gives only the barest outline of what teachers and schools need to do, and what will be of most interest to you are the codes of practice and guidance that help you to make decisions and put the law into practice in your own circumstances. However, you need to be aware of some of the most important Acts that govern aspects of your work.

The Children Act 1989 set out teachers' responsibilities to protect children from harm. This is a very wide-ranging piece of legislation and it is supported by a great deal of guidance. Among the most important topics in this guidance is the recognition of child abuse. Schools are required to designate a member of staff to liaise between the school and other agencies in cases of suspected child abuse (see Chapter 20). Before you begin work in a school, you will need to prioritize finding out who this member of staff is and what systems operate within the school for the communication of concerns.

The Health and Safety at Work Act 1974 sets the basic framework for health and safety both of pupils and staff. You will need to familiarize yourself with the requirements both of the Act itself and of the particular policy of the school in which you work.

A number of pieces of primary legislation govern schools' and teachers' responsibilities in terms of inclusion. The Race Relations Act 1976 and Race Relations (Amendment) Act 2000, the Sex Discrimination Act 1975, the Disability and Discrimination Act 1995, and the Special Educational Needs and Disability Act 2001 all cover very complex areas of provision and are discussed in the appropriate chapters in Part 4 of this book.

An area of law that frequently concerns new teachers is that which relates to pupil behaviour and discipline, in particular the physical restraint of pupils. There are a number of relevant pieces of legislation. The School Standards and Framework Act 1998 requires schools to have a behaviour policy and individual teachers need to work within that policy. The Human Rights Act 1998 requires that treatment of pupils should not be inhuman or degrading. The Education Act 1997 gives more detailed information about the legality of keeping pupils in detention after school and of the use of physical restraint. It gives guidance on what is meant by the use of 'reasonable force' and in what circumstances this might be deemed necessary.

You will obtain more detail about the law in each of these areas from the *Bristol Guide* (Document Summary Service, 2017) listed under Further Reading and from the teaching unions, which regularly publish updated guides to teachers' legal responsibilities. These are available direct from the unions or from their websites (see webliography).

One area of the law that is especially open to legal interpretation is teachers' 'duty of care'. Teachers have a common law duty of care towards their pupils resulting from their position *in loco parentis* (in the place of the parent). This means that they are required to care for their pupils as a 'reasonable parent' would. There is no legal interpretation of this and judgments are based on the large amount of case law that has built up over the years.

It is impossible to lay down hard and fast rules for every circumstance. A teacher must take the same degree of care that a reasonably careful parent would of their own children, taking account of the number of children in the class and the nature of those children.

Regard must be paid to the likelihood of accidents in particular situations, such as in science experiments. Older children can be allowed more freedom and discretion providing that the pupils are in a well-ordered environment.

Task 2.3

Here are two contrasting examples in recent leading cases. In each case, try to decide whether you think the school would be considered liable and what aspects of the situation might have been taken into consideration in coming to these judgments.

- During a lesson, an 8-year-old boy is excused to go to the toilet. He slides down the banisters and falls onto the floor below, injuring himself. Discipline in the school was good and there had been no similar accident (*Gough v Upshire Primary School*, 2001).
- A 15-year-old boy is in the playground five minutes before school and is struck in the face by a heavy leather football. There had been similar incidents before. Heavy leather footballs had been banned but no steps were taken to enforce the ban. There were 30 or 40 members of staff in the staffroom but nobody patrolling the playground (*Kearn-Price v Kent County Council*, 2002).

The decisions made by the courts were that, in the second case, the school was liable, but in the first it was not. In coming to these decisions, they would have considered first whether the danger was reasonably foreseeable. In the primary school, there had been no previous instances of pupils sliding down the banisters and, even at the age of 8 years, the pupil could reasonably be trusted to walk through the school building unsupervised. At the secondary school, however, there had already been similar incidents and so the danger was foreseeable. The second key question is whether the school had taken preventive action that was reasonably practicable. It was thought impracticable to insist that a pupil be accompanied each time they leave the classroom, but not impracticable for staff to be on duty in the playground before school.

As a professional teacher, you will:

- work within the legislative framework;
- know that acting 'reasonably' is the legal cornerstone of all you do;
- know that your school will have guidelines and policies lodged within the legislative framework;
- know that you can gain advice within your school on general and specific matters;
- know that you can gain advice from your professional association. These associations are experts in the application of the law to teaching. They produce general guidelines on the law and specific publications on certain issues and can offer, in cases where it is necessary, specific and specialized legal advice.

The law covers every aspect of schools. It changes frequently and, at this stage in your professional life, you do not need to know all the details, but you do need to know those areas that affect your daily working life. Most of all, you need to understand and carry out the school policies.

When you take up your first post, there are some fundamental things you can do:

- Read the staff handbook. If it is not clear on something – detention, confiscating property, confidentiality, health and safety, off-site visits – ask to see the policy concerned, which has to be available to staff and parents.
- Study the departmental handbook for the same reason.
- Study the scheme of work (SoW) and the assessment and reporting procedures.
- Make sure you are a member of a professional association and receive their legal publication for new teachers.
- Find out at an early stage who the people are, apart from your head of department and head of year, who can provide advice. For example, who is the expert in the school on copyright, information and communications technology (ICT), teaching assistants, health and safety, learning mentors, child protection and SEN?

2.4 The role of school governors

Since the mid-1990s, the development of the roles and responsibilities of governors has quickened relentlessly. Since the Education Act 1988, which gave governing bodies additional representation and unprecedented freedoms, and the advent of Local Management of Schools, governors' responsibilities and powers have been radically strengthened, largely at the expense of local authorities. These changes mean that it is the governors who strategically manage the central legislative framework for their school. The growth in governor training and support, and the number of national and local governor publications, indicate the burden on 350,000 volunteer governors nationally. An increase in central direction over the last twenty years, as reflected in the increase in primary and secondary legislation, for example in areas such as the curriculum and intervention in schools causing concern, has required governors to become involved in considerable detail previously left to head teachers.

The changes to school organization introduced by successive governments have led to a wide variation in the composition of governing bodies between different types of school and the creation of academies (see Chapter 26). The establishment of groups of schools operating as Multi-Academy Trusts (MATs) has further complicated the governance landscape and has, in many cases, changed the composition of governing bodies.

You need to be aware of the type of school you are working in to ensure you understand the composition of your particular governing body. There are also frequent policy changes in this area and the DfE and the National Governance Association provide useful updates.

The key responsibility of governing bodies is to provide a strategic overview for the school's development, albeit within the framework of national policy and guidelines. They have overall responsibility for the budgetary, staffing, curriculum and disciplinary frameworks within which staff work. Although their powers are wide, they are constrained by legislative and policy frameworks. Nonetheless, their responsibilities are extensive and most governing bodies will have constructed an elaborate committee structure to discharge their formal responsibilities. Governing bodies typically work through curriculum subcommittees, which have responsibility for the development, quality, coherence and assessment of the curriculum, a finance subcommittee, which sets budget parameters and monitors spending, a personnel subcommittee, which oversees the school's staffing plan and appoint-ments, and a premises committee, which oversees the school's site development plan. Other committees deal with exclusions, disciplinary hearings, and appeals. It should be clear from this list that governors often have to deal with sensitive, contentious and difficult issues, such as grievance, discipline and occasionally dismissal. Effective governing bodies depend on the commitment of their members to discharge their responsibilities and undergo contin-uous training to update themselves on legislative changes.

Governors are unpaid volunteers drawn as widely as possible from all sections of the community. Schools depend on their governors and good governors can be effective sources of support and expertise for their schools – many governors bring their own experience in business, industry, public service or the voluntary sector to bear on their role. Nonetheless, governors do not have day-to-day responsibility for the management of the school, or of individual staff or curriculum areas: these responsibilities rest with the head teacher and senior staff. Governors' roles are strategic rather than directly managerial. Whether governors have the time or the capacity for the detailed work now required of them is an issue that has not been seriously addressed by successive governments. Recruitment and retention of governors is a major focus of the work of local authorities. In some areas of the country, they are very hard to recruit. Recruitment of governors from minority communities is a particular issue.

As a new teacher, you will have a different perspective on the governing body. You may see the big picture of their roles as removed from the reality of your life. They do, however, have formal and informal connections – though some of them only potential connections – with you. For example:

- They have responsibilities to you as a newly qualified teacher (NQT); they are required to satisfy themselves that your induction is being conducted properly so that you are being given every opportunity to succeed.
- At least one governor may be involved with your appointment.
- They will establish policies and procedures that will have implications for you as a member of staff.
- One of the governors will be identified as a 'link governor' for your department and may be quite closely involved in the department's strategic development.

When you go into school, find out what type of school you are in and ask for a list of the governors by category. Depending on the type of school, there are likely to be different categories of governors including parent, staff, local authority and sponsor governors. However, all governors have the same roles and responsibilities once they assume office. Ask to see agendas and minutes of the meetings of the governing body. Also ask to talk to one of the teacher governors about the work of the governors in your school and how you are represented at meetings.

Most governors are very supportive of the school they serve and act fairly towards the school and the staff. They show a genuine interest in the workings of the school and are keen for it to succeed. New teachers can feel vulnerable if they are teaching the child of a governor, or if a governor comes to spend time in their department, but you should remember that in the vast majority of cases, the governors are there to play a positive, supporting role.

Recommendations for further reading

Department for Education (DfE) (2011) *Teachers' Standards: Guidance for School Leaders, School Staff and Governing Bodies*. London: HMSO. Available at: https://assets.publishing.service.gov. uk/government/uploads/system/uploads/attachment_data/file/665520/Teachers__Standards.pdf.

Department for Education (DfE) (2017) *Governance Handbook: For Academies, Multi-Academy Trusts and Maintained Schools*. London: DfE. Available at: https://assets.publishing.service.gov. uk/government/uploads/system/uploads/attachment_data/file/582868/Governance_Handbook_-_January_2017.pdf.

Department for Education (DfE) (2017) *Governance Handbook and Competency Framework*. London: DfE. Available at: https://www.gov.uk/government/publications/governance-handbook.

Document Summary Service (2017) *Professional Responsibilities and Statutory Frameworks for Teachers and Others in Schools: The Bristol Guide*. Bristol: University of Bristol Graduate School of Education.

Webliography

National Governance Association: www.nga.org.uk

3

Key issues, opportunities and challenges for new teachers

David Middlewood

3.1 Introduction

In the fast-changing world of the twenty-first century, education and schools are as much subject to the constancy of change – the 'not standing still' – as all other areas of our personal and professional lives. It is a particular issue for those working with children and young people, as teachers help to prepare them for a future world in which things are or will be already different from what we knew. Think of when you were, say, sixteen and think how much has changed in that relatively short period of time.

In this chapter, we identify some of the issues that are important for teachers in the educational world as it is now and consider some of the ways that these might be approached. We will look at the issues or aspects of teaching today of which you will need to be aware.

By the end of this chapter, you should:

- know some of the major elements in education and schooling that face teachers and schools today;
- be aware of some of the biggest challenges facing teachers today;
- begin to think about how you might develop your own strategies as to how to approach present-day challenges in education.

3.2 Dealing with multiple accountabilities

Part of being a professional lies in being accountable for what you do, as noted in Chapter 2. Being a teacher involves a somewhat complex network of accountabilities. As someone preparing to be a teacher, you probably feel instinctively that you are first accountable to your pupils and their parents, as well as to the colleagues with whom you work closely, perhaps those in your department. Within your school, your accountability for how well you do will be dealt with through your line manager using the performance management framework operated by the school. Indirectly, through the head teacher, you are accountable to the school governors. Depending on the nature of the school, teachers are also accountable to either the local authority or the sponsor/Board of the Trust or chain of academies of which the school may be a part. The latter may also involve some accountability to other schools and colleagues in that Trust or chain. The external inspection service, Ofsted, will similarly pass judgement on the quality of the school in which you work and, finally, there is a professional body: all members of the teaching profession are ultimately accountable to the Teaching Agency. Many of these are structural accountabilities that are unlikely to impinge on the daily work of a student teacher or, indeed, a new teacher; the key thing is to retain at all times a clear idea of what you are doing and why. In other words, if asked, you should be able to give a clear account of your own practice and reasons why it is what it is. To do this, teachers need to keep up to date with recent research in education, and what is encouraging is how much practitioners are able to access research (for example, through Ofsted publications), as well as contributing to it in no small way today. Examples are given in this book of how to carry out research into your own and others' practice.

It is worth reflecting about personal professional accountabilities. To whom do you see yourself as a teacher being primarily accountable? How does this affect the responsibilities you feel you have towards the people you encounter at work on a daily basis? Your answers to these questions are probably reflected in your responses to the initial perceptions about the purpose of education, as set out in Chapter 1. Look at your responses there and think about how they influence your ideas about accountability.

3.3 Understanding how schools work in organizations

A school is an organization and as such is subject to many of the considerations that affect how organizations operate – in the relevant literature, this is known as 'organizational behaviour'. Although all schools have many things in common, as the various topics in this book show, inform and advise upon, each individual school is in some respects unique. This is primarily because the individuals that make up schools are themselves unique, both individually and as a mix of people. Here, we mention two aspects of schools that can prove crucial in understanding how they work and how a person can operate in them effectively.

The first of these is a school's *culture*, which may be broadly defined as the values and beliefs held and, hopefully, practised by those that work there. It is usually expressed through the way people go about their routines and their approaches to their work. While all schools would probably state that they have similar values of, for example, equity, openness, diversity and achieving individual potential, in reality schools differ in how they try to put these into action. This might show itself in attitudes towards behaviour and discipline, for example, or how different levels of ability in pupils are catered for. Middlewood and Abbott (2017) provide an interesting example of two schools that wanted to operate the same school policy about school uniform but applied the policy using two very different sets of values. Both schools introduced a new uniform to help instil pride in the school on the part of the pupils who wore it. Both schools enforced the uniform rules strictly but, after three years, staff in one school were complaining of spending too much time inspecting sock colours and skirt lengths, taking too many detentions for uniform rule breaches, and believed that the pupils now saw cheating the uniform code as a challenge! The other school had not focused on uniform alone but had developed pupil voice, encouraged independent learning and got parents involved. The first school had treated the uniform as an end in itself and not focused on the values it was meant to represent as the second school had. Some people argue that the culture of a school can be discerned through its ethos, and this is visible through the way visitors are treated, for example. You might want to consider this when attending interviews for a post!

A second aspect of a school's individuality often lies in its micro-politics. This is the reality of life in an organization that cannot be found in any brochures, staff documents or handbooks and is often described as what goes on 'beneath the surface'. It can be useful to think of the school as an *iceberg* (Plant, 1975), where the visible elements are above the waterline, such as the policies, procedures, documents and plans. Beneath the waterline you will find the invisible elements, such as how people feel on a particular day, unspoken feelings, unofficial relationships and attitudes, and so on. Micro-politics is about 'the subterranean conflicts and minutiae of social relations – a subtext of organisational life in which conflicts, tensions, resentments, competing interests influence everyday transactions' (Morley, 2000: 232). Remember that no one can be exempt from micro-politics in a school, and every teacher is part of the minutiae whether they know it or not!

Case Study 3.1

Helen is in her second term of her first year's post in a school when she is given a lift home after an after-school meeting by Elaine, an experienced teacher in another department. Elaine tells her of a proposed new rule concerning behaviour sanctions that the principal is planning to introduce soon, to which she and some others are strongly opposed. She believes Helen will also be against it and invites her to an unofficial meeting of a few staff to discuss how it should be opposed when it is put forward at a staff meeting. She fears there may not be proper debate at the staff meeting and that they need to be prepared. One of the staff she mentions is in Helen's own department and has been helpful to her in her first year.

COMMENTARY: This is classic micro-politics! Staff members often try to draw other colleagues, especially new ones, into various sets or groups in what some call conspiracies and others simply debate! What should Helen do?

Perhaps you could begin by listing the advantages and disadvantages of Helen going to the meeting. If you were her friend, what might you advise her to do? Above all, what do you think is the most professional thing for her to do? On one hand, you might feel there is no harm in going to a meeting to have a discussion; on the other hand, you might think she should not get drawn into any particular group at this stage about something that is not yet official. In any organization, new staff members are often approached to ally themselves to a particular social group before they have had the opportunity to view the whole staff. Note that this is not some kind of wicked stratagem but part of what goes on in any organization – and nearly always for the best possible reasons as seen by those involved. Everyone is involved in the micro-politics of an organization, whatever they say and whether they want to be or not! It is part and parcel of life in any school.

3.4 Achieving a work–life balance

Teaching is a highly intense profession that is demanding physically, mentally, intellectually and emotionally. It has become more so over recent years and was listed by Occupational Stress Ratings (OSR) in 2016 as the second most stressful occupation in England and Wales, behind only social work, with clerical staff and teaching assistants also in the top twenty. Far too many teachers leave the profession (13%) after one year, with approximately a third leaving after five years. Most of those leaving cite a heavy workload and too little time for 'normal life' as the main reasons for their decision. As we have mentioned in Chapters 1 and 2, the rewards in teaching are tremendous and it is ultimately an extremely fulfilling and satisfying career, so it is worth thinking during the training year about strategies for achieving a reasonable balance in your personal and working life (now widely referred to as 'work– life balance'). Obviously, you expect to work extra hard in the early days, as in any new job, while you learn the ropes, but you ought to think about how to manage your work effectively and to avoid some of the circumstances that can cause problems, as you settle into the profession. Any good school should recognize the need to provide support for their staff's emotional health and well-being, and some schools offer specific training sessions on such things as stress management. A small number have counsellors attached to the staff, available for both pupils and adults. In a study of people-centred occupations such as teaching, Donaldson-Feilder *et al.* (2011) found that the concealing of personal emotions at work, which was often necessary for the benefit of those being helped, could be harmful if carried over into the professional's personal life. Based on this, two issues emerged: first, that an outlet for emotions outside of work was essential and, second, that employers should recognize that emotional outlets at work were inevitable. While policies should not be based on them, the researchers pointed out that very few people are entirely consistent emotionally, but that occasionally following the heart instead of the head is the right thing to do.

Your mentor, both during your training and in your first teaching job, can be a valuable outlet for such emotions, particularly at times of high stress (Dunne and Bennett, 1997). Opportunities to talk informally with other colleagues and friends can also be a great help. Ofsted have recognized the pressures of workload and its effects on teachers, and the National Director has reassured teachers that what they are looking for in most areas when they visit any school is not some kind of 'perfect Ofsted' model of operating, but whether a teacher is following the school's own policy, for example, regarding assessment (Harford, 2017). In other words, when the school is subject to an Ofsted inspection, as long as you are doing what the school requires, the pressure is on the school, not the individual teacher.

Obviously, life outside of school becomes critically important in helping teachers keep a sense of perspective, and sometimes the hectic nature of that seems to add to the pressure. Think about questions such as the following:

- Should you give up your favourite recreational pastime during the early years of teaching because of the professional demands of the job?
- Consider your personal record of meeting deadlines. Can you improve on it if needed?
- How good are you at managing your own time?
- What personal concerns outside of teaching do you have that may impact on your professional commitment? Are there specific strategies that may be adopted to manage these?

Everyone's individual circumstances are unique, but there is evidence to suggest that, for example, having outside interests is good for a professional's emotional health. Also, the issue of deadlines is one that is managed by the school and, while a school often cannot have control over external deadlines, it does have control over internal ones. There are two specific people who are the key supports in secondary schools to teachers and whose job it is to help those members of staff who may struggle to achieve a reasonable work–life balance: your line manager and your mentor.

Your *line manager* is normally the head of your subject department, although where such departments or faculties are very large, the task of supporting new teachers may be delegated to a second in department, for example. The line manager is responsible for teacher performance and has regular oversight of how well a teacher is doing. This should also include regular feedback on progress and discussion about where and how to improve. That person is also therefore the one to be consulted about such matters as deadlines, approaches to assessment and clarifying exactly what is required of the teacher if that is needed. It is in the interests of both the line manager and the teacher for the teacher to succeed, so effective advice, guidance and practical support are in everyone's interest. The line manager's role is much more specific than that of the mentor because evidence or data concerning progress will need to be collected for performance management so that the teacher's contribution to the department's and school's progress can be seen. This will often involve formal reports on achievements and progress.

Your *mentor* will be a more experienced member of staff whose job is to support you in ways that enable you to develop your effectiveness and confidence. Depending on the way the school operates, a mentor may have more than one teacher to work with, but the meetings between mentor and mentee teacher are, importantly, on a one-to-one basis and, unless otherwise agreed, the views of and information divulged by the mentee can remain confidential. The differences between mentoring and line managing are shown in Table 3.1.

	Mentoring	Line managing
Role filled by	Senior colleague or peer	Department or subject head
Purpose	Development as a teacher overall	Performance development
Communication	Debate/discuss	Discuss and report
Use of information	Confidential	Performance review
Future actions	Agreed with mentee	Decided by line manager
Who is accountable for progress?	Mentee	Senior leadership

Table 3.1 Differences between mentoring and line managing

3.5 Being part of a diverse workforce

As explained in Chapter 7, there are several other staff members who are not teachers but who play a crucial role in the life, organization and success of a modern secondary school, and it is important that all teachers recognize the contribution they all make to the school. Chapter 7 focuses in particular on the role of the teaching assistant (TA) because of how closely TAs work alongside teachers. The importance of all these members of staff is recognized in legislation on school staffing structures and through the availability of advanced qualifications, such as Foundation degrees and higher-level teaching assistant (HLTA) posts. In secondary schools with large numbers of pupils from deprived or disadvantaged backgrounds, staff might include personnel with various 'social' roles, such as counsellors, home visitors or learning mentors. What you need to remember as a teacher is that these personnel are usually expert in their specific field. Some have the highest qualifications available, but even when this is not the case, they will have been appointed by the school for their close knowledge of the local community and thus of the conditions in which the pupils live. It would be foolish for a teacher to ignore this fact and become involved when such expertise exists that is paid for by the school. At the most human level, such personnel may feel aggrieved if a teacher intrudes on their 'territory' without prior consultation – even if for the best intentions – just as a teacher would be offended in the reverse circumstances. As always, the key to successful practice, for the benefit of pupils, is to work as part of a team. For example, if your class includes a pupil who is working at home because they have been excluded from school, you need to work closely with the school's home visitor to ensure work is taken to the pupil at home and collected for assessment.

3.6 Recognizing the place of pupil voice

All secondary schools have a school council on which pupils are represented and have a voice in some aspects of the school's operations and organization. This is now an official requirement of all schools, as it is in many countries, and is the bare minimum of what is known as pupil voice. (Note that in secondary schools, it is often called 'student voice'.) There are many who see the development of pupil voice as one of the most powerful movements of our time, and one that will grow in significance over the next few decades. In the Nordic countries, which have excellent records of pupil attainment, pupil voice is seen as an integral part of learning about democracy and pupils have access to ministers of education (see Mortimore, 2013). An example of how pupil voice has developed in England and Wales is that when interviewed for a first teaching post, it is now quite common for candidates to be interviewed by a group of pupil representatives, who provide feedback to the head teacher and others who make the final decision. It is therefore important to consider pupil voice and how it can affect teaching and learning.

Legal requirements in England and Wales state that children and young people should be encouraged to become involved in the design and delivery of the services provided for them. Also, relationships between children and adults are changing in western societies (Thomson, 2009), mainly due to earlier maturation, so that adults speaking on behalf of children is no longer considered the norm. Others argue that pupil voice is about the democratization of educational institutions and therefore about active citizenship, preparing young people to fulfil a role in society (Whitty and Wisby, 2007). It is also suggested that pupil voice can help the disadvantaged feel they are legitimate members of a group (for further discussion, see Chapter 25) and can boost the self-esteem of pupils from ethnic minorities, urban environments or working-class backgrounds (Smyth, 2006). It is important that the pupil voice in a school is an authentic one and not tokenistic because, as Fielding (2006) warns, if young people see that it is being used for adult purposes, they may become cynical and disenchanted. Research on school councils by Burnitt and Gunter (2013) found that they seldom went beyond asking for ideas about relatively minor issues in school. Thus, it could be argued that, unless pupil voice is linked to learning, it may not be seen as a genuine means of recognizing pupils' role within the school: 'Listening and responding to what pupils may say about their feelings or reactions as learners can lead to teachers examining and improving their own practice' (Middlewood and Abbott, 2015: 43). Clearly, more meaningful debates about learning that involves pupil voice are essential.

Giving a voice to pupils can also, from the perspective of the individual class teacher, be seen to be closely linked with developments in such initiatives as personalized learning. So, how can the individual class teacher recognize the importance of pupil voice and help it to develop through their own practice?

Task 3.1

Make a list of the various aspects of teaching a lesson on which you might encourage pupils to express their personal views. For each item on the list, consider how you would ensure that those views are seen to be valued, even if you feel they are incorrect or inappropriate.

COMMENTARY: One major area is that of assessment, and you can read about pupil involvement in formative assessment in Chapter 9. Peer assessment may be an important part of this.

Evaluating and reviewing a unit or module of work at its end is an important exercise. Your department may have standard end-of-module evaluation forms for all classes, which can be collated to provide an overall view of the module so that any revisions can be made for its future use. However, it is also valuable to offer pupils a chance to reflect in discussion on a module of work and, in doing so, offer the opportunity for them to give their opinions on such things as whether it was enjoyable and stimulating or boring, which were the most enjoyable parts, and so on.

Another strategy to involve pupils is to ask or nominate pupils to take on specific roles in lessons, either singly or in pairs. For example, two pupils might be responsible for displays in the classroom or on a particular noticeboard. Such roles should, of course, be rotated to avoid any accusations of favouritism.

Perhaps the most fulfilling – but also potentially the most challenging – way of involving pupils is in the area of teaching and learning itself. This can be done through a form of in-house inquiry that requires the pupils to carry out structured research on an agreed aspect of classroom practice. As pupils are in a unique position to observe their teachers on a daily basis, feedback from them that is based on a carefully constructed, mutually agreed investigation into practice can clearly be of significant value to both the teacher and learner.

First, the teacher needs to identify what is to be investigated. For less-experienced teachers in particular, something could be chosen for discussion that both pupils and teacher are concerned about. Ideally, the process would proceed as follows:

1. Teacher(s) and learner(s) identify issue *together*.
2. Discuss and agree research focus.
3. Agree method(s).
4. Carry out research.
5. Analyse data *together*.
6. Report and action agreed *together*.
7. Continuing professional development (CPD) needs identified (if relevant).

8. CPD provided (if relevant).
9. Teacher modifies practice.
10. Evaluation and revisit after agreed period.

Case Study 3.2 shows the possibilities in such inquiries.

Case Study 3.2

Jenni was a teacher in her first year of her first post and was generally pleased with her progress to date. By the second term, she had become aware that her questioning in class seemed to draw responses from about seven or eight pupils per class and they tended to be the same pupils each time. From her training year, she knew that some adolescents can be self-conscious in front of their peers but felt that, with the help of the class, she could discover more. After a discussion with an amenable class of 12-year-olds, Jenni selected four pupils (two very voluble and two very quiet) to work together to devise a questionnaire for all the pupils in the class. The selection of the four was approved by the class as a whole. A questionnaire was devised, with a series of questions and statements focusing on why the respondents might not answer a question in class, might not volunteer an answer, and so on. The questionnaire was completed anonymously.

Upon collecting the completed questionnaires, Jenni and the four pupils analysed the data. Jenni was surprised at the extent to which some pupils were afraid of appearing silly in front of others and how lacking in confidence many were about being able to express themselves when answering a question.

Having reflected, Jenni changed her approach to questioning. She reduced the number of open questions to a very small number and instead directed nearly all questions at individuals. In doing so, she ensured that everyone was asked a question at some point over two or three lessons and, most importantly, that everyone was praised for attempting to provide an answer, whether it was right or wrong. With incorrect answers, she always praised the effort in answering and tried to find a positive in even a quite incorrect response.

Jenni commented that she felt she knew the pupils better and that the learning was seen to be more relevant. Two of her other classes asked if they could do something similar as the word got around.

COMMENTARY: Clearly, careful thought needs to be given as to which classes are suitable for such inquiry, but the process itself, as well as the outcomes, can have significant advantages for everyone concerned in that:

• the teacher has gained insight into their own practice and is able show improvement in that area;

• the pupils have learned valuable research skills from the process;

- the pupils know that their views and opinions will be acknowledged and respected, while they are based on reason and logic;
- the relationship between the teacher and pupils is enhanced through working together;
- the procedures used by the teacher will be more likely to be accepted by the pupils because they will have contributed to any changes.

For a detailed study of such in-house research involving learners, see Middlewood and Abbott (2015: 44–49).

3.7 Planning for learning for life

As noted in Chapter 1, initial teacher training (ITT) is the start of a professional journey during which, as you move through the various stages of your teaching career, you will need to update and develop your skills and attributes on a continuous basis. These will need to be appropriate to the particular stage of your professional life you are at. Establishing attitudes and principles in relation to these during your training and your first year of teaching will help greatly in being able to:

- identify your personal professional needs at any point in time;
- determine the most suitable kind of CPD from which you can benefit most.

Task 3.2

Rank each of the following actions according to the way you believe you learn most effectively (1 for the most effective, 2 for the next most effective, and so on):

Talking informally with teaching colleagues	_____
Personal reading and study	_____
Attending a programme or course	_____
Listening to a speaker	_____
Visiting another school	_____
Carefully analysing your own teaching	_____
Formal appraisals and feedback from senior colleagues	_____
Observing other members of staff	_____
Working in partnership with one other person	_____

Some of these actions will overlap but, when you have thought carefully about this task and ranked the actions, look at, say, your top three or four as a group and your bottom three or four similarly. What does this tell you about yourself as a professional learner? Because we are all different, there are no 'right' or 'wrong' answers. It can, however, be the case that

CPD provided to a group (for example, all members of staff) may not be appropriate for certain of those members. It is all the more important, therefore, that as a professional you become aware of the particular strengths and possible weaknesses you have as a learner. You may decide at a later date to remedy some of your weaknesses.

3.8 Conclusion

This chapter has described and considered several issues prevalent in education that are likely to be encountered by new teachers. It has suggested questions you can ask yourself and offered a few strategies that may assist you.

No two schools are identical and some of the issues discussed may be much more evident in some than in others. For example, pupil voice may be almost invisible in some schools yet widespread in others. However, these are all issues that you will encounter at some point. Developing personal professional approaches to them – and the many others yet to be met – will be important as you develop your contribution to the education of young people and find satisfaction in so doing.

Recommendations for further reading

Middlewood, D. and Abbott, I. (2015) *Improving Professional Learning through In-House Inquiry.* London: Bloomsbury.

PART 2

Core Professional Competences

4

Understanding how pupils learn: theories of learning and intelligence

Daniel Muijs

4.1 Introduction

In this chapter, we will discuss the main theories of how children learn. This is, of course, an important issue in teaching, as to be effective we need to try and teach in a way that reinforces how people naturally learn. The theories of learning and intelligence are many and diverse, and we cannot look at all of them in one chapter. What we will do instead is to focus on some of those theories that have been most influential in education over the years.

By the end of this chapter, you should:

*   know about the main theories of how pupils learn: behaviourism; Piagetian and Vygotskian learning theories; IQ theory; the theory of multiple intelligences; and cognitive science;
*   be able to make judgements on the relevance of these different theories to teaching and learning;
*   be able to reflect on the extent to which these theories contradict or build upon one another.

4.2 Behaviourism

The first major theory of learning we will discuss is called behaviourism. Behaviourism was developed in the 1920s and 1930s by psychologists such as Skinner, Pavlov and Thorndike. Although now somewhat outdated, this theory still has a strong influence on educational practice, if not theory.

Behavioural learning theory emphasizes changes in behaviour as the main outcome of the learning process. Behavioural theorists concentrate on directly observable phenomena using a scientific method borrowed from the natural sciences. The most radical behaviourists, such as B.F. Skinner, considered all study of non-observable behaviour ('mentalism') to be unscientific (Hilgard, 1995; O'Donohue and Ferguson, 2001). In recent years, however, most researchers and psychologists in the behaviourist tradition, such as Bandura (1985), have expanded their view of learning to include expectations, thoughts, motivations and beliefs. Learning, according to behaviourists, is something people do in response to external stimuli.

This was an important change from previous models, which had stressed consciousness and introspection, and had not produced many generalizable findings about how people learn.

As mentioned, behaviourists imitated methods used in the natural sciences, especially experiments conducted with animals – including rats and dogs – as well as humans. This is because, being against 'mentalism', behaviourists think that it is largely external factors that cause our behaviour. The basic mechanism through which this happens is conditioning. According to behaviourists, there are two different types of conditioning:

- *Classic conditioning* occurs when a natural reflex responds to a stimulus. An example of this comes from another behaviourist's – Pavlov's – experiments with dogs. In order to process food, dogs need to salivate when they eat. As all dog owners know, what happens is that dogs start to salivate even before eating, as soon as they have smelt or seen food. So, the external stimulus of food will cause the dog to salivate. It has become a habit: that is the response that is conditioned. When confronted with particular stimuli, people as well as animals produce a specific response.

- *Behavioural or operant conditioning* occurs when a response to a stimulus is reinforced. Basically, operant conditioning is a simple feedback system: if a reward or reinforcement follows the response to a stimulus, then the response becomes more probable in the future. For example, if every time a pupil behaves well in class they receive a reward, they are likely to behave well next time. (Note, however, that although animal behaviour follows reliably from a stimulus, this applies to a lesser extent among humans.)

Rewards and punishments are therefore an important part of behaviourist learning theory. Initial experiments with dogs and rats convinced these psychologists of the importance of the use of rewards and punishments to elicit certain desired behaviours, such as pushing a lever, in these animals. Over ensuing decades, these findings were further tested and refined with human subjects and became highly influential in education. Pleasurable consequences, or *reinforcers*, strengthen behaviour, while unpleasant consequences or *punishers*, weaken behaviour. Behaviour is influenced by its consequences, but it is influenced by its antecedents as well, thus creating the ABC – Antecedents-Behaviour-Consequences – chain. Skinner's work concentrated mainly on the relationship between the latter two parts of the chain (Skinner, 1974; O'Donohue and Ferguson, 2001), and these findings still form the basis of many behaviour management systems in schools, as well as much of the research on effective teaching (see, for example, Muijs and Reynolds, 2003).

While this movement remains highly influential, behaviourism has come to be seen as far too limited and limiting to adequately capture the complexity of human learning and behaviours. The idea that learning occurs purely as a reaction to external stimuli has proved to be inadequate. Activities such as recognizing objects ('this is a ball'), sorting objects ('this is a rugby ball, this is a football') and storing information are clearly 'mentalist' activities: they occur in the head. Although, of course, an external stimulus (perception of an object) is present, behaviourist theory cannot account for the information processing that occurs when we are confronted by stimuli. Behaviourism also cannot account for types of learning that occur without reinforcement – in particular, the way children pick up language patterns (grammar) cannot be explained using a behaviourist framework. Behaviourism also presents problems when the learner is confronted with new situations in which the mental stimuli they have learnt to respond to are not present. The fact that behaviourists do not study the memory in any meaningful way (they only talk about acquiring 'habits') is another major problem if we want to explain learning. If we want to truly understand how people learn, we have to be 'mentalists' and look at what is going on inside the brain as well as measuring reactions to external stimuli.

Should we totally discount behaviourism? As already mentioned, behaviourism has been heavily criticized over the years. Much of this criticism is justified. Behaviourism is clearly too limited a theory of learning to properly account for how we really learn. Not all the criticism is justified, however. Some of it seems to emanate from a dislike of the findings rather than a close look at the evidence. Behaviourism has little place for the role of free will and human individuality. This is never a popular view and, as we have seen, this determinism is clearly overdone in behaviourist theories. However, that does not mean that it is entirely inaccurate. While we always like to believe that we are entirely free, our behaviours can to an extent be predicted, in some cases by behaviourist models. That this is true is attested to by the continued usefulness of behaviourist methods in teaching, such as the use of rewards. Not liking certain research findings does not make them wrong, and it is not the job of research and science to simply tell us what we want to hear. Recently, it is fair to say that neo-behaviourist theories have become popular among scientists looking at the role of evolution in the way we behave. If you read the work of Richard Dawkins (1989), for example, there are clear links with behaviourist psychology.

Task 4.1

Can you think of anything you know or can do that you have learnt in a way that conforms to behaviourist learning theory? Can you think of anything that you learnt in a way that clearly is *not* behaviourist? What does that tell you about behaviourist learning theories?

4.3 Piaget and Vygotsky

Jean Piaget: learning as qualitative change

As well as the behaviourists such as Skinner and Watson, two other pioneering psychologists that have had a lasting influence on how we view learning are Piaget and Vygotsky.

Jean Piaget (1896–1980) was a Swiss psychologist who began his important work on how children develop and learn before the Second World War. In contrast to the behaviourists, who developed most of their theories using laboratory experiments and rarely looked at the real-life behaviours of children, Piaget's theories were developed from observation of children.

What these observations taught him was that, in order to understand how children think, one must look at the qualitative development of their ability to solve problems. Cognitive development, in his view, is much more than the addition of new facts and ideas to an existing store of information. Rather, children's thinking changes qualitatively; the tools that children use to think change, leading children and adults, and indeed children at different stages of development, to possess a different view of the world. A child's reality is not the same as that of an adult (Piaget, 2001).

According to Piaget, one of the main influences on children's cognitive development is what he termed *maturation*, the unfolding of biological changes that are genetically programmed into us. A second factor is *activity*. Increasing maturation leads to an increase in children's ability to act on their environment, and to learn from their actions. This learning in turn leads to an alteration of children's thought processes. A third factor in development is *social transmission*, learning from others. As children act on their environment, they also interact with others and can therefore learn from them to a differing degree depending on their developmental stage.

According to Piaget (2001), learning occurs in four stages:

1. *The sensori-motor stage (0–2 years)*. The baby knows about the world through actions and sensory information. They learn to differentiate themselves from the environment. The child begins to understand causality in time and space. The capacity to form internal mental representations emerges.
2. *The pre-operational stage (2–7 years)*. In this stage, the child takes the first steps from action to thinking, by internalizing action. In the previous stage, the child's schemes were still completely tied to actions, which means that they were of no use in recalling the past or in prediction. During the pre-operational stage, the child starts to be able to do this, by learning how to think symbolically. The ability to think in symbols remains limited at this stage, however, as the child can only think in one direction. Thinking backwards or reversing the steps of a task is difficult. Another innovation that starts to take place during this phase is the ability to understand conservation. This means that the child can now realize that the amount or number of something remains the same even if the arrangement or appearance of it is changed (for example, four dogs and four cats is the same amount). This remains difficult for the child in this phase. In this phase, the child still has great difficulty freeing themselves from their own perception of how the world appears. Children at this age are also very egocentric. They tend to see the world and the experiences of others from their own standpoint.
3. *The concrete operational stage (7–12 years)*. The basic characteristics of this stage are: (1) recognition of the logical stability of the physical world; (2) the realization that elements can be changed or transformed and still retain their original characteristics; and (3) an understanding that these changes can be reversed. Another important operation that is mastered at this stage is classification. Classification depends on a pupil's ability to focus on a single characteristic of objects and then to group the objects according to that single characteristic (for example, if one gives a pupil a set of pens of different shapes and colours, they will be able to pick out the round ones). Pupils can now also understand seriation, allowing them to construct a logical series in which A is less than B, which is less than C, and so on. At this stage, the pupil has developed a logical and systematic way of thinking that is, however, still tied to physical reality. Overcoming this is the task of the next phase.
4. *The formal operational stage (12+)*. In this stage, which not everyone reaches, all that is learned in previous stages remains in force, but one is now able to see that a real, experienced situation is only one of several possible outcomes. In order for this to occur, we must be able to generate different possibilities for any given situation in a systematic way. Pupils are now able to imagine ideal, non-existing worlds. Another characteristic of this stage is adolescent egocentrism. Adolescents tend incessantly to analyse their own beliefs and attitudes, and often assume that everyone else shares their concerns and is in turn analysing them.

Piaget's theory has been hugely influential but has been found wanting in a number of areas. His stages of learning are clearly too rigid. A number of studies have found that young children can acquire concrete operational thinking at an earlier age than Piaget proposed, and that they can think at higher levels than Piaget suggested, even to the propositional stage that Piaget believed only adolescents or adults could reach. Piaget also underestimated the individual differences between children in how they develop, and that part of the explanation for these differences is the cultural and social background of the child. Piaget also did not take much notice of the way children can learn from others, seeing learning as largely dependent on their stage of development. Notwithstanding that, Piaget's theories have stood the test of time well, and are still a useful way of looking at children's development.

Lev Vygotsky: the social side of learning

Lev Vygotsky (1896–1934) was a Russian psychologist, who worked at around the same time as Piaget (although he died at a younger age) and was influenced by Piaget's work. During his lifetime, he was not that well known in the West, but after his death – particularly in the 1960s – he became increasingly influential.

Vygotsky's main interest was the study of language development, which he believed initially develops separately from thought, but starts to overlap with thought more and more as the child grows up. According to Vygotsky, a non-overlapping part still remains later in life, with some non-verbal thought and some non-conceptual speech remaining even in adulthood (Vygotsky, 1978; Moll, 1992).

A major difference between Piaget and Vygotsky was that Vygotsky did not think that maturation in itself could help children acquire advanced thinking skills. Vygotsky, while seeing a role for maturation, believed that it was children's interaction with others through language that most strongly influenced the level of conceptual understanding they could aspire to (Vygotsky, 1978).

Vygotsky strongly believed that we can learn from others, both from our peers and those of an older age and higher developmental level. One of the main ways this operates is through *scaffolding* in the *zone of proximal development* (ZPD). The latter concept, one of Vygotsky's main contributions to learning theory, refers to the gap between what a person is able to do alone and what they can do with the help of someone more knowledgeable or skilled than themselves. It is here that the role of teachers, adults and peers comes to the fore in children's learning, in that they can help raise a child's knowledge to a higher level by intervening in the ZPD. This can be done by providing the child's thoughts with so-called scaffolds, which, once the learning process is complete, are no longer needed by the child. Children are not all equally *educable* in this respect, some being able to learn more in the ZPD than others.

Thus, for Vygotsky, it is *cooperation* that is at the basis of learning. It is *instruction*, formal and informal, performed by more knowledgeable others, such as parents, peers, grandparents and teachers, that is the main means of transmission of the knowledge of a particular culture. Knowledge for Vygotsky, like for Piaget, is embodied in actions and interactions with the environment (or culture), but unlike Piaget, Vygotsky stresses the importance of *interaction* with a living representative of the culture.

While Piaget has been criticized as being too strongly focused on developmental learning, Vygotsky's work is seen as suffering from the opposite problem. Vygotsky wrote little about children's natural development and the relationship of that to their learning (Wertsch and Tulviste, 1992). Vygotsky's theories are also in many ways rather general and overarching and have not been fully worked out (that Vygotsky died at the age of 37 is one reason for this). Vygotsky's contribution lies mainly in his attention to the social aspects of learning, which clearly need complementing by what current research is teaching us about brain functions.

This view of learning as socially constructed strongly influenced the so-called constructivist theories that have followed since then and influenced classroom practice. His ideas about pupils' learning in their ZPD have been influential in the development of collaborative learning programmes.

Task 4.2

How do you think the theories of Piaget and Vygotsky could influence teaching? What can teachers do to take into account the importance of the ZPD?

4.4 IQ theory

Another theory that has had a lasting influence in education (whether this has been for the good is debatable) is intelligence quotient (IQ) theory. IQ theory is mainly interested in the concept of intelligence, which is seen as determining people's ability to learn, to achieve academically and therefore to take on leading roles in society. IQ theorists, such as William Stern (1871–1938), who was one of the developers of the theory in the early part of the twentieth century, claimed that core intelligence was innate. Many psychologists in America and Britain supported that conclusion. Tests of intelligence were often developed for specific purposes such as screening for the US army or immigrants. Psychologists including Terman and Binet developed instruments designed to test people's innate 'intelligence', which was analysed using the most recent statistical methods such as factor analysis, developed by Thurstone and Spearman. These analyses showed that all the items (questions) in those tests essentially measured one big factor, called 'G', or 'general intelligence'. Therefore, the theory states that people have one underlying general intelligence, which will predict how well they are able to learn and perform at school (Howe, 1997).

A major point of discussion is whether intelligence, as measured by IQ tests, is innate or learned – and to what extent. The initial theories largely stressed the innate nature of intelligence, seeing it as an inborn property. Subsequent research has, however, clearly shown that IQ can be raised through educational interventions, which means that it cannot be totally inborn. The successful Cognitive Acceleration in Science Education (CASE) programme in the UK, for example, does just that (Adey and Shayer, 2002). Another fact that points to the mutability of IQ is that average IQ test scores have been increasing steadily over the past decades, in all countries where they have been studied (Flynn, 1994). When testing someone's IQ, we are therefore testing their educational level at least as much as – if not more than – whatever innate ability they may possess. Also, it has become clear that children's IQ test scores are strongly influenced by their so-called cultural capital – that is, their cultural resources (how many books they read, what media they access, and so on). This in turn is strongly determined by their parents' socio-economic status, or their position in the social class system (Gould, 1983; Howe, 1997; Muijs, 1997).

As well as the issue of whether IQ is innate or acquired, IQ theory as a whole has been heavily criticized for many years now. Such criticism has been levelled at a number of things. The first of these is the methods used to measure intelligence, which produced G. While I do not wish to go into a discussion of statistics here, it is fair to say that the factor analysis method these researchers developed was specifically designed to come up with one big underlying factor – and usually does. Using different methods, you are likely to find far more factors. Therefore, in many ways it is pre-existing theories that led to the development of methods designed to confirm IQ theory (Muijs, 2004). The theory of intelligence also focuses purely on 'academic' intelligence, and so disparages other skills and abilities. As we will see, recent theories have taken a different approach (Gardner, 1983). The idea that there is one measurable factor that distinguishes people has also been widely misused. One of the earliest uses of IQ tests was to compare intelligence among groups in society, which were then said to be differently intelligent (and by implication more or less suitable to take on leading roles in society). The findings of these studies tell us far more about the societies in which they were carried out than about the 'intelligence' of different groups (which, as a matter of fact, does not differ significantly). Thus, in the USA, research concentrated on differences between racial groups; in France, it focused on differences between the sexes (men scoring higher than women); and, in the UK, the spotlight was on differences in social class (the upper classes being more intelligent than the working class) (Blum, 1980; Gould, 1983).

Notwithstanding these criticisms, it would be wrong to dismiss IQ theory altogether. There is evidence that an underlying general aptitude influences how well pupils perform on a variety of subjects. There is a far stronger correlation between pupils' performance in maths and English than is often realized, for example. As we will see later, if conceptualized as just one of a number of possible 'intelligences', the study of the kind of intelligence measured by IQ tests may have some merit.

Task 4.3

Do you think there is such a thing as intelligence? Is it inborn, acquired, or both? In what ways do you think IQ theory has influenced educational practice?

4.5 The theory of multiple intelligences

As we saw in the previous section, the theory of IQ stresses the existence of one overarching intelligence, a view that has become increasingly controversial with time. For many decades, however, no alternative theory was able to challenge the dominance of IQ theory in the study of ability and intelligence. This changed, however, in 1983 with the publication of *Frames of Mind* by Howard Gardner (1983), in which he set out his theory of 'multiple intelligences' (MI).

Gardner's view is very different from that of IQ theory. According to him, people do not have one general intelligence, but are characterized by a range of intelligences instead. So, rather than being globally intelligent, I may be particularly strong in certain areas, for example mathematics, while someone else may be particularly strong in another area, for example physical sports. To this end, Gardner (1983, 1993) distinguishes nine main types of intelligence.

4.6 Cognitive science

What many of the older learning theories (such as behaviourism and the theories of Vygotsky) were not able to incorporate was any idea of how the brain works (owing to limitations in research methods at the time). More recently, however, cognitive research and the neurosciences have progressed greatly, and are informing learning theory and education to an ever greater extent. To some degree, these new methods are confirming theories that we discussed earlier, including Vygotsky's views on learning, but they are also offering us important new insights.

Cognitive science – the study of how the mind works – combines research from a number of different fields, including psychology, neuroscience and computer science (in particular, the study of artificial intelligence). Technological advances have both led to major scientific discoveries in this area and to great public interest, especially in the visually attractive presentation of brain imaging results. Cognitive science has led to significant breakthroughs in understanding the different functions of the brain and how specific processes, such as visual processing, work. All of this has implications for our understanding of learning but has, unfortunately, also led to a lot of misconceptions and provided further material for educational snake-oil salesmen. Translating data from the laboratory to the classroom is not straightforward, not least because whereas cognitive scientists typically study the functions of the brain in isolation, in reality the different functions interact with the environment in complex ways. Willingham (2008) gives the example of overlearning: cognitive science suggests that learning is better retained when we continue to practise something even if we have full mastery of it. However, this is not likely to have a very positive effect on the motivation of our pupils! So, in this section we will discuss some of the things we can learn from cognitive science, but also what we can't.

One of the first major theories of learning that explicitly based itself on our emerging knowledge of the brain was cognitive information processing (CIP) theory. Especially important in this theory is the role of memory in learning processes. The memory consists of three parts: the *sensory buffer*, the *working memory* and the *long-term memory* (Figure 4.1).

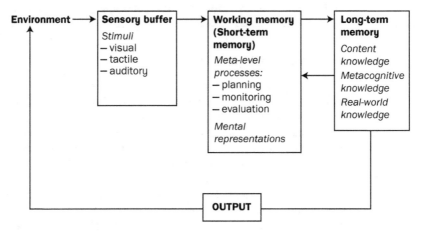

Figure 4.1 The structure of memory

The memory works as follows: one's experiences (tactile, visual or auditory) are registered in the sensory buffer, and then converted into the form in which they are employed in the working and long-term memories. The sensory buffer can register a lot of information but can only hold it briefly. Some parts of the information in it will be lost, other parts will be transmitted to the working memory. The working memory is where 'thinking gets done'. It receives its content from the sensory buffer and the long-term memory but has a limited capacity for storing information, a fact that limits human mental processes. The working memory contains the information that is actively being used at any one time.

The long-term memory has a nodal structure, and consists of neural network representations, whose nodes represent chunks in memory and whose links represent connections between those chunks. As such, nodes can be equated with concepts, and links equated with meaningful associations between concepts. Together these form schemata, or clusters of information. Activating one item of the cluster is likely to activate all of them (Best, 1999). This means that memorization and making connections are two crucial components of learning, according to CIP theory. Making connections is particularly important. The brain has literally millions of neurons that can be linked in neural nets in an indeterminate number of ways.

These structural characteristics of the brain have some important pedagogical consequences. In particular, if working memory is where information processing occurs, the limitations of working memory will be of great importance to learning. This, indeed, is the basic thesis of the so-called cognitive load theory, which suggests that the limited capacity of the working memory places a limit on the amount of information that can be processed at any one time. These limitations only apply to new information that has not been stored in long-term memory. This type of information can only be stored for a short period of time. This is not the case for information from the long-term memory, which can be retrieved for an indefinite time and in large quantities. Thus, it is important that learning tasks do not overload working memory, something that is often a problem with individual and discovery learning approaches (Kirschner *et al.*, 2006). Rather, a structured approach, akin to mastery learning, or an approach whereby cognitive load is limited through collaborative group work (with different pupils taking on different parts of the load) may be more appropriate and may account for the lack of effectiveness of discovery-oriented approaches among pupils with low levels of competence or prior knowledge as found in a lot of effective teaching research (Muijs and Reynolds, 2010).

The functioning of the short-term memory is not independent of the long-term memory. The more information about a specific area or skill that is contained in the long-term memory, the easier it will be for the working memory to retrieve the necessary information for quick processing. The processing of information in the working memory (or learning) is influenced by the extent and speed with which prior knowledge (in the broad terms defined here) can be accessed. Working memory processes are therefore in part determined by the extent of prior knowledge, as well as the extent to which prior knowledge is organized in a way that makes it easily accessible. These processes are open to change, and practice and learning can increase them, which in turn is linked to achievement in maths and reading (little research exists on other subject areas) (Molfese *et al.*, 2010). Of course, this potential for change means that popular sayings on the actual number of chunks of information that can be processed are not very helpful.

The way memory works has been found to be somewhat different from what we intuitively expect. For example, repeatedly re-reading a text or practising something a lot immediately after we have learnt it is not as effective as we think. We believe we are learning and

memorizing, but actually we quickly lose what we have learnt. More effective strategies are ·
spacing out our practice of new skills or knowledge, or interweaving it with practice of a
different skill and testing ourselves on what we have learnt (Brown *et al.*, 2014). The fact
that learning proceeds through making connections in long-term memory also means that
we require a solid knowledge base, contrary to the view that we do not need knowledge in
the age of the internet and constantly accessible information.

Another key finding from cognitive science relates to the importance of emotions in
learning. Emotions can both help and hinder learning. On the positive side, emotions help
us to recall information from the long-term memory, through allowing any information
received through the sensory buffer to be perceived as positive or as a threat. Research
suggests that the brain learns best when confronted with a balance between high challenge
and low threat. The brain needs some challenge to activate emotions and learning. This is
because if there is no stress, the brain becomes too relaxed and cannot actively engage in
learning. Too much stress, however, will lead to anxiety and a 'fight' response, which are
inimical to learning. A physically safe environment is particularly important in reducing
overly strong levels of stress (Sousa, 1998).

There are also a number of ideas that have been peddled as 'brain-based', but which do
not stand up to empirical scrutiny. Learning styles is one such area. Other so-called 'neuromyths' include the idea that we can neatly distinguish left- and right-sided brain functions,
that we only use 10% of the brain, and programmes such as the preposterous 'Brain Gym',
which remains popular in some schools in the UK and Europe. Unfortunately, one recent
(albeit small-scale) study found that such neuromyths were believed by almost 50% of the
teachers surveyed (Dekker *et al.*, 2012).

As a field of research, cognitive science is constantly developing, and it is highly likely
that further developments will in future strongly inform our views on learning, as well as
our teaching strategies. However, one caveat does apply: while I have presented a number
of basic findings, this research area is diverse. Findings from different studies are not
always in agreement and are usually far more subtle than one may outline in an introductory text. Also, it is dangerous to try and translate findings directly from brain research to
the classroom. This type of research should clearly inform us, but we need to take into
account that it has been conducted for very different purposes and will always need to be
matched to educational research findings on effective classroom teaching before it can be
translated into effective classroom strategies.

Task 4.4

What do you think the findings of cognitive science research mean for classroom
practice? Do they change what we previously thought about learning from the theories
of Piaget, Vygotsky and behaviourism?

4.7 Conclusion

In this chapter, we have looked at some educationally-influential theories of learning and
intelligence.

Behaviourism was mainly concerned with how we learn from external stimuli. Using experimental methods, behaviourists looked at how behaviour can be conditioned, for example by providing rewards and punishments.

Piaget used observation to develop his theories of learning. His key concept was *maturation*, the unfolding of biological changes that are genetically programmed into us. A second factor was *activity*. Increasing maturation leads to an increase in children's ability to act on their environment and to learn from their actions. An important finding of Piaget's work is that growing up does not just mean knowing more, it actually entails a change in how we think.

Vygotsky concentrated on the ways in which learning is a social process, based on interaction with others, both one's peers and those of an older age and higher developmental level. This process operates through *scaffolding* in the ZPD. The ZPD is the gap between what a person is able to do alone and what they can do with the help of someone more knowledgeable or skilled than themselves. Scaffolding refers to the way others can help us to bridge that gap.

IQ theory focuses on the concept of intelligence. According to IQ theorists, there is one underlying, general intelligence that determines our capacity for learning. More recently, Gardner developed his theory of *multiple intelligences*. Rather than just the one intelligence, according to Gardner there are nine. His theory has not gained much empirical support, however.

Cognitive science is increasingly influential in our understanding of learning and is producing valuable findings for educators. Key lessons include the importance of the *structure of memory* to learning, where we need to make sure that we encourage the making of connections in long-term memory and develop the necessary basis for learning through knowledge stored in the long-term memory. The important role of emotions in learning was also stressed.

Recommendations for further reading

Brown, P.C., Roediger, H.L., III and McDaniel, M.A. (2014) *Make It Stick: The Science of Successful Learning*. Cambridge, MA: The Belknap Press.

De Bruyckere, P., Kirschner, P. and Hulshof, C. (2015) *Urban Myths about Education*. Amsterdam: Elsevier.

O'Donohue, W. and Ferguson, K.E. (2001) *The Psychology of B.F. Skinner*. Thousand Oaks, CA: Sage.

Piaget, J. and Inhelder, B. (2000) *The Psychology of the Child*. New York: Basic Books.

Vygotsky, L.S. (1978) *Mind in Society: The Development of Higher Psychological Processes* (edited by M. Cole, V. John-Steiner, S. Scribner and E. Souberman). Cambridge, MA: Harvard University Press.

Willingham, D.T. (2010) *Why Don't Students Like School? A Cognitive Scientist Answers Questions about How the Mind Works and What it Means for the Classroom*. San Francisco, CA: Jossey-Bass.

5

Planning for learning

Paul Elliott

5.1 Introduction

Planning is the thought process that underpins success. This chapter will first explore the journey that teachers facilitate, from where the pupil is and has been (prior learning) to where they need to be (learning outcomes). Appreciating the range of approaches that can be used to help different types of learners on this journey is important, as is the ability to make conscious decisions about which are most appropriate in particular circumstances. Guidance will be given on how to construct a lesson plan and you will be shown how planning, at a very practical level, can help maximize pupils' learning. Effective planning is also the best way to reduce the stress and anxiety you will experience in the classroom and improve the chance of things going smoothly for you. Only good planning will give you the confidence and clarity of purpose that will encourage pupils to view you as someone in whose lessons they can learn.

When you observe an experienced and successful teacher at work, it can be hard to appreciate how difficult teaching is. The lesson will proceed smoothly, all the necessary resources will be at hand, and the pupils will be interested and engaged in the work. It is only when you try to emulate this performance that you will discover how much experience the teacher drew upon and/or how much effort they put into planning their lesson. Great lessons do not just happen, and they are not a product of good luck. Great lessons are a product of great planning – plus a little bit of inspiration and a tiny amount of good fortune. You can aspire to teach great lessons, but you will only succeed if you put time and thought into planning. The principles of good planning discussed in this chapter are relevant to lessons at Key Stage 3 (KS3), Key Stage 4 (KS4) and post-16.

By the end of this chapter, you should:

- know that good planning starts with establishing 'where your pupils are';
- know that good planning is driven by the learning that needs to happen;
- appreciate that good planning involves being clear about what you want pupils to achieve by the end of the lesson;
- understand that good planning requires you to think about how you can help pupils make progress;
- know that, as a new teacher, planning is something you can best demonstrate by producing a detailed written record of your thinking.

5.2 Establishing where pupils are

The success of your teaching is judged by the learning that your pupils do. Your first task is to establish what they already know, understand or can do: 'where they are now'. Two analogies can make this clear.

- *Bus stops*: Think of yourself as a bus driver. You need to be clear about your destination. However, you also need to make sure that you stop at the right bus stop to pick up passengers. If you do not stop, very few of your passengers will be able to run fast enough to catch the bus.

- *Building bridges*: Imagine that some of your pupils are standing on one bank of a river; other pupils are further back from the river while others are in midstream. The opposite bank is where you would like them all to be. How are you going to get them there? Only a few will be capable of jumping across. The rest will need some help along the way. You need to build a bridge, or a number of bridges, to cater for the needs of all pupils. The bridges need to start where your pupils are and end up where you want them to be. The bridges need to be built carefully and probably in collaboration with your pupils, otherwise some will fall into the river and be lost. Some scaffolding would be useful to construct the bridges.

It should be clear from both of these analogies that your lesson plan needs to take account of what your pupils already know, understand and can do. This applies at the start of a new topic but is also likely to be the case at the beginning of lessons. You may think the content of your previous lesson will be clear in your pupils' minds but remember that since they last saw you, they will have been to several other lessons on different subjects.

How can you find out where pupils are starting? There are a number of tactics that you can use:

Outside the classroom:

- Check what they have already studied by looking at the scheme of work (SoW) and the topics they have been taught prior to you taking the class. Cross-reference this information to the National Curriculum or examination specification(s).

- Look at pupils' work to check the subject matter they have encountered and find clues about their learning and the range of support you will need to give.

- Ask to see assessment data for the pupils in your class (for more on assessment, see Chapters 9 and 10).

Inside the classroom:

- Plan activities that will allow pupils to show their knowledge and express their thinking.

- Question pupils on aspects of the topic with which they may already have some familiarity. Listen carefully to their responses (see Chapter 8).

- Set tasks to find out what they can do before you start (see Chapter 9). These could include pre-tests, quizzes, concept mapping exercises, sorting games, and so on.

- Talk to pupils. Each individual will bring a different level of understanding to your lesson, and this may be revealed in discussion.

Avoid making assumptions about what a class will know or can do. If you do this, or misjudge where they are, you risk losing them by making too big a leap or boring or patronizing them by covering work they have done before.

5.3 Identifying learning objectives and outcomes

Once you have established where your pupils are, the next step is to decide where they need to get to. Think in terms of what the pupils need to know, understand or be able to do at the end of a lesson or series of lessons, rather than what you are going to *teach* them. The input that you make should be determined by the objectives you have identified and by the outcome desired. This approach is sometimes referred to as 'backward design' and the implication of this approach is that you should not be tempted to go with the methods, sources or activities with which you are most comfortable, but with the ones that maximize your chances of meeting your objectives. As Wiggins and McTighe (2005) explain, it is important that you can clearly state in your plan what pupils should understand or be able to do, irrespective of any constraints you may face. It is also crucial that you think in terms of what will characterize success and how you will *measure* it.

Planning can be based on the behaviours that are the desirable outcome of learning. The intended learning outcome for a lesson can be framed in a way that describes a behaviour, preferably a measurable one. However, there will be differences between, and within, subject areas. For example, planning in religious education might be more concerned with non-behavioural objectives, which are more difficult to measure. This might involve introducing objectives related to values, attitudes or beliefs.

It would be easy to devise a learning objective for a history lesson on the English Civil War that read something like:

> *Understand the reasons for the rise of the parliamentarian movement.*

While this may be a desirable outcome for the lesson, it is incredibly difficult to assess whether you have been successful. In contrast:

> *Be able to describe at least three factors that gave rise to the parliamentarian movement.*

This allows you to use questioning, output from class work, homework activities or testing to judge your success. The second version becomes part of the assessment cycle (see Chapter 9) and allows you to evaluate your own performance in terms of what your pupils have learned.

Bloom's taxonomy (Bloom *et al.*, 1956) is a useful way of categorizing the levels of demand in thinking and learning represented by different types of task. The taxonomy categorizes learning outcomes into three domains: cognitive (knowing and understanding), affective (emotional responses) and psychomotor (related to physical skills). The cognitive domain is further broken down into six areas:

1. Knowledge
2. Comprehension
3. Application
4. Analysis
5. Synthesis
6. Evaluation.

It is helpful to draw on this approach during planning, to ensure pupils are being given opportunities to demonstrate what they have learned. For instance, in addition to the word 'understand', mentioned in the English Civil War example above, there are other terms you might use when phrasing intended learning outcomes, but which give only a poor indication of what outcomes might be expected. For example:

know   *memorize*
become familiar with   *appreciate the significance of*

Figure 5.1 shows a range of terms that can be much more useful when trying to identify appropriate learning objectives. Note that these are in themes, related but not identical to Bloom's taxonomy. The terms demonstrate a general increase in demand or difficulty as you go down the table.

Draw	State	Record	Recognize	Identify	
Sort	Describe	Select	Present	Locate information from text	General increase in demand
Decide	Discuss	Define	Classify	Explain what...	
Devise	Calculate	Interpret	Construct	Clarify	
Plan	Predict	Conclude	Solve	Determine the key points from...	
Formulate	Explain why	Use the pattern to...	Reorganize	Explain the differences between...	
Link/make connections between...	Use the Idea of... to...	Use a model of... to...	Provide evidence for...	Evaluate the evidence for...	

Figure 5.1 Useful words to use for defining intended learning outcomes
Source: DfES (2002).

Task 5.1

Choose a topic from your subject that might be taught in one lesson or a short series of lessons. Use the National Curriculum, exam specification or the school's SoW to determine what relevant prior learning pupils might have. Identify the learning that you would expect to take place when you teach the topic and try to devise statements that describe the outcomes in behavioural terms, using Figure 5.1 for guidance. What techniques could you use to assess whether the teaching has been successful?

5.4 How can you help your pupils get there?

Having established where your pupils are starting from (prior learning and attainment) and where you need to get them (intended learning outcomes), you need to determine a number of other things if you are to plan effectively. First, you need to be clear how long you have with the class:

- the length of lessons will be determined by the school;
- the department's SoW may well specify the number of lessons to be devoted to the topic.

These factors will set the framework within which you work. Most departments have a SoW in place for most topics and do not expect a beginning teacher to create one from scratch. The SoW will usually be produced by a group of teachers who have collaborated to identify a route through the syllabus or curriculum that takes account of the learning that should take place, the resources and time available, the location of the school or college, and the ideas and enthusiasms of the staff. However, you will have some degree of flexibility in how you interpret a SoW and should certainly aim to personalize aspects so that you can take ownership of it when you translate it into real lessons. You would be wise to plan to use slightly less time than the SoW indicates, because some of the learning may take longer than you anticipate and things like school trips, epidemics and tests can curtail available time. Time might also be needed to incorporate actions in response to feedback from formative assessment (see Chapter 9).

Pupils can be more efficient learners at particular times of day (Owens *et al.*, 2010) and earlier in the week, so check when lessons are and plan accordingly. Also, check what the pupils have done immediately before your lesson, since this will affect their attention and energy levels.

Homework should be integral to your planning and, used carefully, can allow you to devote time in the classroom to collaborative rather than individual learning. This is sometimes referred to as the 'flipped classroom' (Bergmann and Sams, 2012) in which many of the activities traditionally undertaken during school time are done for homework (for example, reading, answering short questions and watching videos), while lessons allow time for more dynamic, interactive, collaborative and inquiry-based learning opportunities.

Before proceeding too far with your plans, you need to check what resources are available. Resources include props, ICT hardware and software, access to specialist teaching rooms and the support of technicians, librarians, learning assistants and even external guests. In some cases, you may have the chance to plan learning opportunities off the school site, such as theatre visits, geography or science fieldwork, and visits to businesses or religious sites.

How will you assess how successfully your pupils are learning? You will almost certainly be preparing them for some sort of summative assessment, be it an end-of-topic test, a modular exam, a final exam or coursework assignment, and you need to be aware of the attendant requirements and expectations. You have to ensure that your pupils are properly prepared but should avoid 'teaching to the test'. Concurrently, a major part of your planning should focus on how you are going to formatively assess pupils' progress during the topic. This should be guided by the intended learning outcomes, since you and your pupils need feedback on how effectively these are being met. It is also useful if you have some idea of where pupils are meant to be 'going next', since no topic that you teach will stand alone. Even if the factual content is not directly linked to any other part of the course, the development of pupils' skills will be. You need to know how the topic you teach will contribute to pupils' progression.

Really effective planning will also take account of what pupils are doing in other subject areas, especially where the learning in one subject supports pupil learning in another. For instance, work on graphs in mathematics should have some bearing on the graph work that is expected of pupils in science lessons. In this case, both science and mathematics teachers should be aware of each other's requirements and take account of these in their planning.

5.5 Planning for success

A huge amount of time during training is spent planning lessons. At times, this will frustrate and exhaust you, but it is central to your success as a teacher. All your plans must exist in written form to provide evidence of the process you have been through. Mentors, tutors and external examiners will draw on them to inform judgements about your progress towards qualified teacher status (QTS). Your lesson plans will also be scrutinized if the school in which you are working, or the course on which you are training, is inspected. It can be difficult to reconcile the amount of time you spend writing lesson plans when more experienced teachers seem to get away with something far briefer. The truth is that good, experienced teachers are far more practised at teaching than you are, and they automatically internalize aspects of the planning process. Even then they have to put detailed plans on paper when producing a portfolio of evidence to cross the pay threshold, or when their school is being inspected – although, fortunately, there is evidence that such demands may soon be moderated (Independent Teacher Workload Review Group, 2016).

The experienced teachers with whom you work will assist with lesson planning, but ultimately the plans need to be yours. Avoid trying to teach someone else's lesson, unless as a deliberate learning tactic. At the end of the chapter there are some websites from which you can download lesson plans, but you have to tailor them to suit your pupils' and your own needs and strengths. If the plan is not really yours, then you will not have engaged with all aspects of the planning and will not feel fully committed to it.

Planning lessons is a complex business. Let us consider some of the fundamental processes that you need to engage in.

Subject content and skills

First, you need to be clear what it is that your pupils are supposed to be learning. This will relate to specific subject-based information, but also to relevant skills, including those of literacy, numeracy and ICT and desirable habits such as collaboration, respect for peers and democratic decision-making. You then need to check that you have sufficient personal subject knowledge to help your pupils learn. If there are deficits in your knowledge, you will have to address them in advance of the lesson. At the same time, you need to consider how you are going to make your personal knowledge accessible to Year 7, Year 10, and so on; you need to re-shape the ideas and represent knowledge in different ways that will be accessible (Ellis *et al.*, 2002). This is one of the most challenging aspects of planning for new teachers.

Planning for progression

Make sure you understand what pupils already know and where they need to get to (intended learning outcomes). How will you take account of pupils' different learning preferences or multiple intelligences? How will you differentiate your teaching and expectations, so that all pupils can achieve something because of the support you give and the nature of the tasks you set? Some pupils are likely to have Individual Education or Learning Plans (IEPs/ILPs), or equivalent, which you may need to consider (see Chapter 21). How will the more able in your class be challenged and stimulated by your lesson? It helps to consider what you want *all*, *most* or *some* to be able to do (see Chapter 6 for more on differentiation).

Resources

You will need to think about resources at least three times during your planning:

1. Identify the resources available to you that *could* be used to help your pupils meet the objectives and intended learning outcomes.
2. Decide which of these resources is most appropriate.
3. Ensure the resources you want to use will be available. Some, like science equipment, you may need to order; some, like ICT suites or drama studios, you may have to book; and some you may have to collect for yourself – for instance, fresh fungi for an art lesson or leaflets from a medical centre for a personal, social, health and economic education (PSHEE) lesson. An oversight in these areas could be disastrous and very stressful. Check the minutiae, have you got: the key to the room; your flash drive; whiteboard pens; a class set of tablets; spare pens to lend pupils; and something to light the Bunsen burners with?

Resources may need to be organized well in advance of your lesson.

Physical safety should be incorporated into all planning, but for some subjects (for example, physical education, science and technology) this is a big issue and needs to be done overtly, in writing. In these subjects, you will probably receive specialized training in risk assessment. Psychological safety should also be considered: might your lesson contain content or activities that may upset or distress some pupils? In all cases, the responsibility for safety in lessons lies with the usual class teacher, so it is in their interests to check your plan in advance of a lesson. You should have your plan ready well in advance of a lesson for the class teacher and/or mentor to check.

5.6 Structuring a lesson

So far, we have considered planning in a general sense, as it applies to any defined period of learning. For much of your time, however, you will be preoccupied with the planning of specific lessons, so the rest of this chapter is devoted to this.

The underlying sequence of events should be based on backward design:

Identify your objectives and the learning outcomes
⇓
Identify and choose activities that help deliver the learning outcomes
⇓
Determine what you have to do to facilitate those activities

Be clear about the learning that needs to take place in the lesson and then investigate what activities might successfully bring this about, rather than trying to justify the use of an activity you have come across or had suggested to you. Next, think carefully about the lesson's exact structure. Adopting a clear structure for your planning will make the task of helping pupils meet the learning objectives more manageable. Pupils generally respond more positively if you have planned the learning as a set of discrete 'chunks' that will not test their powers of concentration for too long. If you make pupils do any activity for too long – for example, listening to you, writing, discussing, watching a film – you will experience diminishing returns. By incorporating variety, you maximize your chances of maintaining their interest, motivation and momentum. Conversely, there will be times when you have so successfully stimulated pupils' self-motivation, that they just want a solid block of time to get on with the task!

Generally, lessons should have clear beginnings, middles and ends. Too many student teachers get bogged down with the 'middle' and neglect to plan for an effective start to their lesson or a discernible end. The beginning of a lesson may well include a 'hook' with which to grab pupils' attention or a short starter activity that will help them focus and settle. The starter may be designed to remind them of what has been learned previously or provide an introduction to what is to come. The middle of the lesson should comprise the main activity/ activities and be followed by some sort of plenary activity where the teacher and pupils

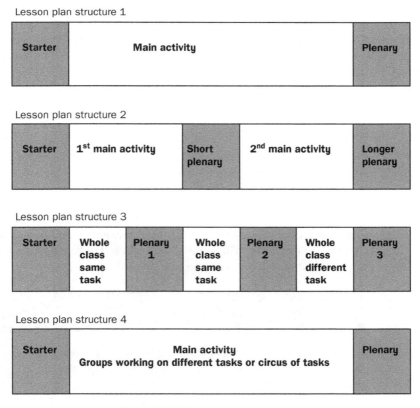

Figure 5.2 Model lesson structures
Source: Adapted from DfES (2002).

reflect on what has been learned. A lesson should not necessarily contain only three phases, but these components are a useful tool in planning. Figure 5.2 represents various ways of structuring a lesson, but each is built on the principle of starter, main activity, plenary.

5.7 Starting a lesson

Before your lesson, your pupils may have been stimulated – for example, through practical activity – and may find it difficult to settle. At the other extreme, they may have come from a stuffy, overheated classroom in which they were bored. If they have come to you after a break, then anything is possible! You may not have seen them for days, in which case the topic of your last lesson may have dimmed in the memory. In all cases, your challenge is to get them learning. Some experienced teachers have their class so well trained that taking attendance is an effective way of creating a calm, ordered start to a lesson. As a student teacher, starting a lesson this way can present a class with an opportunity to challenge your authority. Even if you can do it effectively, it is still a pretty boring way to start a lesson. It is much easier to take attendance once pupils have engaged with a motivating task.

In most circumstances, it is wise to reassure your pupils that you have a plan by sharing your agenda and the objectives of the lesson. Since you cannot guarantee that all pupils will be paying attention, it is worth reinforcing this visually. The learning objectives you have identified for the lesson are unlikely to be in a suitable format for sharing directly with pupils, but can easily be translated into pupil-friendly language, displayed on a board and explained to them. You can also flag up any new or recently introduced key words at this stage. Pupils will respond better if you give them this overview of the structure of the lesson, so that they understand what is expected of them.

It is in your interests to start your lesson in a way that focuses attention quickly on the main theme of your lesson. Plan something that:

- you can start quickly;
- will stimulate your pupils' interest; and
- will build bridges between relevant prior learning and today's lesson.

There are many tactics that can be used to start a lesson in a way that quickly engages pupils' attention, helps them to focus on the theme or purpose of the lesson and its objectives, but which do not take too much time. Table 5.1 offers a range of activities that can be employed to start lessons in ways that will achieve these aims. Try to employ a variety so that the starts of your lessons do not become predictable.

Task 5.2

Identify appropriate intended learning outcomes for a single lesson in your subject. Identify some of the tactics in Table 5.1 that could be used to get the lesson off to a good start. Choose two contrasting alternatives from the table and prepare in detail, identifying any necessary resources. When you come to teach the relevant topic, choose which starter activity to use and on the second occasion you teach it, use the other starter. Compare the responses.

Technique	Features
Sequencing	Put something on paper that has a sequential order to it. Give pupils envelopes containing the cut up sequence for them to order
Card sort	Prepare sets of cards that can be paired up. Pupils work in small teams to see who can correctly pair them fastest
Continuum	Pupils to position themselves on an imaginary line representing the range of views from one extreme to another (e.g. from *personal firearms should be banned* to *anyone has a right to carry arms*) or degree of comfort with a skill set (e.g. from *extremely competent with spreadsheets* to *not sure what a spreadsheet is*)
Traffic lights	Pupils have a red, amber and green card. Teacher asks a question and provides a possible answer. Pupils hold up relevant card: red = false, green = true, amber = uncertain. This could also be done using electronic devices such as clickers
Mini-whiteboards	Teacher asks questions and pupils have to write the answer quickly on mini-whiteboards and display them to the teacher
Five things	Give me the five key questions/key things/most interesting things/ most important things about . . . Teacher (or pupil) records the answers, which can then be used to recap prior learning
Visual/audio stimulus	The teacher shows something thought-provoking (e.g. a piece of art, an artefact, a short science demonstration, a YouTube clip, a news headline) and asks pupils to give their immediate response or raise questions about it

Table 5.1 Examples of starter techniques

5.8 Main activities

The main activity or activities in a lesson provide a time when you are probably not centre-stage. Activities with the greatest educational value are very often not teacher-led, but teacher-facilitated. The teacher is then free to check that pupils are on-task and give them valuable individual attention. The activities need to be carefully planned so they enable pupils to meet the intended learning outcomes and are accessible to all. Having identified a suitable activity ('task'), you need to think about how long pupils will need to complete it ('time') and whether you want them to work as individuals, in pairs, groups of three or more, or as a whole class ('team'). These are crucial decisions because they will affect the type of learning that takes place and have implications for classroom management and behaviour. Once you are clear about the activity, how long it will take and how pupils will be grouped, plan how all this is going to be communicated to the pupils. It may be useful to remember the task–time–team triangle while planning to make sure that you have considered all three aspects (see Figure 5.3).

Remember to make use of a good variety of techniques to suit multiple intelligences and the range of preferred learning styles in your class (see Chapter 6). You need to develop

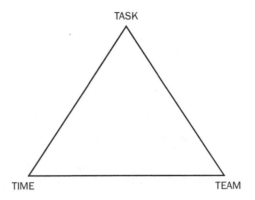

Figure 5.3 The planning triangle

empathy for those pupils who learn in a different way from yourself, so that they are not disadvantaged in your lessons.

You should also consider the nature of evidence the activity will generate and how it can demonstrate whether learning and progression have occurred. Evidence may come from the way in which pupils engage with the activity, the output or both. The quality and quantity of evidence you collect will be influenced by the way in which you communicate with pupils during the activity (see Chapter 8) and the subject that you teach. This will influence the range of opportunities for pupils to demonstrate what they have learnt, but you should plan to incorporate activities within lessons and across a series of lessons that enable pupils with different learning styles and aptitudes to show what they can achieve (see Chapter 6).

Once the structure of your lesson is in place, you need to review timing. Some student teachers find it difficult to get this right at first. The most common problem is running out of time. There are various reasons for this and they include:

- Underestimating how long tasks will take. Until you get some experience of the speed at which pupils can be expected to work, this is difficult to get right, but observing lessons and practice will help.
- Failing to give pupils a clear indication of task-time-team parameters, leading to confusion, uncertainty and lack of pace. This problem can be avoided by good planning.
- Failing to plan for all aspects of the lesson, for example, clearing away, setting homework, having a plenary.

Task 5.3

Read through the following case study and before you read the commentary that follows, identify all the ways in which Brittany's planning let her down.

Case Study 5.1

Brittany was looking forward to teaching the Year 10 history group that she had been observing from the start of her placement. They were a lively group, but there were enough interesting characters to make the prospect of working with them exciting. Her mentor advised her to plan lessons that would keep the class calm and to avoid activities that would require them to leave their seats. He gave her a list of films that he usually showed during the course of the unit on the Cold War and advised her to make full use of them. She chose to use one of the films in her first lesson with the class, believing that it would be a good way to engage their interest in the topic. She only reviewed the first five minutes of the film herself because her mentor had recommended it and its title appeared to be relevant. After a brief introduction to the unit and then the topic of the film, she went to connect her laptop to the projector only to realize that she had left the connector cord in the department office. Flustered, she asked one of the pupils to go to the room and recover the cord. By the time the pupil returned, the other members of the class were busy talking with one another and it took her a while to regain their attention. At first the pupils were attentive when the film began, but as it wore on their attention waned and they began to engage in low-level talking. Brittany wanted to stop the film, but her only plan for the latter stages of the lesson had been to engage the class in a discussion about the film. Unable to think on her feet she let the film drag on to the bitter end and was then faced with trying to lead a discussion with a now bored and fidgety class.

COMMENTARY: Brittany made several mistakes that could have been avoided with better planning. From her own initial observations of the class, she should have appreciated that they would need engaging lessons that might include legitimate opportunities for movement and self-expression. This demonstrates the importance of planning from where your pupils are, not only in terms of their knowledge but also their learning preferences. Because she had not made time to fully review the film, but had simply accepted her mentor's suggestion, she had no idea whether the film was at an appropriate level for the class, contained relevant content or was likely to engage them. She should have reviewed the whole film, evaluated its relevance to the curriculum and considered whether it was at the right level for her class. If Brittany had concluded that it was worth showing, then she should have thought about activities that could have been done before, during and after the film to maximize the benefits of her class watching it. She should also have given at least some thought to what alternatives strategies might work and to have planned a back-up activity in case her timing of the lesson was out. Even if she had properly reviewed the film in advance, during the lesson Brittany may still have realized that the film was not engaging the class, in which case she should have had the confidence to stop it and take the lesson in a different direction, but because her planning had been half-hearted she was not able to do this because she had failed to consider alternative ideas or fall-back activities. Her idea of leading a 'class discussion' is also an indication that her plans were poorly thought out because this technique is rarely satisfactory – much better to plan more structured opportunities for pupils to engage in discussion (see Chapter 8). Forgetting to pick up the connector cord is typical of the small planning oversights that can easily be made, but which not only interfere with your plans, but also undermine your self-confidence and your pupils' confidence in you.

5.9 Bringing a lesson to a close

How you end a lesson, or a discrete portion of a lesson, can have a profound effect on the overall quality of the learning that takes place. If you plan carefully how you will finish your lesson, or a portion of it, you can maximize the chances of pupils meeting the intended learning outcomes. The term 'plenary' is widely used to describe this phase of a lesson.

Plenaries have a number of uses. They are:

- an opportunity to draw the whole class together;
- a chance to review what has been learnt so far, including progress against intended outcomes;
- a time to direct pupils to the next stage of learning (signposting);
- a time to help pupils reflect on how they have learnt (metacognition);
- an opportunity for the teacher to make formative assessments, identify and explore misconceptions.

Pitfall	Suggested solutions
The class runs out of time and never gets around to a plenary	• Ask a pupil to be a timekeeper • Stick to your planned times, even if some activities have not been completed • Plan the plenary in detail
Pupils feel the lesson is over when the main activity finishes and do not take the plenary seriously	• Signpost what will be expected of pupils in the plenary • Involve pupils in delivering the plenary • Do not allow main activities to run until the bell rings
'All I need to do is get them packed away, sitting in their seats and repeat the objectives and set the homework'	• Over a course of lessons vary your plenaries to re-engage attention • Set homework at the beginning of the lesson
'It's become dull because it's always the same routine'	• Plan for variety • Design each plenary to fit the lesson and use it to revisit the objectives • Use it to whet the pupils' appetites for the next lesson
'You end up repeating everything and nothing is gained'	• Ask pupils to articulate the key points or consequences of the lesson • Ask pupils to apply the learning to a new context • Ask different groups to apply the learning indifferent ways
'The learning is implicit in what has been covered'	• Ask pupils to identify the factors that have helped to achieve the lesson's objectives

Table 5.2 Plenaries: common pitfalls and possible solutions

Source: Adapted from KS3 strategy training materials in DfES (2003b).

Successful lessons do not end with the teacher calling over the noise of pupils packing away: *'That's all we've got time for today, don't forget to bring your homework in next lesson'*. As you can see from Figure 5.2, even if there are other plenary phases during a lesson, there should certainly be one at the end. In your lesson plan, you should allow time for reflection so that pupils leave your classroom feeling that they have completed something and gained from the experience. This will build their confidence in you as someone who can help them learn. Ending lessons effectively is something that even many experienced teachers struggle with. Table 5.2 shows some plenary pitfalls and possible solutions.

5.10 Other planning issues

As well as planning your lesson so that it starts effectively, has appropriate main activities and a purposeful ending, there are a number of other factors that you need to consider and incorporate into your planning:

- The need to accommodate the special needs or exceptional ability of one or more pupils. Overlooking this can undermine your plans for the whole class.
- Opportunities for pupils to develop generic skills within the lesson, especially those relating to literacy, numeracy and ICT.
- Opportunities for your lesson to contribute to relevant cross-curricular themes such as education for sustainability.

5.11 The best laid plans . . .

Ideally, by the time your lesson starts, your plan should be so familiar to you that you do not need to consult it during the lesson. If you need subject knowledge crib sheets, keep them separate, for example on index cards or a Smartphone, so that they are easy to consult. Try to keep to your planned timing, especially allowing time for the end-of-lesson plenary. You may need to modify the plan during the lesson to take account of rates of progress, rates of learning, management issues caused by behavioural problems, interesting inputs from pupils, and so on. Ironically, good planning will give you the confidence to deviate from your plan.

5.12 When it's all over . . .

Once a lesson is over, it is tempting to transfer your attention to the next. First, however, you should try to learn from the experience you have just had. Part of this evaluation should focus on the lesson you planned as well as the lesson you delivered. How suitable did the plan turn out to be? Which parts of your planned lesson worked and which did not? Did you deviate from your plan and if so, why? Were the objectives met and do the outcomes support your verdict? To develop your practice, you need to make the time to ask these questions and answer them honestly.

5.13 Conclusion

In this chapter, we have learned that while lesson planning can feel like a chore, it is an essential and multi-faceted activity that underpins successful teaching. Establishing where your pupils are starting from and understanding where you want them to get to is crucial and should precede any detailed planning. This knowledge, rather than factors such as your personal preferences, convenience or precedent, can then drive your planning so that you end up delivering lessons that are tailored to your pupils' needs. Good planning is worth all the effort because it enables you to start a lesson with confidence, which in turn will encourage your pupils to believe in you as someone who can help them to be successful learners.

Recommendations for further reading

Aberson, M. and Light, D. (2015) *Lesson Planning Tweaks for Teachers: Small Changes that Make a Big Difference*. London: Bloomsbury Education.

Bergmann, J. and Sams, A. (2012) *Flip Your Classroom: Reach Every Student in Every Class Every Day*. Washington, DC: International Society for Technology in Education.

Brown, K.J. (2009) *Classroom Starters and Plenaries: Creative Ideas for Use across the Curriculum*. London: Continuum.

Ellis, V., Butler, R. and Simpson, D. (2002) Planning for learning, in V. Ellis (ed.) *Learning and Teaching in Secondary Schools*. Exeter: Learning Matters.

Fautley, M. and Savage, S. (2014) *Lesson Planning for Effective Learning*. Maidenhead: Open University Press.

Haynes, A. (2010) *Complete Guide to Lesson Planning and Preparation*. London: Continuum.

Wiggins, G. and McTighe, J. (2005) *Understanding by Design*. Alexandria, VA: Association for Supervision and Curriculum Development.

Wright, T. (2008) *How to be a Brilliant Trainee Teacher*. London: Routledge.

Webliography

BBC Schools: www.bbc.co.uk/schools/teachers – a variety of resource types, including lesson plans, work sheets and ideas for making use of BBC media.

TES: www.tes.co.uk/secondary-teaching-resources/ – lesson plans and other resources submitted by teachers.

Teacher Planet: www.teacherplanet.com – a North American site where teachers share lesson plans for a wide range of topics.

6

Using differentiation to support and extend learning

Kate Mawson

6.1 Introduction

Differentiation is at the core of quality teaching; it isn't something that we 'add on' or something aimed solely at the gifted or those with learning challenges. We differentiate in classrooms and in the school as a whole in order to address the needs that all pupils have, regardless of the opportunity afforded to them prior to reaching us. This chapter will highlight some of the differences there are between pupils, as well as research underpinning school and classroom approaches to differentiation. You will be helped to understand your role as a class teacher in providing differentiated learning and examples will be provided of differentiation strategies that you might employ in order to support and extend the learning of your pupils.

By the end of this chapter, you should:

- know what differentiation is and why it is an essential element of effective teaching;
- be aware of the role of differentiation in national policy;
- be familiar with different ways of differentiating in the classroom and at school level;
- understand the issues raised by differentiation.

6.2 Case studies

To set the context for what follows in this chapter, here are four case studies. The following are descriptions of pupils from the same Year 9 tutor group.

Case Study 6.1

Aisha is a high achiever in most areas of the curriculum. She performs particularly well in mathematics and science, and has very good literacy and language skills. She achieved a Level 6 in English, maths and science in Year 6. Aisha grasps new concepts very quickly, however the material is presented, and she can be impatient with what she perceives to be repetition. She likes to establish basic principles and to work from definitions; she is less interested in anecdotes or personal responses. Her strong analytical skills mean that she is often in a position to take a lead in group work, but she finds it difficult to work with those who grasp theoretical ideas more slowly or have priorities that are different from hers.

Case Study 6.2

Kayla generally gets on well with people and is popular with her peers. Teachers find that she is happy to make constructive verbal contributions in lessons but that her attitude changes and she 'acts the fool' when they set a written task. In Year 7, she got off to a bad start with some teachers because she was invariably the last to arrive at lessons and would usually give some excuse about being lost or having forgotten what time it was.

Kayla's difficulties stem from the fact that she suffers from dyslexia. Her difficulties with literacy were recognized early in Key Stage 2 (KS2) and most of her teachers were sympathetic and supportive, with the result that she did much better than originally expected. Provision was made for a reader/scribe in her maths and science lessons and for part of her English lessons. She achieved higher results in maths and science than she did in English.

Kayla finds it difficult to read from the board, especially if she is some distance from it, and cannot copy from the board at any speed. She finds it difficult to communicate her ideas in writing and gets frustrated when this is the only way to demonstrate her understanding. Structuring a piece of writing is particularly difficult for her. She reads competently but slowly and often stumbles if asked to read aloud.

Case Study 6.3

Ben's performance data on entry to secondary school indicated that he was working below expectations in maths and English. He had a reading age of 14 months below his chronological age. He did, however, do better in science. His Year 6 primary school report described Ben as a quiet child who needed to develop greater confidence in his own abilities. Ben has been placed in low sets for maths and English and a middle set for science. His reading age is now 10 months behind his chronological age following an intensive reading course in Year 8. Although Ben has made progress in KS3, he is unlikely to be in line with average attainment in the core subjects at the end of KS3.

Ben finds it difficult to concentrate during teacher expositions and doodles when required to listen for any length of time. He responds positively when visual stimuli are used to help him understand new concepts. Ben is left-handed and writes slowly and awkwardly, producing poorly formed script. In subjects that require extensive reading and writing, Ben is poorly motivated, slow to start tasks and gives up easily when he encounters difficulties. Written work is rarely completed. Ben does not seek help either from his peers or his teachers. In fact, he is at pains to avoid drawing attention to himself and always appears to be working assiduously whenever a teacher approaches. Ben does not enjoy group tasks, especially group discussions, and contributes little when he is obliged to work in a group. Although Ben's fine motor skills are poor, making intricate tasks difficult, he nevertheless enjoys practical activities. Ben likes investigating how things work and designing and making things.

Ben has an older brother, an able, confident boy in his final year in the sixth form. Throughout his school career, his parents and teachers have had expectations of Ben based on his brother's achievements. Unfavourable comparisons have dented his self-esteem.

Case Study 6.4

Rhys is a gifted young man who attained the highest KS2 results in his school; he is listed as eligible for pupil premium on the register. He is well-liked by other children and is respectful and courteous to staff. Rhys has a number of out-of-school interests, including playing online strategy games and volunteering at his local church's elderly people centre. As an avid reader, Rhys regularly demonstrates knowledge of many new topic areas and has an impressive vocabulary and reading age. His talents are varied, and he enjoys captaining the Year 9 rugby team as well as sketching and drawing. Rhys increasingly finds the work presented at school too easy and, occasionally, staff report that he spends time daydreaming or drawing secretly under his desk during activities. Recently, the standard of his homework has slipped and appears messy and rushed. His expected grades are high, and all teachers report that he is on target to meet them, although Rhys' mum never manages to attend parents' evening appointments to discuss his progress.

Task 6.1

Analyse the aptitudes and needs of each case study pupil. Now pick a topic that is taught at KS3 in your subject. Imagine that you will be teaching this topic to a mixed-ability group containing the four pupils described above. How might you adapt your basic scheme of work/individual lesson plans to cater for the needs of Aisha, Kayla, Ben and Rhys?

Spend some time thinking about the characteristic features and demands of your own subject. (For example, English literature involves reading closely and reflecting on texts to analyse features such as theme, imagery and characterization. Mathematics involves solving problems by thinking logically and sequentially about the application of general principles. Design and technology may require measurement skills, while drama demands fluency of the spoken word.)

Identify the following:

- distinctive features/demands of your subject;
- types of learners who may be well-suited to studying your subject;
- types of learning difficulty or learning preference that are likely to provide particular challenges for learners in your subject.

6.3 What is differentiation?

Differentiation calls on a teacher to recognize that the pupils in their classroom differ from one another in a variety of ways, including readiness, interests and learning profiles, and to respond to these differences with learning experiences matched to demonstrated individual pupil need (Tomlinson, 2014). The exercise you have just completed replicates the kind of thinking required to plan for differentiation – or the provision teachers and schools make to help each child achieve their full potential. Successful differentiation, then, entails teachers developing insight into individuals' needs and difficulties. It involves identifying the barriers to learning faced by some children and devising means of removing, or at least minimizing, them. It also entails identifying potential: the strengths and interests that each child brings to learning and finding ways to capitalize on these, including strategies to challenge those who have the potential to reach the highest level of attainment.

Skilful differentiation relies on the sound diagnosis of what is required to improve learning, and this is why differentiation and assessment are best viewed as activities that work in tandem. The best way to build a detailed picture of a child's learning profile is through formative assessment (see Chapter 9). Assessment helps a teacher to understand where a pupil currently is with their learning and to decide on next steps: what kind of experience, support or challenge will help them to progress. Information derived from assessment provides the basis for action and that is why differentiation and assessment are such closely related processes. Differentiation is not a set of instructional strategies but is a pupil-focused approach that values and plans for diversity in order that every pupil can succeed. Differentiation has been shown, even in small doses, to have a positive impact on pupil achievement and attitudes towards learning (Brighton et al., 2005).

All pupils are unique, and it is easy to identify differences between any pair of pupils. However, not all differences between pupils are relevant to their lives as learners. It is helpful as you go forward to have some idea about categories of difference that might affect the way you plan for pupils' learning.

Educational differences

At a very obvious level, pupils' learning in any lesson is affected by what they have already learnt in previous lessons. This will be influenced both by the teaching that they have experienced and by the way in which they responded to it. Pupils in your class will have:

- attended different schools at KS2;
- been in different classes for your subject last year;
- undergone different experiences in classroom learning – for example, they may have been absent from lessons, worked with different partners, paid different degrees of attention both in class and to homework or attended to different aspects of the lesson;
- been more or less successful in achieving the learning objectives;
- been exposed to varying degrees of support at home both in terms of help with school-based endeavour and in the process of developing and encouraging aspirations.

Most of the information about pupils' prior achievement that has been mentioned is available to you as the class teacher, if you know where to look for it and are prepared to spend a little time interpreting it. Some is not available, however, no matter how assiduous you are in collecting assessment information, and so there will always be a need to make ongoing assessment during the lesson and to adapt your plans accordingly. For example, you may need to provide support during the lesson for Ben when you find that he did not complete a unit of work from last year on which you were relying as background for the current topic. You may need to provide a more challenging task for Aisha when you find that she has encountered all the ideas in your introductory exercise already. Equally, you may have no idea that Kayla's stepsister regularly takes her to the cinema and her knowledge of a particular film version of the latest twentieth-century text you are studying far outstrips that required by the curriculum. Rhys may have no interest in what you are teaching as he covered it for a KS2 film critic writing competition, which he won, hosted by a local university.

Adaptability is key to becoming a successful teacher. As you enter the profession, you will develop this ability and it will become one of your most effective strategies as a leader of learning. In the beginning, however, you may need to predict these additional requirements and have two or three activities prepared in advance to support or challenge your pupils. Tailor work to their needs from the outset by harnessing your knowledge of what they already know.

Your understanding of a pupil's prior learning is essential to ensuring successful differentiation and some time spent assessing the learners at the beginning of a topic or unit is highly recommended. It is worth noting that one in every five primary pupils transfers to secondary school below the minimum expected level in reading, writing and mathematics. In 2015, this equated to 115,000 pupils (Standards and Testing Agency, 2015), and so many of your differentiation strategies may be around the literacy and numeracy levels of your lessons. You also need to be prepared in every learning episode for the eventuality that some pupils will already be confident with the learning you have planned, and so you must provide work that challenges the most able in order to develop a deeper understanding. In order to be differentiated upwards, the opportunities you provide for these pupils must be *different* not just *more* in number. Avoid rewarding children who complete the work you set with yet more work.

Psychological differences

It is a common shorthand in some schools to speak of pupils with 'high ability', 'low ability' or 'middle ability'. However, this terminology masks a great number of uncertainties and complexities about pupils' learning potential. The very existence of a characteristic that can be termed 'general ability' or 'intelligence' is hotly contested (see Chapter 4). In terms of differentiation at the classroom level, the notion of general ability, or even that of attainment in a general sense, is not particularly useful. It may help you to predict who will achieve a high score in the end-of-year assessment, but it doesn't tell you how to provide for the high- or low-attainer.

Can they work effectively on their own or do they need a lot of input from an adult? What kind of problems or tasks will they excel at or find difficult? You should also remember that pupils have variable needs across different subjects due to the nature of the requirements of those subjects and so the differentiation a teacher finds is required in French may be very different from that required in geography. It is important that we treat children as individuals within our subjects as well as across the subjects.

As teachers, you will be dealing with children and adolescents who are not yet adults. Some of the neurological differences in the brain prior to adulthood include a limited capacity for the following: long-range planning, mental flexibility, abstract thinking and holding in mind related pieces of information. This staged neurological development of the young people in our classes and schools is important to consider as we differentiate the learning opportunities we provide.

Social, cultural and gender differences

There are differences between pupils' interests and cultural experiences that can be linked to their sex and ethnic background. The teacher has the difficult task here of being continuously aware, in particular, of how these interests and experiences might differ from their own. For example, an art teacher who bases a lesson on designs of playing cards may find that the lesson is inaccessible for a number of pupils. Some pupils in the class may be unfamiliar with playing cards and others may find them offensive on religious grounds because of their association with gambling.

Gender or, more accurately, sex differences have significant effects on attainment in the classroom, in some circumstances stemming from the physical differences evident in boys and girls such as girls' finer motor skills in art and boys' bodily height and muscularity – which tends to lead to separate teaching in PE – to other circumstances including statistical differences in subject choice. A well-differentiated curriculum should involve opportunities for boys and girls to explore areas that they may not feel high self-efficacy towards (such as reading and writing for boys and science and maths for girls). These opportunities should promote achievement and appreciation of the unfamiliar or uncomfortable subject matter in order to widen the choices for both sexes.

Specific needs

Some pupils have been identified as having learning needs that make special provision necessary, or as having special educational needs (SEN). Such pupils benefit from early identification of potential barriers to learning and differentiation strategies designed to remove or minimize their impact (for more detail, see Chapter 21). For example, the school's special educational needs coordinator (SENCo) has provided the following advice to Kayla's teachers:

'It is recommended that Kayla sits near the front in lessons where she can more easily read from boards and is more likely to build a positive relationship with the teacher through verbal interactions. Kayla will particularly benefit from opportunities to consolidate and demonstrate her understanding in ways that do not require a written response. Where possible, written tasks should be short and employ techniques such as writing frameworks to help her organize her response. Teachers should avoid asking Kayla to read in class, because she is very embarrassed about her difficulty with this. Giving homework well before the end of a lesson will give Kayla time to copy it down correctly.'

Effective differentiation is not the production of a detailed education, health and care plan for every pupil, although for some this is an entitlement; instead, it is the professional judgement of the teacher acted on in such a way that learning is accessible for all. Special educational needs can take a great many forms and it is not possible to do justice to them in this chapter. You will find more information in Chapter 21, which looks at SEN in greater detail. It is worth drawing attention here, however, to the fact that more able, gifted and talented pupils can also be considered to have SEN.

Task 6.2

Think about Rhys in your lessons. How will you ensure he is engaged and making the same expected progress as the rest of your pupils? What barriers to his learning might need to be overcome due to his pupil premium status? Is there more you could do for him other than getting him to support other learners in the room?

6.4 Differentiation and planning

It is sensible to consider how differentiation affects the types of planning undertaken by student teachers: the medium-term planning of units and scheme of work (SoW) and the short-term planning of individual lessons. Some aspects of differentiation are best planned for in the medium term. For instance, it may not be possible to cater for a wide range of preferences within a single lesson, and to attempt to do so would fragment the planning. Therefore, it is helpful to think about catering for different preferences as part of your overall planning for a SoW rather than attempting to tackle this on a lesson-by-lesson basis. Similarly, as well as having objectives for individual lessons, it is important to clarify longer-term aims for a SoW, distinguishing between essential knowledge, skills and concepts that all pupils will be expected to learn, additional materials that most pupils will assimilate, and more advanced ideas and skills that some learners might master.

A similar process should take place at the level of individual lessons where it can be useful to distinguish between key, support and extension materials:

- *Key material* refers to information, concepts and activities that are essential for all learners to address in some way.
- *Support material* refers to provision that supports pupils who find the key materials difficult for physical, psychological, emotional, behavioural or linguistic reasons. Support materials are not necessarily easier, but they will have been developed with access in mind.
- *Extension materials* take the key materials to a higher or more complex level and are developed for those who do not find the key materials sufficiently challenging.

Differentiation can be considered in relation to lesson content, processes and products. The most commonly used differentiation strategies are Support, Outcome, Resource, Task and Team (SORTT). We describe each of these differentiation strategies below.

Differentiation by support. In-class support could be provided by you or by assistants. At the planning stage, decide how your own time and that of assistants will be deployed (see Chapter 21). Some pupils will need help at the beginning to get going with tasks, others will need help intermittently, and others will need support throughout. Consider non-adult-led support through help desks, pupil learning leaders or resource banks. The use of peer support and lead learners can be particularly effective. For example, in PE classes, a lead learner can be identified and given the opportunity to develop instructional and coaching skills while supporting their peers through the task.

Differentiation by outcome. Pupils work on similar tasks but the tasks are open-ended to allow for different outcomes. For instance, in a science lesson pupils might be required to present the arguments for and against gas-fired power stations, with a choice of presentational formats on offer, including a poster, an audio recording of a speech and a written report. As long as the assessment criteria for the task are clear, all pupils should be able to achieve the highest possible outcome regardless of the format they choose.

Differentiation by resource. Pupils do similar tasks but use different resources. For instance, all pupils produce a descriptive account of weathering during a geography lesson, but some base their account on reading about the process in written sources and others, such as Ben, base their account on watching a video.

Differentiation by task. Pupils use similar resources but complete different tasks. For example, all pupils use the internet to research a topic in media studies but high-attaining pupils, such as Aisha and Rhys, compile a report that requires them to synthesize and evaluate their findings, whereas lower-attaining pupils with SEN such as Kayla follow structured guidelines and search for answers to specific questions. Pupils with learning difficulties often find tasks more manageable when they are broken down into a series of small steps.

Differentiation by team. Pupils work in different sized groups for different tasks, including the class as a whole, smaller groups of 5–6 pupils, as pairs or as individuals. You may mix this up during a topic, across a SoW or within a single lesson. Think about allocating roles to individuals within groups as well as the make-up of each group. Are you going to group by gender or attainment? Or might you set up groups with a mix of attainment?

The above strategies can, of course, be used separately but they are more often used in conjunction with one another. Indeed, differentiation often involves a cluster of interventions designed to support and challenge children in their learning. For instance, Kayla's teachers make a point of monitoring her progress closely whenever she has to follow written instructions, a task that is made easier by seating Kayla near the front of the classroom. In science and mathematics, Aisha often works with a small group of high-attaining pupils focusing on open-ended, investigative tasks where there is scope for taking risks in learning and devising creative solutions to problems. Rhys regularly finds himself employed as the lead learner in the classroom to support pupils like Ben.

Clearly, differentiation as part of lesson planning should focus on the detailed provision teachers make to meet the specific needs of individuals and groups within a class but the requirements of all children have to be considered at the lesson planning stage with differentiation embedded in the process – and not seen as the addition of a few support and extension activities that can be tacked on after a lesson plan has been finalized. Thus, when Kayla's teachers set written tasks, they have to consider whether it would be appropriate for her – and other children who find writing difficult – to complete the same basic task by working in a different medium, possibly by word-processing a response or by producing an audio version. Alternatively, such children may be provided with a writing frame to enable them to complete the task or they could annotate a diagram rather than producing an extended prose response.

There are various organizational considerations to make, too. For instance, Kayla benefits from sitting near the front of classes where she can more easily read from boards and has frequent opportunities to interact with teachers. Giving homework well before the end of a lesson gives Kayla time to copy it down correctly. Differences in temperament and attainment make it difficult for Aisha and Ben to cooperate on group tasks, so the composition of groups requires careful consideration.

Differentiation at the lesson level is also shaped by feedback from ongoing formative assessment (see Chapter 9). For instance, in mathematics, before they started their work on addition of fractions, a class completed a pre-test. The results of the test suggested three broad starting points for this new topic. The understanding of equivalence of fractions needed to address addition was in place for over half of the group. However, over a quarter of the group had misconceptions that would have to be eliminated before they could tackle the work and a small group were already competent in addition of simple fractions with similar denominators and needed to extend their understanding. Pupils were assigned to groups based on their results in the pre-test and completed tasks tailored to their needs. The use of feedback to set individual and group learning targets is another example of the close relationship that should exist between assessment and differentiation.

It is important to remember that, where learning has been differentiated, assessment criteria and longer-term objectives can remain constant so that, while different outcomes are recognized and valued, we also ensure that all pupils make the required progress without limiting them by presenting a watered-down version of the curriculum.

Task 6.3

Consider these common methods of instruction. How many ways can you think of to differentiate them? Remember to include differentiation for support and extension and consider the SORTT acronym as you go through the list.

- Teacher exposition
- Question and answer
- Modelling/demonstration
- Worksheets
- Reading a text
- Watching audio-visual material
- Internet research

6.5 Differentiation, personalized learning or mastery

So far, we have focused on what teachers can do inside their classrooms to help pupils to achieve their full potential. However, in the first decade of the twenty-first century, differentiation became subsumed by a policy initiative: *personalized learning*. It was, however, highlighted by Kulik *et al.* in 1978 when demonstrating that high pupil achievement was an outcome of personalized instruction, the forerunner of personalized learning. Personalized instruction has repeatedly been shown to be more effective than the traditional lecture, or chalk and talk approach (Klishis *et al.*, 1980). Personalized learning is, however, a nebulous concept that has been variously defined. The name seems to suggest that each pupil should follow an individualized learning programme. Despite this, teachers have been urged to view personalized learning as a 'philosophy' that has been embraced by some schools for many years. It entails:

> . . . tailoring education to individual need, interest and aptitude so as to ensure that every pupil achieves and reaches the highest standards possible, notwithstanding their background or circumstances and right across the spectrum of achievement . . . giving every single child the chance to be the best they can be, whatever their talent or background.
>
> (DfES, 2006)

Thus, although personalized learning addresses the needs of all children, including those who are more able, gifted and talented, it has been promoted as playing a particular role in raising the aspirations and attainments of disadvantaged children. The Gilbert Review (DfES, 2007: 6) suggested that:

> Put simply, personalising learning and teaching means taking a highly structured and responsive approach to each child's and young person's learning, in order that all are able to progress, achieve and participate. It means strengthening the link between learning and teaching by engaging pupils – and their parents – as partners in learning.

The five components of personalized learning are:

1. *Assessment for learning* and the use of evidence and dialogue to identify every pupil's learning needs.
2. *Teaching and learning strategies* that develop the confidence and competence of every learner by actively engaging and stretching them.
3. *Curriculum entitlement and choice* that delivers breadth of study, personal relevance and flexible learning pathways through the system.
4. *A pupil-centred approach to school organization* with school leaders and teachers thinking creatively about how to support high-quality teaching and learning.
5. *Strong partnerships beyond the school* to drive forward progress in the classroom, to remove barriers to learning and to support pupil well-being.

One issue already alluded to, that personalized learning is a nebulous concept that has been variously defined, led a team from Sussex and Cambridge universities and the UCL Institute of Education to investigate the personalized learning approaches of a number of schools in 2007. They concluded that 'there was widespread uncertainty as to what was meant by "personalised learning"' (Sebba *et al.*, 2007: 18).

With personalized learning falling out of favour, and possibly misunderstood by many, there appeared to be a need for an approach to learning capable of raising academic standards across all schools. Mastery learning, which was first put forward as a theory by Bloom in 1968, is very much in evidence across many recently developed instructional models and school-based interventions; indeed, changes to the National Curriculum, which came into effect in September 2014, mean that the curriculum is underpinned by the concept of mastery learning (see Chapter 13 for more on the curriculum). Research has consistently linked some of the practices of mastery learning to highly effective instruction and pupil learning success (Guskey, 2009; Marzano, 2009; Rosenshine, 2009).

In 2016, the British Government announced that 8,000 primary schools would receive £41 million over four years to support the mastery approach. Mastery learning can be described as 'how a child can apply much of the curriculum as a whole in more complex and in-depth, cross-objective, multi-modal methods. It demonstrates how skilfully a child can apply their learning. Mastery is not just knowing a fact, but it is using that fact in increasingly more complex situations' (Holland Junior School, 2018). Unless a learner attains typically 80% in the current unit, they are not allowed to progress and additional work including tuition, peer support, small group discussions or homework is provided so that they can reach the expected level.

Evidence from meta-analyses collated by the Education Endowment Foundation shows a five-month learning gain when pupils are taught using mastery learning techniques, but this is an average and there tends to be a cluster in the results. Some research shows advances of six months, with a large body of research demonstrating no advance whatsoever. Mastery learning appears to be a promising strategy for narrowing the gap, as lower-attaining pupils increase by one or two months on average. This is similar to the critique of Bloom's mastery learning in that both Arlin (1984) and Slavin (1987) questioned whether mastery learning simply shifts learning from high to low achievers. They suggested that mastery learning sacrifices coverage for mastery, emphasizing that rapid coverage is likely to be of the greatest benefit to high achievers and high mastery of greatest benefit to low achievers.

The danger of all three approaches is that the most able – the gifted, the talented or the highest attainers (whatever label we afford to this group) – are overlooked in the classroom. When teachers differentiate, they tend to focus their efforts more on the struggling learners, believing that gifted pupils do not need differentiation (Brighton *et al.*, 2005). Unfortunately, some teachers in heterogeneous classrooms tend *not* to view gifted pupils as in need of differentiation and so provision for these pupils is regularly lacking.

As you develop a repository of mastery learning techniques, an understanding of personalized learning components, and numerous ways of differentiating units of work, lessons and activities for pupils with SEN, you should aim to provide just as much challenge for your more able, gifted and talented pupils. In order to effectively 'teach up' to these more able secondary school pupils, you require not just a knowledge of these techniques but also excellent subject knowledge. Focus on improving your own subject knowledge as well as your pedagogic knowledge throughout your career. According to Hertberg-Davis, excellent subject knowledge is a prerequisite for effective teaching:

> . . . to differentiate the curriculum in meaningful ways for all students, and in particular for gifted learners, teachers need a deep understanding of the scope and sequence, big ideas, resources, and unanswered questions of a discipline.
>
> (Hertberg-Davis, 2009: 252)

6.6 Organizational approaches to differentiation

Schools also have a part to play in recognizing pupils as individuals and ensuring their provision caters for different learning needs. Traditionally, differentiation has been seen as a response to ability, and so at school level it has involved the use of organizational strategies – 'setting' and 'streaming' being the most common.

Setting involves allocating pupils to ability groupings on a subject-by-subject basis, allowing for variations in performance from one subject to another. Higher sets will, in theory, be set more demanding work using more sophisticated learning materials and more complex tasks. The 1997 White Paper, *Excellence in Schools* (DfEE, 1997a), marked a shift in official thinking about organizational differentiation strategies, requiring schools to consider setting, unless alternative approaches could be shown to be more effective. Despite this official endorsement, concerns about setting remained. There are dangers that pupils placed in lower sets will be 'labelled' by themselves, their peers and teachers. Pupils can lose motivation when they are placed in the 'bottom set', and disaffection quickly spreads throughout the group creating an almost unteachable class. Setting can unfairly limit teachers' expectations for pupils in lower sets and sometimes leads to an inequitable distribution of resources, both financial and human. (For more information, see the *Teaching and Learning Toolkit* [EEF, 2018].)

Streaming involves allocating children to a stream for all or most parts of the curriculum. It is an approach grounded in the notion of ability as 'general', that pupils will perform at a similar level in the various subjects that make up the curriculum. This is an outmoded view and it is unusual for streaming to be adopted today. Where it is adopted, this is often for pragmatic reasons to do with ease of timetabling.

Whatever mechanism is used for allocating pupils to classes, it is important to recognize that every group, however finely set, will contain children with a range of prior attainments and learning preferences. The only difference between a school practising 'setting' or 'streaming' and one using 'mixed ability' groups is in the spread of attainments and needs to be found within each group.

In addition to, or in some cases instead of, setting or streaming, some schools have experimented with grouping pupils differently according to emotional requirements or sex. For example, vulnerable Year 7 pupils arriving at a large secondary school from very small primary schools are sometimes grouped together with less staff changeover and more static rooming, allowing pupils to settle more easily into secondary school. Some schools have also become increasingly responsive to pupils as individuals; the approaches listed below demonstrate this. The following subsections will convey some of the main ways in which schools are currently responding to the challenge of differentiation.

Target-setting

Target-setting takes place at different levels in schools. Chapter 9 considers target-setting as a feature of classroom life – the individual learning targets that are negotiated by teachers with pupils on an ongoing basis to enable children to progress in a subject. This day-to-day target-setting takes place within a framework of whole-school target-setting. Many schools run target-setting days where the timetable is collapsed to provide time for individual consultations between subject teachers, pupils and their parents. The aim of such meetings is to review a child's progress and potential and to establish targets for the medium term (for example, the end of a Key Stage or year). Once individual targets have been agreed, the information is collated and shared among relevant staff. Overall progress can then be monitored, for instance by a pupil's form tutor, year head and school assessment coordinator. Continuous monitoring allows schools to quickly detect when an individual's progress exceeds or falls below expectation – and to agree an appropriate intervention strategy.

Mentoring

Many people perform the role of mentor for secondary pupils, including older pupils in a school, members of a school's senior management team, university students and business mentors from local workplaces. Although the role and responsibilities vary from scheme to scheme, mentoring represents an attempt to identify underperforming individuals whose learning may benefit from being in a mentoring relationship.

Support for the curriculum

The National Curriculum established pupils' entitlement to a broad and balanced curriculum. You will encounter a host of initiatives designed to support a broad and balanced curriculum by removing barriers and facilitating access for children with learning difficulties. For pupils who require additional challenge, the curriculum is extended in various ways. For instance, enrichment programmes may supplement the curriculum for high-attaining pupils, whereas low-attaining pupils may be provided with in-class support from a teaching assistant. Alternatively, pupils may be withdrawn from classes either for parts of the week or for certain subjects and taught by specialist SEN teachers or assistants. Sometimes pupils are withdrawn for several weeks at a time during which their education takes place in a special unit attached to a school. Chapter 21 explains how the work of other adults in the classroom may be organized.

6.7 Conclusion

This chapter has provided a brief introduction to the many ways in which differences between individuals can impact on their learning and to some of the approaches adopted by individual teachers and schools in response to these differences. Responding to individual differences is possibly one of the most difficult aspects of a teacher's role and, if taken seriously, will provide you with challenges for the rest of your career – challenges that, through continuous development of both your subject and pedagogical knowledge and through engagement with educational research, you will tackle with relish.

Recommendations for further reading

Cowley, S. (2018) *The Ultimate Guide to Differentiation*. London: Bloomsbury.

Department for Education and Skills (DfES) (2007) *2020 Vision: Report of the Teaching and Learning in 2020 Review Group (The Gilbert Review)*. London: DfES Publications.

Kerry, T. (2002) *Learning Objectives, Task-setting and Differentiation*. Cheltenham: Nelson Thornes.

McNamara, S. (1999) *Differentiation: An Approach to Teaching and Learning.* Cambridge: Pearson.
Pollard, A. and James, M. (2004) *Personalised Learning: A TLRP Commentary.* Swindon: ESRC.
Tomlinson, C.A. (2014) *The Differentiated Classroom: Responding to the Needs of All Learners,*
    2nd edn. Alexandria, VA: ASCD.
Weston, P., Taylor, M., Lewis, G. and MacDonald, A. (1998) *Learning from Differentiation.* Slough:
    NFER.

7
Working with parents and school support staff

David Middlewood

7.1 Introduction

To be an effective teacher, you need to be able to work with various other adults to provide the best possible service for your pupils. In other words, as a teacher, you need to see yourself as a member of a team some of the time in order to improve the educational outcomes of your class. Many of these adults will be your professional colleagues – teachers and assistants, and various support staff – but others will be those external to the daily working of the school, such as social workers, specialist support service agencies, health workers, and so on. Perhaps the most important of all, however, are parents, who are the key adults in a young person's life. In this chapter, when the term 'parents' is used, it encompasses all those in a parent or carer role, including step-parents, foster parents, absent parents and carers, and does not preclude grandparents and others in similar roles or circumstances if they provide support to a young person.

By the end of this chapter, you should:

- understand why working with parents is so important;
- be able to develop your own ideas about the role of parents and their relationship with the school;
- be aware of the various ways in which parents may be involved with the school;
- appreciate the range of attitudes that different parents may hold towards the school and teachers;
- know how to develop professional strategies to enable effective working relationships with parents of your pupils;
- understand the roles of school support staff and their importance;
- be capable of developing strategies for working effectively with various support staff.

7.2 Why are parents so important?

There are perhaps three good reasons why parents are the most significant 'others' in any young person's learning journey:

1. They are the *first* educators of children, before any formal schooling starts, and it is widely accepted that this period is one of the most important in a person's life. Parents

remain in a relationship with their children throughout their own lives. Many teachers will admit that their own parents still refer to them as their 'boy' or 'girl' – even in middle age! The teacher–pupil relationship, on the other hand, ends when the pupil leaves school.

2. It is widely acknowledged that parental support is one of the most significant factors in pupil achievement and progress at school. Desforges and Abouchaar's (2003) review of many studies confirmed this. Progress can be hampered when relationships between home and school are anything other than positive.

3. Finally, although it seems obvious to say so, parents are the providers of children to the school – no children, no school!

Attitudes to the role of parents in the education of children differ from country to country, often depending on history and culture. Even in the United Kingdom, although there are statutory issues that all schools must address in organizing home–school links, the attitudes and application of policies vary from school to school. Briefly, the role of parents may be viewed as follows:

A. parents as consumers of a service provided by the school;
B. parents as partners, with the teachers as the experts and the parents as their supporters;
C. parents as co-partners in learning, with each partner having a distinct and complementary role to play in the child's education;
D. parents as part of the learning process that encompasses the 'triad' of school–pupil–parent (Coleman, 1998).

Of course, there may be elements of each of these in any school's approach, but it is important for any new teacher to know, first of all, what the statutory requirements are that need to be fulfilled in dealing with parents whose children they teach or tutor and, second, what the school's specific policies and philosophy are in this area.

Task 7.1

As a new teacher, you should read carefully the school's documentation regarding each of the following:

*   Its formal statement about its home–school agreement, setting out clearly what the school is entitled to expect from the parents and what parents can expect from the school.
*   Information about parents' consultation meetings during the school year, giving the dates and times and the format to be followed.
*   Written reports for parents on the progress of their children, when these are due and the format to be followed.
*   Other information about proposed events for parents, such as open days or evenings, and curriculum sessions.

> Of these, you will certainly be contributing to the consultation meetings and the written reports. Once you have consulted the above documentation:
>
> • Consider what picture you are forming about the school's overall attitude to home–school relationships. Does it approximate to any of A, B, C or D as described?
> • Are you clear about the procedures that are to be followed in any contact with parents?

7.3 Ways in which parents can be involved with the school

There are a number of ways in which individual parents are able to become involved in their children's school, some formal and some informal. Some of the more formal ways, in addition to those mentioned earlier, include:

• standing for election as a school governor;
• becoming a member of the school's Parent–Teacher Association (PTA) or equivalent group; in some schools, all parents are automatically deemed to be members of such a group, but individuals can stand for election to its committee;
• joining in fund-raising or publicity events organized by such groups;
• responding to and even contributing to newsletters that are sent out to parents;
• attending special events organized for parents, such as curriculum evenings that spotlight a particular subject or a new development in the school's curricular provision, making an appearance at sports events, or supporting arts and drama productions;
• supporting events that are jointly organized by the school and parents on topical issues of concern, such as cyber bullying, substance abuse, eating disorders, and so on.

Other less common ways of becoming involved may depend on the level of support that the school normally gets from its parents and the extent to which it feels it can develop this. A good school gets to know its local community and adapts its approach to parents accordingly. For example, schools serving localities where parental literacy levels are low often provide the means to enable those parents to improve their skills in a way that is not patronizing. Some schools offer classes in basic parenting when they feel the need is there, usually ensuring these are led by people other than teachers. In more rural areas, where parents can feel isolated, schools might organize parent/child revision sessions for pupils in their examination years and facilitate a network of villages to enable local support groups to operate.

Other examples include targeting parents who are particularly disadvantaged in various ways. Schools that have parents whose first language is not English, and the children therefore only speak that language at home, have established workshops for these parents that often involve the children as well. In areas of significant unemployment, some schools have developed courses for parents to help them improve their employability skills. In Chapter 24 you will find more detail on ways in which schools help to work with parents to raise the attainment of pupils in disadvantaged circumstances.

Many of the above initiatives are often carried out by community schools, some of which have what is known as extended provision and/or adult learning facilities available on site. However, it is possible for any school to arrange them, for the benefit of their pupils and parents.

7.4 The range of parents' attitudes to the school

For all parents, the most obvious way they are involved with a school is through their own children and, no matter how much we speak of 'the parents', they are not an entity as such any more than 'the teachers' or 'the pupils' – everyone is an individual. Just as you are expected to know the standards and needs of individual pupils, as a teacher you also need to deal with their parents in a similar way. Although, of course, one can generalize as to whether parents are supportive or not, each parent is entitled to be treated as an individual mother or father of their son or daughter.

Let us now consider a couple of attitudes that can be found in the following remarks:

'The parents you most need to see are the ones that never come into the school!'

This implies that the pupils who cause most concern to teachers, through poor work or behaviour, or failing to work to their potential, have parents who tend not to come to consultation meetings or respond to communications from school.

Case Study 7.1

Karl is a Year 9 pupil in your class. His attendance record is below average and he has truanted internally from your lessons on two occasions. He does not make any effort to catch up after his absences. He does attend detentions, which he is given as sanctions. You believe his ability in your subject is good but not outstanding and that he is achieving well below this level. Letters home to his parents have received no reply. Neither of his parents attended the recent parents' consultation evening. He has a sister in Year 7 who is apparently doing reasonably well, although the parents did not attend her consultation meeting either. Questions directed to Karl about this are met with a shrug of the shoulders; he will not discuss it further.

- Make a list of the possible reasons why Karl's parents do not reply to letters.
- List possible reasons why Karl's parents do not attend parents' evenings.
- Make a note on anything else you think you or the school may be able to do to improve Karl's attendance and educational outcomes.

COMMENTARY: Your reasons probably include practical ones such as inconvenient timings of parents' evenings, or letters home not being delivered. However, other possible reasons include:

- poor quality of literacy at home;
- perception of the school as an alien institution that should be avoided;

- a belief at home that education is relatively unimportant and success at school is not essential;
- family tensions at home, including possible sibling issues.

Overall, the likelihood is that the parents' attitude to school is one of fear or embarrassment, rather than hostility (the fact Karl attends detentions suggests that confrontation is not being sought). Whatever the action taken, it should not be based on a belief that the parents do not care about their son as a person.

> '*You can't expect the parents of secondary pupils to be as keen as those of primary pupils.*'

This implies that secondary schools must be realistic and accept that parents have less interest in and involvement with the school as their children get older. This can be very misleading if seen simplistically and only from the school's point of view. In fact, what is true is that parents' relationships change as their sons and daughters enter adolescence, and these changes are reflected in various ways. For example, many teenagers do not like to be seen out with their parents, especially in front of their peers. They are therefore less keen on their parents coming to school.

This does not mean that such parents are necessarily less interested in their children's progress at school, or that the children no longer have need for their parents. Different ways have to be found of showing that interest and meeting those needs. Recognizing this can help a new teacher in their understanding of both pupil and parental viewpoints. For example, at a consultation meeting conflicting accounts of a pupil's behaviour and personality can arise. A parent may describe a pupil as 'talkative', 'lively' and 'chatty' at home, whereas you find them to be very quiet and that they rarely speak in class – or it could be the other way round of course! You need to reflect, for example, on:

- Does it matter? Perhaps they just behave differently in different contexts?
- Does your new knowledge of the pupil affect the way you deal with them at school? Should you change anything?

Unless you think the pupil's learning is being impeded by what you now know, it is probably wiser to say nothing to the pupil (even though parents may mention it to them). If their learning is being impeded, then you now possess valuable knowledge to assist you in your teaching of the pupil, perhaps encouraging them to respond more in class, for example.

Another type of encounter with parents involves a complaint – you will experience this at some point! We suggest you try applying the following principles, even if you find yourself in a difficult situation:

- *Listen* to what is being said! Even if you are certain the complaint is unjust or inaccurate, it needs to be aired. The parent will only become more upset if they do not feel they have been heard.
- *Get the facts straight.* The facts are the real basis of any complaint; did this or that actually happen or not happen?

- *Find something positive to say about the pupil.* If everything you say is negative, the parent may become convinced that you are prejudiced against their child.
- *Do not allow things to become personal.* Although it may seem a personal affront, complaints are usually the culmination of a growing dissatisfaction about something that may not even be connected with the school. Concentrate on the *what* not on the *who*.
- *Find things that you can agree on.* This is crucial for any resolution.
- *Agree at the end on some future action.* This may be referring the matter on, changing something on one or both sides, or simply agreeing to meet again at a later date.

Although dealing with complaints or apparent indifference can be tricky, some parents are inclined to be over-protective of, or over-ambitious for, their children. It can be equally stressful when dealing with such parents. Over-anxious parents only add to the pressure on their children, although this is not the intended outcome. Unfortunately, the pressure on young people to do well in external examinations is greater in some countries than others – this is especially true of the USA, Japan and the UK. The crucial thing for you as a teacher is to avoid adding to the pressure on the child, for example by deferring to the parents' wishes. As a professional, you will know whether the child is working to the best of their ability.

Case Study 7.2

Louise is a pupil in your Year 10 class. She works conscientiously and always hands her work in on time. She regularly achieves good marks and grades for her work, which is neatly presented at all times. She has never given you cause for concern regarding her behaviour in class. At a parents' evening, both her mother and father attend and you are surprised that they are concerned that Louise is not doing as well as they had hoped and that 'if she doesn't watch out, she will not be able to get the top grades she needs to get to Oxbridge, like her brother'. They ask if she can be given extra work, and if there is anything they can do to help her get better marks. They ask you to give them regular updates on her progress. They politely imply that you are perhaps not demanding enough of her and ask you to be 'tougher' on her.

What are your options here?

- Ignore the whole thing as she is progressing well in your view.
- Set extra work as requested, explaining to Louise that her parents had asked for it.
- Ask colleagues whether they have also been approached by Louise's parents.
- Have a quiet word with Louise about the situation and be guided by what she wants.
- Other?

Whatever you decide, after consulting your colleagues, remember the reference to Louise's 'highly successful' brother. How significant do you think this might be and what could it mean for any action taken?

7.5 Developing strategies for working with parents

To help you to develop strategies to build relationships with your pupils' parents, try completing the parent side of the chart that is Task 7.2.

Task 7.2: The teacher–child–parent triad

Teacher(s) can bring:		Parent(s) can bring:
Professional skills and expertise (e.g. in pedagogy and assessment)		
Professional knowledge of educational system		
Professional knowledge of child development (based on training and experience)	C	
Knowledge of child's academic experience (including rate of progress and measured attainment)	H / I	
Knowledge of child's behaviour at school (including peer relationships)	L / D	
Professional relationship of teacher/ learner		
Professional commitment for a fixed period		Parental commitment (potentially for a lifetime)
Professional values (including those of school culture)		

As you gain experience through your early dealings with parents, you may find it helpful to amend, update or add to your list in the light of that experience. Bearing this in mind, there are probably some useful principles and points to note when working with parents, including:

- *Listen to what they are saying.* As noted, their perspective is as valid as your own and those of your teaching colleagues. Remember that children spend more of their time at home than they do at school in any one year, so parents' observations are based on a great deal of knowledge. Of course, they may be biased, but this is precisely where your professional viewpoint can help to provide a more accurate overall picture of the young person.

- *Avoid jargon* as much as possible when communicating with parents, whether face-to-face or in written form. Carefully explain any acronyms you use.

- *Use praise.* As noted earlier, it is important to be positive – even in extreme cases, find something positive to say so that the picture received by the parent isn't wholly negative.

- *Do not stereotype pupils or their parents.* Everyone is entitled to be treated as an individual and labelling anyone as 'aggressive' or 'awkward', for example, is denigrating and counter-productive, as 'it undermines any claims that the judgements involved are unbiased' (Middlewood and Abbott, 2017: 125). Stereotyping by race, gender or sexual orientation is particularly offensive and must be avoided at all costs, even by implication.

- *Keep your focus on the child as a pupil.* While you may have your own opinions about the children you teach, you occupy the role of their educator and your comments ought to reflect this. Any suggestions for improvement should to be related to raising the standards of their work and making progress. Of course, their behaviour in class and in school in general will need to be addressed if it is affecting their learning.

- *Offer suggestions as to how a child can progress.* Parents may look to you to for your professional expertise, so you should be able to offer suggestions. Some parents will ask how they can help, so be prepared to offer up some ideas – the more simple and practical the better!

- *Base everything on evidence not impressions.* Base your judgement of any child on evidence not a general impression. This is good professional practice anyway, as improvement usually comes through small practical steps.

7.6 School support staff

In England and Wales, since schools took over the management of their own resources in 1992, the number of support staff has trebled, while teacher numbers grew by 10% (Bush and Middlewood, 2013). These staff are now an important part of the school's workforce and you will need to have an effective working relationship with them. The various categories of support staff include:

- administration and clerical workers;
- those helping in technical areas;
- staff responsible for the school environment;
- those providing catering services;
- members of staff directly involved with teaching and learning and child development.

We only have space here to discuss the last of these categories in any detail, but it is worth mentioning that some key principles apply whenever and with whoever you come into contact at school. First, you need to act professionally at all times, even when you find yourself working with someone whose personality clashes with yours. Second, remember that everyone is busy at school and will have many things to do, as well as their own personal issues to manage. Third, you are an adult in a place of learning for young people, thus you are a role model and need to conduct yourself accordingly. If the pupils see members of staff openly disagreeing, it is inviting them to act in the same way. Therefore, if you are in a department that, for example, has a technician as a member of its staff, your relationship with that person should be professional at all times, as with school office staff, cleaners, lunchtime supervisors and anyone else you meet in the course of your work. Ultimately, all members of staff ought to be working in the interests of the pupils.

7.7 Teaching assistants

There is now widespread recognition, following research into the best use of teaching assistants (TAs) in schools (Blatchford *et al.*, 2007), that simply having more TAs does not automatically raise the levels of attainment of pupils who need help. What is crucial is the effective use of TAs. Each TA needs to be recognized as an individual member of staff who brings special skills to support the learning of pupils and to do this by working closely with the teacher(s). You are most likely to work with a TA in a class where they are supporting a pupil with some kind of special learning need, whether that be regarding literacy, numeracy, behaviour or something else. If you do, it is important that you read Chapter 21 of this book, which discusses special educational needs (SEN), the way schools organize provision for this and the various strategies that exist. Here, we focus specifically on the teacher–TA working relationship, and how it should be managed for the benefit of the pupils(s) concerned.

The main thing to remember is that the chief responsibility for making the relationship work is yours. TAs are paid much less than teachers, their contracts are often short term in nature, they may be part-time, and career prospects are often unclear. Since both you and the TA are there to help pupils in need, show that you value what the TA brings to this partnership. For example:

- Talk to the TA before any lesson to plan how the support will operate in class.
- If the TA is unable to attend departmental meetings (and many cannot because of their contracts), tell them anything relevant that was discussed.
- Value the TA's role as being important in its own right – not just someone who carries out the teacher's instructions.
- Show that you value the knowledge they have about individual pupils. Because they work with individual pupils, TAs come to know those individuals very well indeed, better than you will be able to, with many pupils to manage.

The most effective partnerships involve mutual learning, and a new teacher can learn much from an experienced TA. Emira (2011: 171) showed that the partnership worked best when the school – as well as individual teachers – are able to 'maximise the use of [TAs'] skills, allow them to express their views and make them feel they are valued team members'. Working with a TA can help you gain useful experience about some of the help that some pupils need to improve their learning. Also, some TAs see their role as a stepping-stone to gaining full teacher status, and if this is true of a TA whom you find yourself working with, you may be able to discuss issues of mutual interest that benefit the two of you.

Whilst you should value the TA's contribution, it is the teacher who is ultimately responsible for the pupils' progress, so it is crucial that you are kept fully informed about each supported pupil in your class. If, for example, a pupil is withdrawn from your class for a period to work on a one-to-one basis with a TA, find out from the TA how they are progressing, because the aim eventually is for them to return to your class, and you need to be fully up to date on how they should be managed at that point. If you become too dependent on the TA, you may feel at a loss when their support is withdrawn, often because of funding cuts or it is considered their support is no longer needed.

Case Study 7.3

You are told there will be a new pupil in your Year 8 class whose family has just arrived in the country. He can speak only a few words of English but he is having extra lessons after school and you will have a TA who is fluent in his language in your lessons who will be able to sit with him to interpret and translate as appropriate.

Think about this potentially tricky situation, then undertake Task 7.3.

Task 7.3

Plan your meeting with this TA:

- When will you try to arrange this for?
- What will you want to be the outcomes from the meeting?
- What information do you want from the TA?
- What information do you intend to give to the TA?
- Is there anyone else you should involve in your discussions?
- Are there any issues that you need to be particularly aware of or sensitive to in this case?

COMMENTARY: You should certainly consult the Learning Support Department or its equivalent in the school to find out if there is a specific policy or strategy that the school follows in such circumstances. Find out what you can about the specific TA who will work in the class with you and the pupil. Try to arrange to meet that TA before the lesson to:

- Agree on what you ought to be aiming for on behalf of the pupil.
- Find out the TA's knowledge of the lesson's content.
- Perhaps learn one or two simple words or phrases in the pupil's first language.
- Have some way of communicating between one another so that you are alerted if anything needs to be clarified during the lesson.
- Agree how you and the pupil are going to be introduced to each other and how the pupil and TA will be introduced to the other pupils.

- Agree on any interaction with other pupils that the lesson may involve and how the TA should respond.

- Find out about any cultural and language issues that might be relevant to reduce the risk of misinterpretation.

- Agree how you and the TA are going to assess how things have gone and how progress will be evaluated.

Never assume the pupil has low learning ability because they cannot speak English! This, sadly, is a very common error and an easy trap to fall into. It can be very embarrassing if the person later turns out to be a highly gifted scientist or mathematician who just happened not to speak English at first!

Finally, remember to ask the TA after the lesson how they felt it went and what you might have done to improve it.

Such situations as this will be common in some schools and very rare in others, of course, depending on the school's environment. As a mainstream teacher, you are not expected to be a specialist in SEN, but you do have a responsibility to every pupil to help them perform to their full potential. Working closely with a TA who has expertise and experience in the field can be extremely valuable to any teacher. The key to the partnership being successful is perhaps, above all, communication. TAs like teachers who talk to them, and the more teachers and TAs converse together, the more the pupil is likely to gain. Since the teacher and the TA sometimes share confidential information about a pupil, this can help to create a professional bond between them. As mentioned earlier, mutual learning is important and one important example of when the TA's input will be crucial for the teacher as a professional is at a parents' consultation session. It will normally be you, the teacher, who has to respond to parents' queries about their son's or daughter's progress – and the TA won't usually be present!

7.8 Conclusion

In this chapter, we have looked at the importance of working with a variety of adults who have a legitimate interest in the young people you teach. We have focused on parents as the most significant of these adults, but also examined the need to develop positive professional relationships with a range of other staff who work in a school, with an emphasis on TAs. The key to being effective in all these areas lies in good communication between those concerned. It is not possible, or even necessarily desirable, that you like each person that you encounter, but it is essential that you manage to develop some kind of professional relationship with them as individuals, even when a conflict arises – as it occasionally does in a busy school. The reason for this is simply that the interests of the pupil are central to everyone's concern. By focusings on this at all times, you are doing what you came into teaching for in the first place!

Recommendations for further reading

Harris, A. and Goodall, J. (2007) *Engaging Parents in Raising Achievement: Do Parents Know They Matter?*, Research report DCSF-RW004. London: DCSF.

Sharples, J. and Webster, R. (2011) *Making Best Use of Teaching Assistants: A Self-assessment Guide*. London: Education Endowment Foundation.

Webliography

Child Trends, *Parental Involvement in Schools*: www.childtrends.org/indicators/parental-involvement-in-schools – suggests ways in which the extent of parental involvement may be estimated.

Time, *Why Parenting is More Important than Schools*: http://ideas.time.com/2012/10/24/the-single-largest-advantage-parents-can-give-their-kids/ – suggests how parents talking with their children at home can enhance the school performance of the children.

8

Communication in the classroom

Paul Elliott

8.1 Introduction

Communication skills lie at the heart of your success as a teacher. Here we will consider the non-verbal communication that occurs in the classroom, the features of verbal communication and take a detailed look at the art of questioning.

By the end of this chapter, you should:

- appreciate that your communication skills will play a major part in determining how successfully pupils learn;
- appreciate that part of your job is to develop pupils' own communication skills;
- be aware of the scope for non-verbal communication in the classroom;
- be aware of the power of questioning as a teaching tool;
- be able to identify features of good practice in questioning technique.

8.2 Communication and power

Communicate effectively with pupils and they will respond positively, but it is important to remember that communication is a two-way process. When you are planning lessons and teaching, you need to consider not only what you intend to communicate to the pupils, but how you will nurture their communication skills – what you expect them to communicate to you, how they are going to do this and how you might respond. You also need to listen carefully because pupils' questions and answers provide an important source of formative assessment (see also Chapter 9).

Consider the following questions. How do pupils know . . .

- The objectives/intended learning outcomes of your lesson?
- How they will meet them?
- Whether they are on target to meet them?
- When they have met them?
- What they need to do to progress?

And . . .

- How do you know what your pupils know?
- How do you spot their misconceptions and misunderstandings?
- How can you promote deep learning and effective communication?

You cannot answer these questions without dialogue taking place. If communication involved one-way traffic from teacher to pupils, teaching would be easy. Unfortunately, the traditional strategy of *filling empty vessels with knowledge* has proved ineffective – dialogue is key.

Successful teachers plan what they are going to communicate. They seek to promote communication between their pupils and themselves, as well as among their pupils. A common mistake that *student* teachers make is to talk too much, which causes pupils to turn off from what they are saying and miss the main messages. With careful planning of communication, teachers can facilitate quality learning with a minimum of words.

Everyday conversation is characterized by some particular features. Listen to a conversation between two of your friends whilst thinking about how their conversation is structured. It will probably be punctuated by hesitations, interruptions, incomplete sentences that fade away and lots of facial interaction (even when one or both parties is partially sighted). This is very different from many verbal classroom interactions involving teachers. Typically, teachers tell pupils: when to talk, when to stop talking, what to talk about and how well they have done it. In the classroom context, much of the talk is centred on one pupil at a time and the teacher demands the class pays full attention to what is being said. Either the teacher is talking or a pupil selected by the teacher is responding to a question or prompt from the teacher. This means that the teacher is in a very powerful position – rather like the conductor of an orchestra.

By using the power of your position appropriately and wisely, you can build good relationships with pupils. When pupils trust you, you are in a good position to help them learn. To build such trust you need to communicate with:

- respect, courtesy and politeness;
- clarity – keep sentences short, simple and focused;
- appropriate vocabulary, in terms of complexity and degree of formality;
- the aim of building pupils' confidence and willingness to participate;
- honest and useful feedback.

If your communication lacks any of these features, pupils will either fail to understand what it is you are trying to communicate or, worse, feel anxious or threatened by it. Remember, you are the person in a position of power in the classroom, you are the person who possesses most knowledge, and you therefore have the responsibility to communicate effectively and appropriately. Sometimes teachers tell pupils they have not listened properly when, in fact, it is the teacher who has not communicated clearly.

A growing number of educationalists argue there is great value in promoting classroom dialogue in ways that challenge the traditional power relationship between teacher and pupil. Wells (1999) believes that dialogic inquiry, where teachers and pupils collaborate in a search for answers, is a process that leads to a much richer learning outcome. This is an approach that supports inquiry-based learning in which the teacher plays the part of facilitator rather than the so-called 'sage on the stage'. In this role, a teacher may be heard asking questions such as:

'Does anyone have any thoughts about how we could we test Samantha's theory?'
'I wonder if there are any other ways we could try and solve this problem?'
'How could we explore the strengths and weaknesses of this design?'
'What do we need to do to . . . ?'
'Gosh, that is a really interesting idea. Might that be useful in helping to explain . . . ?'

8.3 Non-verbal communication

When we think of communication in a classroom, the first thing that probably comes to mind is verbal communication initiated by the teacher. Classrooms are full of teachers talking to pupils: explaining, questioning, instructing, praising, chastising, advising, and so on. This verbal communication is central to your work as a teacher, and most of this chapter relates to this skill, but there are other forms of communication between teachers and pupils and their importance should not be underestimated.

Simply through your presence in a classroom you are communicating with your pupils. In various ways, we send subtle signals to our pupils about:

- how we feel about ourselves;
- how we feel about them;
- how we feel about the subject matter of the lesson;
- how confident we are;
- how well organized we are;
- how competent we are likely to be at helping them learn.

These subtle messages are transmitted as a complex medley of signs and signals. Compare the two sets of signs and signals in Table 8.1 that exemplify positive and negative messages.

Positive	Negative
Well-organized resources	Struggling to organize resources
In the classroom before pupils arrive	Arrives after pupils
Cheerful, pleased to see pupils and be in school	Ignores pupils or scowls at them Moans about it being Monday morning
Calm and confident	Flustered and tense

Table 8.1 Signs and signals

Fortunately, teaching is a profession where there is room for individuality, which should include the celebration and acceptance of diversity: pupils need diverse role models to reflect the make-up of society and their own identities. Conversely, the further you stray from pupils' expectations, the more you may struggle to be taken seriously; so, think carefully about how others are likely to perceive you. For a student teacher, it can be helpful to try and conform to pupils' expectations of what a competent teacher should be like. Should you expect to simply be yourself in the classroom? There is no simple answer to this question. Try observing experienced and successful teachers at work and then follow them into the staffroom after the lesson. As the staffroom door closes behind them, you will often see that they metamorphose from the classroom version of who they are, their 'teacher self', into their 'real self'. The two persona will not be unrelated, but they won't be identical!

Part of the communication between you and your pupils is in the form of body language. This is a complex language, but one in which it is well worth developing fluency. As with other forms of communication, it is about teachers' and pupils' behaviour. Neill and Caswell (1993) explore the subject in more detail. As a teacher, there are some simple guidelines that will help you:

- stand or sit confidently;
- try to keep still – shifting about distracts pupils and may be taken as a sign of nerves;
- however nervous you are feeling inside, try to avoid fidgeting with your hands;
- show pupils the palms of your hands and make confident, slow gestures with them while you talk;
- be positive and expressive with your face – smile and nod regularly when pupils say or do anything positive;
- have the confidence to approach pupils for an intimate discussion of their work, but avoid invading their personal space;
- with smaller pupils in particular, it is much better to be down at their level rather than lean over them when having a one-to-one interaction.

The way that you use your body will not only influence the way that you are perceived, but also the way that you feel. If you can *act* confident, even when feeling nervous, you are likely to end up *feeling* confident.

8.4 The teacher's territory

The confidence with which you use the teaching space will also send a message to your pupils. Do you feel safest behind the teacher's desk? Would you prefer to avoid going any-where near the back row? It is natural to feel this way when you start teaching, but it is behaviour to avoid if you are to communicate the right message to your pupils. However nervous you feel inside, there should be no 'no-go' zones in your teaching space. Pupils should feel like welcome guests in your classroom; you should not feel like a guest in theirs.

Just as it is important to get your body language right, it is important to get your use of classroom space right: cower at the front and pupils will sense your fear. Here are some general guidelines that are worth remembering:

- moving confidently around a classroom 'marks' it out as your territory;
- using posters, pictures and display work to personalize classrooms not only creates a more stimulating working environment but marks it as part of your territory;
- addressing a class from different places in a room (this can be difficult in smaller rooms) shows them that you are confident and at ease in the space;

- talking to a class from the back of the room 'turns the tables' on those pupils hoping for a quiet life at the back;

- moving amongst pupils to check their progress is important – it should be done soon after the start of a task to check that pupils have understood what they have to do;

- whatever the layout of the room, you should encourage all of the pupils to look at you while you are addressing the class; this may mean that some or all will have to move around in their seat.

Regarding the latter point, some pupils may be reluctant to look you in the eye. This may be because they are on the Autism spectrum or because their culture has taught them that it is disrespectful to look directly at an adult. Do not be too quick to interpret it as discourtesy or insolence.

Some habits are best avoided:

- *Moving around the room as you speak*: the changing point of focus will distract pupils from what you are saying.

- *Turning your back on pupils for very long*: if you stop to speak to one pupil, make sure that you scan the room regularly to check that everyone else is on task.

- *Obscuring pupils' views of information on boards*: you do not want to become the excuse for pupils stopping work!

Task 8.1

Draw a sketch map of a room in which you have taught or in which you are going to teach. Think about how you could use the teaching space effectively and confidently. Mark on the map all of the places that you could stand or sit while addressing the class; these need to be places where you can scan the room easily and make eye contact with pupils. Think also about suitable places in the room to place resources, to carry out demonstrations, or to get pupils to engage in role play or other activities.

8.5 Types of teacher talk

Teachers need to talk to pupils for a variety of reasons. Their talk falls into three general categories: cognitive, procedural and managerial. *Cognitive* teacher talk concerns the content of the curriculum and should include the majority of the dialogue, questioning and elucidation engaged in by the teacher. *Procedural* talk concerns how the work in the lesson is to be done; it is about the nature of tasks, the teams in which pupils are to carry out the tasks and the timing of the work. *Managerial* talk relates to behaviour management, the giving of notices unrelated to the curriculum, and so on.

All three categories of talk are essential, yet much attention has been drawn to the need to shift the balance from procedural and managerial talk towards more cognitive talk. It has been suggested that two-thirds of lessons involve talk, two-thirds of that talk is teacher talk and two-thirds of teacher talk is about management and procedure rather than content

(Norman, 1992; Cazden, 2001). Many new teachers are guilty of spending too long introducing content and explaining tasks, to the extent that pupils become bored and lose track of what is being said. With careful planning, you can ensure that what you say to a class is clear and concise so that pupils remain focused and are quickly engaged.

8.6 Visual reinforcement

When you are in the role of student, do you listen intently to every word that your instructor says? In reality, everyone's mind drifts occasionally, so there is no reason why your pupils should be any different. Making sure that key information is not only said but displayed on a board or screen enables pupils to get back on track without the disruption of asking you, or a neighbour, what they have missed. This can be as simple as writing a page number on the board when you have asked your class to read something from a book.

8.7 Pupil talk

Meaningful dialogue between pupils is crucial if you are to establish a learning community in your classroom. A range of pedagogical techniques promote productive talk between pupils. These include techniques such as Think-Pair-Share, Jigsaw and Envoys. The pupil-to-pupil talk encouraged by these techniques is valuable for pupils for the following reasons:

- It's a chance to learn from and teach each other.
- It builds confidence, giving pupils a chance to verbalize their ideas and practise using subject vocabulary.
- It is less daunting than talking to the teacher, especially in front of the rest of the class and when one's ideas are still being formulated.
- It allows ideas to be tested in an intimate setting before going public with them.
- It builds social skills.
- It helps pupils develop the ability to express themselves coherently and persuasively.

8.8 Your voice as a tool

You need to use your voice with precision and care if you are to get the best out of it. It has to last you a long time, so it is important that you use it in a way that will avoid damage. Your voice is the main tool of your trade – think of it as a scalpel rather than as a sledgehammer!

Your voice has unique characteristics that make it distinct and you have the ability to vary the way in which you speak. It is desirable to practise varying how you use your voice to achieve different effects and emphases. For example, some people have voices that are easier to listen to than others, but there is a lot you can do to maximize the potential of your voice. Volume, speed, pitch, projection and expressiveness are examples of the features of your voice that you can try to vary to achieve maximum impact.

At times you will need to get a class's attention. Some teachers achieve this effectively without using their voice, for example by giving a visual cue such as raising their hand or using a signal such as a bell or gong. If you do raise your voice, once you have gained attention you can dramatically reduce its volume. If you insist on talking to a class with the volume of your voice raised, you will provide pupils with the cover needed to start their own conversations. Speaking at a volume that pupils at the far side of the room can only hear clearly by concentrating on what you are saying makes it harder for pupils to start unauthorized conversations.

Nevertheless, you should avoid shouting. Pupils *hate* teachers who shout, and you will end up with noisy classes and a sore throat. Loud teachers create loud classrooms. You need to be able to make yourself heard on the other side of a classroom, but you should aim to do this by learning to *project* your voice, not by shouting. Before speaking, take a deep breath, be clear in your mind what you need to say, and then say it with clarity and conviction. Consider the tone of your voice as you speak so that you sound as if you are a person of authority rather than someone who is pleading with a class. A common mistake made by new teachers is to talk too fast. If you do this, pupils may struggle to follow you – and sooner or later may give up trying. Speak clearly and try using pauses to emphasize key points and to allow pupils to digest what you have said.

Voices with a lower pitch tend to carry more authority and sound more confident (Anderson and Klofstad, 2012). Speaking with a higher pitch can make projection in the classroom difficult and, when someone is under stress, their vocal pitch will tend to rise further, making the situation worse. If you have a relatively high-pitched voice, try practising using the lower end of your natural range. Your training institution may also be able to arrange coaching to help you do this, and we would recommend the British Voice Association as a useful source of advice.

8.9 Less is more

Teacher talk is very important, but it is the *quality* of what a teacher says, not the *quantity*, that matters. A lesson dominated by the sound of the teacher's voice is seldom a successful lesson (Hattie, 2012). One survey of secondary schools (Sage, 2006) found that some lessons involved teachers talking for 90% of the time! When a teacher says the minimum needed to interest pupils in the subject and explain the nature of a well-planned, engaging task or series of tasks, it can provide a powerful learning experience. Take time to plan what you are going to say and ensure that it is clear, unambiguous and at a level appropriate to the listeners. Avoid unnecessary detail and repetition, check pupils' understanding and allow them the chance to check that they have understood you. Then let the pupils get on with the task. Once pupils are on task, you can circulate to talk to individuals or small groups. It is during these more intimate exchanges, when you engage in dialogue with your pupils, that much of the highest quality learning and formative assessment takes place and you will be able to build effective working relationships.

Task 8.2

The next time you plan a lesson, think carefully about what you need to say. Try scripting part of what you are going to say and then edit the script down to the minimum that is needed to communicate clearly the cognitive, procedural and managerial aspects of the lesson. Aim to deliver the lesson with the minimum spoken input possible. Why not record the lesson and then evaluate how successful you have been?

8.10 The art of questioning

It is ironic that teachers spend so much time asking questions. It makes more sense for pupils to ask most of the questions, since it is teachers who have the knowledge and expertise. However, there are very good reasons why teachers should ask questions, most of which can come under the umbrella of 'assessment for learning' (see Chapter 9), for example:

- to establish what pupils already know about a topic or what skills they already have;
- to promote pupils' cognitive engagement with a topic;
- to check what pupils have learnt;
- to check the effectiveness of their own teaching.

There should also be opportunities for pupils to ask questions and engage in dialogue with the teacher. While they need to be able to ask the teacher questions, pupils can also benefit from asking each other questions. The ability to ask effective questions is a skill that needs to be nurtured in pupils. There are various strategies we can use to help pupils to identify, phrase and ask appropriate questions. Here are some ideas that you could try in the classroom:

- Get pupils to work individually, in pairs or in threes to devise questions relevant to the topic for the teacher to answer. Make the process anonymous to encourage pupils to pose questions they might otherwise feel too embarrassed or lacking in confidence to ask and then either: (i) have them place their questions in a box during one lesson for answering in the next, or (ii) tell pupils to fold up their question papers and place them into a large box. You can then draw out a selection to answer on the spot.
- Create a climate of enquiry by encouraging pupils to ask questions and speculate during the lesson. For example, chunk lessons, providing opportunities for pupils to raise questions at the end of each phase.
- Give pupils 'answers' and ask them to suggest what the questions were.
- Use the 'hot-seat' technique. This is where pupils, rather than the teacher, take turns at fielding questions from classmates. To avoid causing anxiety, it may be best to have two or three pupils in the hot seat at a time.

8.11 Types of questioning

It can be argued that the only reason to ask questions is to raise issues about which the teacher needs information or to stimulate pupils' cognitive engagement (Black *et al.*, 2004: 13). To this end, there are various categories of question that you can ask, which place different demands on pupils and achieve different things, so you need to develop an awareness of how you are using questions. Certain questions can be considered 'low-order', meaning that the cognitive response they elicit is relatively undemanding. Some questions merely require the pupil to *recall* something and so test existing knowledge or observations. For instance:

'Which is the fourth planet in the Solar System?'

This sort of question is often used at the start of a lesson to assess existing knowledge, but used too extensively pupils can become bored or feel patronized. It is important to develop a wide-ranging repertoire of questions that require higher-order thinking. Slightly more demanding is the *comprehension* question:

'Why is Mars colder than Earth?'

Then there is the *application* question, which requires pupils to apply their knowledge to different situations:

'Why are we unlikely to find liquid water on Mars?'

Higher-order questions make greater cognitive demands and require pupils to analyse, synthesize and evaluate. An *analysis* question might be:

'Why would the conditions on Mars make it hard for life to survive?'

A *synthesis* question demands that the respondent makes use of several pieces of knowledge to produce an answer. For example:

'What would we have to think about if planning a trip to Mars?

An *evaluation* question requires the respondent to synthesize various pieces of information in order to make a judgement of some kind. For instance:

'Is the cost of sending people to Mars justified when there are so many problems on Earth?'

These different types of question have been categorized according to Bloom's (1956) Taxonomy of Educational Objectives (see Chapter 5).

Task 8.3

Choose a specific topic from your own subject area and devise six questions representing the categories exemplified.

You may have heard of *open* and *closed* questions. Lower-order questions tend to be closed. That is, there is only a limited number of correct responses and often just one. Higher-order questions tend to be open; pupils can make a wide variety of appropriate responses. Open and closed, higher- and lower-order questions should have a place in your repertoire. However, prioritize asking open questions that require elaborated answers in which pupils have to explain their thinking (Gipps, 1994).

8.12 Planning questions

It is best to plan your questioning strategy in advance. Link it to the objectives for the lesson and design it to achieve specific things. For instance, you may want to use questions to establish what is already known, to stimulate thought or to set up the major themes of the lesson. You should also use questions to check learning and to reinforce learning that has taken place. Black *et al.* (2004: 11) found that many teachers do not plan classroom dialogue in a way that maximizes pupils' learning. By planning questions in advance, you can think about the way that you are going to ask them and take account of a range of options:

- *The sequence in which you will ask them.* It may be important to ask questions in a logical sequence. In most circumstances, it is wise to start with lower-order questions and build up to asking higher-order ones.
- *The language you will use.* Avoid ambiguity and try to get the level of vocabulary right for the class.
- *Designing questions for particular pupils or groups of pupils.* It is important to involve all pupils in questioning, not just the most able. Try to differentiate your questions so that some are suitable for all.

Good planning will make you more confident during the lesson and better able to question effectively, think on your feet, ask supplementary questions and engage in effective dialogue with pupils.

8.13 Asking questions

Having planned your questioning strategy for a lesson, it is important to think about how you actually ask the questions. Whether you are asking questions of a whole class, a small group or just one individual, there are some basic principles of good practice to bear in mind. As with other communication with pupils, you need to appreciate that their use of language is almost certainly going to be less sophisticated than your own, so questions need to be clear. The younger the pupils and the less sophisticated their language skills, the truer this will be. Bear in mind that speech, language and, more broadly, communication skills continue to develop as young people move through adolescence and into adulthood (Hartshorne, 2011). This means that you need to be selective with the vocabulary you use and the way you structure sentences, depending on the age group you are teaching. That said, part of a teacher's role is to introduce pupils to unfamiliar vocabulary and to develop their literacy skills, so be ready to spend time explaining vocabulary or turns of phrase that you have chosen to use.

Having asked your question, it is vital to allow pupils thinking or 'waiting' time. It is very common for a new teacher to fail to do this because they are anxious to get the 'right' answer so that they can move on. But think how you would feel if someone was firing questions at you and failing to give you time to consider your response. By giving several seconds of thinking time, you provide pupils with better opportunities to make a positive contribution to the lesson, raising their self-esteem, making them feel good about being in your lesson and becoming more engaged in their learning. If you do not get a response, try repeating the question to give more thinking time and allow those who were not concentrating to refocus. You may also offer prompts or clues to encourage pupils. There is a danger that some pupils will feel they have not had time to think or contribute because the teacher habitually accepts answers from those who raise their hands quickest or shout the answers out.

In a whole-class setting, decide which questions to target at individuals or small groups and which to broadcast for anyone to address. Broadcast questions may only get responses from the most confident pupils. Whilst this can be useful in helping to roll out your structured lesson, if you neglect to involve other pupils it will leave them feeling isolated and you may miss the fact that the majority have lost the thread of the lesson. Remember that questioning is a powerful tool in formative assessment. It is vital to get into the habit of addressing some of your questions to individuals and small groups. It is much easier to do this once you have learned pupils' names but, in the meantime, you can employ other techniques, including:

- asking questions in sequence around the class;
- asking for a response from one of a group – for example, 'Can anyone on the back-left table tell me . . .';
- asking pupils to remind you of their name before they answer, turning the session into an opportunity for you to learn some names.

As tempting as it may be, avoid asking only those pupils who are keen to answer, who are sitting immediately in front of you, who need to be kept occupied or whose names you can remember.

Pupils sometimes need longer to think about higher-order questions, especially those requiring them to reflect on issues or consider their own opinions. Help pupils get the greatest benefit from such questions by providing an opportunity to discuss their answers before replying. A useful approach is to first ask them to consider their response privately for a short time, then to ask them to discuss their ideas in groups of two to four and, finally, for a spokesperson from each group to share their ideas with the whole class. This is sometimes known as Think-Pair-Share (T-P-S) or the Private-Intimate-Public (P-I-P) approach, and it is an excellent way of involving all pupils in responding to a question.

Increasing numbers of schools and teachers are choosing to operate a 'no hands-up' policy, as advocated by Black *et al.* (2004). This avoids the common scenario in which a minority of keen and confident pupils answer the majority of questions. Allowing thinking time and then expecting anyone to answer if called upon means the teacher can avoid using simple recall questions and instead concentrate on questions that promote critical thinking. If using this technique, it is important to promote a culture whereby pupils can excuse themselves from answering the question by saying, for example, 'I need a bit longer to think about it'.

Questioning is an important assessment technique, but how do you know whether all the members of a class know the correct answer to your question? Rather than getting pupils to respond verbally, you can get them to respond visually to good effect. If individual pupils or small groups each have a small dry-wipe board, you can ask them to write answers on the boards and hold them up for you to see. You can also create a class set of true/false, yes/no cards or traffic light cards (red = no, orange = unsure, green = yes) and get pupils to indicate their response to statements that you make. Even simpler is to ask them to put 'thumbs up' to represent 'yes', 'thumbs down' for 'no' and 'thumbs horizontal' for 'not sure'. All of these techniques allow you to scan the classroom and get an impression of how confident the class is with the material and whether there are individuals that may need extra help with the work. If the technology is available, you can use classroom response systems, such as clickers, to the same end or, if most of your pupils have smartphones, make use of an online tool such as Poll Everywhere (www.polleverywhere.com).

8.14 Receiving answers

It's not just how you ask questions that is important, but also how you receive responses. Try to avoid answering your own questions (it is surprising how often novice teachers do this!) because it has the effect of:

- frustrating pupils who needed more thinking time before responding;
- suggesting that you did not expect anyone to be able to answer;
- denying pupils the opportunity to test their own understanding and develop their own communication skills.

After asking a question, it is also tempting to take the first appropriate answer and move on, but this can be a mistake. Allowing more than one pupil to answer your question before you respond gets more ideas into the public arena and gives a better feel for the understanding of the whole class. It is also good practice to invite pupils to evaluate each other's answers. This encourages greater pupil participation and active listening whilst allowing the teacher to spend more time listening, gaining a fuller picture of understanding within the group.

You have choices to make when responding to pupils' answers. First, decide whether to make a verbal response to a pupil's contribution. Generally, of course, you should, but there may be situations when it is best not to, for instance when a clearly facetious response has been made. Sometimes answers may anticipate something you plan to come to later and you may be unable or unwilling to adjust to accommodate a change in sequence, in which case it is best to acknowledge the contribution and note that you will come back to it later. It can be useful to repeat an answer or the key element of it because this allows other pupils to keep up and gives them a second chance to listen to the answer or, indeed, to hear it for the first time if the respondent has a quiet voice (or they were not paying attention the first time!). You may wish to rephrase an answer to make the point more clearly or concisely. It is also a good idea to praise contributions. If pupils receive praise for answers, they will be encouraged to make future contributions.

There will be occasions when the answers that you receive are factually incorrect. In these cases, you will generally need to correct the pupil, but this needs sensitive handling or you may demoralize them and deter them from making future contributions. Consider the following:

'Thanks for that, it's a really good suggestion, but it's not quite right . . .'

is much better than:

'No, that's not what I'm looking for . . .'

In most cases it is a mistake to allow factual errors to pass because it may be assumed by pupils that they are correct. Wrong answers can be just as useful as correct answers in providing clues to pupils' thought processes, so you need to listen carefully to them.

Some pupils will give you responses that are part-way to answering the question and, in such cases, it can be worth taking the time to gently probe the pupil and encourage a fuller answer:

'That's an interesting idea, could you say a bit more about it?'
'That's an interesting answer, can you tell us more about what you have in mind?'

Providing such opportunities may reveal the pupil was not on the right track after all: a valuable thing to establish.

As you can appreciate, all these different ways of responding to pupils' answers require you to be alert to and aware of what you are doing.

8.15 Encouraging dialogue

Wolfe and Alexander (2008: 2) suggest that by encouraging pupils to use reasoning and argument, you introduce them to critical inquiry and the idea that it is acceptable to question the status quo.

Teachers who want to free themselves from the constraints of the traditional power relationship in the classroom need to think about how they are going to promote a dialogue with their pupils. At the heart of this approach is enquiry-based learning, including the idea of the teacher as less an authority figure and more a fellow learner, a facilitator or an expert witness. This model entails being willing to give more control to pupils, with lessons driven by their questions, ideas and enthusiasm. This approach can create and nurture a learning community and has the potential to produce much deeper learning.

Alexander (2005) identified the following key features of dialogic teaching:

1. It involves collective activity where the teacher and pupils work together on tasks.
2. It involves a reciprocal arrangement whereby the teacher and pupils share and listen to each other's ideas and views and consider alternatives.

The teacher must support pupils by engaging in the sorts of good practice when asking questions and receiving answers described in Sections 8.13 and 8.14. Resultant learning should accumulate into a coherent line of thought and enquiry, planned by the teacher to purposefully address specific objectives. A useful technique for encouraging all pupils to contribute ideas in a respectful environment is the *talking circle*. This traditional Indigenous practice from North America can work well in the classroom. The teacher and pupils sit in a large circle, so that no one is at the head of the class. A stick, or some other object, is passed around the circle, and only the holder of the stick is allowed to speak. Other participants are expected to listen, but not make verbal or visual responses. It is a good way to get full participation and lots of ideas and opinions aired.

8.16 Avoiding questioning pitfalls

Questioning is a very powerful tool for promoting learning. A successful question and answer session can feel exhilarating and serve effectively to consolidate learning or move it forward. There are some common mistakes though, in addition to those discussed, that can cause such sessions to stall or lead to management problems. In general, it is best to avoid:

- asking questions requiring yes/no answers, unless the whole class is required to respond with visual signals such as yes/no cards;
- asking questions in ways that encourage calling out. Good examples of these are questions that begin with the phrases 'Who can tell me . . .' and 'Does anyone know?' (Think about these questions and you will see that the instinctive responses are not ones that you would want.) It is much better to turn the question into an instruction: 'Raise your hand if you can tell me . . .';
- over-using 'response-seeking' questions (Black and Wiliam, 1998a), an approach that entails fishing for a desired response, ignoring or rejecting unwanted answers, and then moving on once the desired response is obtained. This promotes a surface approach to learning, encouraging guessing and the unthinking regurgitation of information that is poorly understood. It is also unhelpful to teachers because it fails to detect whether meaningful learning has taken place.

8.17 Theory into practice

You should now appreciate the importance of planning for effective communication. Remember it is about more than just what you say – it is also about how you say it, how you use your body and the space in which you teach. You will also know that questioning is a powerful tool, but that you have to develop awareness of its finer points if you are to build successful relationships and promote learning.

Read through the following case study and, before going on to the commentary, think about what advice you would give Tariq.

Case Study 8.1

Tariq, a new teacher, asked his mentor to watch a lesson with his Year 8 science class, an introduction to the Periodic Table, and to give specific feedback on his use of questioning. Tariq had planned the main questions he wanted to ask and these generally progressed from some simple, closed questions to help his pupils remember the content of the previous lesson, to more open, higher-order questions. Careful thought was given to ensure that the language he was going to use would be appropriate to the age and sophistication of the class. His aim was to get pupils to the point where they could think about how the Table can be used to make predictions about the behaviour of different elements, prior to carrying out a class practical in the subsequent lesson. To achieve this, he realized that he needed to gradually progress to questions that gave opportunities for pupils to demonstrate comprehension and analysis. In discussion after the lesson, Tariq said that he felt that he had successfully structured his questioning to ensure a progression in cognitive complexity during the lesson. While his mentor agreed with aspects of this overview, she pointed out that almost all of the questions Tariq had asked had been broadcast to the whole class and that more than 90% had been answered by just six pupils in a class of 28. She asked him how he knew that all 28 pupils were engaged in the lesson and how confident he was that they had all understood. Tariq could not provide an answer.

COMMENTARY: While Tariq had made some good progress in his use of questioning, he had made the mistake of focusing solely on the questions he wanted to ask, whereas he should also have thought about how to ask them and how to elicit pupils' responses most effectively. He had also failed to provide pupils with the chance to ask questions of their own. His mentor advised him to remember to make sure that, in future, some of his questioning was targeted at named individuals as a way of making sure that answers were obtained from a broader range of pupils. She also suggested that he give pupils longer to respond to the more open, challenging questions; give pupils a chance to discuss possible answers in pairs or small groups before responding; and provide a chance for pupils to ask him questions. Finally, she invited him to observe her Year 9 class where she was making use of traffic light cards during a review lesson as a way of checking the understanding of all members of the class. When Tariq saw this technique, he resolved to make himself a set of cards to try out in his next lesson.

8.18 Conclusion

In this chapter, we have seen how appropriate visual communication, use of voice, questioning techniques, and strategies for promoting effective communication by all pupils can contribute to successful learning outcomes. The way that you communicate in the classroom and how you foster communication by and among your pupils goes a long way to defining how your pupils perceive you and your skills as a teacher. Taking time to think about communication at the planning stage and then being mindful of what you do during lessons are important steps towards becoming a successful teacher. While honing your own skills is critical in determining this success, whatever your subject specialism you also have a responsibility to help develop your pupils' ability to respond to questions, discuss their ideas and acquire new vocabulary. As with many aspects of teaching, you should aim to continue reflecting on and improving your communication skills throughout your teaching career.

Recommendations for further reading

Alexander, R. (2017) *Towards Dialogic Teaching Rethinking Classroom Talk*, 5th edn. Cambridge: Dialogos.

Anderson, R.C. and Klofstad, C.A. (2012) Preference for leaders with masculine voices holds in the case of feminine leadership roles, *PLoS One*, 7 (12): e51216.

Black, P. and Wiliam, D. (1998) Assessment and classroom learning, *Assessment in Education: Principles, Policy and Practice*, 5 (1): 7–74.

Black, P., Harrison, C., Lee, C., Marshall, B. and Wiliam, D. (2004) Working inside the black box: assessment for learning in the classroom, *Phi Delta Kappan*, 86 (1): 1–21.

Churches, R. (2010) *Effective Classroom Communication Pocketbook*. Alresford, UK: Teachers' Pocketbooks.

Hattie, J. (2012) *Visible Learning for Teachers: Maximizing Impact on Learning*. New York: Routledge.

Mercer, N. and Hodgkinson, S. (2008) *Exploring Talk in Schools*. London: Sage.

Wragg, E.C. and Brown, G. (2001) *Questioning in the Secondary School*. London: Routledge-Falmer.

Webliography

The British Voice Association: https://www.britishvoiceassociation.org.uk/

9
Using assessment for formative purposes

Ruth Dann

9.1 Introduction

Teachers use a variety of approaches to assessment, including different viewpoints on impact and outcomes. Understanding assessment is both complex and multi-layered yet, without grasping what it is and why being 'assessment-literate' needs to become part of your pedagogical practice, you will not be able to be an effective teacher.

This chapter is organized so that it will help you in key phases of your developing practice as a beginning teacher. The focus is on formative assessment, which is the assessment that occurs in the dynamic of everyday teaching and learning and can provide evidence that will enable adjustments by both teachers and pupils to promote learning. Additionally, formative assessment (which embraces assessment for learning [AfL]) is examined in ways that will challenge your own thinking, relating it to theory, policy and practice. Finally, the chapter draws on a broad evidence base to help support you as a reflective practitioner, enabled by informed thinking in assessment.

By the end of the chapter, you should:

- understand the purpose of formative assessment (AfL) in relation to both teaching and learning;
- know how to select appropriate strategies that can be used as part of formative assessment;
- relate key aspects of your own practice, planning, teaching and evaluation to assessment;
- understand the role of both the teacher and pupils in formative assessment (AfL);
- have an informed evidenced-based perspective for the judgements that you make about assessment.

9.2 Distinguishing formative and summative assessment

Conceptually, framing assessment in a particular way is typically linked to the purpose for which it is to be used. Some assessment tools and techniques, however, can be used for a variety of purposes. Hence it is important to be clear what characterizes different assessments (such as formative or summative), the levels of detail required (in relation to individual pupils), and the fairness and accuracy that the assessment seeks. *Formative assessment* has developed from Scriven's (1967) original ideas of 'formative evaluation', which was concerned with continuous curriculum improvement largely through teacher adaptations. Subsequent developments have yielded broader notions of formative assessment focused on evidence on pupil achievement that may 'be used as feedback to modify teaching and learning activities' (Black and Wiliam, 1998b: 40). *Summative assessment* is typically regarded as assessment that measures attainment over a preceding period of time and therefore summarizes learning (Harlen, 2005: 208). Typically, summative assessments are presented as overall scores or grades. The purposes for which they are used are often varied and can cause tensions and confusion. (For example, GCSE – General Certificate of Secondary Education – results are designed to provide certification for pupils, but in England they are also used to measure teacher performance and school success.)

The use of summative assessments for accountability purposes (measuring the effectiveness of, for example, a school or teacher) is also linked to what has been termed 'high-stakes' assessment. This means that the results of assessments have significant consequences. In England, as well as other countries such as the USA and Australia, high-stakes summative assessments tend to dominate assessment practices and distort the processes of teaching and learning (Lingard, 2010; Tanner, 2013; Goldstein and Moss, 2014; Hardy, 2015). Thus, the stakes for ensuring pupil outcomes in test results have been raised in an assessment data-driven accountability system. Even though this relates to summative assessment, there have been implications for formative assessment when the focus of formative assessment is distorted to prioritize the end points of summative assessment. This often means that the immediate learning needs and next steps of pupils are overlooked. The relationship (often not intended) between formative and summative assessment is therefore an important component in any attempt to understand either.

As a new teacher, assessment is an area that may well present a challenge. The role of any teacher must be to ensure that each child receives a broad and balanced curriculum. However, in a professional capacity, external pressures and standards must also be heeded. Formative assessment is concerned with the ways in which teaching and learning are best matched in the classroom so that they can be adjusted for the best outcomes. Such outcomes will include those that are demanded by summative assessments. However, these come at the *end* of a period of learning. The focus of classroom formative assessment usually needs to be far more sharply focused on specific goals and targets that incrementally build towards what is required for summative assessments. In 2015, the Department for Education in England (DfE, 2015a) removed the national assessment levels that had been used since 1998 in both primary and secondary schools, right up to the start of GCSEs. One of the key reasons identified in the report highlighted the negative impact of national summative levels in classrooms. These levels were being used daily by teachers, sometimes in individual lessons, when the original intention was for them to be outcome measures, at the end of a Key Stage. Use of these levels was seen to distort everyday teaching and learning towards summative (rather than formative) outcomes. The national levels were consequently removed so that the impact of summative assessment would not take over classroom formative assessment practices. This evidence, which revealed that summative assessments frequently dominate formative practices, is an important starting point for building your own knowledge and skills in the field.

Formative assessments are specifically designed to yield information that will allow for adjustment to future teaching and learning. Black and Wiliam (1998a), in their seminal review paper, made it clear that formative assessment embraced judgements about both teachers and pupils and could therefore influence subsequent teaching and learning. Whereas summative assessment is focused on judgements about a preceding period of learning, formative assessment uses assessment judgements to inform the next steps of learning. Thus, the assessment judgements that provide essential evidence, central to enacting formative assessment, are for both teachers and pupils to use. They are as much a tool for reflecting on your own teaching development as they are for developing pupil learning. Formative assessment can usefully be seen as the connecter between teaching and learning – it yields important information that needs to be productively used.

Task 9.1

What is the problem with the planning suggested in the following example?

Context: A student teacher of English, in her final placement, starts a new text that will be the core 'modern' text used as part of the GCSE syllabus. The first lesson in her series draws directly from the exam board specification.

Lesson objective: 'Show understanding of the relationships between texts and the contexts in which they were written' (taken from AQA, 2014: 13).

Task/activity for the lesson: To write a brief account based on the preface in the book, as to why the author might have written this book.

Pupil learning outcomes: Provide at least two reasons why the writer wrote the book.

COMMENTARY: Details from the exam board specification should certainly be used to plan a scheme of work (SoW). However, it is too broad and too vague to be the guide for one specific lesson. The important thing to recognize here is that formative assessment is a process that is designed to help steer the learning journey along its course – it is about the steps along the way. Therefore, in a lesson such as the one outlined in Task 9.1, the focus needs to be much more firmly rooted in the possible ways of making interpretations, linked to previous knowledge. It would also need in particular to teach strategies that would help explore and surmise perspectives and interpretations that the pupils need to develop. Trying to catapult pupils to final destinations (exam outcomes), which overshadows the learning and teaching processes along the way, is highly problematic. It is an all-too-often familiar example of how summative assessment requirements come to dominate classroom teaching and learning and the process of formative assessment. The relationship between formative and summative assessment is difficult but one that needs to be balanced. It should be a consideration of whole-school policy.

9.3 Grasping the essence of formative assessment for classroom practice

The Assessment Reform Group (ARG) promoted the notion of AfL, providing a steer towards an emphasis on formative assessment, including that of pupils' learning (rather than the focus being more concerned with only the adjustment of teaching). Their definition of AfL was 'the process of seeking and interpreting evidence for use by learners and their teachers to decide where the learners are in their learning, and where they need to go and how best to get there' (Broadfoot *et al.*, 2002: 7). The term AfL is widely considered the equivalent of formative assessment in much contemporary assessment literature. The two terms are used interchangeably in this chapter. Ten key principles were highlighted on a poster for effective practice of AfL and it is worth using these as the starting point for developing your own practice. In essence, the ten principles of AfL (reordered so they move from the teachers' actions to the pupils) state that it:

1. is part of effective teaching and planning;
2. is key to classroom practice;
3. is a vital professional skill;
4. embraces all educational achievement;
5. enhances understanding of learning goals;
6. relates to how pupils learn;
7. supports learners to know how to improve;
8. promotes the development of self-assessment;
9. recognizes that assessment has an emotional impact;
10. fosters motivation. (Broadfoot *et al.*, 2002)

Implicit in these ten principles are four key themes. These relate to: (i) teachers' professional and practical skills (1–3), which this chapter is designed to address; (ii) understanding curriculum goals and purpose (4–5); (iii) promoting aspects of understanding pupils' learning (6–8); and (iv) considering the impact of assessment for the future (9–10). It is intended that, by the time you have fully engaged with this chapter, you will have a strong grounding in all the themes that these ten general AfL principles promote.

9.4 Using formative assessment in your learning

Following the ARG's principles, the many other iterations of how AfL should be regarded and developed can help to inform your planning. Wiliam (2011: 46) usefully highlights five key strategies for AfL:

* 'Clarifying, sharing, and understanding learning intentions and criteria for success

* Engineering effective classroom discussions, activities, and learning tasks that elicit evidence of learning

* Providing feedback that moves learning forward

* Activating learners as instructional resources for one another

* Activating learners as the owners of their own learning.'

Embedded in the ARG definition of AfL (Broadfoot *et al.*, 2002) are three focal areas for formative assessment:

1. Where the learners are in their learning   [Now]
2. Where they need to go   [Next]
3. How best to get there   [Steps to be taken]

These AfL strands may be incorporated into a single lesson but may also be used across a series of lessons. Critical for AfL is that all three of these strands are considered. Furthermore, who is involved in understanding each of these three focal areas is important. Task 9.2 is designed to further support you in developing these ideas.

Task 9.2

Look at a recent lesson plan of yours. Did you consider the three focal areas of formative assessment in your lesson, and did you look for and consider evidence to support each?

AfL focus	Source of evidence	Teacher understanding	Pupil understanding and differing needs
Where the learners are in their learning			
Where they need to go			
How best to get there			

9.5 Strategies and tools for AfL: are they fit for purpose?

There are many formative assessment strategies and tools you can use, and the Times Educational Supplement AfL toolkit is a growing resource (TES, 2009). However, you need to carefully consider why you are using a particular AfL tool or technique. Bennett (2011) warned that formative assessment can risk becoming little more than tools and techniques with not enough emphasis being given to the adaptations and adjustments that are required to shape future learning and teaching. One of the greatest dangers in the use of AfL (and indeed all assessment) is that the tool or technique becomes an end in itself (see Chapters 10 and 15 for further discussion). If an AfL action/activity does not provide evidence on which to base better-informed decisions, then you are not carrying out AfL (Wiliam, 2011: 43). The following task builds on the previous tasks but requires careful consideration as to which of the three key strands of AfL is the focus. As you build your own repertoire of AfL strategies, it is worth noting which strand it best serves.

Task 9.3

Recall an AfL strategy that you have observed or used. Perhaps consider something connected with questioning that relates to Section 9.8 later in this chapter.

Which AfL strand was it addressing and who was involved? Think in particular about the actions or responses that were required by participants.

AfL observed/ used	Establishing where the learner is now	Making clear where the learner is going next	Establishing the pathway between learning 'now' and 'next'	Who is involved and what are their roles?

How was the assessment evidence used to adjust/improve teaching/learning?

9.6 Putting AfL strategies into practice

The key requirement for successful AfL is to relate learning 'now' to learning 'next'. Many attempts have been made to tease this out offering tried-and-tested approaches for teachers to use. In recent years, teachers have often used tightly controlled strategies that clearly specify learning intentions and success criteria that are shared in each lesson. These may be clearly visible for students on screens, boards and in books. Indeed, it is important that there is clear direction for teaching and learning. However, what is less well recognized and explored is how the outlined trajectory of the curriculum, with its targets and required outcomes, becomes aligned with pupils' aspirations and learning.

Despite a national curriculum, and assessment and examination outcomes, there are still clear messages that too many pupils do not achieve at the required level. This is not only an issue in England, but in the USA and Australia also. Using formative assessment effectively in classrooms offers the potential for both teaching and learning to be better adjusted, and more importantly for these adjustments to be more accurately related and synchronized between pupils and teachers. Fundamental to understanding AfL is how this operates in the classroom. There are some essential considerations here as you develop your lesson planning, which may have already challenged your thinking from Tasks 9.2 and 9.3.

- How will you know what pupils already know?
- What will you do if there is a range of knowledge and skills across pupils that you teach?
- How can you plan so that there is appropriate challenge for each pupil?
- How will your lessons support learning, and ensure that pupils are engaged in the learning process?

Formative assessment is the mechanism through which all of these can be addressed. However, solutions are not always straightforward, as formative assessment relates to the complex process of teaching and learning, where evidence that might suggest what will work does not always work for everyone in each and every context. Figure 9.1 may help to make sense of the important relationship between teaching and learning within AfL.

It considers existing pupils' knowledge and skills (now) and how they might relate to the learning challenge that the taught curriculum offers (next).

What Figure 9.1 (and Figure 9.2) seeks to illustrate is that there is an optimal zone in which new learning challenges relate to existing knowledge and skills. If the challenge of new learning is too great (or appears to be too great), pupils are likely to lessen or avoid completely any engagement with learning. If it is too low, they are likely to be bored or, if compliant, they are likely not to reach their potential. Thus, the way in which teachers and

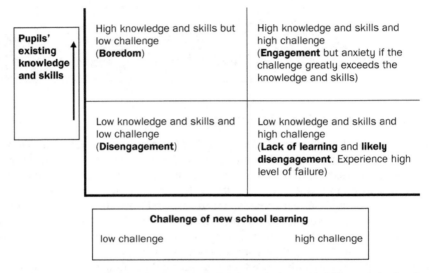

Figure 9.1 Relationship between existing knowledge and skills and the level of challenge of new learning

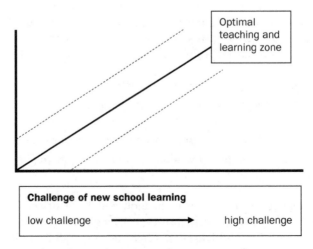

Figure 9.2 Optimal teaching and learning zone within formative assessment

pupils use assessment evidence for formative purposes must be within optimum limits. Indeed, AfL can partly be seen as a way of trying to ensure that this zone is both identified and sustained. This may require different approaches for different pupils and contexts (Dann, 2016).

A clear message for anyone developing their skills through informative assessment is that it is a relational process (Basford and Dann, 2017). Control of the learning that takes place in the classroom cannot be a result of your planning and teaching alone. AfL embraces both teacher and pupil understandings together with adjustments to learning and the curriculum. As Figure 9.2 illustrates, trying to ensure teaching remains in an optimal zone requires a close relationship between what is taught, pupils' knowledge and pupils' response.

Task 9.4

Identify a recent lesson you have taught and reflect on the following questions:

- How did information about pupils' existing knowledge and skills feed into your lesson planning and preparation? Could this have been developed further?
- In what ways did the lesson provide challenge for the pupils you were teaching? Was the lesson too demanding or insufficiently challenging for some pupils?
- In what ways can you change the demands of the challenge? This might mean lowering the challenge, further supporting pupils' perceptions of their own self-efficacy, or scaffolding their learning differently.
- In what ways were the pupils enabled to relate their existing knowledge to new learning?
- Were there adequate steps taken within the lessons to support all pupils to align their learning with the lesson's intentions?

9.7 Feedback within formative assessment

In identifying formative assessment as being in some way relational, communication between teacher and pupil is important. Communicative processes that interweave the components of the journey from where the learner is now, where they are going and how to get there requires careful consideration. Feedback is one of the central techniques used within AfL (Sadler, 1989; Black and Wiliam, 1998a). Its role and impact in teaching and learning has been high profile within an evidence-based approach to teaching. The Education Endowment Foundation (EEF, 2018), linked to the Sutton Trust Toolkit, identifies feedback as having one of the highest 'effect sizes' of all possible interventions used in teaching (+8 months). This suggests that pupils can make up to 8 months' gains in learning from such an intervention. Research evidence certainly points to the 'power of feedback' (Hattie and Timperley, 2007). However, closer scrutiny reveals a far more complex picture than is frequently painted. Indeed, Wiliam (2016: 115) maintains that his initial optimism for its high effect size 'may have been a mistake'. The arguments here are not straightforward. There is certainly evidence to show that feedback can have a positive impact on learning, but there is also evidence to show that feedback may have a negative impact. Kluger and DeNisi's (1996) research revealed that a third of the feedback had a negative effect. In contrast, Askew and Lodge (2000: 6) identify some forms of feedback as 'killer feedback', recognizing the damaging effect they can have on learning.

There is general agreement in the literature that successful feedback should be timely, targeted and clearly identify steps forwards that are within the cognitive reach of each pupil. Less effective – or even damaging – results stem from a range of feedback practices, including feedback that: addresses the person rather than the learning; is dominated by marks and grades only; is overly corrective (highlighting every error with little or no encouragement); does not offer ways to improve; and is not given in a timely manner. As Black (2015) reveals, as teachers adopt formative assessment practices, there is a very different relationship between teaching and learning.

In the school in which you teach, there are likely to be specific polices connected with written marking and feedback. These may include its style, frequency and length. Ensure that you are familiar with these policies. However, it is important that you ensure the type of feedback is suitable for what you hope to be achieved from it. The national report on marking following the national consultation on workload (DfE, 2016a) revealed that there were considerable unnecessary marking practices, which mainly seemed to be satisfying a perceived need for evidence of accountability. Ensuring that marking and feedback are 'meaningful, manageable and motivating' (2016a: 5) was identified as a priority. It was clear that one size does not fit all.

Feedback might usefully be given verbally sometimes. It may even be the case that different pupils will benefit from different approaches to marking and feedback. There is a balance to be achieved here. How can the marking and feedback be manageable, and in what ways does it best enable pupils to adjust their learning?

Task 9.5

Look at some marking and written feedback that you have recently undertaken. What strategies and techniques did you use? What difference have they made to pupils' learning?

In considering the effectiveness of any feedback strategy, you need to evaluate its manageability for the teacher as well as the way in which pupils use it.

What might you need to adjust in relation to manageability in your own workload or in the teaching day for pupils to effectively receive and respond to feedback?

9.8 Questioning as an AfL technique

Chapter 8 addresses how questioning can be effectively used as a vital teaching skill. Questioning can be used in your teaching to provide instant formative assessment evidence on how pupils are responding to what you are teaching. It can also be used in short quizzes and mini-tests to gauge pupils' progress. It provides information that can help you pace a lesson or pitch it higher or lower as you proceed. In addition to your own skills in constructing suitable questions that reveal the information that will help you adjust your teaching, it requires responses from the pupils. This may require appropriate 'wait times' so that pupils have thinking time, giving everyone the chance to respond on a personal white board or with an answer card (A, B, C, D); 'think-pair-share' times where pupils talk to one or two others first with their ideas, so that everyone has a chance to respond; or questioning that is differentiated and targeted at different groups of pupils. The purpose of such questioning is to help reveal what the pupils know, or perhaps what they are finding difficult. Maybe a particular set of questions can usefully be constructed at the planning stage to be asked at a 'pivot point' in the lesson. This might be the point at which you decide whether to continue further with more new teaching or recap and consolidate. Or, it could be when you move some pupils on to one activity and others to something different, or for some pupils to have further support. In relation to Tasks 9.2 and 9.3 before, questions posed by the teacher in the introductory phase of the lesson are often used to establish what is known and how the pupils are connecting with the new ideas being taught, in the moment of teaching. It can also be used to help pupils understand their own thinking better and to learn with others.

9.9 Pupils' responses to AfL

Pupils' school learning is only one part of their 'lifeworld'. Some pupils are more equipped than others to make clear distinctions between what is required for school learning and when they can appropriately game-play within school, so that they can hear, understand and respond to the school's call for 'successful learning'. Others will find this more difficult. Therefore, feedback strategies will necessarily need to be adjusted for different pupils' needs. Furthermore, pupils need to develop their own skills in using assessment to promote their own learning. Part of the intention of formative assessment is that the information it yields will be used by pupils as part of their own learning processes. Effectively it becomes 'Assessment as Learning' (Dann, 2002, 2014) as the information from formative assessment is incorporated into each pupil's own learning development and strategies. There are some important things you need to consider if this is to be supported in the classroom. These can be categorized as follows: motivational, cognitive, strategic and regulatory. They are briefly outlined below as a starting point for your own thoughts and subsequent application.

Pupil motivation and AfL

If pupils are to progress in their learning, it is important that they have some notion of needing to know something new. They require some desire to change their current knowledge and understanding. This may be described through ideas such as motivation or curiosity. They also need to believe that they *can* learn new things (self-efficacy). Essentially this drive for learning is fairly individualistic and will differ in strength between pupils (Dann, 2018: ch. 6). Nevertheless, as a teacher you need to try to make your teaching as accessible as possible to differing ideas and ideals for future learning from a pupil's perspective.

Cognition in AfL

If AfL is aimed at providing evidence that will help pupils adapt their learning to develop new learning, it primarily serves a cognitive process. The context of learning, together with the AfL information, requires the pupil to internalize new information. Pupils need to develop their own understanding of what they know and what they are trying to alter in their learning. AfL is therefore an additional tool to promote learning and builds on some of the concepts that you will have read about in Chapter 4.

Self-assessment skills are part of AfL; in other words, how pupils understand judgements made about what they already know, need to know, and the gap between the two. Fundamental in seeking to help pupils to be more aware of their own learning needs are the processes of meta-cognition and meta-learning. Meta-cognition relates to the way in which pupils are able to think about their own thinking. Meta-learning involves consideration of how learning is planned, enacted, reviewed and improved. It requires pupils to notice their learning, talk about their learning, reflect on and experiment with their learning (Watkins *et al.*, 2007: 128–129).

Pupils' strategic learning and AfL

In our school system, the focus of learning is important. Pupils need to understand that the curriculum is constructed around the National Curriculum framework and that, at the end of their compulsory schooling, examinations will offer them certification that can be used to access further training and/or education. Pupils can strategically use the information from AfL to help develop their learning in ways that will help them achieve the best outcomes. Keddie (2016) highlights how pupils are able to game-play by navigating their way through their learning so that they amass the capital to achieve the outcomes that will serve them best in a market-orientated education system. However, this also means that some pupils, for whatever reason, won't be so successful or interested in playing such a game.

Pupil self-regulation and AfL

Pupils organize their learning in many ways: cognitively, motivationally, behaviourally and strategically. Essentially self-regulation in learning is an organizing concept in which pupils shape and pace their learning. The way in which pupils use information from AfL to adapt their existing learning is a key part of the self-regulatory process. Teaching, and the learning environment, can certainly influence self-regulation, yet ultimately it is controlled by the pupil.

Task 9.6

In what ways have you supported or promoted pupils' skills and understanding in using AfL evidence to adjust their own learning?

Consider using a self-assessment strategy such as pupil self-marking against stated criteria. Or, ask the pupils to identify what has improved in their learning over the last few lessons (this is called 'ipsative' or 'self-referenced' assessment) and what remains to be developed further. Or, ask the pupils to rate their own learning using a simple scale.

For example: 'My grasp of the concept *X* is', or 'My understanding of *X* is':

1	2	3	4
Very good	**Good**	**Still developing**	**A problem for me**

How do you support pupils to act on the judgements they make and to set new targets? (Think about the concepts of meta-cognition and meta-learning and how these may help pupils to use AfL.) How do you understand pupils better (or differently) from their self-assessments?

9.10 Conclusion

AfL is focused on the future. It continually seeks to understand the learning that has already occurred, the teaching and learning that is being enacted, and the future direction of new or applied learning. It will help you and your pupils to identify next steps (realistic targets) that will enable learning to continue in the optimal zone (see Figure 9.2). As a new teacher, your own skills and assessment literacy will be developing. Hopefully this chapter will in some way serve in this process. As Wiliam (2016) points out, grasping the processes and principles of formative assessment is one of the best tools for your continuing professional development. Furthermore, formative assessment is about pupils' futures. Supporting pupils in the skills of understanding and reflecting on their own learning by using AfL evidence is an excellent tool for equipping them to develop their own learning for a sustainable learning future.

Recommendations for further reading

Black, P. (2015) Formative assessment – an optimistic but incomplete vision, *Assessment in Education: Principles, Policy and Practice*, 22 (1): 161–177.

Dann, R. (2018) *Developing Feedback for Pupil Learning*. London: Routledge.

Wiliam, D. (2011) *Embedded Formative Assessment*. Bloomington, IN: Solution Tree Press.

Webliography

Association for Achievement and Improvement through Assessment (AAIA): https://www.aaia.org.uk/

Assessment Reform Group: http://nuffieldfoundation.org/assessment-reform-group

Times Educational Supplement (TES) AfL Toolkit: https://www.tes.com/teaching-resource/assessment-for-learning-toolkit-6020165

10

Using assessment data to support pupil achievement

Isobel Ashmead

10.1 Introduction

It is Sunday evening and the last thing you want to do is mark some pupils' work; however, this is the life of a teacher. Marking is an intrinsic part of the teaching role. It enables teachers to quantitatively verify (and report on) the progress of their class; it will enable you to assess the attainment and achievement of your pupils on a lesson-by-lesson basis with visual data. Although this may seem obvious, the way pupils are assessed and even the way we measure attainment has been, and is, in a state of flux. What does not change, however, is the primacy of your task as a teacher: to ensure pupils learn and then measure what they have learned and thus achieved.

This chapter will give a detailed outline of how assessment is done such that achievement and attainment can be measured. As a secondary school teacher, you will be involved and held accountable for the progress that pupils make from the age of 11, as they start Key Stage 3 (KS3), until they reach the age of 16, at the end of KS4, and then onto KS5, the end of compulsory education. The methods of measuring achievement and attainment have changed significantly in the last few years and it will not be until 2022 when achievement using all the new measures, as explored in this chapter, is due to be fully embedded at KS4. Thus, it is important to remember that methods of assessment will be changing at least until this point; both the old and new measures will be explained.

It is important to remember that assessment by a teacher will occur throughout a good lesson. Assessment is not just the final process but should be seen as a *circular* process that involves planning the appropriate work, ensuring pupils understand what is being done and then further assessing the progress made. This means assessment is more than just marking a test or a piece of work; rather, in a lesson it will involve discussion and questioning, both to test understanding and to move the learning process on.

Chapter 9 focused on the importance of formative assessment in developing teaching and learning strategies. This chapter will focus more on assessment as a test of learning gained and ways in which schools have to adopt and adapt particular assessment policies. The principles of a good assessment, recording and reporting system will be explored because this should not vary between schools.

By the end of the chapter, you should:

- be aware of the range of assessment data that is available to teachers, especially given the importance of data protection measures;

- understand the ways in which schools use assessment data;
- know how schools undertake target-setting;
- be aware of recent changes to the way in which progress is measured.

10.2 Attainment and achievement

At this point it is useful to consider the difference between 'attainment' and 'achievement'. *Attainment* is the level reached against a set of criteria or score that is given for a particular assessment. *Achievement* is seen as the progress made against the prior attainment of the pupil. This may be against the initial attainment that the pupil reached at the end of the previous Key Stage; usually, in the case of secondary school pupils, this is their KS2 score. In addition, from 2016, the school may be judged against the national levels of progress based on the prior attainment of their cohort.

Within a school, assessment systems may vary as a pupil moves between KS3 and KS4 and, before the introduction of the current National Curriculum (NC) in 2015, this was the case. Prior to the NC reforms, at KS3 pupils were assessed using descriptors, which equated to levels of attainment. At KS4, they would then have been assessed against the grade criteria for their qualifications. There was a statutory duty to report the KS3 level to parents and the government, although this had been reduced to reporting only core subjects before the 2014/15 changes were made. The removal of descriptors enabled schools to choose their own assessment scheme, and this has led to a variety of different methods being used at KS3 and KS4 in different schools.

Assessment at KS4 has also changed for individual pupils. This is because grades awarded for GCSEs has and is changing, with the replacement of grades A*–C with 9–1.

At KS5, assessment and attainment is usually measured against the criteria for the qualifications being studied, but schools are assessed for the progress – or *achievement* – that pupils have made from KS4. Again, there have been moves away from simply measuring attainment and, with the changes at KS4, these will take time to embed.

The major changes to the assessment framework that are taking place mean that there will be different cohorts of pupils with varying measures being used to judge progress within a school for a number of years. In addition, as Ofsted has said, there is no preferred or correct method of assessment and reporting of achievement during the pupil's time in a school (Ofsted, 2018a). As a result, schools have adopted different practices. However, all will have some way of recording attainment and achievements and then meeting their statutory duty to report to parents. Schools will use a variety of management information systems (MISs) to collect and record data about attainment and achievement.

10.3 Prior attainment and baseline data

When pupils enter schooling in England and Wales, they are assigned a Unique Pupil Number (UPN), which stays with them through school. Secondary schools receive data from feeder primaries and, using the UPN, the Department for Education (DfE) website. From feeder primaries, this data is transferred as paper and electronic files. These files will include varying assessment data, dependent upon what they have collected and entered into their systems, but usually include the results of statutory KS1 and KS2 test results.

In addition, the files may include reading and spelling levels, often age-related. These can be useful to secondary schools but, because there are so many different methods for testing spelling and reading, the receiving school may often choose to retest pupils either on induction or as soon as they start at the school. This then provides baseline data, where further retesting following teaching can show achievement.

The way pupils are assessed at KS1 and KS2 has changed. Before 2016, pupils at the end of KS2 were assessed in English and maths. They were given tests in reading and writing (and latterly spellings), as well as maths, to give them levels in English and maths, as calculated against NC criteria. As well as tests, Year 6 teachers also had to record a Teacher Assessment, although the tests were the more usual method secondary schools used as their baseline. Pupils were given a level between 2 and 6 and this was subdivided as follows: 'a' represented the top portion of the level, 'b' the middle portion and 'c' the lower portion. Schools could also get the raw scores, although these were not reported to parents. A '4a' was seen as the average level of attainment, although the national expected level was a Level 4. For secondary schools, below Level 4 meant the pupil had an attainment of – that is, they were reaching the level of – a low-ability pupil, whereas a Level 5 indicated they had the attainment of a high-ability pupil. These labels were important as schools were measured on the *achievement* of each ability cohort.

Since 2016, pupils are no longer awarded NC levels at KS2. Instead, they are assessed and given scores that are standardized against a score of 100. Maths and English are tested, but with a refined spelling, punctuation and grammar test as part of the English element. The scores range from 80 to 120, with 120 being the highest level of attainment. In 2016, despite the scores being standardized, the average was 103 (Standards and Testing Agency, 2016). Secondary schools now had to decide their own boundaries for what was low, middle and high achievement, as no definitions were provided.

Knowing these levels and scores, most secondary schools will make this information available to teachers as it provides an indication of ability. In many schools it will be used to set pupils into particular classes so that appropriate teaching, building on prior knowledge, can take place immediately.

However, some schools will choose to do their own retesting, considering they need more detailed information than a raw score or level to make a judgement about the appropriate teaching that should take place. Some schools use other tests such as cognitive ability tests (CATs), which seek to measure other aspects that may not have been assessed through the KS2 tests, such as intelligence tests involving puzzles. The test scores are measured against database scores from previous years and exam outcomes from nationwide samples covering thousands of pupils. These then provide a baseline set of information for a school to assist in providing appropriate challenge through teaching and, when necessary, support when a pupil struggles and has a low score on a particular element of the test. Access to these scores may be used to set appropriate targets. Analysis of the various elements of the tests can be useful for teachers, particularly where there are skewed scores, meaning a pupil does better in, for example, non-verbal tests than verbal ones, which could mean a pupil may have underachieved on the KS2 tests because of their poor reading levels.

Many schools use spelling and reading tests, a variety of which are available commercially. As schools receive 'catch up funding' for pupils not meeting expected levels at KS2, and as there is the suggestion of resisting tests officially, schools need standards by which they can measure progress over time. Reading and spelling tests often give an age-related score, so a pupil in Year 7 with a reading and spelling age of an 8-year-old will struggle with the texts written for Year 7 pupils. Differentiation will be needed to enable them to learn across the curriculum. Intervention programmes put in place will aim to ensure the pupil catches up so that their reading age, for example, is more in line with that which is expected, or so that they make faster progress and achievement.

Task 10.1

In your placement school, speak to the member of staff in charge of assessment about the ways in which the school is responding to the changes taking place in recording pupil data and the tests that have been introduced.

10.4 Target-setting

Once a baseline has been established, or KS2 scores are known, it is common practice in secondary schools to set appropriate targets for attainment. Schools will use different sets of data but the DfE now, more than ever, places much greater emphasis on the achievement of pupils in the league tables for schools. Therefore, it is important to set challenging targets for all pupils, regardless of ability and prior attainment. As schools are held accountable for their KS4 results, many schools are setting targets for the end of KS4 but with 'flight paths', or expected levels of attainment at various points, either by term or by year for each subject.

Schools are able to set their own targets for pupils, but they should ensure that the targets will enable pupils to achieve at least the average, or better than average, national achievement, based on the prior attainment at KS2. This will be explained in more detail in the remaining part of the chapter and, given KS2 scores have changed, it is difficult currently to benchmark what will be expected outcomes.

Thousands of schools across the country set their targets using a database run by a not-for-profit organization endorsed by the government, the Fischer Family Trust (FFT). The FFT has a database of KS4 results against prior attainment for different cohorts of pupils by pupil characteristics, such as gender, and whether they have special educational needs (SEN) or are in receipt of free school meals (now known as 'disadvantaged pupils', though this refers to a range of groups eligible for Pupil Premium funding). The database also looks at the level of achievement by percentile: it calculates what grades pupils got in the top achieving schools (5th percentile), then high achieving schools (25th percentile) and finally average achieving schools from different KS2 scores. Schools using the service can set the benchmark at the target level they have chosen, as the system will give suggested end of KS4 targets for a range of subjects. Schools will use the system in varying ways. Some schools will issue targets to teachers and pupils. Some will allow teachers to set their own targets for the pupils using the data provided. Data can be exported from the system and placed in the school's MIS.

Some of the baseline testing systems mentioned here will also enable target-setting, as they provide information based on previous pupils' achievement from the initial test scores. Again, schools may choose to share or use a range of different sources of data to set targets.

Once targets have been set, schools decide whether to report these to parents. Given the fluctuations in the systems used, many schools will have data they hold that will give KS4 predictions but, lower down the school, they will only report to parents whether the child is in line to make the progress expected. This is a change from what occurred prior to

2016, when pupils and their parents had KS3 levels and these were used as the assessment scheme by most schools. Some schools will report a 'flight path' to parents and pupils, which is becoming increasingly popular, especially given the way the grading of qualifications has changed. Some schools predict different flight paths based on the attainment at KS2, giving them names such as 'Gold', 'Silver' and 'Bronze' and, as long as the pupil is on or above their line, they are making good or expected progress.

At KS5, targets are set, although the principle of using prior attainment is maintained, this time using KS4 results. Again, there are a variety of MIS and software packages available using nationwide databases. The FFT provides KS5 targets, but another database that gives targets and analysis of performance is called Alps. Neither of these databases is free to schools though, but because they use large samples, they provide reliable information, which may warrant the investment.

Once targets are set, these should link to one's teaching. On an individual lesson basis, this should feed into lesson objectives for learning and more formative assessment. Target-setting, if done properly, should motivate and challenge pupils to do their best. Some schools will have a variety of targets, such as expected levels of attainment and aspirational targets. Targets need to be realistic to be motivational but at the same time one needs to be careful not to set targets that place so much pressure on the pupil that they feel they are bound to fail. This is particularly the case with the most able pupils given straight-A grades (or the new 9s) across all subjects. In some cases, schools will deliberately avoid issuing such targets. This can be for various reasons, but one of the main warrants is that it can place additional pressures on the pupil, which can be detrimental. Conversely, settling for targets that are very low can be demoralising. A good assessment policy will look to discuss targets with all stakeholders to provide the right motivation for the pupil to achieve at their best.

Task 10.2

Consider how the process of target-setting is likely to impact on your lesson planning and classroom teaching.

10.5 Assessment in the classroom

Targets alone do not guarantee achievement. However, looking at prior attainment and targets should provide a road map for teaching and thus learning. At its simplest, this should include setting appropriate learning objectives. In many cases, these will be linked to assessment criteria set for the subject. Levelled lesson objectives inform the pupil and help create the steps to learning. It is good practice to have several linked and differentiated levels that will provide challenge and enable the learner to see progress. Sometimes these objectives will be written as 'Must', 'Should' and 'Could'. The levelling of objectives will vary according to school policies relating to assessment. Some schools have brought in new levelling systems whereas others use GCSE criteria throughout KS3 and KS4, the exam boards having come up with skills-based criteria for their new specifications. These are certainly easier to apply at KS4 although, given that the first 9–1 grades will only be issued in 2017 for English and maths, it is difficult, currently, to know where the standards lie. Experienced teachers will probably rely on trying to convert from old levels and grading criteria for some time.

Teachers will assess a pupil's work in a variety of ways. Schools will have a marking and assessment policy, which will usually state what work should be marked, how it should be graded, how frequently work should be assessed and the type of feedback that should be given to pupils.

In addition to teacher marking, good teaching should provide opportunities for peer and self-assessment. In these cases, grading criteria, mark schemes and model answers can be used. These help the pupils to see what is required and where common mistakes are made. Although informal, these assessment opportunities sometimes are less threatening and more supportive for pupils. However, pupils do like their teacher to check that peer assessment has been done correctly.

Feedback on what learning was demonstrated and where achievement was good is useful and motivational. Correcting work can enable pupils to learn from mistakes but there needs to be a balance in the amount of annotations applied, otherwise the pupil may look at a page and think they have got everything wrong. Ticks enforce where things are done well. The colour for marking may be prescribed: some schools suggest green is seen as a more 'supportive' colour for marking.

There has been much discussion and research on whether grading work aids progress. Some pupils will only look at the grade given and not read the comments written. However, there are ways around this, such as writing the grade within, or at the end of, sentences. In addition, many schools are adopting feedback loops whereby a teacher has to write a positive comment or 'What Went Well' (WWW) and an 'Even Better If' (EBI) statement. Pupils are then given time to improve, or are tasked to make the improvement to, their work either when assessed work is handed back or as a homework task.

Many schools will have assessment policies where termly assessments are put in place. These will be done by all pupils at the end of a unit of work. Schools can decide how they will be assessed but tests usually have score marking, which might then be converted into percentages and then compared against KS4 criteria, if this is what the school is using. Tests such as these serve a number of purposes. If marked properly, they should provide formative assessment to pupils. Tests do enable judgements of progress over time, or achievement. This is useful for the pupil and the teacher, who can then plan how to move learning forward or what interventions have to be put in place to secure improvement. Given the move to terminal or end-of-year assessment and the removal of modular assessments at KS4, schools are reintroducing yearly exams as a preparation for recall over longer periods of time. This is also the case at KS5 where AS exams are largely being phased out in preference for the terminal A2 exam.

10.6 Assessment for accountability

Assessment data is also used to hold teachers and institutions to account. The former could be referred to as 'internal accountability'. This will include analysis of 'progress' that pupils are making over time in your class. It can be used in judgements of your lesson for performance management, including successful completion of your NQT year, that is linked to pay progression. In addition, some of the assessment data you collect is likely to be reported to parents. In both cases, it is therefore important that you follow the school's assessment policy with regard to what assessment data has to be collected, how often and what systems need to be used to store the data.

It is your responsibility to show that pupils are making progress in your class. This will be in a lesson but, with regard to more formal assessment, over time also. Maintenance of assessment records was traditionally done in a mark book. Many MISs have electronic mark books, but you will need to see what works best for you or is required by your school. Electronic systems are useful as data can be extracted and sent to others easily, either prior to a lesson observation or as part of the school's reporting cycle. However, marking books next to a computer is sometimes not always easy and some prefer to maintain a paper copy, in a tangible mark book, or to use a combination of the two. You will have to share your records with others. It is good practice to record baseline data and the targets that you are working towards, as this enables you and others to judge the progress of individual pupils. Regular marking is also key. If you get behind, it is difficult to catch up, so plan your time carefully.

Some teachers record marks in the pupils' books over time. This could be in a grid at the front or graphically. This shows the pupil what progress they are making over time.

Schools vary in the regularity that teachers have to share their assessment data. Most secondary schools will report to parents once a term, although the statutory duty is to report once per year. When reports are due, you will be asked to submit your assessment of the pupil. This could be the grade they are working at or, in the case of KS4 and KS5, their predicted grade. This would be based on assessments you have done. Annually, you have to report what a pupil can do and set a target for improvement. Schools will vary in terms of what you will be asked to use to make your judgement. In some cases, you will give the latest test score. However, this may mean a fluctuation in grades over time. More common is the view that you should use test grades, in-class performance and, possibly, coursework grades. From these you make a *summative* judgement.

Your data will be entered into an MIS, which can be used to generate the reports and assess performance. These systems vary in their complexity but, as mentioned before, the system may report the proportion of pupils that are on track in relation to the 'flight path'. They will also work out the average grade for the class, which enables comparisons to be made between classes, teachers and subjects. A class and subject residual can be calculated to decide whether a pupil or class is doing particularly badly, suggesting that interventions need to be put in place. This may be the way your performance as a teacher is judged – do pupils do better or worse in your class than they do in other lessons?

Subject reports are often generated to assess the progress pupils are making towards targets. Clearly, your assessments form part of this data. It is likely you will have a discussion with your line manager about the performance of your subject.

Task 10.3

When you are on school placement, find out how the assessment manager in your school draws together assessment data and find out the cycle for such data to map pupil progress in Years 7 and 8.

What steps are taken to challenge pupils who are not performing at least to expected levels of performance and to extend those who are exceeding expectations?

10.7 External accountability

Although you may not be directly involved in the collation of statistics for school league tables, it is important that you have an understanding of what is used and how the figures are calculated. In many cases, this now has an impact on the curriculum that the school offers, as schools are held accountable for pupil performance against a range of measures.

The headline figures have been and are changing. The move to new GCSEs assessed on a scale of 9–1 has meant there will be a mixture of calculations used until 2019, with the full change not being due to be implemented until 2021/22. In addition, to measure progress, new figures have been developed. The qualifications that count in the league tables that are used for state-funded schools have changed. The qualification has to be of a particular breadth and standard. All qualifications that do count in league tables are given a point score. The simplest grading is the GCSE, where they are awarded 9–1. However, non-GCSEs, which award Distinction*, Distinction, Merit and Pass, are given equivalent point scores, which are then used in the calculations.

The simplest measure is called the 'Basics'. This is the percentage of pupils in a year group that achieve a 'Good' pass (Grade 5 or better) in both English (either literature or language) and mathematics. Initially, only attainment above Level 5 was to be reported. However, in spring 2017, the government announced that a Level 4 (equivalent to an old 'C' grade) pass would be recognized as the basic standard, and so it may be that schools' results for *this* measure will be published.

The new 'headline' measures, which were introduced in summer 2016, are Progress 8 (P8) and Attainment 8 (A8) scores (DfE, 2017c). These have had a significant impact on the KS4 curriculum, as it encourages the school to ensure pupils take what is considered to be a broad range of qualifications. Pupils are assessed on their performance across a range of eight subjects (A8 score), which is then compared with their KS2 score and worked out nationally to see if they have achieved above-average progress. This is their P8 score. Above average will give a positive score and below average a negative score. A score of 1 means that the student achieved, on average, one grade higher than their peers nationally, with the same KS2 score. Hence, they have made good progress.

The calculations are more complicated, as it is not simply eight qualifications, but some of these are prescribed and have to be taken by all students. The eight must be made up from three different groups of subjects. These groups are sometimes called 'buckets', 'baskets' or simply 'P1, P2 and P3', as shown in Table 10.1.

The scores for these subjects are then added up to give the Attainment 8 (A8) score. The Progress 8 (P8) score is worked out by dividing the A8 score by 10 (as English and maths are double weighted) and comparing with the national performance based on prior attainment. This is harder to calculate, as you do not know what the national score is. MISs are being developed to work this out but can only go on previous years' data and, with changing qualifications, this will take time to stabilize. However, the P8 score is important, as this will be used by stakeholders such as Ofsted. A P8 score of –0.5 for the school is seen as unacceptable progress. In addition, confidence levels are used, which give greater accuracy. This is now the key measure and replaces the percentage of pupils who achieve five A*–C passes including English and maths.

Schools are also measured on the percentage of pupils who achieve 9–5 passes in English language and literature, maths, two sciences, a language and either geography or history. This is known as the English Baccalaureate (EBacc) measure. It is effectively being replaced by the P8 score. The percentage of pupils achieving passes in two languages and the percentage achieving the triple sciences is also published.

Bucket or group	Subjects	Number of subjects	Special notes
P1	• English language and literature • Maths	Must have both a maths and an English grade. Counts as 2 subjects	These subject scores are double weighted, although the English score will only be doubled if both English language and literature are studied. The best English grade is counted. The second grade may go into P3
P2 – known as the EBacc bucket	• Biology • Chemistry • Physics • Double award (so worth 2) science • Computer science • Geography • History • Modern foreign languages	3 subjects from this group	The aim is to ensure breadth in key subjects. This has been controversial, as neither religious studies nor ICT GCSE count, with the latter being dropped as a GCSE
P3 Open bucket	Any other GCSE equivalent qualification on the approved list	3 subjects from this group	English literature or language could be included or additional subjects from P2

Table 10.1 Subject groups

Task 10.4

Consider what impact the changes in external accountability outlined in the preceding and the developments in the KS4 curriculum are going to have on your subject area.

10.8 Conclusion

These are changing times for assessment, reporting and recording in schools. As a classroom teacher, you need to ensure you assess in line with your school's policy. The key thing is that assessment is not the end point of learning but should also be the beginning and middle, to ensure the pupils in your care achieve their potential. Chapter 15 will develop a number of issues introduced in this chapter and will provide a range of strategies to achieve maximum attainment and achievement for all pupils.

Recommendations for further reading

Blandford, S. and Knowles, C. (2013) *Achievement for All: Raising Aspirations, Access and Achievement*. London: Bloomsbury.

Wiliam, D. (2017) *Embedded Formative Assessment*, 2nd edn. Bloomington, IN: Solution Tree Press.

Webliography

Dylan Wiliam: http://www.dylanwiliam.org

National Foundation for Educational Research (NFER): http://www.nfer.ac.uk

Curriculum, Evaluation and Management (CEM) Centre at the University of Durham: https://www.cem.org/

Fischer Family Trust (FFT): https://fft.org.uk

UK Government, School Performance Measures: https://www.gov.uk/government/collections/school-performance-tables-about-the-data

11

Positive approaches to supporting pupil behaviour

Lynn Reynolds and Ian Abbott

11.1 Introduction

Promoting positive behaviour in the classroom and supporting teachers with this task is high on the agenda of educational reform. All teachers need to be able to understand and manage behaviour in the classroom effectively to promote learning and the well-being of learners. Naturally, this is an area of concern for many student teachers at the start of their teaching career, as well as experienced teachers, given that there is an expectation that schools will provide a safe, orderly environment and that teachers are accountable for pupils' academic achievement (Rosas and West, 2009). Most student teachers are looking for 'practical things that will work in the short term as one of their main objectives is understandably to get order in order to teach' (McNally *et al.*, 2005: 180), possibly leading to a neglect of the central principles that should guide practice. Effective classroom management is underpinned by good professional practice and entails:

- high expectations of all pupils;
- the delivery of well-prepared lessons appropriately informed by the use of formative assessment and thus matched to pupils' learning needs;
- opportunities for pupils to succeed and to have both academic and social successes recognized;
- teachers who offer good role models and whose behaviour promotes mutual respect;
- systems that support the individual teacher.

The teacher's role is to promote positive learning behaviour and to respond effectively to incidents of undesirable behaviour. Teachers develop a toolkit – strategies that they employ almost automatically, with some doing this more effectively than others – and this resource is constantly replenished from the experiences they have every day. Successful teachers continue to develop their understanding of behaviour management and the associated skills throughout their career, regularly reflecting on their own practice.

The focus in this chapter is on proactive planning to nurture a positive learning environment, and thus on prevention, rather than reaction and punitive responses. Newly qualified teachers (NQTs) need to have constructive relationships with learners based on high expectations, awareness of relevant legislation, respect for diversity and commitment to achievement.

Self-awareness, adaptability, identification of professional needs and commitment to professional development are key attributes for teachers entering the profession. Student teachers have their own beliefs, drawing on their experience as learners, from the workplace and family contexts. These beliefs will shift during training and beyond as each individual builds their own toolkit and finds ways to align beliefs with practice (Roehrig *et al.*, 2009).

For most children, part of the process of growing up involves challenging, or at least *renegotiating*, relationships with parents and teachers who have been authority figures. In addition to the difficulties of adolescence, some young people bring 'baggage' into school from difficult lives outside of school. Teachers need to be sensitive to pupils' experiences and see their behaviours in context, rather than 'labelling' them as disruptive. The ways in which we categorize pupil behaviour are notoriously imprecise and subjective and the behaviour that one teacher finds infuriating may be seen by a colleague as good fun.

Task 11.1

Remember some of the things you or your friends did at school – good and bad! List five things that you would now consider to be 'good behaviour' and five things that you would consider 'bad behaviour'. Then, write beside each of these how this action impacted on your learning. Is good behaviour always linked to a useful learning experience? Similarly, is bad behaviour always linked to a poor learning experience? List five characteristics of the learning behaviour that you would like to promote in your classroom.

Now read the following quotes:

- 'We tightened a pupil's head in a vice.'
- 'We locked a teacher in a store cupboard.'
- 'We climbed through the loft hatch and banged on the ceiling of the classroom below.'
- 'We coated the drawer handle of the teacher's desk with syrup.'
- 'I organized a pupil rebellion in which we refused to attend lessons.'

Who do you think these miscreants were?

two head teachers, two university lecturers, and one chief education officer!

By the end of this chapter, you should:

- know how to take a critical look at policy and theory supported by research findings;
- have developed an understanding of the characteristics of learning behaviour and how to promote this;
- have considered a range of strategies for positive classroom management.

11.2 Behaviour policy

A consideration of how government policy has developed is important, as it reflects shifting perceptions of what constitutes 'good' behaviour and the link between behaviour and learning. Major developments such as the National Curriculum (NC), league tables and testing have served to reconfigure the expectations of pupils and teachers alike. As education has become increasingly politicized, behaviour has come to the fore triggering government reports (e.g. DES, 1989; DfES, 2005c; DfE, 2016f, 2017f). The Elton Report (DES, 1989) focused on addressing standards of behaviour that were perceived to be declining. As well as acknowledging the impact of pupils' backgrounds on behaviour, there was clear reference to the role of the school and 'the quality of its leadership, classroom management, behaviour policy, curriculum, pastoral care, buildings and physical environment, organisation and timetable and relations with parents' (DES, 1989: 89–90). The term 'classroom management' has steadily replaced 'behaviour management' to acknowledge a teacher's role in planning engaging lessons, pitched at the right level and delivered well.

Following this, the Behaviour and Attendance strand of the National Strategies (for more information, see https://www.stem.org.uk/rx35z6) aimed to support teachers with behaviour and attendance training and materials. These materials helped forged a link between these elements of the classroom and teaching and learning, strengthening the understanding that pedagogy and practice underpin improved behaviour. Although the National Strategies came to an end in 2011, the materials are still useful, and widely used in schools, with programmes such as SEAL (Social and Emotional Aspects of Learning) giving explicit guidance on how to encourage behaviours such as group work to support positive learning behaviour (DfES, 2005b). The Bennett Review does not include specific reference to SEAL but does take into account 'the circumstances and the needs of each student when managing behaviour issues' (DfE, 2017f: 37).

Alongside these changes, the New Labour government expressed a commitment to the inclusion of all learners (in mainstream if possible) with the document *Excellence for All Children* (DfEE, 1997b), which created a potential source of tension for pupils and teachers. *Every Child Matters* (DfES, 2003a) strengthened the move towards working with the individual child to meet their needs: 'We all share a duty to do everything we can to ensure that every child has the chance to fulfil their potential' (2003a: 6), thus paving the way for 'personalized learning' (DfES, 2004). An increasing expectation that schools and teachers would be responsive to individuals, rather than expecting individuals to fit in, was developing. This was underpinned by an expectation that the teacher would have a 'heightened awareness of how individuals achieve best and be prepared to change practice based on this' (Ellis and Tod, 2009: 27).

Media interest resulted in another review focusing on behaviour in 2005, the Steer Report (DfES, 2005c), which resulted in *Higher Standards, Better Schools for All* (DfES, 2005a). The key findings highlighted the importance of:

- a consistent approach to behaviour management;
- effective school leadership;
- strong classroom management, learning and teaching;
- transparent rewards and sanctions;
- appropriate behaviour strategies and the teaching of good behaviour;

- planned staff development and support;
- effective pupil support systems;
- collaborative liaison with parents and other agencies;
- well-managed pupil transitions;
- appropriate organization and facilities.

There is little here that is different from the earlier Elton Report (DES, 1989) with research findings supporting these points (Watkins and Wagner, 2000). However, it marked a definite move towards a more secure link between behaviour, teaching and learning, perhaps reflecting the impact of the National Strategies in strengthening pedagogy.

The need for guidance on the discipline of pupils had been addressed by the Education and Inspections Act 2006, which gave official guidance on the 'rights and responsibilities' of those involved. The Coalition government later made their commitment to addressing behaviour concerns very clear with *The Importance of Teaching* (DfE, 2010b). There was a different emphasis here, focusing on 'discipline and respect', giving schools more freedom to exclude difficult pupils, and increasing the rights of teachers to search pupils and issue detentions – here behaviour was linked to pupil safety rather than learning. Ofsted will inspect and guide schools as to effective and ineffective practice particularly with respect to bullying (DfE, 2010b). There was little mention of learning and a clear message that the government would be less prescriptive about how this is managed in the classroom. Recent publications from the Department for Education (DfE) have stressed the importance of developing a whole-school approach and the need for ongoing training and support for teachers (DfE, 2016f, 2017f). In particular, these publications stress the importance of having clear policies and strategies in place across the school rather than depending on staff operating in isolation, however well trained they might be. A successful approach to maximizing positive behaviour in the classroom begins with committed and visible school leaders who set high expectations and adopt consistent practices that are clearly communicated to everyone in the school.

Task 11.2

Read section 4 of the Bennett Report (DfE, 2017f). Consider how you can incorporate the approaches and strategies into your own teaching practice. How do they compare with what you found in your placement school?

11.3 Background theories

Approaches to addressing the complex issues involved in managing classroom behaviours are informed by a wide range of theories about what causes pupil misbehaviour, how to assess behaviour and what interventions are effective.

This section will look briefly at three fundamental underpinning approaches to the issue of pupil behaviour. You are advised to follow this up with further reading (see, for example, Ayers *et al.*, 2000; Porter, 2000; Roffey, 2011). Theories link to different stances about the social world and human behaviour, and you will be able to make links between your own belief systems and some of these ideas.

Most teachers make flexible and eclectic use of strategies that derive from each of these approaches but have a strong preference for strategies that fit with their own ideas of effective classroom management.

Behavioural approaches

The behavioural model addresses the observed behaviour rather than seeking explanations in cognitive or psychological causes. (You can read more about behaviourism as a theory of learning in Chapter 4.) Behaviour is influenced by the antecedents – the environment in which the behaviour occurs – and is reinforced by the response it gets. The model therefore uses an ABC formulation:

A for Antecedents
B for Behaviour
C for Consequences

Changing behaviour may involve changing the antecedents (e.g. reorganizing seating arrangements), observing precisely the frequency and context of the behaviour, and looking at what reinforces it. To increase the incidence of good behaviour, the teacher needs to notice and respond to this positively, while unwanted behaviours should be dealt with by use of sanctions but not rewarded by lots of attention.

Whole-school approaches such as 'Assertive Discipline' or 'Discipline for Learning' seek to enable teachers to respond consistently to behaviours with a clear tariff of responses. Within the classroom, a discipline plan allows for clear rules that are taught to the pupils, positive recognition of pupils for following the rules and a system of consequences for not following the rules. Much effective behaviour change has been achieved through these approaches, not least because they are accompanied by training of all the teaching and support staff, the development of a coherent policy, and consistency in application of the approach.

There are some concerns that arise with this approach, including whether the pupils internalize the better behaviour or it is bound to the context. For some, it works well. Better behaviour may enable better learning; thus, better educational achievement and consequent improvement in self-esteem will enable some pupils to pass through difficult periods. Others, especially those who are having a difficult time outside school, may require approaches that give them more space to look at feelings, and programmes such as SEAL can be very useful in this instance. It is important to note also that behavioural engagement is just one aspect of being engaged in the lesson. Emotional and cognitive engagement is also essential for effective learning to take place (Fredricks et al., 2004).

Cognitive approaches

A further set of theories attaches importance to the child's experience and to understanding its impact on behaviour. Cognitivists believe that young people's perceptions, their understanding of a situation, their emotional state, the stage of their development and the context, all impact on their behaviour. Interventions are targeted at helping them think through irrational, distorted or impulsive responses. Pupils with behavioural problems may not have the cognitive skills they need for appropriate interactions with their peers or with teachers and other staff. Problem-solving training and social learning approaches can help pupils develop new behaviours.

How people feel about themselves determines their self-esteem and this plays a signifi-cant part in the ability of pupils to be effective learners, as pupils with low self-esteem are vulnerable to failure and to criticism. A young person with high self-esteem can take risks in their learning and in their relationships. Low self-esteem means playing it safe and avoid-ing trying out new things. There are ways in which teachers can help protect and develop the self-esteem of vulnerable pupils:

- learn pupils' names and use them;
- use praise – specific and personal;
- reprimand the behaviour, not the person;
- repair the relationship;
- apologize if you are wrong;
- look after your own self-esteem;
- develop sensitive practices – for example, let pupils choose whether they read aloud;
- do not show pupils up by making comparisons and/or mocking them.

The ecosystemic model

The ecosystemic model is based on systems theory, which sees the school as part of inter-connected systems, each part influenced by change in the other parts. Porter (2000) char-acterizes this as one of the 'democratic' theories. These look at young people and teachers as equal actors in the teaching and learning enterprise and as each having rights to have their needs met, albeit in different roles. Relationships lie at the heart of these theories, and the emotional needs of participants in learning are included in the framework. That differ-ent people have different understandings of the same events is central to the ecosystemic model. Any event may be subject to various interpretations, with some more likely than others to enable progress.

To change the situation, we need to look at where it is stuck and seek ways of under-standing it that will encourage change. Teacher and pupils can get locked in a negative cycle: this theory would encourage the teacher to look at the situation from the pupils' perspectives and seek ways to cooperate with them. The assumption is that there are differ-ent interpretations of a situation, each equally valid, and the behaviour of teachers and pupils draws on those interpretations. The technique for thinking about a problem from a different perspective is called 'reframing' and requires the teacher to think of alternative explanations for the behaviour and ways in which they might respond differently. Teachers who took part in research by Tyler and Jones (2002) found that, in spite of initial resistance and scepticism, there was an improvement in dealing with entrenched problem behaviours and that they and their classes were more relaxed.

Pupil participation has received considerable interest in recent years as part of the growing understanding of the potential power of consultation with pupils or pupil voice to reduce barriers to learning (Flutter and Rudduck, 2004). For this to be successful, pupils' ideas need to be encouraged and, importantly, listened to. Pupils want a learning environment that fosters a sense of agency and ownership, as well as collaborative learning within social contexts (McIntyre *et al.*, 2005). This latter study mapped the success of teachers who 'listened' and adapted, as well as the continuing frustration for those who failed to engage with pupils' ideas.

11.4 Strategies for classroom management

Task 11.3

As you read through this section, try to link strategies with the theoretical frameworks outlined before. Note where they fit neatly and where they cross over.

Think about your own beliefs and how well these approaches suit the sort of teacher you want to be.

Teachers need strategies to enable them to plan for positive behaviour, to prevent the onset of poor behaviour, and to respond effectively when such behaviour occurs. Although most young people want to learn and resent their learning being impeded by other pupils' disruptive behaviour, the same pupils are able and willing to take advantage of a chance to reduce a lesson to chaos.

The Elton Report (DES, 1989: 69–70) stated that 'teachers' group management skills are probably the single most important factor in achieving good standards of classroom behaviour' and that 'those skills can be taught and learned'. This is still highly relevant today. Skills and strategies are essential and can be learned through 'the right kinds of training, experience and support'. Applying them depends on a pragmatic assessment of the context; it is not the purpose of this chapter to offer strategies as blueprints. Instead, you need to consider them, try them out, add those that work for you to your toolkit, and pursue further skills and continuous professional development through reading and observation of experienced colleagues.

Task 11.4

Think of someone you thought was a good teacher from your own school days.

- Make a list of the key features that you think made them memorable.
- Identify how many of those features were linked to lesson content, to classroom management skills and to personality. Any other categories?
- What qualities or skills of that teacher do you share?
- What qualities or skills of your own would you like to develop?

The interactions between a teacher and the pupils in any particular classroom are determined by key features that you as a classroom teacher can influence, a number of which will be considered in the following sections. The books by Sue Roffey (2011) and Bill Rogers (2015), listed in the recommended reading section of this chapter, provide a fuller overview of these.

Whole-school policy

The Behaviour and Attendance strands of the National Strategy sought to strengthen and develop whole-school approaches to behaviour, requiring all schools to review their policies about behaviour and attendance and identify areas for improvement. As well as including specific support for schools in particularly challenging circumstances, the Strategy focused on whole-school perspectives, identifying and sharing best practice in order to develop consistent and effective policy to secure positive behaviour and attendance.

Whole-school behaviour policies also address the school's response to issues of bullying, including racial and sexual harassment. *Learning Behaviour: Lessons Learned* (DCSF, 2009a) offers a comprehensive review of the Steer Report with a strong focus on how behaviour and learning policy should be developed within schools along with the identification of good practice. Consistency, pupil participation and consultation with parents were just some of the points that emerged from this useful document. Current government policy has focused on behaviour as part of the broader policy aim to bring about widespread school improvement and is clearly seen as a whole-school issue (DfE, 2017f). The roles and responsibilities of head teachers have been clearly identified and the role of the school leader is seen as vital in developing positive behaviour. The government has identified that improvements in behaviour throughout a school can lead to a range of benefits (DfE, 2017f: 6):

- 'students achieve more academically and socially
- time is reclaimed for better and more learning
- staff satisfaction improves, retention is higher, recruitment is less problematic'.

Policies underpin school rules or codes of conduct, which are usually expressed positively, signalling what is required, rather than a list of 'don'ts'. Thus, 'Walk in the corridors' is seen as more positive in promoting the desired behaviour than 'Don't run', which focuses on the negative. In many schools, you will see a written 'Code of Conduct' displayed in strategic locations that provides a shared framework for promoting good behaviour.

All experienced and trainee teachers must be familiar with their school policy on behaviour and attendance and use it in a consistent fashion to encourage a whole-school understanding of good behaviour.

High expectations

Teachers' expectations have an impact on pupils' behaviour and on their learning. High – but *realistic* – expectations should inform your approach, and you need to signal this in the way you address pupils both as a group and individually.

The negative impact of 'labelling' is seen as a key influence on negative outcomes for some pupils, particularly the most vulnerable – and remember that the 'acting-out' or 'acting-up' pupil may be vulnerable, although it may not feel like that to you. Labelling links to the idea of positive and negative expectations and of a self-fulfilling prophecy.

Case Study 11.1

Think about the following scenario:

- The teacher expects Jaz to behave badly, probably because he has been warned in the staffroom.
- Every time Jaz steps out of line, the teacher notices because it confirms negative expectations, even though Jaz is no worse than other pupils.
- By the end of the lesson, the teacher is convinced that Jaz is a troublesome pupil, thus confirming the original expectations.
- At the same time, Jaz feels that she can do no right even though she knows her behaviour has been no different from that of anyone else.

COMMENTARY: You are likely to encounter this type of labelling from well-meaning teachers during your placement. How would you as a trainee teacher deal with this situation?

The sibling phenomenon is associated with labelling theory. Pupils may arrive in secondary school already labelled by their association with their older siblings, again, often in the staffroom. There is a difficult balance to strike between the information that is useful to know about your pupils as a new teacher and the labelling effect that staffroom talk may encourage. Your own professionalism and judgement is critical. Of course, pupils have expectations too. The research into pupil voice has added to our understanding of what pupils expect from teachers – and their views are well worth listening to (Haydn, 2007). When asked about teacher characteristics, pupils rated subject knowledge, the ability to explain things well, being friendly and talking normally as most important. Other factors included teachers who were polite, not being absent, marking homework and having a sense of humour.

Positive relationships

Gaining respect from pupils and establishing authority happen within the context of the relationships built by the teacher. These relationships need to be based on the knowledge that you have the right to manage the class. Genuine liking for, and interest in, young people is important and pupils will be aware of this at once. Listening to pupils carefully, using names and learning about their personalities and enthusiasms are very important in showing an interest in your pupils – as well as planning lessons that will engage them.

How you present yourself is similarly important. A calm sense of determination that you are in control of the lesson and expecting the best from your pupils will contribute to a positive outcome. There is no set ideal of a teacher but, however you do so, whether through changes in attire, posture or language, you do need to look like you are in charge, and for some this can be difficult. It is important to create an identity that signals 'grown-up in charge', both to pupils and to yourself. A culture of good behaviour has to be established

and it is 'important for staff and students to see exemplary behaviour' (DfE, 2017f: 51). As noted in Chapter 8, body language and voice are important tools in managing a class effectively. Video recording the lesson and reviewing it with a colleague is an invaluable tool in helping you determine what you 'look like' as a teacher. It also helps you to identify what 'learning' looks like in your classroom and whether your classroom management techniques are encouraging the type of learning that you had hoped for.

The teacher's self-conviction is an important signal to pupils while the opposite, self-doubt, is an open invitation to create trouble. The conviction underlying this chapter is that warmth and genuine engagement with pupils are important qualities and valuable tools. However, student teachers often find that a natural desire to be chummy with pupils, particularly at the outset during initial visit days, sets up relationships that are hard to shake off when they become responsible for managing the class. While the old adage 'don't smile 'til Christmas' seems grim these days, it is prudent to adopt a 'teacher persona' from the outset, even when it feels awkward.

Rogers (2015) carefully considers and suggests ways in which positive relationships can be developed. The right verbal cues must be used and there are some simple rules that can make a significant difference such as using the word 'thanks' rather than 'please': 'Everyone looking this way, thanks' carries an expectation of what is directed rather than a request. Another useful tactic is to focus on the expected or required behaviour: 'Jack, facing this way, thanks' communicates the required behaviour concisely. Non-verbal prompts are often used to strengthen the verbal cue and may also be used instead of a verbal prompt. Non-verbal prompts can help avoid unnecessary tension; however, the success of this rests on the pupils understanding the prompt, and thus the consistency with which the teacher has used this previously.

Planning for classroom management

Planning for classroom management is as much a part of lesson planning as subject content. There are some key questions that you need to ask yourself (Haydn, 2007: 74): How much or what type of control do you want during the lesson? How will this shift throughout the lesson? Kaufman and Moss (2010) have shown that trainee teachers often struggle with the difference between organizing the lesson and managing the learning, both of which have an impact on behaviour. Organization includes understanding the physical environment and factors such as pupil movement. Using technology effectively is something in particular that requires both careful organization and a consideration of the desired learning.

Most effective teachers anticipate and prevent disruption by careful planning for key stages of the lesson:

Beginnings of lessons

- Try always to be there first, properly prepared, with everything you need.
- Control the entry to the classroom by standing at the doorway to greet pupils, remind them of the rules (for example, 'coats off', 'bags at the back').
- Have an initial activity ready for them to get on with, already projected on the whiteboard or on the desk, so that they are occupied while you settle everyone and get the main lesson started.

Transitions between activities

- Make sure every pupil stops what they are doing to listen to your instructions; do not talk over them.
- Give clear instructions; check they have understood.
- Make sure you give clear guidance about how much time they have – try using one of the online stop clocks that are freely available.

Handing out resources and equipment

- Use reliable pupils to hand out books and equipment, otherwise it holds up the flow of the lesson.
- Find the time to speak to the teaching assistant before the lesson to discuss the potential for any organizational support.

Dealing with interruptions by minimizing their disruptive impact

- Politely ask someone who comes in to wait while you get to a point where you can talk to them.
- Plan how you will respond to requests to leave the room (check whether there is guidance on this in the school behaviour policy).
- Respond to disruptive behaviour by talking quietly to the pupil individually, avoid public showdowns and, if necessary, ask them to see you after the lesson.
- Use the language of choice: 'If you cannot work quietly here, then you will have to work elsewhere'. The important feature of this is that there are no free choices; all choice has got to be within what is expected in your classroom.

Ending lessons

- Anticipate so that there is plenty of time left for reviewing learning, setting homework and clearing up.
- Warn the group that they will go when you tell them, not when the bell rings.
- Make sure that pupils leave chairs tidy and pick up litter.
- Provide positive feedback on the learning, progress and behaviour, if appropriate, that has occurred in the lesson.
- Let pupils go in groups or rows, when they have tidied up and are ready and quiet.

Routines and rules

Bill Rogers has a user-friendly approach to setting up rules, routines and responsibilities. He makes the important point that you are establishing routines right from the beginning. If pupils carry on talking when you are talking, then you are establishing that it is acceptable. While Rogers' work includes dealing with very difficult behaviour, his emphasis on routines, on clarity, on reinforcing desired behaviour and on dealing with problems in the least intrusive way is useful for most situations.

Establishing rules in discussion with the class provides a sense of ownership that can be further strengthened by careful use of inclusive language: 'In our classroom, we . . .'. Posting them on the classroom wall provides a point of reference and allows for an early preventive reminder ('Rosie, remember our rule about . . .').

Task 11.5

Write a list of classroom rules, no more than five in total, to cover the key features of: entry to the classroom and readiness for the lesson; movement within the classroom; getting teacher's attention; teacher's cues for whole class to attend; responses to and behaviour with other pupils; closure systems for ending a lesson.

The rules should be easy to understand and suitable for putting up on the classroom wall. Make sure they are expressed positively. What are your expectations across the age range? Will all pupils adhere to the same rules?

Planning to meet the needs of all pupils

This is a challenge and an opportunity for teachers in the current climate of inclusion (see Chapter 21). Inclusion embraces the idea that the school community should be representative of and include all the community members of school age: thus, teaching approaches and management strategies need to be based on the individual learning needs of pupils. Differentiation and the planned and effective use of classroom support are key elements in preventing disruption. Work pitched at too low a level will bore pupils and at too high a level will make some defensive and anxious. Key to achievement is participation, as pupils have an active role to play in their own learning, closely linked to pupil voice, which was discussed earlier.

Rewards and sanctions

You should notice pupils being good and respond to desirable behaviours as well as to academic achievements. Use praise generously and specifically, so that the pupil (and any others in earshot) knows what was praiseworthy. However, do not devalue praise by giving it where it is not deserved. As pupils get older, it is more appropriate for praise to be more private, as public praise may have a negative effect.

Praise is rewarding, as is positive written feedback on work or in homework books. Some teachers write letters to parents to acknowledge good behaviour. Giving pupils responsibility can be used to reward good behaviour. Some schools have whole-school or year systems that can be used to acknowledge merit for positive behaviour as well as for good work.

You should recognize 'baggage', although no matter how carefully you plan a lesson, you cannot control the baggage that a pupil may bring with them from home, from an earlier lesson or from relationships with peers that may make them disruptive. As well as establishing routines and rules, teachers need to be ready to respond when disruptive behaviour occurs.

Teachers need to relate to whole-school policy and responses to poor behaviour need to take into account the whole-school policy. Serious problems will invoke the school systems, which probably include referral to year head or senior management, time out, detentions, letters home and, as a last resort, exclusion. There should be clear lines of support for students and new teachers in a school that spell out how to get help to deal with major difficulties. Find out at an early stage what the back-up systems are and how to access them.

You should respond early and lightly, as most disruption can be dealt with within the classroom by the teacher. Your first reaction to the early signs of disruptive activity should be very low on a tariff of responses. Many behavioural problems can be spotted early and deflected effectively with small interventions. A suggested tariff of interventions is as follows:

- the 'look';
- proximity control (moving closer to the disruptive pupil);
- praise to person adjacent who is on-task;
- private word (this is less confrontational if delivered from the same height, thus crouching rather than towering over);
- re-statement of task;
- rule reminder: 'remember our rule about . . .';
- direct questions: 'What are you doing?' 'What should you be doing?' (Avoid 'Why are you doing that?' questions);
- offer choices: 'If you do not put the mobile phone away, I will have to ask you to stay at break'.

When low tariff interventions have not succeeded in dealing with problem behaviour and tensions rise, teachers need to employ strategies to remain calm. Angry or exasperated responses can easily exacerbate tense situations and shouting will not help. Instead:

- Take a few deep breaths to calm yourself.
- Own what you are feeling: 'I am angry because . . .'.
- Use assertive language: 'I don't swear at you. That language is unacceptable here'.
- Lower your voice as soon as possible.
- Allow cool-off time for both parties: 'We will follow this up tomorrow morning'.
- At a meeting with the pupil, explain what made you angry at the time, listen to the pupil's perceptions, refer to relevant rules, discuss how to make reparations or deal with a similar incident next time.
- Repair and rebuild the relationship.

Support for the teacher

You need to ensure that you have systems of support in place as a student or a new teacher. Some or all of the following will be useful to you:

- A member of the senior management team usually has responsibility for pastoral and discipline matters.

- The special educational needs coordinator (SENCo) or, in some schools, behaviour support specialist teacher, will have particular knowledge about pupils with behavioural difficulties and their needs.
- School mentors can offer advice, demonstrate skills, and point you in the direction of other skilled teachers.
- Peers can offer excellent support, including peer observation as a basis for discussion about your approach.
- Reading, making use of websites, watching DVDs and trying out new ideas can all be helpful.
- Use stress-busting techniques such as exercise, relaxation, playing in a band or talking to friends!

Task 11.6

Think about the following situation and how you would react:

You are teaching in your first week of school placement when Ryan, a pupil you have not met before, comes in and walks deliberately and slowly across the front of the room between yourself and the pupils you are addressing.

Consider how your reaction to the situation would be affected if you knew that:

- Ryan is a regular troublemaker who frequently tries to 'needle' teachers;
- Ryan has been asked to take a message around the school by his head of year;
- Ryan is six feet tall;
- Ryan is small for his age and his mother says he is very nervous – often too frightened to come to school;
- Ryan has Asperger syndrome (a form of autism);
- it is a science lesson and you are demonstrating a potentially dangerous experiment;
- your mentor has warned you not to stand any nonsense from this group, and especially not from Ryan, who rarely comes to school;
- the class laughs uproariously;
- the class falls silent.

Underlying teachers' responses to pupils are sets of assumptions and presuppositions that can get in the way of responding to pupils' needs and building positive relationships. If you, as a teacher, strive to avoid jumping to conclusions, are sensitive to pupils' needs, and *listen carefully* to what they have to say, you stand a good chance of promoting positive behaviour and avoiding disruption and conflict.

11.5 Conclusion

This chapter has introduced you to some ideas about managing pupil behaviour in a positive and planned way. The central resource in this process is you, the individual teacher and your skills, working within a framework of the school community, its ethos and its policy on behaviour, which is in turn informed by government policy. Your skills will take time to build up and you will learn most from reading about and observing a range of practices and selecting approaches that fit the sort of teacher you are becoming.

Good teachers reflect constantly on their own practice and seek ways to develop new approaches that fit with their value system and suit their personal style. Bromfield (2005) points out that recognizing your concerns is a prerequisite for finding solutions. It is tempting, and easy, to blame the pupils when a lesson goes wrong. The trouble is that this does not help you to make the sorts of changes that might improve things. A teacher can change the lesson plan, vary seating arrangements, alter the order or content of the lesson, or vary the activities or the pace to meet the needs of a particular group or a group at a particular time. Flexibility to respond to the context is an important part of the teacher's skill, and preparation for a range of eventualities is invaluable for beginning teachers.

Recommendations for further reading

Bromfield, C. (2005) PGCE secondary trainee teachers and effective behaviour management: an evaluation and commentary, *Support for Learning*, 21 (4): 188–193.

Department for Education (DfE) (2011) *Getting the Simple Things Right: Charlie Taylor's Behaviour Checklists*. London: DfE.

Department for Education (DfE) (2016) *Behaviour and Discipline in Schools: Advice for Headteachers and School Staff*. London: DfE.

Department for Education (DfE) (2017f) *Creating a Culture: How School Leaders can Optimise Behaviour (The Bennett Review)*. London: DfE.

Haydn, T. (2007) *Managing Pupil Behaviour: Key Issues in Teaching and Learning*. London. Routledge.

Kaufman, D. and Moss, D. (2010) A new look at preservice teachers' conceptions of classroom management and organization: uncovering complexity and dissonance, *The Teacher Educator*, 45 (2): 118–136.

Roffey, S. (2011) *The New Teacher's Survival Guide to Behaviour*, 2nd edn. London: Sage.

Rogers, B. (2015) *Classroom Behaviour: A Practical Guide to Effective Teaching, Behaviour Management and Colleague Support*, 4th edn. London: Paul Chapman. Very useful practical approach to effective behaviour management, looking at setting up systems with a new class, dealing with challenging pupils, managing anger – pupils' and our own – and strategies for when things get difficult.

Webliography

National Union of Teachers (NUT): www.teachers.org.uk – the NUT provides guidance and resources for teachers on managing pupil behaviour.

Education Support Partnership: www.educationsupportpartnership.org.uk – there are a number of practical guides and resources relating to managing pupil behaviour available from this organization.

12

Using digital tools to support learning

Michael Hammond and Sarah Younie

12.1 Issues in using digital tools in school

This chapter discusses the use of digital tools in teaching your subject. We present three case studies of student teachers using such tools in schools and this is followed by a discussion of planning to use technology in your teaching. We go on to raise some wider issues concerning the use of ICT in secondary schools and we point you to further sources of information.

By the end of this chapter, you should:

- be aware of different motives for using digital tools in school;
- know how to assess the contribution of digital tools to teaching and learning;
- be able to plan for using digital tools in your own teaching;
- be able to contribute to critical discussions on the role of digital tools in teaching and learning.

12.2 Case studies of the use of digital tools

In this section, we will consider three examples of student teachers using technology in their placement schools. These examples illustrate a range of applications as well as different levels of planning. We use them to consider the planning, implementation and evaluation of technology in teaching, and how classroom experience can be used to inform future planning. These examples or 'case studies' are necessarily rooted in the teaching of particular subjects, but they raise general issues concerning technology for teaching, so please do not skip them even if the subject context is unfamiliar.

Task 12.1

Before reading the commentary that comes after each case study, ask yourself:

- What does technology contribute to pupils' learning?
- What are the strengths and weaknesses of each teacher's approach?

Case Study 12.1

Anthony, a student teacher of English, was worried about several aspects of his teaching and fretful about his relationships with pupils, which were often confrontational. He freely admitted to becoming interested in the use of technology as a means to get his pupils interested in working in class and, in his own words, 'bring them over to my side'. He booked a computer room and planned a lesson based on the pupils' understanding of *Romeo and Juliet*, the play they had been reading. The pupils would be asked to prepare a 'pitch' trying to persuade a production company to make a film of the play. For this, the pupils would use presentation software. Anthony had used the software many times before and felt confident about being able to demonstrate its use and deal with any problems the pupils might have. He asked a colleague, a student teacher of computing, to give him a short demonstration of how to logon and save work on the school network. This colleague volunteered to be on hand to deal with any technical hiccups that might occur during the lesson.

Anthony prepared his presentation to explain the aims of the lesson. He set the pupils to work in pairs at their machines. He monitored their work and tried to prompt them into recalling the key events of the play and move them away from investigating Clip Art and other images and embellishing text. At the end of the lesson, he asked for volunteers to talk through the work they had done in front of the rest of the class. His evaluation of the lesson was not extensive or formal. However, he felt the lesson had been a great success, as the pupils seemed much more positive and his relationships with them had been far less stressful. Nevertheless, although the pupils had been 'on-task', he was not quite sure what they understood the task to be. They had spent a lot of time 'playing on the computer' rather than addressing his learning goals. He could see that the pupils would need more time to finish the presentation, something he had not predicted, and decided to try to book the room for his next lesson with them.

COMMENTARY: This case study hardly represents an ideal model of introducing technology into your teaching, but it is consistent with the haphazard way in which many teachers get started. It is worth remembering that computers and computer programs are not always produced with schools in mind – teachers sometimes have to adapt widely available tools for their own use and settings. This may sound like an indictment of Anthony, and of schools in general, but it is not meant to be. Anthony faced a challenge in the classroom, so he looked around and used what was available to try to address the issue. Having said that, his planning of the lesson was rudimentary. He took pupils' skills very much for granted. Fortunately, he chose a software application that had a 'low entry threshold' (one pupils could start using without long and detailed explanation) and one with which they were, in fact, familiar. Again, he was fortunate in getting a colleague to support the technical side of the activity – any hitches would have been very difficult to address himself.

However, Anthony was unsure of the learning goals of his lesson and hence did not set out his objectives very clearly. He could have structured his introduction more clearly and provided a 'mock-up' of the kind of presentation he was looking for, thereby modelling expectations for his pupils. He could, for example, have explained that he wanted to see a synopsis of the plot and a statement about why the play would still be relevant to today's audiences. He could have encouraged his pupils to focus on specific scenes or on how language was being used to persuade. On the positive side, he did ask pupils to work in pairs. This had the advantage of reducing the number of pupils asking for technical assistance, since they were encouraged to help each other. More importantly, however, it seemed to prompt the pupils to discuss their ideas together and their understanding of characters and themes in the play, an example of 'dialogic' learning as, for example, discussed in Chapter 8. Pupils were asked to present their work using bullet points, so there was not a lot of waiting while one entered text and the other watched.

Anthony saw the lesson as a success since pupils had been on-task, or at least they had not disrupted his lesson or his teaching. He was very preoccupied with his own role as a teacher and relied on his 'gut' feelings to evaluate the lesson. Of course, the introduction of technology is not a guarantee of increased motivation, but it is a common observation – and a commonly reported finding – that many pupils enjoy using computers (see, for example, Deaney *et al.*, 2003; Younie and Leask, 2013: 57–83). Why this is the case is not always clear, as pupils often find their enjoyment of technology difficult to articulate. However, they do seem to take satisfaction from making decisions and seeing the consequences of those decisions on screen. For example, in Anthony's lesson, pupils could add and delete text, insert images, and introduce sound and animation quickly and easily. The use of the computer opened up opportunities that would have otherwise been unavailable using pen and paper. Digital technologies more generally have an *expressive* quality, which seems to motivate pupils. Many, though by no means all, young people feel at home with digital tools, and Anthony wanted to show that his world as a teacher was not as removed from that of his pupils as they might have otherwise thought.

It was doubtful whether Anthony's subject teaching aims in the lesson had been fully met or even properly articulated. His pupils were as much focused on *format* as *content*. He learnt valuable lessons from this class, however. In doing this kind of work again, he would need to focus pupils' attention on the content of their work. Next time, he would stress the need for a simple, uncluttered and consistent background and work to a series of writing 'frames' to help pupils plan their presentation. He would need to think about timings, to make pupils aware of the timescale to which they were working and to book the room over two lessons, not one. As time at the computer is limited, he might provide a template and a bank of images and film clips for pupils to work from. He realized that the first time round he was fortunate to have support but, in the future, he might have to be more self-reliant and would need to prepare in more detail. He would also need a contingency plan in case the network crashed – this was something he had only thought about once pupils had told him of its unstable performance. At a later point, he might expand the range of digital tools that he used and the kinds of activities he could ask pupils to carry out. For example, pupils could be asked to provide a short news report of an event in the play for a local radio in the form of a podcast, to role-play and film a particular incident from the play, or to write a series of 'tweets' to advertise the play, focusing on why the play still has relevance today. These outputs could be uploaded to a school virtual learning environment (VLE) or learning platform, or other internal social network for pupils to share.

Case Study 12.2

Baljit, a student science teacher, had a specific focus on her pupils' subject learning in her use of digital technology. She was aware that her pupils had spent a long time collecting data manually in their laboratory work and were not sufficiently focused on drawing conclusions from experiments. She felt it was important that pupils could 'tell stories about data' if they were going to develop their information-handling skills. She planned two lessons based on software with which she was familiar from training events she had attended. In the first lesson, she introduced data logging software to help pupils explore the many variables involved in determining the speed of a vehicle rolling down a ramp. Trolleys and ramps were set up in the laboratory with light gates to measure the speed of the trolley as it reached the end of the ramp. Pupils released the trolley from different points on the ramp and measurements were taken and entered on a spreadsheet. Graphs of the results were displayed. To support her pupils, Baljit gave a short demonstration on using the software and provided a brief help guide. Each group of pupils was asked to discuss their results and to provide an explanation of why the speed of the vehicle changed with the distance it had travelled. As an extension, pupils could look at the relationship between speed and other variables such as the height of the ramp or distance travelled on leaving the ramp.

In the follow-up lesson, Baljit gave her pupils an opportunity to extend their work on interpretation of data. She set up a circus of activities using temperature sensors. The first investigated the effect of surface area on cooling. Here, temperature sensors recorded the temperature of two hot potatoes – one large, one small – every five seconds. A second experiment involved wrapping a temperature sensor in cotton wool and comparing the cooling effect of different liquids, including alcohol and water. A third investigation examined the insulating properties of different materials by recording the temperature of water inside containers insulated by cotton wool, paper and other materials chosen by the pupils themselves.

Pupils were asked to focus on the key variables in each experiment, to describe the relationship between these variables and provide an explanation to account for any relationships they had identified. In fact, each experiment raised challenging scientific concepts, which Baljit would need to develop later. For now, she was concerned that pupils generated and justified their own hypotheses about the events they were investigating.

Baljit evaluated the two lessons as successful as she had uncovered many misconceptions about interpreting data, which she was able to address in whole-class discussion and in one-to-one work. Addressing pupils' misconceptions is a crucial aspect of subject teaching in science – and other subjects too. For example, in listening to pupils talking about the trolley experiment, Baljit had found many of them mixed up ideas of acceleration and speed and could not distinguish between mass and weight.

In the science lessons, the pupils had supported each other in using the software. The area that worried her most was the social dynamic within groups and dealing with whole-class discussion at the end of the activity. Not all pupils had contributed to the discussion and she had not left enough time to develop her response to pupils' ideas.

COMMENTARY: Unlike Anthony, Baljit had planned her use of technology in detail, and she had a clear idea of how it could contribute to pupils' learning about science. In this case, the automatic features of the computer program gave pupils opportunities to capture data over very short periods, something they could not do accurately by hand and eye. The software took away the repetitive graph-drawing work and allowed pupils to focus on the higher-order skill of interpretation. The use of digital technology was nicely staged so that all pupils could experience using the data-logging software before the circus of activities. The software had a relatively low entry threshold and any difficulties were addressed through help sheets, peer support or occasional teacher intervention.

This case study illustrates how a very simple and long-established approach to computer-based data collection can work really well to support teaching of higher-order skills. However, pupils are unlikely to take advantage of opportunities for reflection and discussion without teacher intervention. Although Baljit had built discussion into her planning, she would need to fine-tune her approach during her placement, for example by developing ideas for exploratory talk during her whole-class discussion and organizing more formal plenary sessions.

Case Study 12.3

Carlton, a student teacher of geography, was enjoying his school placement and receiving good feedback on his teaching. His major area of concern was how much time he seemed to spend setting, chasing up and marking homework. The results seemed disproportionate to the effort he was putting in. He worked in a school that was highly committed to using digital technology for learning and had attended an after-school session that had introduced him to the learning resources on the school's VLE or 'learning platform'. Already one department had built up a substantial set of presentations, forums and links to outside sites. He wondered if he could build a similar site for his pupils to support them in their homework, or what he now wanted to call 'learning tasks'. Going further, perhaps he could create online quizzes that would provide automatic feedback, including tips for better understanding of a topic, for pupils.

After much discussion with the ICT coordinator, he scaled down his plans. He would focus on one topic, population growth, which he was covering with a GCSE class. He would post his presentations to the VLE, provide links to BBC and Geography Association resources, many of which contained images and short video clips, and create a closed discussion forum, which he would monitor. He would try to guide pupils to and through the material by setting weekly tasks that they would report back to him and their peers via the discussion forum. These tasks were mini investigations that required pupils to access and draw relevant conclusions from online resources. He would encourage pupils to email each other or email him at any time if they needed help.

The innovation met with mixed results. One good thing was that using the learning platform turned out to be easier than he had imagined because he had a model from which to work and support within the school. The key point was that he was able to upload his classroom presentations. He could also write additional material of his own, but it was important for him to avoid overdoing this – he could save time by linking to external sites for pupils to access. Looking at his records, he found that more pupils were completing their homework than had previously done so, and he felt less stress in cajoling pupils, not least because no one could say they had lost their hand-outs or could not contact him to find out what to do. However, much of the work the pupils submitted was cursory and, where extended, there seemed to be a lot of copy-ing and pasting of text from the websites he had provided. The discussion forum had not taken off, though some pupils had posted and responded to messages about a recently reported decline in birth rates in India, a topic he was covering in class, and two pupils had emailed him to ask for clarification about what was expected for the homework task. This might not seem very much, but he reflected that it would not have happened without the forum.

At the end of his placement, Carlton sought more formal feedback from the pupils and designed and carried out a questionnaire survey. He discovered that web access was not a problem for most pupils – they could access his site at home or through school machines during lunchtime or at the end of the day. He gained a better idea of pupils' widespread use of networked environments and how they juggled access to the VLE or learning platform with participation in their preferred social networking websites.

Pupils were positive about the innovation; they liked the idea of text communication and the greater access to pictures and moving images. However, many did not actively take part in discussion and, when it came to websites, they frequently found the text too difficult to understand, something he had not fully considered.

COMMENTARY: Like Anthony, Carlton was attempting to use digital tools to motivate his pupils as much as to address specific subject learning objectives. Carlton had latched on to the idea of developing online support through work he had seen in another subject. None-theless, the potential contribution of VLEs to his subject teaching was considerable. It would provide pupils with 'anywhere, anytime' access to a much wider range of learning materials and access to class discussion beyond the classroom.

There were limitations in his planning, however. First, he had not thought in advance how those without access to the internet would fare – in the event, this did not appear to be a serious difficulty, but it might have been. He had not communicated to his pupils what was involved in the shift from setting homework to providing 'learning tasks'. The latter he associated with pupils making choices, so that they made choices in the resources they accessed and worked through them at their own pace. However, he had not modelled how this would happen, nor had he been precise in what he wanted pupils to do with the resources once they had been located. Here, there was a major difficulty with pupils' information-handling skills. He assumed that pupils were advanced information handlers because they appeared to be confident using networked environments in their everyday lives. In fact, they lacked the knowledge and skills to be able to analyse the information they accessed. They could not identify key points within a text or transform information for another audience.

The discussion forum was another challenge. It had been helpful for some pupils, but he had not made his expectations clear, for example by explaining the value of exchanging ideas, the number of posts they should, as a minimum, contribute, and the need to respond positively to each other and avoid personal asides. Finally, he had not considered the idea of mobility and that many of his pupils were using devices such as tablets and smartphones rather than stand-alone computers. This would create more opportunities for pupils to participate, but expectations and guidance would need to be offered: with greater mobility, pupils might find it more natural, or at least more accessible, to use a Facebook page, or something similar, rather than the school VLE.

The innovation left him with more questions than answers, but Carlton decided to pursue his investigation further, as there were both practical and pedagogic positives to come out of the innovation on which he could build.

12.3 Planning your use of digital tools

The case studies reveal the starting points some student teachers had for using ICT and some of their experiences. Table 12.1 summarizes the opportunities these teachers saw in the digital technology and the planning and evaluation they carried out.

We now raise some key questions for you to consider in planning the use of digital tools in your subject(s).

What can digital tools contribute to teaching my subject(s)?

First and foremost, consider what you are expecting the use of digital technology to contribute to your teaching. For example, digital tools may enable:

- storage of information (including multi-modal resources and using Cloud-based storage) and access to information (including 'anywhere, anytime' access through mobile devices);
- automatic functions (for example, logging data and recalculating within spreadsheets);
- interactivity between user and software (for example, an interactive quiz on the interactive whiteboard [IWB]) or between users (for example, discussion forums and social media);
- provisionality (for example, rapid deletion and reformatting of text).

A further feature of technology is the speed at which functions are carried out so that it allows the user to do things it would be very difficult to do otherwise. As discussed in Case Study 12.1, technology also has an expressive quality so that it is seen – at least initially – as new and potentially exciting.

A key issue to consider is what can these attributes of digital tools help you to do in your teaching. Anthony wanted to use the storage and interactivity of the technology to engage pupils in his lessons, but very much focused on pupil motivation and his own discomfort with the group. In a similar way, a student teacher who feels under constant pressure when carrying out whole-class teaching might look to engage pupils in creating multimedia presentations to enhance pupils' attention. Of course, in both these cases, the use of digital tools will open up new opportunities that may not have been anticipated. For example, Anthony found it natural to use pair work around the computer, something he was normally more

Case study	Problem/ opportunity	Planning	ICT knowledge/skills	Contribution of the technology	Implementation	Methods of evaluation
Anthony	Address motivation of pupils	Minimal	Familiar with software, assumed pupils would know how to use it	Expressive of relevance, provisional nature of text (easy to alter)	Computer room, pair work, some whole-class teaching	Monitoring, teacher-focused
Baljit	Focus pupils on interpreting data	Extended – learning goals explicit	Familiar with software, demonstrated use to pupils	Automatic data collection and display	Laboratory, group work, whole-class starters and plenaries	Scanning class, use of question and answer, plenary, pupil writing
Carlton	Develop out-of-lesson learning	Broad but learning goals not made clear	Taught how to use the software, assumed pupils would know how to use it	Storage of multimedia resources, interactivity through electronic communications	Machines accessed in school and at home, pupils have high level of control over what and when to access resources	Monitoring, questionnaire survey

Table 12.1 Summary of issues about the use of ICT in the three case studies

resistant to doing. Similarly, early users of IWBs were often more willing to get pupils in front of the class to demonstrate to their peers in a way they would not consider when using a conventional whiteboard (for example, Armstrong *et al.*, 2005). In the second example, Baljit was much clearer in her mind about the cognitive contribution of data-logging tools and how they could contribute to refocusing pupils' learning on higher-order skills.

The conclusion from the case studies is that, as you plan your use of technology, you need to think carefully about how particular digital tools can support learning. Very often, student teachers focus on the behavioural or affective contribution of learning. This is rightly so – try learning to teach without paying attention to pupil engagement! However, this is not paying full attention to what digital technology can offer or indeed what teaching is about. As you plan your lesson, consider how you expect digital technology to contribute to pupils' understanding of a topic and how you are going to convey your expectations of learning outcomes to them. You will not get it right first time, so learn from the feedback of your pupils, both explicitly and via your own observations, and adapt accordingly. This process of critical reflection on your practice is an important habit to develop, and will enhance your professionalism, now and throughout your career.

Are pupils supported in crossing the ICT skills threshold?

You will want to ensure that pupils have access to and can use the technology. This means that pupils need the knowledge and skills to use the software – if they do not, provide simple demonstrations and help sheets in support. Use peer support in the classroom rather than running around trouble-shooting at the computer/mobile device. Think carefully if you are planning to use software or mobile applications ('apps'), which have a high entry threshold. For example, using photo manipulation software or other less-used programs will be a challenge for most pupils. Avoid the assumption that pupils are confident and skilled with technology simply because they use social networking sites or appear proficient in using their mobile phones.

Do you have confidence in your own knowledge and skills?

Enthusiasm, learning by trial and error and a willingness to admit to lack of knowledge go a long way in working successfully with digital technology. But a key lesson from the case studies is to make sure you know how to use the appropriate software for your school – you can become unstuck if the school is using an earlier or later version of a program with which you are familiar. Remember, too, that saving material on school networks is not always intuitive. Ensure that you have technical support for your first attempts in working with pupils. With the advent of mobile technologies and the use of Cloud-based storage and access, make sure you are familiar with the range of apps that may be useful for teaching your subject area. Many teachers use teacher blogs and Twitter chat-groups, ones specifically set up 'by teachers, for teachers', to find out about suitable apps. Blogs may be signposted in your professional subject association website and in practitioner publications such as the TES.

How and when will pupils have access to the technology?

All three teachers in the case studies had to plan around access to computers. Carlton assumed pupils had out-of-school access; you will need to check this for yourself. If you intend on using the internet, make sure you are familiar with the school policies concerning appropriate use and the extent of the security firewalls. In school, you will need to book a computer room or organize access to mobile devices or departmental resources.

What do you see as the pros and cons of each approach? If you have a limited number of digital tools, then pupils will need to work in pairs or groups. Is this desirable in the lesson you are planning or is it a constraint? Something really important to consider is the use of mobile devices and understanding the issues concerning online security, ethics and digital identity as well as practical considerations of which apps to use to support your teaching and learning. The UK Child Exploitation and Online Protection Command (CEOP, 2014) identified five areas in which the ethics of safe online behaviour ('e-safety') should be considered: guidance on posting things online; communicating with strangers; pressures to behave in certain ways as a result of online communication; seeing things online that might be disturbing; and issues of reporting. This highlights the need for us all to explore what technology is available and how it can be used and misused.

Have you planned work away from the digital tools?

The same rules apply to using technology as in any other lesson. If you think whole-class starters and plenaries are a good idea, then use them when the lesson involves technology. Move pupils away from the computers, or ask them to have 'screens down' if they are using mobile devices, so you have their full attention.

Have you planned a contingency?

Have you got contingency materials if the network fails? Can you quickly adapt if getting started takes much longer than you thought (for example, the network is slow, pupils have forgotten passwords or their skills are not as you imagined)? Can you use the computers or mobile devices for a follow-up lesson if required?

How are you going to monitor and evaluate pupils' use of digital technologies?

The case studies showed that question and answer, intervention with groups, and plenaries are all good monitoring tools. How can you use your monitoring and evaluation of pupils' work to inform future planning? Would a short questionnaire survey on pupils' use of digital tools be appropriate?

Task 12.2

Plan for the use of technology in a lesson in school. Address all the questions in the preceding section.

Where can I find out more about using digital tools in my teaching?

All of the issues discussed in this chapter are covered in depth in a range of academic and practitioner reporting (see, for example, Hammond, 2014; Selwyn, 2017; Younie and

Bradshaw, 2017). Looking back, there appears to have been three 'drivers' for the use of digital technology in schools, and these drivers can be classified into three areas: economic, cultural and pedagogical. The *economic* argument highlights the vocational value of digital skills and competences in a global economy. In short, young people need to be confident and knowledgeable about digital technology uses if they are to find work. The *cultural* argument highlights the pervasive role of digital technology in socio-cultural practices such as using social media and online buying and selling; young people need to broadly know about developments in technology to become competent digital citizens and participate effectively in many areas of contemporary society. The third driver for putting digital technology in schools is the *pedagogical* rationale, the belief that the affordances of digital tools can be seen to enhance learning and teaching.

These different agendas for digital technology take-up appeal to different audiences: economic and vocational arguments appeal best to governments and policy-makers, social and cultural arguments often appeal to those trying to reform education, while the pedagogical focus is aimed at classroom practitioners (Younie and Leask, 2013). Of course, you are more likely to be interested in the third rationale and, for teachers, digital tools offer variety in classroom practice, provide opportunities for collaboration, and enhance pupil motivation and engagement. However, it is important to realize that there are wider arguments about using digital technology so that, for example, Baljit's pupils were not just learning about cause and effect in science but were also learning something about being a scientist in the digital age. The trick is to foreground the pedagogic focus for the use of technology without losing sight of its added value.

In looking at the pedagogic potential of technology, some education evangelists argue that digital technology has a *transformative* effect, helping shift us from teacher-led instruction, which is didactic in nature, to a more constructivist approach that allows for enquiry-based learning. This belief, or hope, was reported as critical when we spoke to early adopters of digital technology in English schools (Hammond *et al.*, 2011) and many commentators continue to argue that technology might be a 'catalyst' for change by pushing us to reconsider the nature of learning and teaching. To date, however, technology has enabled a series of small-scale innovations but not the shift that was expected. The reasons for this limited impact has been debated at length, but a recurring theme is that, in spite of investment, there are still many constraints on using digital tools (see, for example, Hammond, 2014; Male and Burden, 2014; and, for a more dated study but one specifically focused on student teachers, Hammond *et al.*, 2011). Reported constraints on teachers include limitations on accessing technology in classrooms; a level of 'inertia' around innovation (for example, few teacher training partnerships are yet to provide detailed modelling of online discussion with pupils); and the mismatch between the opportunities that digital tools offer and the expectations associated with traditional high-stakes pen and paper assessment. Crucial to any debate is understanding the importance of the role and agency of the teacher in the classroom: you are the gatekeeper to when and where technology should be used (see Leask and Pachler, 2014).

12.5 Conclusion

In this chapter, we have highlighted the importance of pedagogy when using technology, and our thinking draws on the idea of technological, pedagogical and content knowledge (TPaCK), put forward by Mishra and Koehler (2006). Put very simply, the idea here is that an effective teacher is likely to have a good understanding of their subject (*content knowledge*) as well as a good understanding of how to teach the subject and the kind of problems pupils will have in understanding key concepts (*pedagogical knowledge*). A teacher making effective use of digital technology has, in addition, a good understanding of both how to use this technology (*technological content knowledge*) and its contribution to teaching and learning (*technological pedagogical knowledge*). TPaCK is then a mix of knowledge of your subject, knowledge and skills of teaching, and knowledge and skills of technology use. In the case studies, only Baljit could be said to have effectively developed TPaCK. We have found TPaCK a useful concept to help us think about technology and its contribution to learning. In particular, it reminds us to see technology in a wider context and is a way of understanding the quality of teaching and thinking about digital technology. However, we do not think that TPaCK can be sensibly measured and would not wish to try to do so.

In developing your knowledge and skills with digital tools, be aware that there is a growing range of computer software and mobile apps for teaching specific to your subject. You will find your subject association a reliable source of advice on their use. In addition, there are very many teacher blogs, MOOCs, Twitter groups and online professional communities of practice for teachers, including MirandaNet (https://mirandanet.ac.uk/), which shares innovations in digital technology among practitioners. Finally, for more on online safety, the CEOP resources provide a good starting point (see http://ceop.police.uk and http://www.thinkuknow.co.uk/). The Byron Review (2010), though now a little old, contains lasting guidance on understanding the risks associated with sharing personal information and, for a more general discussion of key issues, see Bradshaw and Younie (2017).

As digital technologies develop, and the number of apps increases, the skills required of teachers to be able to navigate, make sense of and select what might prove useful in the classroom is a growing challenge. One answer is to harness the teaching community to share those tools and resources that are most effective for professional practice and to link up via social media. As teacher online networks become more mature, so does the support that the profession can provide for itself. Developments in digital technology offer amazing opportunities to support learning and teaching, both in the classroom and beyond the school, as we move into a period of continuous mobile connectivity, and the very real opportunity for 'anytime, anywhere' learning. We need to work together to understand these opportunities and channel the use of technology in ways that support teaching and learning.

Recommendations for further reading

Armstrong, V., Barnes, S., Sutherland, R., Curran, S., Mills, S. and Thompson, I. (2005) Collaborative research methodology for investigating teaching and learning: the use of interactive whiteboard technology, *Educational Review*, 57 (4): 457–469.

Bradshaw, P. and Younie, S. (2017) *Debates in ICT and Computing*. London: Routledge.

Byron, T. (2010) *Do We Have Safer Children in a Digital World? Review of Progress since the 2008 Byron Review*. Nottingham: DCSF Publications.

Child Exploitation and Online Protection Agency (CEOP) (2014) *Think U Know*. London: CEOP. Available at: https://www.thinkuknow.co.uk/11_13/need-advice/ [accessed 10 August 2016].

Deaney, R., Ruthven, K. and Hennessy, S. (2003) Pupil perspectives on the contribution of information and communication technology to teaching and learning in the secondary school, *Research Papers in Education*, 18 (2): 141–165.

Hammond, M. (2014) Introducing ICT in schools in England: rationale and consequences, *British Journal of Educational Technology*, 45 (2): 191–201.

Hammond, M., Ingram, J. and Reynolds, L. (2011) How and why do student teachers use ICT?, *Journal of Computer Assisted Learning*, 27 (3): 191–203.

Leask, M. and Pachler, N. (2014) *Learning to Teach Using ICT in the Secondary School: A Companion to School Experience*. London: Routledge.

Male, T. and Burden, K. (2014) Access denied? Twenty-first-century technology in schools, *Technology, Pedagogy and Education*, 23 (4): 423–437.

Mishra, P. and Koehler, M.J. (2006) Technological pedagogical content knowledge: a framework for teacher knowledge, *Teachers College Record*, 108 (6): 1017–1054.

Selwyn, N. (2017) *Education and Technology: Key Issues and Debates*. London: Bloomsbury.

PART 3

Secondary Schools and the Curriculum

13

What should we teach? Understanding the secondary curriculum

David Lambert

13.1 Introduction

The curriculum is one of the most obvious aspects of schools. Not only does the curriculum describe what pupils learn, but the daily routine of secondary schools, given formal expression as the timetable, is marked by the division of the curriculum into subjects for study: English; mathematics; science; personal, social, health and economic education (PSHEE); music; art; humanities, and so on. Teachers are organized into curriculum teams, either through conventionally described school subjects ('the biology department' or 'the English department') or through broader curriculum areas ('the humanities faculty' or 'the language area') and, of course, some teachers are members of more than one team. Student teachers themselves are trained, above all, to teach a secondary school subject, normally defined in terms of their own degree specialism, or closely related to it. The curriculum, in many ways, defines what school is about and what teachers do, thus providing them with a large part of their professional identity. We all know what goes on in school: pupils learn and teachers teach. But what they learn, and what they teach, is defined by the curriculum.

As we shall see, however, the curriculum is far from straightforward and, in many ways, is one of the most complex and least obvious aspects of school life whilst, paradoxically, often taken for granted as a 'given' aspect of school life. Understanding the curriculum involves far more than understanding the list of subjects that goes to make up the school timetable. It involves exploring questions about what is taught; how it is taught and organized; about the relationship and the balance between knowledge, skills and attitudes; and, more controversially, why the things that are taught in schools have been selected. These are difficult and complex issues, not just because there is always more material that could be taught than there is time available to teach, but because they raise fundamental questions about the purposes of school education itself.

After reading this chapter, you should:

- have developed a clear understanding of different ways of thinking about and organizing the curriculum;
- have formed ideas about what the school curriculum is for;

- have begun to explore how the curriculum is changing;
- have begun to think about your role and responsibility to interpret and enact the curriculum in your subject.

13.2 Curriculum debates and disputes

Before exploring the organization and structure of the school curriculum in England in detail, it is useful to identify some of the underlying debates about the curriculum that shape policy at both national and school level, resulting in pressures on the curriculum. Three are of particular importance. They are to do with the purposes of the curriculum, learners' entitlement and who should decide what is in the school curriculum.

Perhaps the most fundamental issue in discussions about the curriculum relates to debate about its purposes (see Reiss and White, 2013). The school curriculum is one of the main ways in which a society socializes its young into knowledge and ways of thinking. Any curriculum is a selection from all the things that might be taught, and the way in which a curriculum is developed will depend on ideas about its purposes. Disagreements about the purposes of the curriculum are often ferocious. Children learn different sorts of things in schools: they build up knowledge of facts and theories, develop skills and acquire attitudes. There are those who regard the primary purpose of school education as the acquisition of certain types of knowledge. Some emphasize the importance of the school in inducting children into a cultural heritage, emphasizing the significance of making great literature, music or art accessible to the next generation. The American cultural critic, E.D. Hirsch (1996), argued strongly that 'cultural literacy' – providing access to a common-core, knowledge-rich curriculum – is a central mission of schooling. There are those who see the primary purpose of school education as being the acquisition of transferable 'skills for work', preparing young people for the demands of the workplace in a globally competitive job market. There are those who stress the significance of school education in developing learners' sense of their own capacities, abilities and well-being.

Of course, a simple response to these debates is to argue that the curriculum must serve several purposes: it must transmit usable knowledge, develop practical skills and produce well-rounded individuals. However, the balance we give to these different goals will shape both the organization of the curriculum and the teaching of individual subjects. For example, we might debate both the place of music in the school curriculum and the extent to which the subject should be concerned with talent-spotting musical giftedness, developing the skills of concentration and collaboration, and offering all young people opportunities to enjoy the capacity to make music or express themselves creatively.

A second issue relates to learners' entitlement. Most of us have views, even if we cannot articulate them clearly, about the basic entitlement that should shape young people's experience of school, those fundamental things that we expect schools to teach everyone. Politicians often talk about the importance of 'the basics'. By this, they normally mean that they expect every child to be taught to read, write and attain basic numeracy. In the nineteenth century, this conception of entitlement led to the idea that schools were fundamentally about the 'three Rs': Reading, wRiting and aRithmetic. Although this sense of 'the basics' is still prevalent – for example, in the emphasis on synthetic phonics in early literacy teaching – few would now regard this as an adequate account of the basic curriculum entitlement in a complex, advanced society. Most teachers and educationists would extend the list!

Task 13.1

What did you not learn at school that you wish you had? What did you learn at school for which you have since found no use?

What would you include as compulsory elements in a curriculum for children who will be adults in the middle of the twenty-first century?

Your own list might include some or all of the following. You might think facility with information and communications technology (ICT) is a basic entitlement – an addition to the entitlement that could not have been foreseen by Victorian advocates of the three Rs. You might consider that schools have an obligation to prepare pupils for the world of work by teaching them a range of transferable skills, including the abilities to work collaboratively in groups, to apply knowledge to the real world and to take responsibility for their own learning (to 'learn how to learn'). In a society in which many adults will change employment frequently, you might conclude that an essential component of the curriculum is to lay the foundations for lifelong learning.

Looking at other areas, you might consider that schools fail their pupils if they do not prepare them for independence in adult life: this might include the teaching of basic cookery skills and home maintenance, or the rudiments that will enable them to organize and plan their adult lives financially. Given the notorious difficulties that parents have in exploring issues relating to sex education or drug and substance abuse with their own children, your entitlement curriculum might include PSHEE. You may also take the view that in a complex, multicultural and diverse society, schools have an obligation to undertake some political and citizenship education that crucially tackles prejudice in relation to ethnicity, gender and sexuality. Finally, you may well feel that the ability to make sense of the world through an understanding of a range of specialist subjects is also an essential component of the curriculum.

This list of potential entitlements is, by now, long. It is difficult to argue that any of these areas is not essential. For example, are you content with school leavers who have no understanding of how our democracy works, how to boil an egg or strategies to prevent sexually transmitted diseases? But it is also apparent that the list of entitlements has become almost impossibly large, and that there are some aspects of the list better undertaken elsewhere – such as in the home or workplace. Schools cannot do everything and, in building a curriculum, choices have to be made. If the entitlement is too great, then there is no room for choice, and some pupils might become disaffected by having to learn things that they do not see the point of. If the entitlement is too narrow, then schools run the risk of premature specialization – that is, ruling out for pupils important elements of education on which they may later need to call.

There is also the risk of the emergence of different curricula for children perceived to have different 'needs' or capacities, resulting in their labelling, for example, as 'academic' or 'non-academic'. The debate about entitlement is a long one. The Education Act 1944, which made provision for a free secondary education for all children, introduced different types of school providing different types of entitlement curricula to supposedly different types of children. 'Grammar' schools offered an academic curriculum to the supposedly most 'able' 15–25 per cent, technical schools offered an applied curriculum to those deemed at 11 to be technologically oriented, and secondary modern schools offered a 'practical' and 'vocational' curriculum to the rest. One of the main impetuses for the reform that introduced comprehensive schools, which reached its peak in the 1970s, was recognition that this sort of divisiveness from the age of 11 was inadequate, ineffective and unfair. Despite the widespread promotion of curriculum specialism for secondary schools – specialisms now include technology, science, mathematics and computing, performing arts and humanities – the principle of selection by 'ability' or 'aptitude' has not re-established itself in the secondary system. The debate never disappears completely, however, and in 2016 Prime Minister Teresa May announced her intention that the government support the reintroduction of grammar schools and selection by ability. It remains to be seen whether this politically expedient policy has any real impact.

Debates about *entitlement* intersect with debates about the *purposes* of the curriculum. We might argue, for example, that all young people have a shared entitlement to a broad, balanced curriculum throughout their schooling. At the other extreme, we might argue that the entitlement curriculum might differ for different groups at different stages of their schooling, dependent on interest, attainment and motivation. There is currently an extended debate about the 14–16 curriculum following the Coalition government's decision in 2010 to define an 'English Baccalaureate' (EBacc) based on pupils who secure examination success at 16 in English, mathematics, science, a modern or classical language, and history or geography. Introducing the EBacc, the Secretary of State for Education argued that these subjects encapsulate the irreducible academic core of a good general education (DfE, 2010b). His critics argued that it was backward looking to define a modern qualification in which success at history and Latin secured success, but success in IT and engineering did not. Critics also pointed to the lack of artistic and creative dimensions to the EBacc. To get a flavour of the debate, see, for example, the work of Sir Ken Robinson.

The debate about the EBacc is a case study in disagreement over the purposes of the curriculum and about what counts as 'worthwhile' knowledge. But it also raises questions about who should define the content and structure of the curriculum. Mathematics is a part of the compulsory curriculum for learners from 5 through to 16 and, at the time of writing, there are tentative proposals to develop entitlement to mathematics as part of the 14–19 curriculum. Nonetheless, some mathematics educators have argued that the subject is not well-served by its 'privileged' status, and that learners should be given choice as they mature about whether to learn mathematics. Once we have decided which subjects should be taught and when, there are similar debates about purposes, which often translate into bitter disputes about particular issues within school subjects. For example, whether in a multicultural society the balance of school history should focus on British history or global history, whether and how Shakespeare should be a compulsory element in the English curriculum, and so on. There is no 'right' answer to questions like these, which depend on different views about the purposes of the curriculum. You will encounter these debates in the teaching of your own subjects, and you will doubtless find that your position in relation to these debates will evolve as you gain greater knowledge and experience of teaching.

The third area of disagreement, then, is *who should decide* the content of the curriculum? It could be argued that teachers should decide the content of the curriculum: they, after all, have professional expertise in the management of pupil learning. This, indeed, was the belief that underpinned curriculum policy-making in England between about 1944 and 1988.

David Eccles, Conservative Minister of Education in the early 1960s, spoke of the 'secret garden of the curriculum, into which ministers wandered at their peril' (Abbott *et al.*, 2013b), and government largely devolved responsibility for curriculum development to the Schools Council, which had a majority of teacher professional association representatives. Alternatively, it could be argued that parents should be able to control the content of the curriculum: we might argue that it is parents who know best about their own children's needs. Indeed, the Coalition government from 2010 determined to increase 'choice' and diversity in schools, enabled state schools to 'academise', and even extended rights to parent groups who wished to set up so-called 'free schools' (DfE, 2010b). By 2017, the majority of secondary schools in England were academies or free schools, which means they were free from any statutory obligation to follow the NC (see next section). These developments have heightened debates about the extent to which parents should exercise influence, or even control, over the curriculum. Schools are required to consult parents over the content of sex education provision, and parents can exercise the right to withdraw their children from religious education and sex education in school. We might regard other groups as having an important part to play in decision-making regarding the curriculum: religious and community groups, universities and employers and, perhaps most radically of all, the pupils themselves.

There is, of course, another key influence on the curriculum: the elected government of the day. At different times, and in different ways, government has claimed to represent the views of parents, employers or other social groups in its planning for the curriculum, and a number of studies have explored the ways in which government reflects different influences in its curriculum policy (Graham, 1993; Elliott, 1997; Chitty, 2002). But there is no doubt that, between the mid-1980s and the end of the first decade of the twenty-first century, successive governments attempted to wrest control of the curriculum away from teachers and the profession at large. As we have seen, and shall discuss later, there are signs that curriculum responsibility (to select what is taught and how it is taught) is now being returned to teachers – at least at the level of political rhetoric. However, as Hargreaves and Shirley (2012) showed, this new 'freedom' may be illusory so long as hefty, quantitative accountability measures remain in place, encouraging teachers to teach to the test.

13.3 The National Curriculum

In retrospect, it is surprising how slow government was to take direct control of the curriculum in English schools. Only in the Education Reform Act 1988 did government assume power to introduce a national curriculum. Established between 1988 and 1991, the NC has been substantially revised on four occasions. The first was in 1994, in response to widespread teacher protests about what was seen as an unworkable, very detailed initial specification. Subsequent revisions in 2000 and 2006/7 were part of scheduled reviews. In 2014, the NC was subject to an extensive reform of its structure, format and organization, designed to define with greater precision an irreducible 'core' in each subject and to allow schools greater freedom to develop their own curriculum. Indeed, and paradoxically, free schools and academies are not required to follow the NC at all (of course, independent schools have never been subject to the NC regulations). This means that the NC is the lawful requirement of only a *minority* of secondary schools in England.

Currently, the NC provides a basic curriculum structure and subject framework for schools, and few schools – even independent schools – choose to ignore it completely.

Before the most recent reform, Tim Oates (2010) argued that the NC in England had lacked the stability of some other national curricula. As we explore the NC, you might want to consider the balances it now strikes between entitlement and choice, different purposes and the various power groups that attempt to influence it. The basic structure of the NC is set out in Box 13.1.

Box 13.1: An overview of the National Curriculum

Aim (3.1 extract)

'The national curriculum provides pupils with an introduction to the essential knowledge they need to be educated citizens. It introduces pupils to the best that has been thought and said, and helps engender an appreciation of human creativity and achievement'.

(Statutory Guidance: National Curriculum in England: Framework for Key Stages 1 to 4)

Key Stage 3 (11–14 years)

Core subjects: English, mathematics and science.

Foundation subjects: ICT, history, geography, citizenship, art and design, music, PE, design and technology, and modern languages.

Plus RE, careers education and sex education (statutory but outside the NC)

Key Stage 4 (14–16 years)

Statutory subjects (English, mathematics, science, ICT, citizenship, PE, work-related learning, RE and sex education)*

Entitlement areas (which must be made available to students who wish to study them: arts, design technology, humanities and modern languages)

Diplomas (Level 1 and Level 2), various BTEC qualifications and OCR Nationals (see Chapter 19.

*GCSE is graded from 9 to 1, with 9 being the top grade (starting with English language, English literature and maths in 2017). Grade 4 or higher in English, mathematics, two sciences, history or geography and a modern or ancient language makes up the English Baccalaureate (EBacc). AS-Levels taken in the relevant subject before the end of KS4 also count.

Compulsory schooling is divided into five Key Stages, from Foundation (introduced in 2000) to Key Stage 4 (KS4), which includes children up to 16 years of age [informally, some schools refer to the sixth form (16–18 years) as KS5]. At each stage, curriculum requirements set out the content requirement for each subject. Controversially, the 2014 reforms abolished official targets for pupil attainment – formerly expressed through so-called 'level descriptions'.

Learning to teach your subject, no matter how closely it is tied to the NC, is a demanding task for new teachers. There is content to master and issues of planning to overcome.

The formal requirements of the subject curriculum must not only be addressed through well-focused teaching, they must also be addressed in ways that engage and support the learning of all pupils. However, the NC does not describe the full range of the *whole school curriculum*. The NC itself is probably best thought of as a part of the whole-school curriculum, for many elements of the latter lie outside the NC's formal requirements. Religious education (RE), although a compulsory element of the school curriculum for all pupils in school from ages 5 to 19 since the Education Act 1944, is not a part of the NC. Ironically, before 1988, RE was the *only* subject schools were required to teach. But, in 1988, it was felt to be too controversial for the government to *prescribe the content of* RE.

Schools are also at liberty to add subjects to the curriculum. For example, some secondary schools add Latin to the KS3 curriculum, others add Mandarin and yet others business studies: these decisions reflect different assumptions about the most effective way to enhance or develop the curriculum. More radically, schools may decide to restructure the curriculum around organizing themes, intersecting with and 'integrating' the requirements of the subjects that make up the NC. Arguments continue about the merits of integrated curricula, but it is probably true to say that teaching this way places considerable organizational demands on teaching teams.

At KS4, much of the provision is outside the NC, which requires only the teaching of an Extended Core (see Box 13.1). Thus, history, geography, art and music are elements of the NC at KS3 but not at KS4, while vocational elements of the curriculum, such as work experience or vocationally related courses, are likely to feature at KS4 for some students.

The post-16 curriculum (see Box 13.2) lies entirely outside the NC (save for the quaint legal requirement, in practice often ignored, for post-16 pupils in schools to study RE). Nevertheless, the issues of entitlements and purpose – and who should decide – have been the

---

Box 13.2: Post-16 education (sometimes referred to as KS5)

From 2015, Post-16 examinations – for most students AS- and A-Levels – were reformed.

- Assessment is mainly by exam, with other types of assessment used only where they are needed to test essential skills (such as fieldwork in geography).
- AS- and A-Levels are assessed at the end of the course. AS-Level assessments typically take place after one year of study and A-Level assessments after two. (Note: courses are no longer divided into modules.)
- AS- and A-Levels are decoupled – this means that AS-Level results will no longer count towards an A-Level in the way they used to.
- (However) AS-Levels can be designed by exam boards to be taught alongside the first year of A-Levels.
- The content for the new A-Levels has been reviewed and updated. Universities played a greater role in this process through the A-Level Content Advisory Board.

Other Post-16 qualifications include the International Baccalaureate, the European Baccalaureate, Diplomas (Level 3), various BTEC qualifications, OCR Nationals, and a variety of workplace-based training and education programmes.

subject of much debate, just as for the compulsory years. Is the post-16 curriculum meant to contribute to the *general education* of the vast majority of the cohort that now remain in formal education until 18 years? Or, as in the past, is it meant to prepare pupils either for higher education, work-related training or, indeed, the world of work?

One of the key reforms leading to the A-Level specifications introduced from 2015 has been to appoint A-Level Content Advisory Boards. Dominated by university academics, these groups are designed to restore a closer connection between A-Level school subjects and the related academic disciplines. The government's concern to restore 'rigour' to public examinations has also influenced reforms of GCSE specifications, which will make greater demands on teachers and pupils in terms of the range and depth of specific content.

With the relaxation of NC requirements on schools, noted earlier, we might say that unofficial government policy has been to ensure that the whole-school curriculum in secondary schools is driven by the requirements of A-Level and GCSE. Indeed, some schools have responded by beginning the teaching of GCSE specifications already in Year 9 (the final year of KS3). This is a controversial policy because it appears to distort and narrow the school curriculum (another manifestation of 'teaching to the test'). On the other hand, it could also be said that there is great merit in teachers attempting to plan and organize the secondary school curriculum from Year 7 to KS5 as a coherent and progressive framework through which pupils are enabled to make progress.

Task 13.2

Read the NC Order for your own subject (if you are training to teach a non-NC subject, use a GCSE or other examination syllabus in your subject). How does this document reflect wider ideas about the content and purpose of the curriculum?

13.4 Beyond the National Curriculum

The NC can thus be seen as just one element that helps shape the whole-school curriculum. Schools are increasingly encouraged to use curriculum freedoms to give a distinctive 'flavour' to *their* curriculum that reflects the ethos of the school, for example, or its specialist status. Schools are asked to articulate the basis for their curriculum planning and to take responsibility for developing distinctive elements to the curriculum. The school's *planned* curriculum, therefore, is a sophisticated tool consisting of both detailed subject plans and whole-school policies and coordination. Hence, although an important aspect of the senior leadership of the school concerns curriculum planning, curriculum leadership also has to be devolved and distributed. It is interesting to note that Ofsted have recently admitted that inspections of schools need to address curriculum leadership more seriously. As Amanda Spielman, Ofsted's Chief Inspector, commented (2017):

'Given the importance of the curriculum, it's surprising just how little attention is paid by our accountability system to exactly what it is pupils are learning in schools, particularly as we have been through a period of significant curriculum upheaval . . .

The taught curriculum is in fact just one among 18 matters for consideration in reaching the leadership and management judgement, making it somewhat of a needle in a haystack. I believe that lack of focus has had very real consequences.'

Looking to the future, Spielman's intentions for Ofsted are quite clear:

'We will look at how schools are interpreting the national curriculum or using their academy freedoms to build new curricula of their own and what this means for children's school experience. We will look at what makes a really good curriculum. And we will also look at the problems, such as curriculum narrowing, and what we can do to tackle them.'

The planned curriculum, therefore, will need to be much more than a list of content. It will need to clarify the aims of the school's curriculum and identify mechanisms for translating those aims into practice, defining knowledge, skills and concepts. It will also need to identify an 'organizational' framework for achieving these aims, as well as a set of assessment and evaluation arrangements for establishing the effectiveness of the curriculum – for the *planned* curriculum typically differs from the *delivered* curriculum. No teacher ever quite teaches what the plans suggest in their curriculum statements. There are a number of reasons for this, some of them quite accidental and unpredictable. At the whole-school level, these include changes in staffing and long-term staff absences. At the individual teacher level, there may be unexpected opportunities to become involved in curriculum development projects, or local and national initiatives, which provide new perspectives and even teaching materials. Finally, the curriculum *experienced* by individual learners may differ markedly from pupil to pupil, and from class to class. Again, this can happen for a variety of reasons, perhaps due to the school's decision to differentiate provision for different groups, or simply through the deployment of scarce teaching resources (for example, which pupils are taught by well-trained, experienced subject specialists, and which are not).

Task 13.3

Explore the range of possible curricula that different learners at KS4 might follow at www.aqa.org.uk, https://qualifications.pearson.com/en/about-us/qualification-brands/edexcel.html and www.ocr.org.uk. Why do you think schools are so strongly committed to choice in curriculum for pupils post-14? What dangers might lie in a wide range of choices?

We have seen that the school curriculum is a complex construction, comprising several interlocking layers: the whole curriculum, the NC, the planned curriculum, the delivered curriculum and the experienced curriculum. However, to understand more fully the quality of pupils' experiences of school, we can draw on one further concept: *the hidden curriculum*. The hidden curriculum is the term generally used to describe the implicit, often unintended and very subtle messages schools convey about behaviour, learning, knowledge and achievement. The hidden curriculum is very powerful, but often difficult to pin down. It consists of the assumptions about how teaching is to be conducted, conveyed unconsciously through, for example, the way classrooms are organized and work is presented. Messages about the sorts of achievements that are worthy of praise are communicated through notices and honours boards that can be seen around schools and in the kinds of achievements that are praised in newsletters. But even in the way teachers talk with pupils – and each other – can communicate messages about relationships and attitudes, which can have a profound impact on what the school expects from its teachers and pupils.

Furthermore, there are often hidden messages about an implied hierarchy of subjects. For instance, school reports are normally presented loose leaf, with English, science and mathematics at the front and art and music at the back. Underlying messages can also be detected in the organization of staff handbooks and in how well-equipped different subjects are. Some commentators have argued that this is not just about a hierarchy of subjects and achievement in schools, but something more fundamental about schooling, conveying messages about what counts as knowledge in our society, and how that knowledge is organized and presented.

Task 13.4

What other ways might there be in which schools communicate a hidden curriculum to learners? How can teachers become more aware of the hidden curriculum? How important is the hidden curriculum to (a) pupils and (b) parents?

13.5 The curriculum, teachers and teaching

There are always enormous pressures for change on the school curriculum. This is partly – but only partly – policy- or government-related. It also reflects serious questioning about how best to educate young people for a rapidly changing world. Whilst everyone – parents, employers, community groups and pupils included – can have an opinion on this, perhaps it's teachers as a professional group that can be expected to have a particularly valuable viewpoint. Because the curriculum is so closely tied up with teachers' professional identities, it is an important – and, as we have seen, complex – idea that teachers need to keep under consideration. For one thing is clear: in a rapidly changing world, the school curriculum needs to be dynamic and responsive as well as remaining true to some cherished and enduring principles – for example, of truth, justice and fairness.

Some argue that schools should be resolutely 'traditional' in the curriculum they offer, pursuing selections of knowledge as a worthwhile end in itself. In such schools, the knowledge on offer often appears 'given' and predetermined, and the teacher's job is effectively to 'deliver' this to pupils almost on a 'no questions asked' basis. The curriculum becomes the 'script', probably well-served by approved textbooks and an examination system that puts a heavy premium on the recall of facts, laws and principles. It is, to be frank, the form of curriculum that is observable in many systems around the world to this day. It is the one that many readers of this book may even recognize from their own school days. But this form of curriculum has been heavily criticized over many decades. It represents what has been described as a 'banking' model of education whereby facts and ideas are deposited unproblematically into (what is assumed to be) the relatively empty heads of the pupils. Teachers, and the curriculum, become associated with control – of thought and behaviour. If this were the future curriculum, then it is an inadequate scenario, not only in relation to what we know about how children learn (see Chapters 4 and 5) but in terms of inducting young people into the world of knowledge, which is dynamic, evolving and socially manufactured.

In their discussion of possible alternative curriculum scenarios, Michael Young and colleagues (2014) refer to such a traditional 'knowledge-as-given' curriculum as Future 1 (F1), characterized by a vision of knowledge that is grossly under-socialized (see Box 13.3).

Box 13.3: The 'Three Futures' scenarios

Future 1: 'traditional': Content as 'given'; a curriculum of 'delivery'; inert; fixed; often alienating to pupils. Under-socialized knowledge.

Future 2: 'progressive': Content as arbitrary; flexible; a curriculum focused on 'learning'; generic skills and competences. Over-socialized 'learning to learn'.

Future 3: 'progressive': Content is neither 'given' nor arbitrary. It is dynamic and linked to disciplinary procedures and processes. This is a curriculum of 'engagement' – with 'powerful knowledge' enabled though appropriate powerful pedagogies.

Some of the many critics of F1 argue that it is the subject-based nature of this curriculum that constrains thinking, and that the challenges of the modern workplace and the contemporary world call for a different kind of curriculum thinking. For example, the school curriculum might instead be oriented around the application of complex knowledge to new problems, requiring a thematic or problem-based approach. Furthermore, policymakers and school leaders are increasingly under pressure to develop curriculum solutions to what are seen as pressing educational difficulties, such as the disaffection from schooling found among working-class boys or the persistent differences in attainment among different ethnic and social groups. These pressures frequently lead to calls for the curriculum to demonstrate more 'relevance' to the world of work and to use the curriculum as a tool for combating issues such as social exclusion or poor health. These pressures can translate into specific curriculum innovations, some of which are discussed in detail elsewhere in this book. In broad terms, the focus shifts from the knowledge contents of the F1 type curriculum to an orientation on generic, transferrable skills and competency outcomes. These are the key attributes of a Future 2 (F2) curriculum.

If F1 is characterized by under-socialized knowledge, the risk of outcomes-oriented, F2 curriculum thinking is that pupils are introduced to knowledge that is grossly over-socialized. The idea of the social construction of knowledge is taken to a relativistic extreme whereby teachers appear to place emphasis on the learning activity or process. In other words, attention is diverted away from the epistemic quality of *what* is being learned. Gert Biesta (2017) has been a leading voice pointing to the considerable weaknesses of curriculum thinking based upon a focus on learning outcomes, rather than deliberation on the significance of what is being taught.

Thus, F2 curriculum thinking, as a response to the limitations and inadequacies of F1, could be seen as being deeply flawed. This is because it appears to turn away from what we take to be the school curriculum's profound purpose, which is to induct children and young people into knowledge domains and ways of thinking that are able to extend and enhance their intellectual capabilities. But schools are in the knowledge business and, of course, teachers are knowledge workers. In this context, Michael Young (Young and Lambert, 2014) has helpfully introduced the intriguing idea that specialist subject knowledge might be thought of as 'powerful knowledge' – not as a 'given' and an inert accumulation of facts, as in F1, but as dynamic, evolving, systematic and, above all (being derived from specialist subject communities), *conceptual* (see Box 13.4).

Box 13.4: Powerful knowledge: a summary

Powerful knowledge is usually:

- evidence-based;
- abstract and theoretical (conceptual);
- part of a system of thought;
- dynamic, evolving, changing – but reliable;
- testable and open to challenge;
- sometimes counter-intuitive;
- something that exists outside the direct experience of the teacher and the learner;
- specialized (in domains that are neither arbitrary nor transient).

Asking in what way your subject produces powerful knowledge is a productive and useful activity. For one thing, it encourages you to think through how the selection of contents on the specification or scheme of work link together, the significance of particular concepts and perhaps some of the subject's stories about how we have come to know this or that.

In 2008, Michael Young wrote that:

'Powerful knowledge refers to what the knowledge can do or what intellectual power it gives to those who have access to it . . . [It] provides more reliable explanation and new ways of thinking . . . [It] can provide students with a language for engaging in political, moral and other kinds of debates' (Young, 2008: 14).

In other words, concerns about F2 do not necessarily have to push us back to F1, as if this were the only way to think about a knowledge-led curriculum. There is an alternative, known as Future 3 (F3), based upon the idea of powerful knowledge.

There are no lists of powerful knowledge available in different subjects – almost by definition this is not possible to do (we just end up with lists). However, the idea of F3 curriculum thinking is potentially very productive for subject specialist teachers. To ask the question 'in what ways might your subject be thought of as powerful knowledge?' raises several issues that impinge directly on how teachers interpret and enact curriculum documents. For example, how is the subject organized conceptually? What is the history of the subject – the origins of its key ideas and how these have evolved? In what ways does the subject contribute to thought (or specialist ways of thinking)? How do aspects of the subject link together?

The implication for the kind of professional thinking that follows such questions should be clear: an F3 curriculum cannot really be 'delivered' as a simple transmission. Instead, the curriculum, as experienced by the pupils, has to be 'made' to happen by teachers. It is a curriculum of engagement – engagement with the subject's ideas – and therefore heavily reliant on specialist teachers taking responsibility to find ways to engage all young people, in some intellectually defensible manner, with those ideas.

13.6 Conclusion

Schools are certainly becoming more distinctive in the curricula they offer, but those curricula reflect the sorts of choices about content, organization and structure that have been discussed here. As your career develops, these and other issues will be matters for lively discussion and decision-making. The ways in which they are resolved in the schools in which you work will depend on a number of factors. They will, of course, depend on patterns of national policy and local provision. However, they will also depend on the answers you and the teachers with whom you work give to questions about what should be taught, what pupils' entitlement should be, what the curriculum is for, and who has the power and authority to develop the curriculum.

Proposing the curriculum as a key component of teachers' professional identity, as we have done in this chapter, implies that teachers have a profound responsibility to engage in curriculum thinking and work towards an F3 curriculum experience for their pupils. We offer a vision of teachers that is less the 'highly skilled technocrat' (although teachers have to be very skilful) and more the 'curriculum maker', called upon to make difficult and nuanced practical judgements about what to teach and how to teach it.

Recommendations for further reading

Biesta, G. (2017) *The Rediscovery of Teaching*. Abingdon: Routledge.

Hargreaves, A. and Shirley, D. (2012) *The Global Fourth Way: The Quest for Educational Excellence*. Thousand Oaks, CA: Corwin.

Hirsch, E.D. (1996) *The Schools We Need and Why We Don't Have Them*. New York: Anchor Books.

Kelly, A.V. (2009) *The Curriculum: Theory and Practice*, 6th edn. London: Sage.

Oates, T. (2010) *Could Do Better: Using International Comparisons to Refine the National Curriculum in England*. Cambridge: Cambridge Assessment.

Reiss, M. and White, J. (2013) *An Aims-based Curriculum: The Significance of Human Flourishing for Schools*, Bedford Way Papers. London: IOE Press.

Young, M. (2008) *Bringing Knowledge Back In: From Social Constructivism to Social Realism in the Sociology of Education*. London: Routledge.

Young, M. and Lambert, D. (with Roberts, C. and Roberts, M.) (2014) *Knowledge and the Future School: Curriculum and Social Justice*. London: Bloomsbury.

Webliography

Information about the National Curriculum: https://www.gov.uk/national-curriculum/overview

Information about GCSE subject content criteria: https://www.gov.uk/government/collections/gcse-subject-content

14

Spiritual, moral and cultural development

Judith Everington

14.1 Introduction

'Every state-funded school must offer a curriculum which is balanced and broadly based and which:

- promotes the spiritual, moral, cultural, mental and physical development of pupils at the school and of society
- prepares pupils at the school for the opportunities, responsibilities and experiences of later life.'

(DfE, 2014c: 5)

This chapter will focus on spiritual, moral and cultural development. Here, you will find 'official' definitions of these terms. However, when approaching these complex and sensitive dimensions of teaching and learning for the first time, it is important to be aware of the understandings that you have already formed and the feelings that are associated with these. For example, some pupils' experience of school and higher education may have convinced them that they have little or nothing to contribute to one or more of the areas of development. Others will have attended faith-based (for example, Islamic, Roman Catholic or Church of England) schools and may have understandings that are different from those that are currently in secular secondary schools. Through a recognition of preconceptions and existing attitudes, it is possible to set these aside in order to develop a critical openness to new definitions and possibilities.

Whatever your responses to Task 14.1, you may have been inclined to skip over this chapter. Research indicates that student teachers tend to be most interested in those aspects of their training course that have to do with teaching their subject effectively, controlling their classes and forming good relationships with pupils. They take less interest in matters that fall outside these concerns. However, in this chapter you will be asked to consider the view that a teacher's ability to teach, manage and relate to pupils effectively is greatly enhanced by their ability to take account of and draw upon pupils' spiritual, moral and cultural lives, and provide opportunities for development.

By the end of the chapter, you should:

- understand what is meant by spiritual, moral and cultural development in the context of the secular secondary school;
- know the legal and professional requirements relating to spiritual, moral and cultural development;
- understand how spiritual, moral and cultural development can be promoted in teaching and pastoral work;
- know how to obtain guidance on and ideas for promoting spiritual, moral and cultural development.

14.2 Spiritual, moral and cultural development – what's all that then?

'That's RE, isn't it, and assemblies?'

'Moral development sounds like something to do with cold baths and keeping idle fingers busy!'

'Spiritual development is surely a very private thing and I'm worried about interfering in it.'

'I'm interested in the idea of cultural development but my subject isn't "arty".'

Task 14.1

What do you associate with each of the terms 'spiritual', 'moral' and 'cultural' development? Write a list of your immediate thoughts and feelings. Are they largely negative or positive? Where do you believe they have come from?

14.3 Requirements and responsibilities

The quotation at the beginning of this chapter is from the National Curriculum (NC) framework document, which restates the requirement of the Education Reform Act 1988 for the school curriculum to promote pupils' spiritual, moral and cultural development (SMCD). Schools document their provision for SMCD and, before making a final judgement on the overall effectiveness of a school, Ofsted inspectors must evaluate 'the effectiveness and impact of the provision' (Ofsted, 2018b: 40). The definitions of SMCD provided by Ofsted and considered in more detail in the next section make it clear that this is something that must permeate the whole of school life and should be reflected in every aspect of teachers' work, including their relationships with pupils and other people who work in the school. This whole-school perspective is outlined in statements about the school's ethos that appear in its prospectus and, usually, in the 'mission' statements that appear on its website. Although the current teachers' standards do not make specific reference to SMCD, this is implicit in a number of the requirements. For example, teachers must 'demonstrate consistently the positive attitudes, values and behaviour which are expected of pupils' (DfE, 2011a: 10).

14.4 Defining spiritual, moral and cultural development

To what does the term 'spiritual' refer?

In one definition, it is said to refer to 'a dimension of human existence which applies to all pupils' and as 'something fundamental in the human condition which is not necessarily experienced through the physical senses and/or expressed in everyday language' (SCAA, 1995: 3). Other definitions refer to 'our inner life or self, our non-tangible personality [or] our self-awareness' (Bigger, 1999: 6).

Of the three areas considered in this chapter, spiritual development is the most difficult to define. There is a vast body of literature devoted to exploring such slippery questions as 'Is there such a thing as a human spirit?', but what matters for most teachers is having a definition that is clearly related to the context in which they are working.

Some student teachers will undertake one or more of their school placements in faith-based schools and some will eventually take up posts in such schools. In faith-based schools, guidance related to spiritual development will reflect the religious beliefs and values associated with the origin of the school and this guidance will need to be consulted. In this chapter, the context considered is the secular school, which is responsible for the development of young people from a wide range of backgrounds and with a wide range of attitudes to religion – from active atheism, to mild spiritual curiosity, to commitment to a religious faith group or organization. Mindful of the need to provide guidance that is inclusive, those who have offered definitions appropriate for the secular school stress that spiritual development should not be viewed as synonymous with religious development. At the same time, it must include pupils who *will* view spiritual development in relation to their religious development.

In what aspects of their lives do or can young people develop spirituality?

The most recent Ofsted definition includes just four ways in which pupils show their spiritual development (Ofsted, 2018b: 40). These are reflected in an earlier and longer government document that suggests that young people develop spiritually in and through their:

- **beliefs and values:** as they develop personal (for some, religious) beliefs and values, but also begin to understand the beliefs of others and how individual and shared beliefs shape people's lives and identities and lead to decisions and actions;
- **feelings, emotions and inner experiences:** for example, the sense of being moved by beauty or kindness, or angered by injustice; a sense of awe, wonder and mystery – in response to the natural world or to a sense of a reality beyond the material world and the limitations of human understanding;
- **search for meaning and purpose:** for example, asking 'why' when reflecting on hardship and suffering or on the origins and purpose of life, or responding to the challenging experiences of life such as death or loss of love and security;
- **self-knowledge:** an awareness of oneself in terms of thoughts, emotions and experiences and a growing understanding of one's own identity as a unique individual, but also as a member of groups and communities;

- **relationships:** recognizing and valuing the worth of each individual; building trustful relationships with others and developing a sense of the responsibilities that trust entails;
- **creativity:** exploring and expressing innermost thoughts and feelings through art, music or creative writing and using the imagination, inspiration, intuition and insight.

(based on SCAA, 1995: 3–4)

Like most definitions of spiritual development, those above have been arrived at by adult professionals. However, research undertaken in a range of comprehensive schools found that Year 9 pupils' own understandings of 'spiritual' and 'spiritual development' were 'uncannily similar' to the kind of adult definitions provided above. It was also found that, even when pupils struggled to find words, they 'communicated a great depth of under-standing and feeling' in their responses to questions about spiritual matters (Wintersgill, 2002: 8).

Other types of development

Moral development

Like spiritual development, moral development is not easy to define, is the subject of much controversy and debate and, in faith schools, will reflect the religious beliefs and values associated with the origin of the school. However, in the context of the secular school, the guidance offered by government and other authorities has suggested two major strands of pupils' moral development:

1. Knowledge, understanding and (at least implicitly) acceptance of the moral values and codes and conventions of conduct that are promoted within the school and that reflect those promoted in society.
2. Knowledge and understanding of criteria for making moral judgements and the ability to employ these in making one's own judgements in relation to personal behaviour and moral issues.

Between the first and second strands there is a tension and potential for conflict. This reflects one of the most fundamental and enduring tensions within education and within the teacher's role: the tension between 'training' young people to become 'good citizens' and providing them with the tools to think for themselves and make their own judgements and decisions.

At school level, the extent to which there is tension or conflict between moral 'train-ing' and 'empowering' will depend on many factors, including the ways in which moral values and development are presented in school ethos statements and are interpreted by school managers and other members of staff. However, in any school it is difficult to avoid the fact that there will be times when teachers will be enforcing the school's moral values and code, and other times when they will be encouraging pupils to look critically at the moral arguments put forward by adults and develop confidence in making their own moral judgements.

These issues are illustrated by Ofsted's latest definition of moral development, which states that:

The moral development of pupils is shown by their:

- 'ability to recognise the difference between right and wrong and to readily apply this understanding in their own lives, recognise legal boundaries and, in so doing, respect the civil and criminal law of England
- understanding of the consequences of their behaviour and actions
- interest in investigating and offering reasoned views about moral and ethical issues and ability to understand and appreciate the viewpoints of others on these issues.'

(Ofsted, 2018b: 40)

The first of these statements includes elements of the government's 'fundamental British values' (FBV) and, in the next section, which considers these, you will be asked to consider the possibility that the incorporation of some of the values stretches the tension between training and empowerment to breaking point.

Cultural development

The term 'culture' is used and understood in different ways, in different contexts. In everyday speech, to refer to someone as 'cultured' often implies that they are well-educated in and appreciative of the arts. Another common usage of the term is in 'multicultural', although this is being replaced by the more flexible term, 'cultural diversity'. In sociological debate, the term 'culture' is fiercely contested, but there is some agreement that it refers to the expression of the fundamental concepts and values of a community, and that these are subject to continuous development and change.

Attempts to define cultural development in an educational context have drawn upon these differing understandings of 'culture/cultural'. In earlier guidance, Ofsted (2004) made reference to the four central roles for education in the cultural development of young people that were identified in the report of the National Advisory Committee on Creative and Cultural Education, *All Our Futures* (NACCCE, 1999). These included enabling young people '. . . to recognise, explore and understand their own cultural assumptions and values; . . . to embrace and understand cultural diversity by bringing young people into contact with attitudes, values and traditions of other cultures; . . . to adopt a historical perspective by relating contemporary values to the processes and events that have shaped them; . . . to understand the evolutionary nature of culture and the processes and potential for change' (NACCCE, 1999: 48).

It is interesting to compare these statements with Ofsted's latest account of cultural development. You may recognize below where elements of the FBV have been incorporated. Cultural development is shown by pupils':

- understanding and appreciation of the wide range of cultural influences that have shaped their own heritage and [that] of others;
- understanding and appreciation of the range of different cultures within school and further afield as an essential element of their preparation for life in modern Britain;

- knowledge of Britain's democratic parliamentary system and its central role in shaping our history and values, and in continuing to develop Britain;
- willingness to participate in and respond positively to artistic, musical, sporting and cultural opportunities; and
- interest in exploring, improving understanding of and showing respect for different faiths and cultural diversity and the extent to which they understand, accept, respect and celebrate diversity, as shown by their tolerance and attitudes towards different religious, ethnic and socio-economic groups in the local, national and global communities.

(Ofsted, 2018b: 41)

Although it is intended that the aims embedded in these statements should be achieved by the school as a whole, the emphasis on cultural diversity may seem daunting to student teachers whose lives and educational experiences have provided little opportunity to learn about a range of cultures. At the end of this chapter, you will find references to websites that provide material on a wide range of religious and cultural matters and practical guidance on cultural development. During your training, you should be given opportunities to learn about cultural diversity and you may also be able to gain knowledge and understanding through a placement in a school in which a range of cultures is represented.

Task 14.2

- Look back at your initial responses to the terms 'spiritual', 'moral' and 'cultural' development. How do they compare to the previous sections?
- Which of the aspects of SMCD do you feel most and least comfortable with, and most and least equipped to deal with? Make a note of the things that you will need to find out about before and during your training course.
- Make a quick-fire response to the question, 'how could my specialist subject promote SMCD?'

14.5 What does it all mean in practice?

In this section, we will look at the relationship between SMCD and the British values agenda. We will then consider the four overlapping areas of a teacher's work in which there are opportunities for pupils' SMCD: subject teaching; citizenship and personal, social, health and economic education (PSHEE); pastoral work; and assemblies/collective worship. Each area will be considered in a separate section, but in 'real life' there is no clear separation between them, and the opportunity or need to contribute to pupils' SMCD can crop up at any point in a teacher's day. In 'real life', too, the distinction between spiritual, moral and cultural development breaks down. The following case study is intended to illustrate these points.

Case Study 14.1

Spiritual, moral and cultural development in a teacher's day

Dan gets in to school to find a fight brewing between two girls in his tutor group. One is accusing the other of spreading rumours about her 'sex life'. Dan intervenes and reminds both about the importance of respect for others and self-respect.

At the staff briefing, all Year 7 teachers are asked to support the sponsored 'Silly Hair Day' organized by the pupils in aid of Children in Need.

At the Year 9 assembly, an act of collective worship, some of Dan's tutor group read out their own poems on 'Being on the Outside'. The Head of Year follows her short talk with a minute's silent reflection on how it feels to be an outsider, and what each of us can do to break down barriers and enable everyone to feel included.

During the second lesson, a Year 10 pupil asks Dan why they need to spend 'so much time looking at the situation in other countries'. He reminds the whole group that to be at the cutting edge these days, it is crucial to have a global perspective.

At lunchtime, Dan attends a meeting to discuss plans for the cross-curricular field trip to Stonehenge.

In the afternoon, his Year 8 pupils are put into groups to explore and come up with solutions to a conflict between three families who live in adjoining flats but have very different lifestyles and needs.

In the evening, he downloads the lyrics of a song that is well-known to his Year 11 groups and that he will use to help them explore the idea that the effects of a single action go far beyond the intentions of the actor.

- Consider how you would deal with the issues raised in this case study.
- List examples from your own teaching experience of contributing to SMCD.

As a student teacher, you will not have to cope with all of the situations described in Case Study 14.1. However, you will encounter situations like them and you will be expected to demonstrate that you can contribute to SMCD in your work with pupils, as outlined in the following sections.

FBV and SMCD

In November 2014, the Department for Education published 'advice' for maintained schools on 'Promoting fundamental British values as part of SMSC in schools' (DfE, 2014b). In summary, these values are defined as 'democracy, the rule of law, individual liberty, and mutual respect and tolerance of those with different faiths and beliefs' (2014b: 5). The focus here is on SMCD, and it has already been noted that Ofsted's definitions of how development can be shown include statements based on the FBV guidance. In the FBV guidance , the statement that schools should 'enable students to develop their self-knowledge, self-esteem and self-confidence' (DfE, 2014b: 5) can clearly be viewed as an aspect of spiritual development. The guidance that schools should 'further tolerance and harmony between different cultural traditions by enabling students to acquire an appreciation of and respect for their own and other cultures' (ibid.) is clearly aimed at promoting FBVs through pupils' cultural development. Another statement, that schools should enable pupils 'to distinguish right from wrong and to respect the civil and criminal law of England' (ibid.) takes us back to the tension between the aim of providing pupils with the opportunities and tools to explore and make their own judgements about moral and ethical issues and 'training' them to accept the judgements of others. This tension appears in an acute and controversial form in the government's 'guidance' that schools and teachers should 'actively promote' FBVs by 'challenging opinions or behaviours in school that are contrary to fundamental British values' (ibid.). The possibility that anxiety about this expectation might lead teachers to avoid discussions that provide opportunities for the expression of pupils' opinions, or to shut down a discussion in which one or more pupils expresses an opinion that appears to be contrary to FBVs, raises grave concerns about the rights of pupils to free expression of ideas and the ability of teachers to create a safe space in which pupils can express ideas that teachers can work with and respond to, using their professional skills. Much depends on how the words 'challenging opinions' are interpreted, but another concern is that teachers will engage in the kind of classroom confrontation that will lead to a breakdown of respectful and trustful relationships between teacher and pupils and amongst pupils. There is a need to explore and reflect on when and how a teacher might challenge opinions and teacher education courses should provide guidance on and opportunities for this.

Subject teaching

The extent to which subject departments and teachers actively promote SMCD in their planning and teaching will vary between schools. Although subject teaching is not highlighted in government guidance on SMCD, elements of this are referred to in the Purpose of Study statements for many NC subjects and Ofsted inspectors may consider teaching style when assessing a school's provision for SMCD.

Leaving aside external pressures, the report of a Royal Society of Arts (RSA) investigation into provision for SMCD across the UK drew attention to a number of research-based studies that indicate that 'pupils' SMSC [spiritual, moral, social and cultural] development and academic progress tend to go hand in hand' (Peterson et al., 2014: 10). In their own research, it was found that amongst schools that had been judged 'outstanding' for SMCD, most reported that their work on SMCD contributed to strong exam results (2014: 14). An earlier research project, undertaken by secondary school teachers in Bristol, found that when SMCD were planned into lesson objectives, and teaching and learning strategies were geared to achieving these, pupils' discussion and critical thinking skills developed, and they became more engaged and motivated in their learning (Midgley et al., 1999: 3).

How can all subjects contribute to SMCD?

The arts and humanities are often viewed as the natural subjects to promote SMCD. However (and despite teaching that has disguised the fact), there is a long tradition of exploring such matters in maths and the sciences. In subjects that straddle these categories, opportunities for SMCD have been recognized and developed, and support is provided in

SMCD-related websites. Adult perceptions of 'SMCD-friendly' subjects may also be challenged by those of pupils. For example, there is research evidence to suggest that some pupils view PE and sport as important in their spiritual development (Wintersgill, 2002: 6) and this view appears to be supported in an NC 'Purpose of Study' statement for PE, 'Opportunities to compete in sport and other activities build character and help to embed values such as fairness and respect' (DfE, 2014c).

	Spiritual development	Moral development	Cultural development
Maths	Mathematical principles behind natural forms and patterns	Calculation of amount of paper used in the lesson related to the number of trees needed	Analysis/presentation of numerical data on family expenditure in differing cultures
Science	Role of scientific discoveries in changing people's lives and thinking	Why sustainable development is important	Relationship between culture and nature of scientific exploration
Art and design	Exploring ideas and feelings in creative work	The role of art and design in political propaganda	Cultural variations in the representation of universal themes
Design and technology	Aesthetics in the design of a product	Environmental impact of products	Analysis of cultural influences on design
Physical education	Developing pride in skills and an ability to cope with losing	Exploring/developing values of cooperation and inclusion in sport	Performing dances from differing cultures
Modern foreign languages	Expressing personal feelings and opinions in the target language	Reading/responding to 'Problem page' letters in the target language	Learning about the culture of the target language country
Geography	Human responses to environmental hazards	Reasons for changes in the distribution of economic activities	Population distribution and change – why, how and the consequences
History	The power of religious beliefs in people's lives and deaths	'Myths of racial superiority' in events past and present	The development of 'multicultural' Britain
Religious education	Religious/non-religious views of what happens at death	Differing perspectives on the development of 'cloning' techniques	Cultural variations in the interpretation of religious texts
English and drama	Expressing a personal 'vision for the future' in creative writing	Creating dramas that explore conflict between the values of family members	Exploring the content and style of poems from differing cultures

Table 14.1 Topics in SMCD

Whatever the subject, there are two main ways in which SMCD can be promoted: (1) through the topics that are taught, and (2) through the teaching and learning methods used.

Topics at Key Stage 3

At KS3, teachers of most subjects will be covering topics dictated by the NC programmes of study. As noted in the preceding section, the NC 'Purpose of Study' statements for many subjects include elements of SMCD (accessed via DfE, 2014c). For example, in maths, pupils should gain 'an appreciation of the beauty and power of mathematics'; 'Learning a foreign language is a liberation from insularity and provides an opening to other cultures'; and, in English, '. . . pupils have a chance to develop culturally, emotionally, intellectually, socially and spiritually'.

Opportunities for SMCD are more obvious in some subjects than in others but can be identified in the process of interpreting the programmes of study to produce units of work and lesson plans. When the teachers involved in the Bristol-based research set out to plan SMCD into lessons, they found no difficulty in identifying opportunities for development in the content of the existing schemes of work (SoW) and/or in the application of content (Midgley *et al.*, 1999: 2).

Table 14.1 indicates the kind of topics or aspects of topics that can provide opportunities for SMCD, in their content or application of content.

Topics at GCSE and AS-/A-Level

At this level, the topics taught are determined by national criteria and by the examination specification that the department has chosen. In previous years, awarding bodies were required to ensure that specifications included the identification of opportunities for spiritual, moral, ethical, social and cultural issues. For example, in GCSE IT, it was suggested that pupils might explore issues related to privacy and the confidentiality of data, and use the technology to obtain, analyse and report on data related to the distribution of wealth. In business studies, they might consider non-financial reasons why people work in organizations, such as the ethical stances of those who control or try to influence businesses and the workings of multinationals across cultural divides.

Awarding bodies no longer make reference to SMCD in their specifications, but the kinds of SMCD-related topics indicated in Table 14.1 provide a starting point for reflecting on the contributions that exam-level study might make to pupils' development and your training course should provide opportunities for further consideration.

Task 14.3

- What do you think of the suggestions for your specialist subject in the preceding section? How do they compare with the ideas that you suggested in response to Task 14.2?
- What advantages and disadvantages might there be in focusing on SMCD in subject teaching?

Teaching and learning methods

Although the content of some subjects is more obviously related to SMCD than that of others, teachers of all subjects can and do promote these forms of development through their teaching methods. These methods need to be of the kind that encourage pupils to think for themselves. Opportunities to work with others are important, but activities that enable pupils to reflect 'privately' are also needed. Examples of both kinds of activity are:

- expressing opinions and listening to those of others;
- exploring and discussing issues from a range of perspectives;
- simulations, including role plays;
- working collaboratively, for instance to solve problems;
- reflecting privately on issues, experiences and feelings;
- sharing experiences and feelings in 'safety', as in friendship pairs.

In all of these cases, teachers need to create a learning environment in which pupils feel sufficiently secure and confident to express and explore their views, feelings and experiences.

Citizenship and PSHEE are explored in Chapters 18 and 25, but they are considered here because both play an important role in promoting SMCD.

Citizenship

Citizenship became a statutory subject in secondary schools in 2002 and at secondary level there was a clearer relationship between the subject and the promotion of SMCD in previous years than is currently the case. In the current programmes of study, it is at KS2 that pupils are to be taught 'to reflect on spiritual, moral, social and cultural issues, using imagination to understand other people's experiences' and 'that differences and similarities between people arise from a number of factors, including cultural, ethnic, racial and religious diversity, gender and disability' (DfE, 2015c). During your teaching placements, there may be opportunities to investigate the KS2/KS3 transition and what (or if) pupils have gained from a KS2 Citizenship education. At KS3 and KS4, there is currently an emphasis on acquiring a knowledge of political and legal systems and processes and of the rights and responsibilities of citizens (DfE, 2013a). However, there are a number of opportunities to contribute to SMCD. At KS3, pupils should explore the ways in which citizens work together to improve their communities and be given opportunities to participate in school-based activities that provide experience of such work. At KS4, pupils should be taught about human rights and 'diverse national, regional, religious and ethnic identities in the United Kingdom and the need for mutual respect and understanding' (DfE, 2013a).

These opportunities can be provided through any subject, but schools are encouraged to deliver citizenship in a variety of ways. During your school placements, you might be asked to support your tutor group in democratic decision-making. You might be involved in a cross-curricular project, such as creating a 'peace garden' in the school grounds or local community that reflects the identities of visitors. You might also be able to teach or observe a dedicated citizenship lesson on an SMCD-related topic such as human rights.

Personal, social, health and economic education

PSHEE is a non-statutory subject but should be taught in all schools. It is the current government's view that schools should be given the flexibility to create programmes of study that reflect the needs of their pupils (see Chapter 13 for more on the curriculum), but funding is given to the PSHE Association to provide guidance and resources. In the Association's latest outline of the nature and aims of PSHEE, it is clear that a significant contribution to pupils' SMCD is envisaged.

In the PSHE programme of study (PSHE Association, 2017: 9–38), there are three core themes: Health and Wellbeing, Relationships, and Living in the Wider World. 'Health and Wellbeing' learning opportunities at KS3 include recognizing personal strengths and how this affects self-confidence and self-esteem. This identity is affected by a range of factors, including the media and a positive sense of self. Within 'Relationships', one of the key sub-themes focuses on respecting equality and being a productive member of a diverse community. So, for example, pupils are to learn to explore the range of positive qualities people bring to relationships (KS3) and about the role that peers can play in supporting one another, including vulnerable friends (KS4). Within the 'Living in the Wider World' theme, a number of the learning opportunities focus on diversity (ethnic, religious and sexual orientation) and the importance of understanding and combating prejudice and discrimination. In light of concerns about the impact of the government's FBV agenda on teachers, it is interesting to note that, at KS3, pupils should be given opportunities to learn about the potential tensions between human rights, British law, and cultural and religious expectations and practices (2017: 29). This would seem to offer a valuable opportunity for pupils to explore tensions between 'fundamental' values rather than be required to learn and accept particular, prescribed values. However, the extent to which it is possible for teachers to offer such opportunities and at the same time 'challenge' opinions that are 'contrary to' FBVs is an important issue and one that you might wish to discuss in your teacher education seminars or with colleagues in school.

Schools deliver the PSHEE curriculum in a number of ways: through dedicated lessons or tutor group time and PSHEE events, such as a whole-school anti-bullying week or Comic Relief day; through subjects and the pastoral system and assemblies. These latter opportunities will be considered in the final sections of this chapter.

Pastoral care and guidance

Pastoral matters are examined in Chapter 24, but here we focus upon one aspect: 'pastoral casework'. Pastoral casework covers work with individual pupils on any aspect that affects their development and attainment. It includes supporting pupils when they have personal problems, are in need of encouragement, or want to talk about experiences, feelings or issues with which they are grappling. In many schools, it is expected that teachers who act as pastoral tutors will be a 'first port of call' for pupils in their tutor group who want to talk. However, any teacher may be sought out by a pupil in need.

As a student teacher, you will not be given sole responsibility for a tutor group, and all tutors should hand over serious problems (such as suspected child abuse) to senior pastoral staff. Nevertheless, you may find that pupils choose to speak to you about personal matters. You should find guidance on managing these situations in the school's staff handbook, but an awareness of the spiritual, moral and cultural dimensions of young people's experience and development will be important in enabling you to respond to pupils with sensitivity. For example, we have seen that adolescents can be interested in, or deeply concerned about, spiritual matters. In Wintersgill's (2002) research on Year 9 pupils' understandings of 'spiritual' and 'spiritual development' (see section 14.4), a number of pupils who offered lengthy and very thoughtful accounts of their spiritual feelings and experiences made it clear that they would not feel able to share these with their peers. A more recent study found that teachers can help young people of secondary age form, develop and express, in some sense, spirituality and recommended that teachers engage in this (Birkinshaw, 2015). Although teachers of some subjects are more likely to be approached in this way, an awareness of the spiritual dimension of young people's experience may help other teachers to recognize and encourage pupils who need or would benefit from opportunities to talk about spiritual matters.

Young people from religious backgrounds may hide their beliefs, practices and special events from their peers, but may need or just want to talk to someone about these. A teacher who has some knowledge and understanding of pupils' backgrounds, and of religious and cultural beliefs, practices and sensitivities, will be in a position to respond sensitively to these matters.

Moral development issues raised by pupils can be difficult for teachers caught between their 'training' and 'empowerment' roles. However, an awareness of the tension can be helpful, especially when pupils are not in trouble, but want to explore issues with a teacher. A PGCE student of mine found herself drawn into an informal discussion with Year 12 pupils about 'soft drugs'. She recognized the pupils' right to hold their own views and to discuss such matters openly. At the same time, and in line with the current standards for teachers' professional conduct, she was able to raise questions about the 'down-side' of getting involved with such drugs and to keep her personal views to herself!

Assemblies and acts of collective worship

The assembly is a traditional part of school life and, at one time, was synonymous with the act of worship. Now, however, a distinction is generally drawn between the two. Schools can provide 'secular assemblies' whenever they wish but are required by statutory law to provide the opportunity for a daily act of collective worship, a young person's attendance at which is subject to parents' rights to excusal of their child(ren) or other arrangements.

Large group (for instance, year group) assemblies can be a valuable means of bringing pupils together to share an inspirational experience and a sense of belonging to the school community. They are also a useful means of covering aspects of citizenship education and PSHEE. Careful planning and good speakers can produce genuinely moving secular or religious assemblies. However, the involvement of pupils as presenters or even as organizers and leaders of assemblies has the advantage of encouraging pupils to view the assembly as 'their time' – rather than as an opportunity for senior staff to rant about the state of the school site!

Assemblies may include an act of collective worship, although in secular schools it is rarely possible to have more than one large group assembly a week and this leads to difficulties in meeting the statutory requirement for a daily act of worship. However, the law allows for flexibility in the timing of, and grouping for, collective worship, and one option is for tutors to set aside a few moments during the daily registration or tutor period for quiet reflection/worship. In practice, many schools have simply failed to meet the requirement, and this is one reason why head teachers have called for changes in the law and guidance relating to collective worship. Other reasons, shared by many in and outside the teaching profession, have to do with opposition to the very idea that pupils in a secular school should be required to attend an act of worship, or concerns over its having to be 'wholly or mainly of a broadly Christian character' (Education Reform Act, 1988), given the pluralist society in which you will be teaching.

In fact, as touched on earlier, parents have the right to withdraw their children from collective worship and teachers have the right to withdraw on 'grounds of conscience' (for more information on this, see Louden, 2010). In practice, very few parents exercise their right. The reasons for this are complex, but a major factor has probably been the creative way in which schools have interpreted the requirements. Few would accept the idea that young people who have no theistic belief should be forced to participate in religious worship or prayer.

14.6 Conclusion

All pupils are capable of reflecting on spiritual and moral matters, if these are of a kind that have meaning for them and are presented in ways to which they can relate. An inclusive act of worship will allow for a spiritual response from some pupils, and a worshipful response from others. This may mean that pupils will begin by listening to a presentation on a spiritual/moral theme. They may then be invited either to reflect quietly on what they have heard (or on a related thought or question) or to offer their own prayer. The benefits to pupils of this opportunity for a moment's stillness, reflection or prayer make it likely that, even if the law is changed, many schools will continue to build some 'private time' into assemblies.

Task 14.4

- How do you feel about those aspects of a teacher's work that involve guiding pupils in and through matters that are very personal to them?
- Do you have any concerns about how you will be able to remain true to your personal beliefs, values and attitudes and promote the SMCD of your pupils?
- Note down your responses to these questions so that you can give more thought to these later and perhaps share some in your training sessions.

At the beginning of this chapter you were asked to consider the view that 'a teacher's ability to teach, manage and relate to pupils effectively is greatly enhanced by her or his ability to take account of and draw upon pupils' spiritual, moral and cultural lives, and provide opportunities for development'. What do you think now?

Recommendations for further reading

Bailey, R. (ed.) (2000) *Teaching Values and Citizenship Across the Curriculum*. London: Kogan Page.
Bigger, S. and Brown, E. (eds.) (1999) *Spiritual, Moral, Social and Cultural Education: Exploring Values in the Curriculum*. London: David Fulton.

Peterson, A., Lexmond, J., Hallgarted, J. and Kerr, D. (2014) *Schools with Soul: A New Approach to Spiritual, Moral, Social and Cultural Development*. London: RSA Action and Research Centre. Available at: https://www.thersa.org/globalassets/pdfs/reports/schools-with-soul-report.pdf.

West-Burnham, J. and Huws Jones, V. (2008) *Spiritual and Moral Development in Schools*. London: Continuum.

Webliography

Two websites aimed at teachers and offering guidance on SMCD matters and resources are:

- Doing SMSC: www.doingsmsc.org.uk
- SMSC Online: www.smsc.org.uk

An RE site that provides guidance and resources related to SMCD can be found at: RE:ONLINE at http://www.reonline.org.uk/

Insted has a section on race equality and cultural diversity, and provides links to a wide range of websites offering information, guidance and resources: http://www.insted.co.uk/links.html

15

Raising attainment

Sean Hayes

15.1 Introduction

Ensuring that young people fulfil their potential at school should be at the heart of their whole teaching and learning experience. In secondary school, this will largely be determined by the progress they make and how they perform at Key Stages 3, 4 and 5 (KS3, 4 and 5), and if they stay on at school or college post-16. This chapter complements Chapter 10, identifying factors known to affect performance and setting out ways in which teachers can analyse pupil performance data and use this to inform and implement improvement strategies.

Analysing attainment data involves knowing your pupils and getting behind the raw data on performance.

> Successful schools and teachers know how to use their data to make changes to their classroom practice. They peel away the overall school figures to identify pockets of under-achievement within their school and identify the pupils at risk of low performance and potential under-achievement in the future.
>
> (DCSF, 2010: 1)

By the end of this chapter, you should:

- understand the key factors behind variations in pupil performance;
- know how to analyse the range of data that is available to teachers;
- understand the data analysis tools at your disposal and how to use them;
- be able to identify under-achieving and high-achieving pupil groups;
- have gained an overview of the strategies that have been developed to help maximize attainment for all pupils.

15.2 Caveats and health warnings

Teachers should be aware of some important caveats when analysing data on pupil performance. The same groups of pupils rarely under-perform consistently either over time or across the Key Stages. The target groups identified nationally and locally as being at risk of under-performance will not necessarily be the target groups in your school or even in your class. In the same way, the profile of your 'more able, gifted and talented' (MAGT) pupils will not necessarily be the same as that in another school. You should exercise caution when analysing and targeting groups with small numbers of pupils, as it can be difficult to conclude that something is either statistically or educationally significant when referring to a small group. Sometimes it can be a single pupil who is under-performing, and it might be unrelated to them being part of a particular group. It may be due to the nature of their teaching and learning experience or to external events largely beyond your control. Improvement is not always linear or upwards and, in some schools, effectiveness fluctuates from one year to the next.

Remember that data alone will not prove everything about the performance of a school or its pupils. At best, the analysis of data opens up questions and lines of enquiry. You should use the findings from data analysis to provide evidence that tests your interpretation and hypotheses. You will need to use your professional judgement to decide what the data mean and what, if anything, should be done as a result. Quantitative analysis is a valuable approach to use in identifying under-performance and in helping teachers decide how to address it, but it must also be understood that education is a social process and not everything can be explained or resolved by the results of data analysis.

15.3 Raising standards in secondary schools: the challenge

Since the introduction of the National Curriculum, the English education system has become one of the most data rich in the world (see Chapter 13 for more on debates around the curriculum). Central government now collects performance data at individual pupil level across the Key Stages and is able to match those data, using Unique Pupil Numbers (UPNs), from one Key Stage to the next, creating large datasets that enable a comprehensive level of analysis of both pupil outcomes (attainment) and progress (achievement). Within a school, you will encounter several types of attainment data (see Chapter 10). All of these will tell you something about a pupil's level of attainment.

The effectiveness of schools fluctuates from year to year; however, the national pattern of performance at GCSE has mostly been one of year-on-year improvement and, within the English education system, there is an expectation of continuous improvement. What has changed over recent years is the headline indicators used by government to assess the performance of pupils and schools. Before 2008, the headline indicator was the percentage of pupils achieving five or more A*–C grades; and from 2008 to 2015, it was the percentage of pupils achieving five or more A*–C grades (including English and mathematics). In 2016, the headline indicators became Attainment 8 and Progress 8 and these measures are explained later in the chapter. These changes get reported annually by the Department for Education (DfE) in documents called 'Statements of Intent', which were last updated in July 2018 (DfE, 2018a).

The performance of individual pupils in terms of achieving five or more A*–C grades, and five or more A*–C grades *including English and mathematics*, is still important because success against these measures provides evidence for teachers in terms of a pupil's readiness to go on to post-16 courses at KS5. Figure 15.1 shows the national GCSE results from 2001 to 2016 for the percentage of pupils achieving five or more A*–C grades and five or more A*–C grades including English and mathematics. The graph provides a clear illustration that performance at GCSE was improving steadily on both measures from 2001 to 2012 and that performance levelled off in 2013, before dropping in 2014. The drop in GCSE performance in

2014 was largely as a result of significant reforms introduced by the government following the Wolf Report (DfE, 2011c). These changes are explained further in Chapter 19 but the changes that had the most impact on GCSE performance were the decisions to reduce the range of qualifications that could be included in School Performance Tables and to introduce a 'first-entry' rule, which was phased in for the 2014 examinations (Parameshwaran and Thomson, 2015). The first of these changes meant that the number of non-GCSEs that could be included in the 2013/14 Performance Tables was reduced to two, and no qualification could be counted as equivalent to more than one GCSE. Prior to this change, some qualifications, such as Business and Technology Education Council diplomas (BTECs), counted for up to four GCSEs. The introduction of subject discounting meant that multiple entries in the same subject, but in different types of qualification, could no longer be included in Performance Tables, with only one qualification being counted. The first-entry rule only applied to examinations taken from September 2013 onwards, meaning that for the 2014 Performance Tables a pupil's best result from qualifications entered before September 2013 was still counted if it was a better result than their first result from the 2013/14 academic year. However, this will still have impacted on GCSE performance in 2014, 2015 and 2016, when national performance changed only very slightly for the percentage of pupils achieving five or more A*–C grades including English and mathematics.

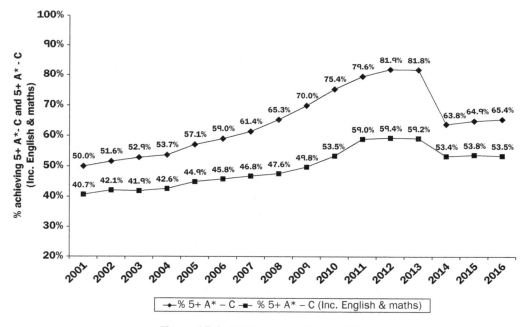

Figure 15.1 GCSE results, 2001–2016

You are likely to be aware of an annual debate that occurs when GCSE results are announced: 'Are standards genuinely rising or not?' In practice, it is not a matter of whether standards are rising or not, but whether they are rising fast enough, and for all pupils. In the period from 2014 to 2016, the percentage of pupils who did not achieve five or more A*–C grades including English and mathematics was around 46% each year and, on that evidence, still too many young people are left behind, too many from specific groups in our society under-achieve, and too many fail to reach their full potential – with all the consequent problems for both individuals and society as a whole.

Task 15.1

Log on to the Department for Education (DfE) website, then locate the School and College Performance Tables web page (https://www.compare-school-performance. service.gov.uk/) and find the latest GCSE Performance Tables for your school and local authority.

What do these tables tell you about the performance of your school in relation to other schools in your area and in relation to local authority and national averages? Study the wide range of performance indicators to help you assess the strengths and weaknesses of your school's performance.

Many factors relating to pupils are known to correlate with attainment. These include prior attainment; level of attendance; the impact of individual teachers; the pupil's intrinsic motivation, including their self-esteem, self-regulation and personal resilience; and, in some cases, external factors such as a disrupted or chaotic home background or other major life events. All of these factors may help to explain variations in an individual pupil's performance and why under-performance has occurred. For example, a pupil might have a prior attainment profile from KS2 that shows that they have achieved the expected standard in reading, writing and mathematics, and they are motivated to learn and be resilient, but a major life event has disrupted their learning. This could be the death of a parent or close family member, which reduces their resilience and could impact adversely on their progress, leading to under-performance at the end of KS3 or in their GCSE examinations. Situations like this will be largely unforeseen, outside the control of the class teacher and will require the effective use of pastoral support to help get the pupil back on track, alongside a programme of work that affords the pupil the chance to catch up with their peers. The impact of circumstances beyond the school was observed by Kerr and West (2010: 25), who recognized that 'children's academic performance cannot be divorced from ... what happens to them outside school – in their families, communities and neighbourhoods'.

Other factors, such as the pupil's attendance record or the role played by an individual teacher, could impact positively on a pupil's progress and attainment. While good attendance at secondary school does not guarantee success, research shows that there is a high correlation between attendance and performance and that pupils with attendance between 95% and 100% are several times more likely to achieve 5+ A*–C GCSE grades including English and mathematics than those pupils with poor attendance (DfE, 2016c). The majority of pupils will perform broadly in line with their ability, their own expectations and the expectations of their teachers. However, some pupils over-perform and exceed expectations while others under-perform, achieving less than they should have. Identifying potential under-performance or performance that is better than expected is the challenge of knowing your pupils and being able to analyse their performance. National data on performance shows some of the specific patterns of inequality of outcomes and the pupils and groups of pupils who are most likely to be over-represented as low or high achievers. The following list, which is illustrative but not exhaustive, has been adapted from Kerr and West (2010) and provides an indication of who those pupils might be:

- On average, White British pupils (both boys and girls) are more likely than other ethnic groups to demonstrate sustained under-achievement and even more so if they live in deprived households.

- Of the minority ethnic groups, Chinese and Indian pupils are generally the most successful and Black Caribbean pupils are the least, though this pattern is far from consistent across the country and patterns of performance by ethnicity tend to change over time.

- Being subject to poverty, as indicated by the pupils being eligible for free school meals, is strongly associated with low attainment. This is more true of White British pupils than for other ethnic groups.

- Children from homes with single and/or unemployed parents and/or parents who have few educational qualifications themselves often do less well at school.

- Children with special educational needs and disability (SEND) and children in care ('looked after' children), who are among the most vulnerable in the education system, are more likely to have outcomes below those of their peers.

These patterns are echoed in the findings from major educational research studies over recent years (Strand, 2015). Attainment gaps in GCSE performance between all the main ethnic groups have narrowed in the approximately ten years from 2004 to 2013. Teachers may find that the groups of pupils who are over- or under-performing in their school are not mentioned in the preceding list. Although the research studies identify broad patterns, the different factors often interact to compound a pupil's advantage or disadvantage. For example, the under-performing group may not just be White British children but White British boys who are eligible for free school meals, or it might be Black Caribbean girls who are also persistent absentees, who all live on the same housing estate. This potential interaction of factors opens up the idea that some pupils are likely to experience multiple disadvantages or advantages, which suggests that the level of analysis that is required might involve a degree of complexity. All of these factors, whether personal to the pupil, external to the pupil, or pertaining to groups of pupils and singularly or in combination, can help explain variations in performance. The data in Table 15.1 shows the performance of some of the main contextual pupil groups at GCSE in England from 2012/13 to 2015/16. Performance is based on the percentage of pupils in each group achieving 5+ A*–C grades including English and mathematics alongside the gap in percentage points between each group in each category. The contextual breakdowns cover: gender; English as an additional language (EAL); disadvantaged pupils, that is, pupils who are eligible for Pupil Premium Grant (PPG) funding; and pupils with special educational needs (SEN).

Although Figure 15.1 shows that GCSE performance had been improving steadily up to 2013, most of the contextual attainment gaps have remained broadly at the same level over the four years detailed in Table 15.1. These national data provide a useful reference point when analysing the results in your school, but you should note that what happened

	2012/13	2013/14	2014/15	2015/16
Gender				
Girls	65.7%	61.7%	61.9%	62.6%
Boys	55.9%	51.6%	52.5%	52.3%
Percentage points gap	**9.8%**	**10.1%**	**9.4%**	**10.3%**
First language				
English	60.9%	56.9%	57.5%	58.0%
Other than English	58.4%	54.7%	54.6%	54.5%
Percentage points gap	**2.5%**	**2.2%**	**2.9%**	**3.5%**
Disadvantaged pupils				
All other pupils	67.9%	64.0%	64.8%	65.1%
Disadvantaged pupils	40.9%	36.5%	36.7%	37.2%
Percentage points gap	**27.0%**	**27.5%**	**28.1%**	**27.9%**
SEN provision				
No identified SEN	70.4%	65.3%	64.2%	63.9%
All SEN pupils	23.3%	20.5%	20.0%	19.8%
Percentage points gap	**47.1%**	**44.8%**	**44.2%**	**44.1%**

Table 15.1 Percentage of pupils in contextual groups achieving 5+ A*–C grades (including English and mathematics) with percentage points gaps

Source: Department for Education (various years).

nationally might not be replicated within your school and the challenge within schools should be to close these gaps, wherever they are encountered.

The next section considers how to identify the contextual and other factors that are correlated with performance, while helping you to carry out your own data analysis to measure their impact on attainment.

15.4 Analysing attainment data

Teachers need to have good assessment data to ensure that they can:

- plan and deliver a relevant curriculum and appropriate lessons;
- set realistic yet stretching targets based on evidence;
- know that learners make the appropriate amount of progress; and
- identify variations in pupil performance.

To make intelligent use of data, teachers need to understand what is available and get behind the figures to explore the strengths and weaknesses in pupil performance. Secondary school teachers should have prior attainment data on their pupils from KS2 standardized test scores, baseline assessment data from any tests that the school administers to pupils on entry – such as cognitive ability tests (CATs) or middle years information systems (MidYIS) – and marking schemes for homework, coursework and ongoing assessments that may be part of a pupil tracking system. Then there will be data from ongoing assessments linked to National Curriculum age-related expectations at KS3 and GCSEs, collectively culminating in their actual GCSE grades at the end of Year 11.

Teachers must know where to get the data from, particularly data on school entry. As a newly qualified secondary school teacher, knowing the key personnel is important when it comes to accessing the relevant assessment data. This will vary between schools but is likely to include: the office manager, for contextual data on your pupils, including information on gender, eligibility for free school meals and which pupils are eligible for PPG; the data manager for baseline assessment information and advice on whole-school marking schemes, target-setting and pupil tracking; and the special educational needs coordinator (SENCo) for information on specific pupils, including the more vulnerable young people and the more able, gifted and talented pupils. Some of these personnel are likely to be the ones who can give you usernames and passwords for external data analysis tools, such as Analyse School Performance (ASP) and Fischer Family Trust (FFT). As a newly qualified teacher, it is likely that you will receive training and induction on the school's management information system. Part of this will include advice on data entry and an explanation of the assessment data available to you for the classes you teach and how you can use this effectively to inform your planning. The data manager will coordinate the data on an individual and whole-school basis.

The prior attainment data from KS2 and the results of any tests that the school administers on entry have been explained in Chapter 10, in terms of how the information can help teachers make judgements about the ways in which pupils can access the secondary curriculum. These purposes can be described as follows:

- to provide diagnostic information on pupils' cognitive strengths and weaknesses and learning styles and preferences;
- to inform any policies that the school has regarding pupil grouping, streaming and/or setting; and
- to establish a baseline for setting targets and measuring pupils' progress to the end of KS4.

The information can also form the starting point for your ongoing analysis of pupil performance and can help you identify pupils at risk of under-performance and to track your high-achieving pupils, who may be more able, gifted and talented. These purposes can be summarized as follows:

- to support pupils who start secondary education already struggling with basic literacy and numeracy who may need support to catch up and possibly tailored interventions;
- to maintain momentum for those at risk of slowing in the progress they make; and
- to ensure that all those who are already high performing continue to be challenged.

For new teachers, the first opportunity to do some data analysis is to build a picture of your class's ability on entry. You can do this by taking their KS2 standardized test scores from the end of primary school to create an ability profile of the pupils, which can be augmented by setting these test scores alongside the pupils' entry test scores (Strand, 2006). The combination of both should provide a broader picture of ability and, if you have entry test scores from non-verbal reasoning tests, these can be very helpful in providing a picture of underlying academic potential, particularly for pupils with EAL. Assessment data also has predictive value and can be used to inform and support pupil and whole-school target-setting. In relation to target-setting, research demonstrates that 'a combination of reasoning [tests] and Key Stage 2 tests together provides the most reliable basis for predicting future performance' (Strand, 2006: 223).

Target-setting at national, local authority, school and pupil level was a feature of government policy for the two decades up to 2010. However, the change of government in 2010 saw a subtle shift in the use of target-setting as a lever to drive up standards. The pre-existing statutory requirements on schools and local authorities to set targets were relaxed, with a shift in emphasis towards giving schools greater control over the targets they might set and a reduction in the number of targets and an element of prescription. This does not mean that target-setting no longer has a role to play. For classroom teachers there will still be value in setting targets for individual pupils within their subject, which will usually be expressed as reaching or exceeding the expected standard at the end of KS3 and a grade for GCSE.

In 2015, the DfE introduced a significant reform to the way in which GCSEs would be graded from 2017, set out in two of their factsheets (DfE, 2017d). The grades A*–G are being replaced with grades 9 to 1, with grade 9 being the highest. Pupils taking GCSEs in England in 2017 will receive a mixture of number and letter grades. English language, English literature and mathematics are the first subjects to use the new system, with another 20 subjects moving to 9–1 grading in 2018, with most others following in 2019. Eventually, all GCSEs taken in England will receive numerical grades. The new grades are being introduced to signal that GCSEs have been reformed and to better differentiate between pupils of different abilities. In the first year each new GCSE subject is introduced, broadly the same proportion of pupils will get a grade 4 or above as would have got a grade C or above in the old system. This means that the old letter-based measure of achieving a grade at A*–C has been replaced by an equivalent measure of achieving a grade at 9 to 4. A useful example of this would be the replacement of the old measure of achieving A*–C grades in English and mathematics with a new measure of achieving grades 9 to 4 in English and mathematics.

The predictive value of FFT data has been explained in Chapter 10 and teachers should be aware that FFT estimates are frequently used by schools as the basis for their target-setting process. One of the functions of the FFT package, known as FFT Aspire, is to provide estimates for the end of KS3 and KS4. The package is highly interactive and schools can choose the level of challenge they want from FFT estimates. Many schools use estimates based on the top performing 25% of schools in England or even the top performing 10% of schools, which builds in challenge and aspiration to the targets and helps drive school improvement. The other main functionality of FFT is to enable schools to analyse their actual performance at the end of KS3 and KS4. FFT Aspire's self-evaluation dashboards allow you to quickly and comprehensively evaluate attainment and achievement in your school. In a suite of six reports, FFT Aspire provides you with a comprehensive evaluation of your school's performance. It identifies strengths and weaknesses across different subjects and pupil groups using a full range of DfE attainment and achievement measures alongside FFT-contextualized progress indicators.

Task 15.2

This task is about analysing performance at GCSE and by completing this task you will have achieved two objectives:

(i) Analysing data in several ways, over time, by context (gender), against targets and national benchmarks; and
(ii) Writing about your analysis in a clear and consistent way.

Table 15.2 provides (fictional) information on the GCSE results of 10 pupils, five girls and five boys, in two GCSE subjects in 2017, English and mathematics. The table also shows the pupils' target grades in each subject.

Pupil	Sex	GCSE English grade achieved in 2017	GCSE maths grade achieved in 2017	GCSE English target in 2017	GCSE maths target in 2017
Anna	Girl	8	7	7	7
Dee	Girl	9	8	8	8
Salma	Girl	5	6	4	5
Mary	Girl	4	3	6	5
Carmel	Girl	6	7	6	7
Barry	Boy	7	7	7	7
Kevin	Boy	8	6	7	7
Javier	Boy	3	2	3	3
Kofi	Boy	4	5	4	4
Tom	Boy	2	3	4	4

Table 15.2 Results of ten pupils in GCSE English and mathematics in 2017

Calculate the percentage of GCSE grades at 9–4 achieved by girls, boys and overall in 2017 and the percentage achieving or exceeding their target in each subject. Then write these percentages into the blank cells in Table 15.3.

GCSE Indicator	2015	2016	2017	2017 National
Girls 9–4 in English	75%	85%		80%
Girls 9–4 in maths	68%	74%		73%
Boys 9–4 in English	51%	55%		65%
Boys 9–4 in maths	66%	63%		71%

GCSE Indicator	2015	2016	2017	2017 National
All 9–4 in English	63%	70%		73%
All 9–4 in maths	67%	68%		72%
All 9–4 in English & maths	60%	66%		64%
All achieving English target	72%	75%		
All achieving maths target	65%	62%		

Table 15.3 The percentage of GCSE grades at 9–4 achieved

Now fill in the gaps in the following narrative based on the GCSE performance information in Tables 15.2 and 15.3. The narrative describes the pupils' performance in English and mathematics GCSEs in 2017.

Girls' performance in English in 2017 has _____ compared with 2016 by ___ % points, while the performance of boys has _____ by ___ % points. Girls' performance in mathematics in 2017 has _____ compared with 2016 by ___ % points, while the performance of boys has _____ by ___ % points. The performance of all pupils in English in 2017 has _____ compared with 2016 by ___ % points, while the performance in mathematics has _____ by ___ % points.

The underlying trend in girls' performance in both subjects since 2015 is _____, whereas the trend in boys' performance in mathematics is _____. The underlying trend in all pupils' performance in English and mathematics combined since 2015 is _____.

In 2017, ___ % of all pupils achieved or exceeded their target in English and ___ % achieved or exceeded their target in mathematics. The underlying trend in meeting targets in English is _____, whereas the trend in mathematics is _____. The pupil who missed their targets by the greatest margin was _____.

Girls performed _____ than girls nationally in English and mathematics in 2017, while boys performed _____ than boys nationally in English and mathematics.

From 2006 to 2016, the DFE and Ofsted made available a powerful analysis tool to teaching staff for analysing patterns of performance in their school – the RAISEonline programme (Reporting and Analysis for Improvement through School self-Evaluation) – but it was discontinued in July 2017 and replaced with a new analysis tool, known as Analyse School Performance (ASP), which is also web-based and interactive. It provides a common set of interactive, online analyses to schools and local authority officers, as well as being used by Ofsted inspectors to raise questions to explore during a school's inspection. Teachers can gain secure access to ASP with a username and password via the UK Government's website: https://sa.education.gov.uk/idp/Authn/UserPassword. ASP for secondary schools contains analysis of GCSE outcomes and offers tabular and graphic representations of a school's results.

The outputs from ASP are based on what are commonly referred to as the headline GCSE measures and, at the time of writing, these are: Attainment 8, Progress 8, the English Bacca-laureate (EBacc); and the percentage of pupils achieving GCSE grades 9 to 4 in English and mathematics. These need some further explanation, so that teachers can understand how to calculate them in their own school. Attainment 8 measures the achievement of a pupil across eight qualifications, including mathematics (double-weighted), English (double-weighted), three further qualifications that count in the EBacc measure, and three further qualifications that can be GCSE qualifications (including EBacc subjects) or any other non-GCSE qualifica-tions on the DfE-approved list. Each individual grade a pupil achieves is assigned a point score, which are then added together to give a pupil's Attainment 8 score. In the years 2017/2019, the DfE will provide tables that enable the scores to be calculated as the system moves incrementally from the A*–G grading system to the 9–1 grading system.

Progress 8 compares pupils' KS4 results nationally with those of other pupils with sim-ilar prior attainment from KS2. There are four steps in the calculation of a Progress 8 score. The first step is to put all pupils nationally into prior attainment groups based on their KS2 results, so that we have groups of pupils who have similar starting points to each other. This is done by working out a pupil's average performance at KS2 across English and mathemat-ics. Pupils' actual test results in English and mathematics are converted into points and an average of the points is taken to create an overall point score. Pupils are then allocated into prior attainment groups with other pupils who have the same KS2 point scores. The second step is to work out a pupil's Attainment 8 score, as explained above. The third step is to calculate individual pupils' Progress 8 scores. Progress 8 is calculated for individual pupils solely in order to calculate a school's Progress 8 score. There is no need for schools to share individual Progress 8 scores with their pupils. The calculation is as follows:

- Take the individual pupil's Attainment 8 score (for instance, Pupil A with a score of 56).
- Compare this to the national average Attainment 8 score for pupils in the same prior attainment group.
- A pupil's progress score is the difference between their actual Attainment 8 result and the average result of those in their prior attainment group.
- If pupil A, for example, achieved an Attainment 8 score of 56 and the average Attain-ment 8 score for his prior attainment group was 55, then his progress score would be +1.
- Then divide +1 by 10 to give an individual pupil's Progress 8 score, which in this example, is +0.1.
- The final step is to create a school level Progress 8 score, and this is done by adding together the Progress 8 scores of all the pupils in Year 11 and dividing by the number of pupils in the Year 11 cohort.

The English Baccalaureate is a school performance measure. The measure indicates how many pupils gained a grade C or above in the core academic subjects at KS4 in any government-funded school. The DfE introduced the EBacc measure in 2010 and, in June 2015, announced their intention that all pupils who start Year 7 in September 2015 take the EBacc subjects when they reach their GCSEs in 2020. However, for the majority of secondary schools up to 2017, not all pupils were entered for all the EBacc subjects. The EBacc comprises the following subjects: English (language and/or literature); mathematics; history or geography; the sciences; and a language. To pass each element of the EBacc, pupils need to achieve grades at A* to C in each of these subjects and in science they need to achieve A*–C in at least two science GCSEs. A pupil counts towards the school's EBacc success measure if they have achieved A*–C grades in all these subjects.

Contextual breakdown of school's Progress 8 scores	Overall Progress 8 scores			Description of benchmark
	Number of pupils	School	National benchmark	
All pupils	300	0.35	0.00	National, all pupils
Gender				
Male	146	–0.02	–0.12	National, males
Female	154	0.72	0.13	National, females
Disadvantaged, FSM, CLA				
Disadvantaged	90	0.10	0.12	National, non-disadvantaged
Other non-disadvantaged	210	0.45	0.12	National, non-disadvantaged
Free school meals (FSM)	86	0.11	0.11	National, non-FSM
Children looked after (CLA)	4	-0.25	0.01	National, non-CLA
Special educational needs (SEN)				
SEN with statement or EHC plan	8	–0.60	0.00	National, all pupils
SEN support	30	0.30	0.00	National, all pupils
No SEN	262	0.40	0.06	National, no SEN
Non-mobile pupils				
On roll in Years 10 and 11	270	0.42	0.02	National, non-mobile
First language				
English as a first language	190	0.32	0.00	National, all pupils
English as an additional language (EAL)	110	0.38	0.00	National, all pupils
Prior attainment (PA)				
Low overall PA	65	0.25	0.00	National, all pupils
Middle overall PA	160	0.40	0.00	National, all pupils
High overall PA	75	0.30	0.00	National, all pupils

Table 15.4 Progress 8 scores for an example (fictional) school from ASP

Table 15.4 provides GCSE performance data for an example (fictional) school from the DfE's ASP tool. The table provides a range of contextual breakdowns of the school's Progress 8 results, including: gender; disadvantage; SEN; pupil mobility; EAL; and prior attainment. The same range of contextual breakdowns are available in ASP for the other GCSE measures: Attainment 8; the English Baccalaureate; and the percentage of pupils achieving GCSE grades 9–4 in English and mathematics.

The additional feature of the performance data in ASP, as illustrated in Table 15.4, is that it includes benchmarks for each sub-group of pupils. The DfE has set different national benchmarks for different subgroups of pupils as they see the process of benchmarking as one that adds challenge and can be used as a lever to improve educational standards. For example, boys are benchmarked against boys nationally and girls are benchmarked against girls nationally. However, pupils with SEN are benchmarked against all pupils nationally because the DfE want to use this to challenge schools to achieve better outcomes for their pupils with SEN, and to narrow the attainment gap between them and all pupils.

In relation to the identification and analysis of low- and high-achieving pupils and pupil groups, ASP has good functionality when used interactively. Users should log on, select their own school and go to the section illustrating scatter plots. These plots allow you to identify groups of pupils and individual pupils who are under- or over-performing. Within ASP, once you have selected scatter plots, you can apply filters. You can use the filter to compare one or more different groups, for instance boys and girls. Alternatively, you can use the filter to look at just one group. These filters are the most appropriate functions to help teachers either identify variations in pupil performance or to test their hypotheses about which groups of pupils might be over- or under-performing.

Task 15.3

What factors would you consider and what measures would you take if the estimates for pupil performance from statistical models such as FFT Aspire, baseline tests and the school's own benchmarking were noticeably different from your own assessments of progress and predictions of the pupils' future performance?

- Is the classroom assessment process robust, monitored and moderated to ensure consistency and equity?
- Are external factors involved – for instance, are some pupils recently arrived from abroad with EAL or are they experiencing instability in their home lives?
- Did they make very good progress in primary school, but their progress has appeared to stall in secondary school?
- What do other teachers say about how they have managed this in the past and what are their predictions for these pupils?
- What are pupils' and parents' understanding of expectations of progress and targets set?
- Are there challenges around behaviour for learning?
- What interventions might you need to put in place to enhance progress?

In the next section, we consider some of the strategies that you might employ to address over- and under-performance.

15.5 Strategies for responding to variations in performance

Once you have identified groups of pupils who have over- or under-performed, the challenge for you is to decide what, if any, strategies you need to put in place to get under-performing pupils back on track and what you need to do to stretch your high-achieving pupils. Some of the strategies that you might employ will be directly related to teaching and learning and the curriculum, which have been covered in other chapters, including Chapters 6, 9, 10 and 13.

One of the unusual features of educational outcomes within the English education system is that some pupils appear to make no progress between one Key Stage and the next. In secondary schools, this has been particularly evident between KS2 and KS3, where data over many years show that between 10% and 20% of pupils stand still – or even regress – in at least one of the three core subjects of English, mathematics and science. Where a teacher encounters this through ongoing pupil tracking and in the end-of-KS3 assessments, one is drawn to evidence of potential under-performance. Sometimes there are valid educational reasons for this, including: the pupil was already struggling with literacy and numeracy at the start of secondary education; the pupil was struggling with the transition from primary to secondary school; or, the pupil lost momentum and their progress began to slow. This phenomenon is often referred to as the 'Year 7 dip', which is not so problematic if the pupil gets back on track in Years 8 and 9 but is a major concern if there is no demonstrable evidence of improvement and progress across the whole of KS3. Educational strategies to avoid pupils making limited or no progress at all include intensive support for literacy and numeracy, regular pupil tracking and assessment, personalized learning, effective use of materials from the DfE on how to ensure that pupils make good progress and, in some cases, one-to-one tuition. However, research (Hayes and Clay, 2007) has shown that this level of sustained under-performance can often be the result of factors other than academic progress and attainment. Earlier in this chapter we referred to the potential negative impact of external events on a pupil's attainment. These could include the pupil being part of a peer group culture that does not value education, through to major life events such as family breakdown, which could result in the pupil experiencing low levels of motivation and self-esteem, leading to low resilience and a reduced capacity for being self-regulating in their learning. Cassen *et al.* (2009), who studied the link between educational outcomes and adversity and resilience, defined resilience in learners as:

> positive adaptation in the face of adversity. It is a process that explains the way in which some individuals achieve good outcomes despite the fact that they are at high risk for poor outcomes. Risk factors are those variables that signal an increased chance of poor outcomes.
>
> (2009: 73)

This chapter has addressed many variables that could lead to poor outcomes and, while some of them may be ameliorated by effective teaching and learning and appropriate educational interventions, personal factors such as resilience cannot necessarily be taught. In the secondary school context, resilience has to be nurtured and developed, partly through whole-school policies, partly by individual teachers and other staff involved in delivering the personal, social, health and economic education (PSHEE) curriculum, and partly through pastoral care (see Chapter 18). For example, schools that manage the transition well from primary to secondary will enhance children's resilience by taking a whole-school focus at this key time in young people's lives.

However, how can individual teachers help young people build resilience once they have identified that they are at risk of poor outcomes? Cassen *et al.* (2009: 10) take the view: 'Interventions through families and schools can reduce disadvantage and promote resilience among children'. One response that a school can take for its pupils, whose potential for low performance might also lead to reduced resilience, is to set up a programme of peer mentoring. Peer mentoring is a form of mentorship that takes place in learning environments such as schools, usually between an older, more experienced pupil and a younger pupil. However, it is important that such a programme is not rooted solely in under-achievement or that it is seen as being done only for ethnic minority pupils or just for one gender. Mentoring should be initiated as a whole-school intervention and pupils should be offered it for a wide range of reasons, so that it is not only seen as a response to under-performance. Cross-age mentoring is generally considered to be more appropriate and beneficial than same-age mentoring in the secondary school context.

It was mentioned earlier that low-performing pupils might be part of a peer group culture that does not value education, so another strategy for teachers would be to encourage and support pupils to change their friendship groups. This would not only get them into a more academically minded group, it would also demonstrate that they were building personal resilience. In research into the reasons cited by pupils from deprived backgrounds as helping them achieve above their estimates at GCSE, several pupils said that changing their friendship group was an important factor (Hayes *et al.* 2009). What the successful pupils in this research managed to do was to build, through their own resilience, a strong academic self-concept and positive peer support. Alongside changing friendship groups, teachers should also work on helping pupils to be more self-regulatory in their learning, which will benefit, in particular, low-performing pupils who have started to become demoralized and demotivated.

Parents often provide support for their children's learning, emotionally, academically or both. Parents continue to be important to their children's education after early childhood, not only in home activities but in their relationship with their children's schools. Parental engagement is really important where early intervention is required when pupils are identified at risk of under-performance. Close partnership working with parents can be crucial to getting their child back on track and engaged with their learning. Parental involvement in a child's schooling is identified as being a more powerful force than other family background indicators such as social class or family size and is estimated to contribute to 10 per cent or more of the variation in educational achievement. Effective parental involvement that supports teachers to raise their pupils' outcomes by as much as 10 per cent could be the difference between success and failure for some pupils. Chapter 7 covers the range of ways that schools can work effectively with parents and other adults in relation to raising attainment.

This chapter has also covered the identification of pupils who might be considered to have over-performed, often referred to as more able, gifted and talented (MAGT). As well as addressing issues of under-performance, it is important that teachers stretch their MAGT pupils to fulfil their potential. The first task for a teacher is to identify their MAGT pupils and, as a new teacher, you may be supported in this by the school's MAGT coordinator. Best practice on managing the education of more able pupils recommends a sharp focus on their identification, support and development, which will bring the energy and aspiration to unlock their potential. In successful schools, the most able pupils typically thrive because school leaders provide a challenging curriculum, making sure teaching is consistently good or better for all pupils throughout the Key Stages. Successful leaders use the information they have from primary schools to ensure that pupils do work that stretches them as soon as they join Year 7. They are intolerant of the notion of a 'Year 7 dip'. This continues throughout the pupils' time at school and culminates in their successful applications to universities, colleges, training providers and employers. An effective approach to this can demonstrate a school's determination to do the best for every child, providing rich opportunities for engagement with parents and enabling children to reflect on and improve their own learning. The development of more able pupils also provides a challenge for schools to take stock of children currently identified as MAGT learners and to consider whether disadvantaged pupils and minority groups are properly represented, challenging preconceptions and embedding inclusive approaches. Work in this area consequently enables schools to take action to narrow attainment gaps and to accelerate the progress of more able pupils.

15.6 Conclusion: what does this mean for me?

As a newly qualified teacher, you will be entering school at a time when the educational system is as data rich as it has ever been. You will be expected to engage with data to help you and the school identify both under- and over-performance and to use this data to put strategies in place to remove under-performance and to stretch the high achievers, so that all pupils fulfil their potential. Hopefully, you can achieve this while playing a part in building a school ethos that recognizes pupils as individuals and celebrates effort and improvement as well as attainment.

The main implications for your practice should be to:

- find out practical information on the context of your pupils and administrative information such as usernames and passwords for the relevant data tools and websites that you will be expected to use;
- understand and use the whole-school systems that are in place for marking, assessment and pupil tracking;
- understand achievement and attainment data and how to use the tools at your disposal to interpret them;
- recognize under-performance and how to implement the range of strategies for addressing it;
- identify your more able pupils and know how to stretch them academically;
- take responsibility for your own continuing professional development and learn from best practice within your school and elsewhere.

Recommendations for further reading

Department for Education (DfE) (2016) *The Link between Absence and Attainment at KS2 and KS4: 2013/14 Academic Year.* London: DfE. Available at: https://assets.publishing.service.gov.uk/government/uploads/system/uploads/attachment_data/file/509679/The-link-between-absence-and-attainment-at-KS2-and-KS4-2013-to-2014-academic-year.pdf.

Department for Education (DfE) (2018) *School and College Performance Tables: Statements of Intent.* Available at: https://www.gov.uk/government/publications/school-and-college-performance-tables-statements-of-intent.

Cassen, R., Feinstein, L. and Graham, P. (2009) Educational outcomes: adversity and resilience, *Social Policy and Society*, 8 (1): 73–85.

Demie, F. (2013) *Using Data to Raise Achievement: Good Practice in Schools*. London: Lambeth Council.

Kerr, K. and West, M. (eds.) (2010) *Social Inequality: Can Schools Narrow the Gap?*, Insights #2 Publication. London: BERA.

Parameshwaran, M. and Thomson, D. (2015) The impact of accountability reforms on the Key Stage 4 curriculum: how have changes to school and college Performance Tables affected pupil access to qualifications and subjects in secondary schools in England?, *London Review of Education*, 13 (2): 157–173.

Sammons, P., Thomas, S. and Mortimore, P. (1997) *Forging Links: Effective Schools and Effective Departments*. London: Paul Chapman.

Strand, S. (2003) *Getting the Best from CAT: A Practical Guide for Secondary Schools*. London: NfER Nelson.

Strand, S. (2015) *Ethnicity, Deprivation and Educational Achievement at Age 16 in England: Trends Over Time*. London: DfE.

Webliography

School and College Performance Tables web page: https://www.compare-school-performance.service.gov.uk/schools-by-type?step=phase&geographic=all&region=0&phase=primary

Analyse School Performance (ASP) – Secure Access: https://sa.education.gov.uk/idp/Authn/UserPassword

Department for Education (DfE) GCSE Factsheet for Parents: https://www.gov.uk/government/publications/gcse-new-grading-scale-factsheets

16

Literacy across the curriculum

John Gordon

16.1 Introduction

Spend any amount of time wandering around a school, down corridors or into classrooms, and the chances are you will encounter some tangible manifestation of what is often termed 'literacy across the curriculum' or 'language for learning' (Ofsted, 2013b). You may see examples of pupils' writing in display cabinets; you may notice laminated cards of subject-specific vocabulary decorating the walls; and you may spot phrases that help pupils structure their writing arranged carefully in sequence on various whiteboards. This chapter concerns schools as environments rich in language and asks you to consider the contribution to literacy development you might make in your own subject discipline.

By the end of this chapter, you should:

- have reflected on what is meant by both 'literacy' and 'literacy across the curriculum' or 'language for learning';
- know about whole-school literacy initiatives since the early 2000s;
- have been introduced to current issues and priorities of policy relevant to literacy;
- consider literacy in relation to your own subject;
- know some current thinking concerning key approaches to reading, writing, speaking and listening that may be helpful to teaching in your subject.

16.2 What is meant by literacy across the curriculum?

You have just read a description of a school environment demonstrating cross-curricular literacy practices in action. What thinking lies behind these signs of literacy across the curriculum (LAC)? Surely it cannot be the case that attention to standards of reading, writing and oral communication in schools is a new idea?

The current National Curriculum states that 'English is both a subject in its own right and the medium for teaching; for pupils, understanding the language provides access to the whole curriculum' (DfE, 2014c: 11). Contemporary interest in the development of literacy (Lewis and Wray, 2000) across the secondary school can be viewed as part of a cycle that follows from the report *A Language for Life*, otherwise known as the Bullock Report (DES,

1975), though just prior to that books such as *Language, the Learner and the School* (Barnes *et al.*, 1969) had considered whole-school language policies. We can trace this back even further, as the Bullock Report begins with some contextualizing historical detail, citing the Newbolt Report's findings that employers were disappointed to find young employees 'hopelessly deficient in their command of English' and that they considered the teaching of English in schools of the day to produce 'a very limited command of the English language' (Board of Education, 1921: 72). Reflecting on the school's role in the same period, in the report *English for the English*, George Sampson (1921: 25) stated: 'all teachers are teachers of English because every teacher is a teacher in English. That sentence should be written in letters of gold over every school doorway'. Whole-school literacy was as important then as it is today, its purposes contested, and its effectiveness alternately criticized or vigorously defended just as they are now.

If pupils' aptitude and facility with language – their literacy skills – have been often debated in terms of the national economy and state of the workforce, discussion has also extended to other concerns. The 1921 quotation describing 'deficient' levels of skill could paraphrase more recent statements concerning adult literacy. A survey undertaken by the Confederation of British Industry (2011) found that nearly half of employers were dissatisfied with what they considered low literacy standards in school leavers. Other studies confirm 'employers are not content with the level of proficiency with spelling, punctuation and grammar possessed by school, college and university leavers' (Macey, 2013: 3). The picture is complicated by the confidence young people report about their literacy skills for employment but their 'very limited understanding' of the communication skills actually needed in a workplace (Clark and Formby, 2013: 9). It becomes evident that literacy is not just about employability, but also about having a repertoire of skills suited to a variety of tasks and situations. Some commentators take the scope of literacy still further, to contend that literacy is about so much more than basic skills. Richard Hoggart (1998), for example, presents a view of literacy as inseparable from social justice, democracy and true citizenship. Similar ideas have been espoused in discussions of 'new literacies' (Cope and Kalantzis, 2000), developed in the context of globalization and the new forms of communication that arise from developing technologies. While literacy increasingly comprises everyday use of digital technologies reflected in education, the *Vision for Literacy 2025* (National Literacy Forum, 2015: 8) also draws attention to diminishing literacy provision through libraries in times of austerity.

The Ofsted survey, *Removing Barriers to Literacy* (2011), made it difficult to conceive of whole-school literacy as anything other than a priority. It highlighted specific pupil groups that made markedly less progress in literacy than others, described inadequate use of assessment data to support progress, and recognized that many secondary teachers simply did not have the benefit of training in fundamental aspects of literacy education that could make a significant difference to pupils' progress. It confirmed literacy as a whole-school issue relevant to every teacher no matter their discipline. Sampson's (1921) view that every teacher is a teacher of literacy holds true a century on.

Bear all of these points in mind as you read this chapter. Thinking about what the word 'literacy' can mean is essential to developing your ability to support pupils in the way they engage with and respond to your own subject area, and to contributing to LAC in a manner that will be enriching both to your pupils and your school. In addition, you will be playing your part in removing potential barriers to literacy, contributing to an inclusive and holistic ethos of secondary education.

Task 16.1

Before you read any further, attempt the following activities:

- Consider and write down your own definition of 'literacy'.
- Identify three activities, common in your subject, that you believe develop pupils' literacy skills and are likely to be applied (a) elsewhere in school and (b) in contexts beyond school.

16.3 Literacy across the curriculum: official guidance since 2010

In 2001, a framework of recommendations for LAC in secondary schools (DfEE, 2001) encouraged a common pedagogy accompanied by abundant resourcing and training for teachers. Its influence remains strong, though recently Ofsted (2011, 2013b) highlighted persistent barriers to pupils' literacy progress. They now take the attitude that no single method guarantees improved literacy in all schools. Concurrently, National Curriculum reforms at primary and secondary levels (DfE, 2014c) reframed expectations of pupil attainment in each phase while use of statistical progress data increasingly informs targeted interventions for various pupil groups (for example, those designated disadvantaged, by gender, or according to ethnicity). The responsibility of teachers to contribute to literacy development is overt in the Teachers' Standards (DfE, 2011a), which require all to 'demonstrate an understanding of and take responsibility for promoting high standards of literacy, articulacy and the correct use of standard English, whatever the teacher's specialist subject'. Ofsted are unequivocal that 'teachers in a secondary school need to understand that literacy is a key issue regardless of the subject taught' (2013b). In 2015, DfE published guidance on reading across the curriculum that noted that research shows that reading for pleasure brings benefits that help pupils achieve more across the whole curriculum (DfE, 2015d: 18). This publication includes a good deal on phonics, and while much of it focuses on Key Stage 2, it throws valuable light on problems and issues encountered by secondary school pupils in their earlier years.

According to Ofsted (2013b), all pupils should have opportunities to 'develop speaking and listening skills as well as activities that integrate speaking and listening with reading and writing', and in each area make 'cross-curricular links with other subjects'. Writing is considered an 'art, craft and discipline' where review and redrafting are fundamental. This conception of literacy extends beyond 'mechanics' and 'calls for thought and understanding, for recall, selection and analysis of ideas and information, and for coherent, considered and convincing communication' (Ofsted, 2013b). These principles are reflected in examination reform (Ofqual, 2017), where memorization and extended writing have increased in importance in assessment that shifts from coursework to 100% examination and where fine-grained grading will emphasize nuances of articulacy at the highest levels of attainment. As the reforms seek to improve pupil attainment and the UK's position in international league tables of literacy attainment (OECD, 2016), they also aim to reassure employers that school prepares young people for the literacy demands of work.

To develop literacy for individual pupils, the reports *Removing Barriers to Literacy* (Ofsted, 2011) and *Improving Literacy in Secondary Schools* (Ofsted, 2013b) outlined the

benefits of interventions informed by a whole-school perspective. They highlighted the continuing gap in literacy attainment between some groups and the rest of the population. Those making less progress in the secondary phase included Black Caribbean boys, children from low-income families and looked-after children. (Consult Chapter 12 for more detail on this and also Chapter 15.) In addition, one in five children leaving primary school does not reach the expected standard in reading and writing with implications for their progress in the secondary phase. More positively, the reports describe schools where these difficulties are addressed effectively. Practices to support improved progress include teachers holding generally high expectations of pupils' achievement, an emphasis on speaking and listening from an early age, a rigorous approach following a planned sequence of guidance, rigorous assessment practice and attention to individual needs. One item to bear in mind for your early practice in this area is that it is very unlikely that you will suddenly find a single solution to literacy challenges; rather, it is likely to involve working through a process of painstaking adjustment as the effect of various strategies is monitored. Variations in pupil achievement will persist and intervention will be an ongoing process.

Several specific actions are identified in the Ofsted reports that you can incorporate into your own teaching. One asserts that where teachers included 'an objective for literacy in all the lessons, senior managers noted an improvement in outcomes across all subjects, as well as in English' (Ofsted, 2011: 7). Additionally, literacy skills were taught in contexts where language demands and use were 'relevant and meaningful' to learners (2011: 6), indicating attention to real purposes. And at the point of planning, there is 'outstanding use of national test and assessment data to raise the expectations of staff and to set sufficiently challenging targets' (2011: 6). Do you know the reading or spelling ages of the pupils you teach? How does this influence the texts you choose to share with them, or the support you offer for vocabulary development and writing?

Other items relate to the role of an individual teacher within the whole school. Of particular relevance is access to and use of data relating to pupils' transition between Key Stages 2 and 3 (KS2 and KS3). Where this data is not shared or acted upon, Ofsted notes that pupils' progress into KS4 may be limited. They recommend schools designate 'at least one senior member of staff with an excellent knowledge of literacy and its pedagogy' (Ofsted, 2011: 6) who can advise on the stages of language development and how and when to provide additional support. They may also coordinate the work of 'learning mentors' who contribute to programmes of intervention in addition to the core timetable for pupils. Although Ofsted saw few instances of systematic phonics teaching in the secondary schools, leading on this may also become part of the secondary phase remit given the continued difficulties many pupils have with decoding (for example, manifest in stilted reading aloud, even before comprehension is taken into account) and encoding (for instance, rendering words on a page with correct spelling). At the very least, there is scope in the secondary phase for a wider appreciation of how to consider these difficulties diagnostically in support of further progress, and for better awareness of the demanding expectations for KS3 pupils manifest in revised testing arrangements at Year 6 (DfE, 2014c) and demonstrated in the spellings they should have secured by the same age.

16.4 Thinking about literacy in your own subject

When you begin to think about how pupils use words in your own subject, think also of what they need to do in your subject that they perhaps do not do in any other area of school life. What *type* of writing are they asked to do? Are there specific *genres* of writing that they must use, such as reports, instructions or diaries? Are there very specific *purposes* for which they write: to explain, to persuade, to describe or to speculate? In what contexts do they usually write: with a PC, in books or on worksheets? The same principles apply to reading. What sort of texts do they commonly encounter? Are these electronic or paper-based? Do these combine words with images, with pictures, maps or diagrams? Again, the concepts of *genre* and *purpose* become relevant: it may be that pupils look at particular forms of text to find equally distinctive types of information. Speaking and listening activity is no different: do pupils talk to hypothesize, to predict or to recount? Do they need to develop skills of negotiation or collaboration? In each arena of literacy, you will ask pupils to do things pertinent to your subject, and perhaps *only* to your subject, within the whole-school setting. By recognizing your role as a teacher of literacy, you will begin to respond to the urgent issues outlined in *Removing Barriers to Literacy* (Ofsted, 2011). A step further is to recognize what literacy means in your subject, to develop expertise in 'literacy for history' or 'literacy for art', for example. Perhaps we should begin to think instead of *literacies* across the curriculum, given that each area makes unique demands of pupils.

Of course, literacy in your subject is not just about what you ask pupils to do. It is also about the attitudes you foster towards language use and the general atmosphere of your lessons. How do you use display space? If you display key vocabulary on classroom walls, do you ever refer to it as you teach, or ask pupils to interact with the information? How do you introduce pupils to pages in books or details in worksheets? Do they have time to scan for information? Do you give helpful directions, for example guiding the group to the third paragraph down? Do you make good use of presentational resources, of an overhead- or data-projector, to display the text that pupils have in front of them on their desks? Do you take care with your own handwriting on the board or in books? How do pupils feel in your lessons about asking about spellings? How do you respond to inaccuracies of pupil spelling that occur when they attempt to use unfamiliar or ambitious vocabulary in their writing? How do you organize pupil talk? Do they share ideas prior to writing, have thinking time before putting pen to paper or finger to keyboard?

Each question here deserves careful reflection. The ways in which you respond, and what you *actually do* as a teacher, culminate to affect how pupils communicate with each other and with you. To some extent you determine the value they attach to words and activity with language, with a bearing too on their propensity and facility to communicate in environments not only beyond your lessons but also beyond the world of school.

16.5 Key words in your subject

A good place to begin in your consideration of subject-specific literacy is at the level of individual words. The important words, often the jargon of subjects, have come to be known as 'key words', and it is often these that you see presented around the school environment, in specially demarcated areas of a whiteboard or across classroom walls. How do pupils come to understand the concepts conveyed by the words, and how do they begin to use them in context, in their own talk and in their own writing?

In her book about the language needs of learners with English as an additional language (EAL), Norah McWilliam (1998) details an excellent and versatile strategy that has merits across subjects and for all learners. She calls it 'rich scripting', a process that involves pupils bringing their existing knowledge of language to bear on words they encounter in subject-specific settings. Sometimes these words may be familiar to them in other contexts but can have very precise meanings and uses within a specialism. McWilliam provides the example of 'peak' in geography, which pupils may already know through everyday idioms such as 'peak performance' or 'career peak'. Other examples might include 'scale', used differently across maths, music and art, possibly known to pupils beyond school as a concrete noun (for example, as in bathroom scales or dragon scales) or as a verb (for instance, 'to scale the rock face'). McWilliam's strategy is about making explicit the associations and resonances of any given word, so pupils can understand better its distinct meaning in the subject context, but also so that in heard speech they can distinguish it from homophones – words that sound the same – so that they fully understand its use in the immediate context (returning to an earlier example, a peak in geography is not the same as a 'peek'). Addressing such subtleties can be helpful in support of learners with EAL, but also valuable in making all pupils alert and sensitive to the nuances of words, in creating language-rich classrooms.

If you use key words on displays to enrich the environment, use them to aid your teaching and to assist pupils. Quick reference to a word in print to support spoken use can be of help to pupils who benefit from visual learning strategies. The connection may help them to assimilate the spelling of the word by seeing its letters and remembering its shape. You may also wish to present different classes of word on different coloured paper, such as yellow for nouns ('bunsen burner', 'test tube', 'tripod') and green for verbs ('react', 'liquefy', 'combust'). If pupils are to be helped to learn about these different classes, a common colour code is probably best adopted consistently across a school.

No doubt you will wish to support pupils in accurate spelling of key vocabulary, extending the very deliberate introduction to word lists pupils will be familiar with from KS1 and KS2. Ensure you appraise yourself of the various ways in which individuals learn spellings: some prefer to see words written down, some need them sounded out, others have to know how it feels to write the word themselves, while others remember through mnemonics or word games (for example, to get the commonly misspelt 'necessary' right, remember 'one collar, two sleeves'). At the same time, try to understand the reasons why words are misspelt. Does the pupil make a guess based, perhaps reasonably, on how the word sounds? Has the word been confused with a commonly used homophone? Does the pupil regularly forget to double consonants where they should?

16.6 Supporting pupils with reading in your subject

It is easy to take pupils' reading in your subject for granted but, bearing in mind that in 2012 England was outperformed by 17 other countries in reading and 17% of 15-year-olds did not reach the minimum standard (DfE, 2015d: 8), this would be unwise.

It is likely that a significant amount of the information with which pupils are asked to engage in your subject is encountered through the verbal mode, in print or on screen. Often written text will be combined with other visual items such as photographs, flow charts or illustrations. Even within written text, graphic elements such as typography, headings and spacing influence how the text is read and sometimes dictate how it should be approached.

If we come to such material as experts well-versed in our specialisms and familiar with their text types, it can be easy to assume that pupils also know how to approach them.

However, we should appreciate that pupils may not understand what we take for granted. Many textbooks, for instance, are not designed to be read from the top left corner then across and down, line by line, every word to be taken in. Instead, they often comprise columns and figures, between which the reader's gaze may move back and forth, and it may be the case that different parts of the page can be rapidly scanned while others require close reading. Such approaches to reading need to be made explicit to pupils, and ideally demonstrated (or 'modelled') so that they all have equal opportunity to access curricular content. It is worth reflecting too on the demands of internet reading, where texts incorporate moving images and sound, and are organized in complex, non-linear arrangements. This will be especially important when setting homework to complete online, for instance through virtual learning interfaces. Where these are new to pupils, they are likely to need some guidance in navigating them and the mode of reading required. Some commentators reflect on such reading in the context of 'multiliteracies' (Kress, 2003) or 'new literacies' (Cope and Kalantzis, 2000), stressing that it is rare for contemporary texts to isolate the verbal mode. It thus becomes important to understand how readers approach and make meaning from a non-verbal item such as a diagram, just as it is useful to consider how it is understood in relation to any accompanying verbal text. Unsworth (2001) is especially pertinent in this respect, offering detailed analyses of specialized school textbooks and identifying distinct grammars of design for each.

Having reflected on how you help pupils orient themselves to the texts relevant to your subject, it is probable that you will want them to read for specific purposes and for particular information. But how do you prevent reading becoming a relatively passive activity, where, even though eyes glance over a page, detail may not be assimilated? 'Directed activities for reading and thinking' or 'directed activities related to texts' [or 'DARTs'; see Guppy and Hughes (1999) for the original idea and https//eric.ed.gov for later amplification] is a term used to describe strategies that marry literacy skills with thinking skills, requiring pupils to engage deliberately and often interrogatively with the texts before them, usually in pairs or groups rather than in silent, individual reading. Examples of DARTs include:

- providing pupils with a prose text that has been disrupted, perhaps with paragraphs presented out of sequence, which pupils must restore to chronological order;

- asking pupils to shape a given number of questions about a text, possibly requiring some that relate to factual or literal details within the text (reading the lines), some that respond to bias or inferred meanings (reading between the lines), and some that consider the text in context, for instance how it came to be written or how it might be used (reading beyond the lines); and

- summarizing the text in a given number of words (necessitating selection of detail) or representing it in a different form (for example, transforming a series of instructions into a flow chart).

All require careful attention to the detail of texts, invite discussion and promote higher-order cognition [according to Bloom's taxonomy (Bloom *et al.*, 1956); see Chapter 5), and most approaches can be applied to a variety of texts across many subject disciplines. They are all likely to influence pupils' engagement with your subject.

Task 16.2

Identify five genres of text encountered by pupils in your subject. For each, try to articulate the reading strategies employed by readers when approaching that genre.

16.7 Supporting pupils with writing in your subject

Pupils write differently in different subjects. In some areas, they are frequently asked to write lengthy extended prose; in some, short answers of only a couple of sentences, even one or two words, may be legitimate. Elsewhere, pupils may be asked to write poems and letters, create newspaper articles or make posters. Expectations of how their work will be presented will also vary. In some instances, much of their writing will be considered 'draft', not intended for public viewing or 'best' formal presentation. At other times, they may be writing for display on the classroom wall, or for sharing on a school website or in a discussion forum. Behind each purpose for writing and mode of presentation lie numerous decisions, assumptions and skills: as with reading skills, these need to be addressed overtly with a class.

Research into the written responses of pupils in examinations (Ofsted, 2003), and more general consideration of their writing across several genres (Lewis and Wray, 1998), has suggested that pupils are not always familiar with the conventions of the types of writing they are asked to do in school. Furthermore, if they have at least some success with any given genre, they often have difficulty sustaining the quality of their writing across a whole piece, with concluding sections often relatively weak. It also seems that facility with different genres can relate to gender. Some findings suggest that boys, through their reading, may be relatively comfortable with quite a range of non-fiction forms, and that girls tend to be more at ease with a broader repertoire of fiction and 'literary' forms (Lynn and Mikk, 2009).

The strategy for LAC offers a range of responses to this background. To ensure pupils are familiar with the conventions of, say, fieldwork report writing in geography or match report writing in PE, it is recommended that teachers provide pupils with 'models' for these types of writing. These are examples of successful writing in the chosen genre, which the teacher can use to illustrate important conventions essential to the text type. This might involve looking closely at the organization of the text, noting the focus of each paragraph and common phrases that contribute to the clarity of the piece, perhaps drawing attention to a sequence ('First . . .', 'Second . . .', 'In summary . . .') or to the juxtaposition of statements ('On one hand . . .', 'Conversely . . .', 'In contrast with . . .'). Each genre will have its own distinct phrases, essential to a pupil's ability to present and develop ideas in writing, and to their likelihood of writing successfully within the conventions of the genre at hand.

Not only can teachers present 'models' so that pupils have a sense of how their finished writing might look, they are also advised to model the *process* of writing in the given genre. This can involve demonstrating the writing process via a whiteboard, overhead projector or interactive board, shaping sentences in front of pupils and articulating the decisions you make as a writer. What thinking lies behind the sentence you have just written? Why is the next sentence important in developing the idea? Why have you decided on those areas of focus for the six paragraphs that make up the main body of the writing?

A complementary approach to the writing process is the use of 'writing frames', formats that provide a scaffold for pupils' own attempts at writing in a given genre. Generally, these identify the key organizational elements of a text, usually through boxes arranged on a worksheet, and include conventional phrases, often connectives, that act as a prompt for a pupil's writing. Such frames can provide a means of differentiating support for writing in your lessons and can be designed to include varying degrees of detail. It is important, however, that the frames do not become inhibitive. If not carefully presented, they can restrict pupils' responses, as discussed by Fones (2001), who describes a process of developing writing frames to support able writers within English without limiting their thinking. Another example of writing frames, this particular instance for science, can be found in Subramaniam (2010).

Task 16.3

Choose one genre in which pupils are likely to write in your subject. Create a writing frame to support them in recognizing the structural features and connectives relevant to the genre.

16.8 Supporting pupils' speaking and listening in your subject

Like writing, the talk-based activity you ask pupils to do can be considered along the lines of genre. In what types of talk do you ask pupils to participate? Do they give talks to an audience, perhaps with presentational devices such as posters, flipcharts or PowerPoint? Are they asked to work through formal debates, opposing teams thrashing out an issue? Do you want them to take part in role plays, for example as members of a community debating an issue at a council meeting? Do they solve problems in groups? Once more, the types of talk they engage in have specific demands, organizational features and distinct turns of phrase, and may also require a certain register of speech (some may necessitate Standard English, in others a colloquial idiom will be more apt).

The same principles of 'modelling' apply. In the case of a formal debate, maybe pupils should see an extract of a debate in the Commons, noting conventions of address ('With respect to the Right Honourable lady . . .', 'Mr Speaker . . .', 'Objection!'); in the case of a presentation to other members of the class, perhaps give a short talk yourself, use examples from video, or invite another pupil (a sixth-former?) to demonstrate. If you are using a complex group work activity, be sure that at the first attempt the process is highly structured and regard it as a model for future work; it will take time for pupils to understand and be comfortable with the procedure. In each case, you may find it helps to give pupils prompt sheets of the key phrases that support discussion, especially in group situations. Do pupils know how to signal polite disagreement with one another or how to put an opposing view without offence or aggression? Can they build on the comments of others ('Just like Mary said, I think . . .'), or open the floor for peers ('Is there anything you'd like to add . . .')? Prompts like these can contribute to pupil talk becoming self-sustaining, with less need for teacher intervention, just as writing frames support individual responses on the page.

Bear in mind the relationship between talking in groups and thinking skills. In this respect, the work of Vygotsky (1986) remains relevant today (see Chapter 4). Especially important is the idea that talk acts as a means of rehearsing, clarifying and refining ideas and these processes support the assimilation of those ideas in the mind of the individual ('intramentally'), aiding understanding and recall. The way in which you organize groups will be very significant, and factors to consider include: the propensity of pupils to share ideas or, conversely, to refrain from involvement; potential clashes of personality; the ability of pupils to manage and sustain their own conversation; and the knowledge and confidence of individuals in relation to the topic in hand. You are unlikely to leave the selection of groups to chance: the decisions you make cannot be separated from principles of behaviour management, differentiation or inclusive education.

Task 16.4

Identify a talk-based task in your subject that could be conducted through group work.

(a) What ground rules do you need to establish for the task?
(b) List phrases that are likely to help pupils organize the discussion, for beginning their contributions and for inviting others to speak.
(c) Try to identify the thinking skills developed as part of the task, with particular attention to those developed through pupils' dialogue that would be unlikely to occur in individual writing activities based on the same topic or idea.

16.9 Conclusion

Whether or not cross-curricular literacy has a profile in individual schools or government thinking, literacy is always an issue for a teacher, whatever their specialism. Moreover, as *Removing Barriers to Literacy* (Ofsted, 2011) describes, it is an urgent matter for many pupils in terms of their immediate engagement in school, but also one with a profound impact on their life-opportunities beyond. It is intimately connected with their enjoyment of and success in a subject, and in turn with their self-esteem. Literacy skills are at the heart of every pupil's ability to find a way into subjects and to access curriculum content. Often, too, they are central to a pupil's ability to succeed in assessments, especially formal and summative assessments, in a system where responses written on paper in silent exam conditions predominate. Ultimately, literacy is about communication and, because communication is about our relationship with others, it is about identity and participation. Literacy is an issue for education in the broadest sense, part of the 'hidden curriculum' as much as the overt curriculum, and always there.

Recommendations for further reading

Klein, C. and Millar, R.R. (1990) *Unscrambling Spelling*. London: Hodder & Stoughton.
Lewis, M. and Wray, D. (eds.) (2000) *Literacy in the Secondary School*. London: David Fulton.

McWilliam, N. (1998) *What's in a Word?* London: Trentham Books.

Mercer, N. and Hodgkinson, S. (eds.) (2008) *Exploring Talk in School.* London: Sage.

The National Strategies (Secondary) (2009) *Key Leaflet: Reading for real, purposeful and relevant contexts.*

Unsworth, L. (2001) *Teaching Multiliteracies Across the Curriculum.* Maidenhead: Open University Press.

Webliography

National Literacy Trust: http://www.literacytrust.org.uk/

17

Numeracy and mathematics across the curriculum

Fay Baldry, Jenni Ingram and Andrea Pitt

17.1 Introduction

Levels of numeracy and mathematical capability are widely recognized as being important at both an individual and societal level. For instance, adults with low numeracy skills are more likely to have lower incomes and poorer health (NIACE, 2011), and low levels of adult numeracy have been estimated to cost the UK economy between £6 billion and £32 billion per annum (Pro Bono Economics, 2014). The Organization for Economic Cooperation and Development (OECD) reports that in England young adults' performance in numeracy is on par with previous generations; however, with levels of numeracy rising in most of its member countries, this equates to a relative decline (Kuczera *et al.*, 2016). Bridging this performance gap by raising levels of numeracy is a constituent part of the UK Government's industrial strategy (HM Government, 2017), and it could be argued that one of the principal responsibilities of all teachers today is the improvement of young people's numeracy and mathematical capabilities.

The uses and meaning of the term 'numeracy' have changed over time, but a distinction that is often made is that numeracy is mathematics that can be applied elsewhere. Modern uses of the word 'numeracy' would include the ability to interpret data in different quantitative representations (for example, graphs and flow diagrams) and have the disposition to engage in mathematical reasoning in a range of contexts (Karaali *et al.*, 2016). Terms such as 'quantitative literacy' and 'mathematical literacy' are also widely used when discussing the interface between mathematics and real-world contexts.

Numeracy and mathematics may appear to be more relevant in some curriculum subjects than others, but all teachers have a role in supporting pupils to develop both the skills and the habits of mind required to be mathematically literate. Indeed, the National Curriculum clearly indicates that developing numeracy and mathematical reasoning is the responsibility of all teachers (DfE, 2013c). Moreover, it is also argued that 'confidence in numeracy and other mathematical skills is a precondition of success across the national curriculum' (DfE, 2013c: 9), so developing pupils' mathematical literacy should contribute to pupils' overall progress.

We begin this chapter by examining a range of definitions and interpretations of the term 'numeracy' and then explore the importance of numeracy and mathematics. Next, we examine some examples of where numeracy and mathematics can be found in a range of curriculum subjects, and how a range of curriculum subjects can support the development of pupils' skills and understanding. We end by offering suggestions as to how you can support the development of numeracy in your own teaching.

By the end of this chapter, you should:

- understand the variety of ways numeracy has been defined and the implications these might have for teaching and learning;
- understand the broader implications of low levels of numeracy;
- be ready to consider the mathematical opportunities and demands in your own subject area.

17.2 What are numeracy and mathematical literacy, today and tomorrow?

There is no common definition of 'numeracy' or what it might mean to be 'numerate'. There is also a range of definitions and uses of terms like 'mathematical literacy' and 'mathematical reasoning', which are often treated as synonymous with numeracy. These definitions and uses are important, however, because they influence policies and practices in schools and employment. In this section, we explore this variation and the implications these might have for teaching and learning.

Task 17.1

- How would you define numeracy?
- What concepts and skills do you think are needed for an adult to be considered numerate?
- What do you think is the relationship between numeracy, mathematical literacy and mathematics?

Numeracy was first introduced in the Crowther Report (CACE, 1959) as a word to represent the mirror image of literacy. The Cockcroft Report (DES, 1982), however, uses the term 'numerate' to imply:

> the possession of two attributes. The first of these is an 'at-homeness' with numbers and an ability to make use of mathematical skills which enables an individual to cope with the practical mathematical demands of his everyday life. The second is an ability to have some appreciation of information which is presented in mathematical terms, for instance in graphs, charts or tables or by reference to percentage increase or decrease. Taken together, these imply that a numerate person should be expected to be able to appreciate and understand some of the ways in which mathematics can be used as a means of communication.
>
> (DES, 1982: 11, para. 39)

However, many people at the time of writing of the Cockcroft Report saw numeracy as the ability to perform numerical calculations and little more. And today, many people continue to perceive numeracy as restricted to numerical calculation and arithmetic.

With the introduction of the National Numeracy Strategy in 1996, further refinements of the meaning of 'numeracy' developed. There, the definition was given as 'a proficiency which involves confidence and competence with numbers and measures ... and an inclination and ability to solve number problems in a variety of contexts' (DfEE, 1999: 4), which again appears to restrict numeracy to working with numbers, but in practice the guidance included examples of generalizing and working with data. The *Numeracy Counts* report, compiled by NIACE (2011), continued to shift the focus from numeracy being about skills to more about mathematical thinking, confidence and comfortableness when working with numbers. This includes decisions about whether to use mathematics in a particular situation, what mathematics it is appropriate to use and how to use the mathematical result within the context in which you are working.

The term 'mathematical literacy' is used across the world in a similar way to numeracy (Vacher, 2014), although definitions and uses do vary. For example, the OECD, in their *Framework for the Survey of Adult Skills*, defines numeracy as:

> the ability to access, use, interpret and communicate mathematical information and ideas, in order to engage in and manage the mathematical demands of a range of situations in adult life.
>
> (OECD, 2012: 33)

The OECD, in contrast, define 'mathematical literacy' within their Programme for International Student Assessment (PISA) as:

> an individual's capacity to formulate, employ, and interpret mathematics in a variety of contexts. It includes reasoning mathematically and using mathematical concepts, procedures, facts and tools to describe, explain and predict phenomena. It assists individuals to recognise the role that mathematics plays in the world and to make the well-founded judgments and decisions needed by constructive, engaged and reflective citizens.
>
> (OECD, 2013: 25)

These definitions seem to imply a hierarchy, with mathematical literacy having a broader and more sophisticated definition than numeracy; so, while some use these terms interchangeably, definitions can vary in scope in terms of mathematics and the roles and responsibilities associated with being a numerate citizen (Karaali *et al.*, 2016). The UK performance in PISA tables is seen as a driver in government policy-making (Jerrim and Choi, 2014), so the OECD definition of 'mathematical literacy' could be of relevance to the English education system. After recent (2014) changes, the National Curriculum no longer defines numeracy explicitly, but it is used in a range of curriculum areas to describe knowledge, skills and techniques.

As these definitions show, being numerate involves more than the mathematical knowledge, skills and techniques needed to solve problems within any particular context. It includes contextual knowledge, such as an awareness of the relationship between the context and the choices of skills and techniques needed, and the confidence and disposition to interpret and find sufficient information in order to make decisions and judgements. These shifts in focus reflect the growing need to see and interpret mathematics in a variety of contexts rather than performing accurate calculations. Most people today carry a calculator in the form of a mobile phone or smartphone, which can perform accurate calculations if they are required, but responsibility for knowing which calculations to perform, what the results should look like and what to do with the result still lies with the individual.

17.3 History of government initiatives relating to numeracy and mathematics

The National Numeracy Strategy (NNS) was developed out of a pilot project in 1996. This was first implemented nationally in English primary schools in 1999 and subsequently extended to Key Stage 3 (KS3) in 2001. Although the focus of the NNS was on mental strategies for calculation and the role of whole-class interactive teaching, all aspects of the mathematics national curriculum were included. Also in 2001, the Department for Education and Skills (DfES) launched a 'Numeracy across the Curriculum' initiative whereby schools with KS3 pupils were expected to run whole-school initiatives and training to encourage subject departments to collaborate to raise standards in numeracy. An Ofsted evaluation in 2005 claimed that, although there was variation between schools, the NNS had contributed to an increase in overall attainment in mathematics. However, in most schools, low priority was given to cross-curricular numeracy and consequently little progress was made with numeracy across the curriculum (Ofsted, 2005).

While the NNS was not a statutory requirement, significant government backing, including Ofsted scrutiny, did result in its wide adoption in schools. In 2011, after a change in government, the strategies ended, and the resources and materials were archived and not replaced. Subsequent government policy has focused on curriculum changes, with a new national curriculum in 2014 and revisions to GCSEs in 2016. The government argued that the reforms would bring more rigour to the curriculum through more demanding knowledge-rich content; a stated aim was to address the attainment gap that international comparisons such as TIMMS indicated exists between the UK and more successful jurisdictions (DfE, 2013b).

In 2015, funding regulations were changed so that pupils who did not achieve a Level 4 (previously a grade C) by the end of KS4, and who stayed in education, were required to continue with a mathematics course, either a GCSE, GCSE equivalent or a stepping-stone qualification dependent on prior attainment (Education Funding Agency, 2016). This is partially in response to an OECD report on their Survey of Adult Skills that stated England's performance is 'well below average for numeracy relative to other OECD countries' (Kuczera *et al.*, 2016: 9); in particular, more pupils are leaving education with low-level numeracy skills than in many other counties. However, Ofsted's initial evaluation was that 'while the policy's intention to improve . . . numeracy levels is well intentioned, the implementation of the policy is not having the desired impact in practice' (Ofsted, 2016: 78).

17.4 The importance of being numerate

There is considerable evidence that levels of numeracy affect societal well-being and economic prosperity at both individual and wider societal levels. For example, adults with low levels of numeracy are more likely to have lower living standards and poorer health (OECD, 2016). Costs for employers, in terms of lower output and productivity, have been estimated at £3 billion per year, and lost government revenue and additional benefit payments have been estimated at £8 billion per year (Pro Bono Economics, 2014). However, there are effects beyond the financial, with evidence suggesting that levels of participation in society, such as engagement with political processes, are also related to attainment of basic skills.

The role of numeracy and mathematical understanding in decision-making has been studied in a range of contexts, particularly in relation to the understanding of risk. Studies have shown that the presentational format of information can affect interpretation, with distortion of risk perception being more pronounced for individuals with low numeracy (Peters, 2008; Reyna *et al.*, 2009). For example, 10%, '1 in 10' and '10 in 100' are not always interpreted as representing the same level of risk, and there are similar issues with information presented as '10% chance of complications' compared with '90% chance of success'. A National Numeracy article reported that nearly half of the people surveyed by Cancer Research were unable to identify which of '1 in 100', '1 in 10' or '1 in 1,000' represented the greatest chance of contracting a disease (National Numeracy, 2015). Studies have also looked for a relationship between patients' numeracy and management of chronic diseases, such as diabetes and asthma, with low numeracy being associated with poorer management (Apter *et al.*, 2006; Marden *et al.*, 2012). Issues directly related to mathematics, such as difficulties in reading a peak flow meter, were identified in some case studies (National Numeracy, 2015) but broader issues, such as numeracy being associated with self-efficacy, were also found (Cavanaugh *et al.*, 2008).

Technological developments continue to contribute to substantial changes in the way we live our lives, including the nature of employment, where the widespread use of technology is transforming the type, rather than the quantity, of numerical skills needed. This includes entry-level or more traditional 'manual' jobs, where technology is extending the range of task expected; for example, stock control can move from a manager's office to the shop floor (OECD, 2016). If a sizable proportion of adults have low skills, then the introduction of new working practices and productivity-enhancing technologies becomes increasingly problematic (OECD, 2016). In a knowledge-based economy, roles characterized by more complex communication and cognitive loads are likely to demand that mathematical skills are embedded in analytical problem-solving, justification of decisions and cross-disciplinary working. In order to compete in this global economy, employers have highlighted the need for an increasing number of numerically literate people to work at all levels within business organizations (HM Government, 2017).

As teachers, we have a responsibility to counteract the widely held view that it is acceptable to have poor standards of mathematics: 'we need a cultural shift in our attitude to maths and numeracy' (NIACE, 2011: 4). Numeracy is more than a 'toolkit' of numerical approaches that pupils can select from to perform calculations; it is a way of thinking that is interwoven into problem-solving, critical analysis and other higher-level cognitive skills. Numeracy impacts on both personal and societal well-being, and we all share the responsibility of raising pupils' understanding of the relevance and importance of numeracy and mathematics as well as their personal proficiency. As the National Curriculum (DfE, 2013c: 9) states, 'teachers should develop pupils' numeracy and mathematical reasoning in all subjects so that they understand and appreciate the importance of mathematics'.

17.5 Numeracy and mathematics within curriculum subjects: authentic contexts for mathematics

Mathematical encounters in other subjects can provide pupils with real and authentic contexts that enable effective learning to occur. These opportunities can support the development of pupils' numeracy and extend the range of approaches pupils can take to the understanding of other curriculum areas. However, context can also be problematic, as pupils need to simultaneously retain an understanding of the context, how mathematics is being used to model the context and the mathematics. Numeracy and mathematics appear in myriad forms and contexts; the following section discusses a small number of cases to act as exemplars as to how mathematical reasoning can be related to other curriculum subjects.

Task 17.2

Reflect on the following question in your teaching experience: What numeracy and mathematics are used in your subject?

Within the National Curriculum subject specifications, numeracy and mathematics appear in a variant of explicit and implicit forms. For example, mathematics is specifically mentioned in science, computing and design technology, whereas geography contains mathematical representations, such as graphs, and history makes reference to the analysis of trends over time. However, even when numeracy and mathematics are more explicitly mentioned, care is needed as different subjects may treat apparently similar concepts in different ways. One simple example that would be familiar to most science and mathematics teachers is that of a line of best fit: in science, it is a line or curve that best fits the data, whereas in mathematics, until GCSE at least, this term only applies to straight lines. Another example is that pupils are expected to calculate inter-quartile ranges from box plots in mathematics, while using dispersion graphs in geography.

Probably one of the most important issues is pupils' confidence and comfortableness in using and interpreting mathematical representations, such as numbers, graphs and tables. Pupils will meet a variety of graphs in mathematics classrooms, but there are shifts in both use and form as pupils move to other subjects. For example, in science, one of the common approaches to analysing experimental results is to plot data as a graph, from which pupils are expected to draw conclusions; in general, pupils would have met those types of graphs in mathematics lessons. This offers an authentic context, as the mathematical representation is an integral part of the scientific process. However, the pupils may also have to negotiate the imprecise nature of results, a factor that rarely has to be taken into account in the mathematics classroom. In geography, data is presented in a wide variety of ways and can include multiple features on one representation. For example, a climate graph often combines temperature and rainfall, using a line graph for average temperature and a bar graph for precipitation. Pupils may have little prior experience of these features, such as the requirement for two scales. Moreover, some aspects may contradict prior experiences, such as gaps being acceptable between bars.

The representation of frequencies is the key feature of many graphs and diagrams. For example, height represents frequency in bar charts and the angle represents relative frequency in pie charts, but in other situations different features, such as colour, width or area can be used. Visual representations of frequency can be provided by, say, circles placed on maps, with area proportional to a population, or by arrows, with width proportional to the flow of goods or energy transfer. While these formats may be more frequently met in subjects like geography and science, automatic computer generation has diversified both form and use. For example, word clouds can present the content of any given text by displaying the words with their prevalence indicated by font size and strength of colour.

These can, for instance, be used in the classroom by pupils in support of their analysis of texts in English (Pearcy, 2016). The interpretation of these types of representation can range from an intuitive 'looking bigger' through to calculations that may require the interrogation of additional information, such as that provided in a key. The underlying mathematical principle, however, is that frequency can be represented in different ways; the inclusion of an explicit discussion of this principle should offer the pupils an opportunity to develop their mathematical understanding.

Pupils will experience a range of contexts where two-dimensional representations of three-dimensional objects are used. For instance, in design and technology (D&T), as in mathematics, pupils are expected to be able to move between orthographic projections (front, side and plan views) and isometric drawings, where angle between projected axes are 120° (see Figure 17.1). Both offer the advantage that measurements can be taken from the drawings, but they are distorted in terms that neither offer the perspective of human vision. D&T does also introduce pupils to more realistic perspectives but providing a context where the ability to take measurements has practical meaning offers an authentic context for engaging with otherwise unrealistic images. The requirement to visualize objects from two-dimensional images features in many subjects. For instance, geography includes the use of isolines, which are lines that link different places with the same value. Examples include contour lines that join places that are the same height above sea level and isobars that link points with the same atmospheric pressure. In science, pupils would meet diagrams that use lines to represent concepts not directly visible, such as forces or magnetic fields. Studies have shown that pupils often struggle with these types of visualizations (Ishikawa and Kastens, 2005; Gilbert, 2008). A cube is a familiar object, and most can 'see' a cube from the representation in Figure 17.1, but this same representation can also be interpreted as a two-dimensional (flat) hexagon split into three rhombi or three inside faces of part of a cube. In many other circumstances, we are asking pupils to visualize less familiar situations and they may need structured support in order to do so.

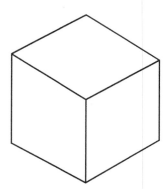

Figure 17.1 Example of an isometric drawing of a cube

A wide range of sources, including numerical representations of situations, could potentially be discarded or misinterpreted in the analysis of issues because of uncertainty over the meaning of the mathematical representations. By developing pupils' numeracy and mathematical reasoning, we are supporting them to both understand and begin to improve interdisciplinary ways of working. Embedding numeracy and mathematics across subjects in meaningful ways can impact on teaching effectiveness, pupils' motivation and developing ways of working. Problems arising in the context of other subjects that genuinely require mathematical approaches to solve can offer authentic situations where the real value of numeracy and mathematics is highlighted. Pupils may be more motivated to learn mathematical skills as they are using them in ways that are relevant to them and where, because of the context, they see a purpose for developing them (Ainley, 2008).

While the UK Government has drawn back from advocating specific cross-curricular numeracy projects, the issues facing the world today are not confined to particular subjects. For example, the problems arising from population growth, sustainability and depleting natural resources all draw any possible solutions from a wide range of disciplines, including mathematics. In the increasingly complex, interdependent and interrelated world in which we live, all levels of working will require non-routine thinking and communication situated in cross-functional environments. A report by the Centre for the Use of Research & Evidence in Education (CUREE) supports the link between effective learning and learning based in context (Bell *et al.*, 2010). So, working in an interdisciplinary manner not only offers pupils the opportunity to prepare for future working practices, it also has the potential to increase pupils' confidence and competence as they widen their experience of using mathematics in context.

17.6 The nature of reasoning

Numeracy is more than a set of mathematical tools that can be used and applied in other subjects. Numeracy is also about reasoning and problem-solving. This includes pattern spotting; modelling, representing and interpreting situations; and communicating effectively. These processes are also fundamental in other curriculum areas. Many of the humanities subjects include exploring how ideas, experiences and values are portrayed and constructed in various sources. While these sources are often textual, there is a wealth of quantitative material that can be used to supplement these sources. Pupils need to be able to critically analyse both qualitative and quantitative sources and see the strengths and weaknesses of the models used to represent different perspectives.

Many of the creative arts subjects involve the use of patterns, sequences and ratios – most obviously, the symmetry of many artistic works or dances, rhythmic patterns in music and dance, and ratio and proportion in art. You can use graphical representations of the structures of plays, which then enables you to compare and contrast different genres. Many will recognize the works of M.C. Escher, appearing frequently in art and mathematics lessons, providing vivid and unusual access into the worlds of transformations, isometries and topology.

In science, while there are many explicit references to quantitative measures and approaches in the National Curriculum (DfE, 2013c), it may also be argued that there are common concepts described in the 'working mathematically' and' 'working scientifically' sections of the National Curriculum. For example, the notion of making predictions, then interpreting data to test those predictions and to draw reasoned conclusions, would fall within the remit of both subjects. This highlights that the links can move beyond common procedural activities and towards common behaviour and ways of thinking.

17.7 Calculations

The NNS encouraged pupils to develop a range of mental and written strategies to choose flexibly between these when faced with a calculation they could not instinctively answer.

These included the use of an empty number line and multiplication using area and grid methods (Figure 17.2).

The 'area' method:

	40	6
50	2000	300
7	280	42

The 'grid' method

×	40	6
50	2000	300
7	280	42

46 × 57 = 2622

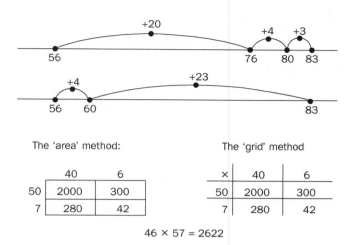

Figure 17.2 Examples of NSS strategies for calculations
Source: DfE, 2013a: 152

The focus did shift with the withdrawal of the National Strategies and the introduction of the 2014 National Curriculum. Mental methods are part of the statutory requirements, but informal representations such as number lines are not mentioned. In terms of written calculations, the focus is clearly on formal methods, with these the only approaches specified (Figure 17.3). However, it is likely that you will encounter pupils who utilize a range of strategies.

Long multiplication

24 × 16 becomes

		2	
		2	4
×		1	6
	2	4	0
	1	4	4
	3	8	4

Answer: 384

124 × 26 becomes

		1	2	
		1	2	4
×			2	6
	2	4	8	0
		7	4	4
	3	2	2	4
	1	1		

Answer: 3224

124 × 26 becomes

		1	2	
		1	2	4
×			2	6
		7	4	4
	2	4	8	0
	3	2	2	4
	1	1		

Answer: 3224

Figure 17.3 National Curriculum written multiplication methods
Source: DfE (2013c: 128).

One of the key skills that pupils need to develop is deciding what method of calculation is appropriate. For some, calculations can be performed quickly and accurately using purely mental skills, while others will require some form of written strategy. However, a third option is using a calculator or a PC to perform calculations. Pupils need to be able to decide when it is appropriate to use a calculator. However, whilst the calculator can perform accurate calculations, pupils still need to choose which calculation to perform, check the reasonableness of the result and interpret this within the context.

17.8 Supporting pupils to be mathematical in your lessons

When pupils encounter mathematical situations in your lesson, you can help them to gain confidence and develop their numeracy and mathematics by:

- discussing the mathematical situation with pupils;
- building in opportunities that draw upon mathematics in an authentic way;
- asking questions such as 'How did you get that answer?', 'How do you know?', 'What does it mean in this context?';
- encouraging pupils to share their ideas and discuss their thinking;
- encouraging explanation, reasoning and justification;
- supporting pupils' own methods of calculating or working, provided they are accurate and appropriate;
- focusing on the conceptual ideas within the mathematics rather than the procedures used to perform calculations;
- listening to pupils;
- talking to the mathematics department in your school to develop coherent approaches to numeracy and mathematics; or
- incorporating genuine data that is often 'messy' rather than artificially 'nice' numbers.

Task 17.3

What opportunities are there for you to support pupils' numeracy and mathematics development in your subject?

17.9 Conclusion

Why have definitions and use of terms such as 'numeracy', 'mathematical literacy' and 'mathematics' continued to evolve? Their prominence serves to highlight the belief of governments and educational and professional institutions in the importance of numeracy and mathematics, with numerous reports indicating the impact on both individuals and the wider community. That their meanings continue to evolve emphasizes that the broad, complex and reflective nature of numeracy and the role of mathematics have yet to be fully embraced by all. We have argued that meeting mathematics in other subjects allows pupils access to those authentic contexts that make numeracy relevant to them.

We have discussed how numeracy and mathematics can enhance the learning of pupils in other subjects and is an integral part of the interdisciplinary approaches that are likely to feature in their future; we would be naïve, however, to believe that new ways of working will be restricted to our *pupils*. As technology develops, we might easily find *ourselves* modelling these very same interdisciplinary approaches, with the knowledge-based subject boundaries being blurred by the increase in demand for non-routine thinking skills.

We therefore conclude it is important for the economic well-being of the country and the life chances of individual pupils that all teachers strive to enhance the learning of numeracy and mathematics in their subjects.

Recommendations for further reading

Ollerton, M. and Watson, A. (2001) *Inclusive Mathematics 11–18*. London: Continuum.

Ward-Penny, R. (2011) *Cross-Curricular Teaching and Learning in the Secondary School: Mathematics.* London: Routledge.

Watson, A., Jones, K. and Pratt, D. (2013) *Key Ideas in Teaching Mathematics: Research-Based Guidance for Ages 3–19*. Oxford: Oxford University Press.

18

Personal, social, health and economic education

Faith Muir

18.1 Introduction

There is an old saying that suggests that the most important things we learn are learnt in nursery school – to line up, take turns and, most important of all, always to flush the toilet. It's a reminder that schools are not simply concerned with the formal, academic curriculum of subjects, but also with pupils' wider development – with their personal, social, health and economic education (PSHEE). We expect schools to play a leading role in the socialization of pupils, preparing them in the most general terms for the demands of adult life, which involves learning to interact effectively with others in a range of settings. It is also about learning to negotiate a path through the intricacies of life in a diverse and rapidly changing society. Moreover, we understand that, while pupils' academic attainments may be powerfully influenced by their cognitive skills and dispositions and the quality of teaching they receive, it is also the case that educational success is affected by self-esteem and the ability to negotiate one's way through the emotional and psychological complexities of childhood and adolescence. These considerations surround schools' work in PSHEE and PSHE (note the absence of 'Economic').

By the end of this chapter, you should:

- understand the aims and current content of PSHEE and PSHE;
- know about some of the methods and issues involved in the organization of PSHEE and PSHE;
- be aware of a range of pedagogic issues and practices concerning the teaching of PSHE and PSHEE.

18.2 Recent developments in personal, social, health and economic education

Personal, social and health education (note the absence of 'economic') has been a non-statutory subject in the secondary curriculum since the National Curriculum (NC) review of 2000. Closely aligned to citizenship, since it became a statutory requirement in 2002, PSHE has continued to help schools fulfil their statutory duties (Education Act 2002; Academies Act 2010) to provide a broadly-based and balanced curriculum that supports pupils' spiritual, moral, cultural, mental and physical development and prepares them for the experiences,

opportunities and responsibilities encountered in their lives. A focused exploration of what is meant by spiritual, moral and cultural development (SMCD) and its interrelationship with PSHE and citizenship is provided in Chapter 14.

The publication of *Every Child Matters* (DfES, 2003a) prompted a major shift in thinking about the potential role of PSHE and how it could help schools contribute to four key ECM outcomes for pupils: (1) enjoy time at school while becoming equipped to achieve their ambitions; (2) gain financial capability skills to achieve economic well-being; (3) stay safe and healthy; and (4) make a positive contribution to society.

Following a further NC review (2006/7), PSHE was renamed personal, social, health *and economic* education (PSHEE) and restructured to comprise two new non-statutory programmes of study at Key Stages 3 and 4 (KS3 and KS4): 'Personal Wellbeing' and 'Economic Wellbeing and Financial Capability'. These identified eight PSHEE teaching strands: sex and relationships education; drug and alcohol education; emotional health and well-being; diet and healthy lifestyle; safety education; careers education; financial capability; and work-related learning including enterprise (Macdonald, 2009). Although the programmes of study were not to last, the foundations of PSHEE as it is today had been clearly defined.

Other initiatives followed, including the SEAL Framework (Social and Emotional Aspects of Learning – in secondary schools from 2007–2010), the National Healthy Schools Programme and the National PSHE CPD Programme, all of which made a positive impact on the status of PSHEE. When the Schools White Paper, *The Importance of Teaching*, was published under the newly elected Coalition government (DfE, 2010b), the value and importance of high-quality PSHEE was further commended, particularly its potential contribution to tackling public health issues and supporting young people's financial decision-making. It called for an internal review to determine how best to improve quality in PSHEE teaching, whilst maintaining that teachers must have flexibility to judge how the subject should be delivered – but made no reference to making the subject statutory.

By the time Ofsted published *Not Yet Good Enough: Personal, Social, Health and Economic Education in Schools* (2013a), the vast majority of schools chose to teach PSHEE in order to fulfil their statutory responsibilities, including sex and relationships education and careers education (introduced in 2012 as a statutory duty for schools to deliver impartial guidance to pupils in Years 9–11). Nevertheless, many programmes lacked rigour, in part due to a lack of teacher confidence in the subject. By 2015, as stated in the House of Commons Education Committee's report, *Life Lessons: PSHE and SRE in Schools* (2015), 40% of schools' PSHEE provision required improvement. Moreover, the Committee noted that the government's strategy for improving PSHEE was weak, not supporting its claim that enhancing the subject's quality was a priority. Crucially, the report recognized that PSHEE must be given statutory status, with SRE forming a core element, in order to ensure provision improved for all pupils. More recently, following calls from many professional and expert bodies (PSHE Association; Public Health England) regarding the need for a whole-school approach to mental health education with *statutory* PSHEE playing a key role, the last government announced (March 2017) that PSHEE should become statutory by September 2019. To this end, the House of Commons Education and Health Committees published *Children and Young People's Mental Health: The Role of Education* (2017) in which they urged the next government to uphold this commitment. Since then, although its future continues to remain uncertain, the Department for Education (DfE) has recently issued a call-for-evidence on changes to the teaching of PSHEE and SRE (December 2017) and Parliament has held a supportive debate on improving the status of PSHEE (February 2018).

> ### Task 18.1
>
> Consider each component of PSHEE. Reflect upon what you think 'personal' may mean, then 'social', and so on. Next, relate these to environments or experiences you anticipate your learners may encounter as they reach maturity and beyond. Note down what you think PSHEE *should* involve and how it differs from 'pastoral care'.

18.3 PSHEE: what's it all about?

The school curriculum is one of the main ways in which schools set out to provide opportunities for all pupils to learn and achieve. The Education Reform Act 1988 saw the overarching aim of the school curriculum as being the promotion of pupils' spiritual, moral, social and cultural development and their preparation for the opportunities, responsibilities and experiences of adult life. This is a challenging task, and one way of thinking about PSHEE is that it can provide the framework that draws together the full range of schools' curriculum work: dealing with issues of pupils' confidence and motivation, supporting them in making the most of their abilities, helping them develop fully as individuals and as members of families and social and economic communities (Ofsted, 2010; DfE, 2010b). In this context, schools' curricula for PSHEE have wide-ranging aims and objectives, but they can generally be grouped into five interrelated areas:

1. Supporting pupils' personal and emotional development, including addressing issues of identity, self-esteem and change, managing feelings, and developing self-confidence, empathy and resilience.
2. Supporting social development, including building healthy relationships in different contexts, becoming a productive member of a diverse community, respecting others' values, attitudes and beliefs, understanding the concept of human rights and responsibilities, and working with others.
3. Supporting physical, mental and emotional health/well-being, including developing and maintaining a safe and healthy lifestyle, managing transition, understanding substance use and misuse, making appropriate sexual and parenting decisions, understanding and managing risk in personal, work-related and social contexts, and knowing how to access help, advice and support.
4. Enabling pupils to take advantage of learning opportunities in school and in their life outside school, addressing issues of decision-making, using critical reflection to clarify values and attitudes, learning and target-setting across the curriculum, developing a 'can-do', enterprising approach and making informed career choices.
5. Supporting their development as critical and informed consumers, producers and citizens, including addressing money management issues, personal budgeting and financial responsibility, employability, learning in work-related contexts and basic business and economic understanding.

It is apparent from these aims that the potential scope of PSHEE in schools is enormous. Guidance is given, in line with all other NC subjects, regarding key concepts, processes, range and content, and curriculum opportunities to be covered. However, each school is invited to develop its own approach, drawing on good practice and setting priorities within the broad framework that relate to pupils' needs, and the range of communities the school serves. In some schools, the task of building a coherent, balanced and well-structured PSHEE curriculum, often with limited teaching time available, has proved challenging; programmes consist of loosely related tasks, each with its own mini-objective. In many schools, there is a taken-for-granted approach to the way PSHEE is planned and delivered, with more concern shown for timetabling and fitting in all the topics that have become traditionally associated with the subject, than reaching an agreed set of overarching aims. Nevertheless, effective PSHEE delivery can be achieved by synthesizing such mini-objectives into broad, holistic aims, which themselves serve as the basis for robust, whole-school curriculum planning.

Pring (1984) introduced a systematic approach to thinking about the place of personal and social education (PSE) – as it was then termed – which still holds true today. In particular, he noted that 'educators' need to understand what it means to be 'a person' if they are to help others grow as persons, and identified four distinctive characteristics of being a person that clearly should underpin the purpose and structure of PSE curricula:

1. A person possesses the capacity to think, reflect, critically engage with – and make sense of – experiences and the values, beliefs and assumptions encountered in life.
2. They can recognize other people as 'persons' in their own right, and are able to relate to them respectfully, appreciating that each holds a distinctive point of view to which it is worth paying attention.
3. A person acts in an intentional and deliberate manner and as such can be held responsible for their actions.
4. Finally, a person is conscious that they are 'a person', with their own distinctive set of values, attitudes and abilities.

PSE was ignored in the original 1998 NC; attempts to develop it in the 1990 NC as a 'cross-curricular dimension' underpinned by 'themes' (economic and industrial understanding; careers education and guidance; health education; education for citizenship; and environmental education) were largely stillborn as schools devoted energies to implementing the NC and its associated testing regimes. From the early 1990s onwards, a continuous, dramatic improvement in the status and position of PSHE in schools developed for a number of reasons. First, a widespread view emerged that the academic curriculum of the NC was insufficient as a framework for thinking about the curriculum as a whole and its relationship to pupils' wider development. These views were linked to general concerns about the place of values in society and the effectiveness of schools in developing young people's values (Haydon, 1997). In 1994, Ofsted published general guidance on *Spiritual, Moral, Social and Cultural Education*, and three years later the School Curriculum and Assessment Authority (SCAA) established a national forum on education and values, aimed at developing general guidance for schools on personal and values education (SCAA, 1997). These developments fed into the NC review of 2000 and to the development of national frameworks for PSHE. These sought to help schools steer a curriculum course through the multiple demands of delivering education for citizenship, health, sex and relationships, alongside a concern to support young people's moral, emotional and personal development. They were supplemented by resurgent interest in schools in the nature of learning across the curriculum and, in particular, interest in ideas such as thinking skills (McGuinness, 1998), emotional literacy (Goleman, 1996) and, in some schools, the development of what the Campaign for Learning called 'learnacy' (Rodd, 2002).

Task 18.2

To what extent do you agree with the government's proposal (April 2017) that schools should include education on social media as part of PSHEE? In your opinion, what should pupils be taught regarding this topic, and why? What skills, abilities and attitudes do they need to develop? What specific problems might emerge for teachers or their schools when planning and delivering this topic?

18.4 Organizing PSHEE provision in schools

Schools vary enormously in terms of the time, resources and importance they attach to PSHEE, not least because of its non-statutory status. In most schools, its coordination has been improved by introducing formal positions of responsibility, and support from a designated member of the senior leadership team. However, the allocation of time, resources and staffing to PSHEE remains a challenge for many schools. One obvious reason for this is that in most – although not all – schools, PSHEE is taught by non-specialist teachers who are not organized into the sort of strong faculties that predominate elsewhere in the curriculum. Delivering PSHEE is a part-time commitment for many teachers, training is not always available and trainee teachers may well receive little guidance on how to teach it. Although some schools may have a specialist or semi-specialist PSHEE team, it remains the case that almost all teachers can expect to teach it at some point in their career – often to pupils for whom they are form tutors. Given the complexity of the PSHEE curriculum, the range of topics that may need to be covered, the need to relate those topics to the needs and expectations of demanding adolescents with complex lives, and the sensitivity of many issues in health and particularly sex and relationships education, this is a daunting prospect.

Case Study 18.1

In a large London secondary school, PSHEE is managed by a team of three senior teachers, responsible for Key Stages 3, 4 and 5 respectively, and taught by form tutors. PSHEE lessons last 30 minutes and are delivered concurrently across all Year groups on a weekly basis to all pupils throughout their time at school. The PSHEE team organizes programme content into half-termly thematic units, which are distributed six weeks in advance to tutors, along with flexible lesson plans and useful support materials.

Content is selected in consultation with colleagues responsible for careers education, SMSC (social, moral, spiritual and cultural) development – with which PSHEE is cross-referenced – religious education and citizenship, and tutors delivering PSHEE. The Student

Voice Forum evaluates the programme's relevance to young people and local community priorities. The team also takes into account school policies and priorities, statutory guidance relating, for example, to SRE and online national PSHEE guidance and advice from reliable external agencies. When dealing with controversial issues of a personal or emotional nature, such as female genital mutilation, the school counsellor is also consulted and will provide a briefing for tutors.

External speakers are invited to contribute, such as health professionals, businesses and community representatives – Year 9 classes learn about pregnancy and parenting from local teenage parents. The school firmly believes that PSHEE should be assessed, not least because this adds to the subject's status for pupils, teachers and parents. They ensure that time for peer- and self-reflection is built into lessons, pupils store their work in folders, which are regularly monitored and commented upon, and older pupils can gain accreditation through courses such as the Young Leaders Award.

- How does the organization and delivery of PSHEE in this school compare with what you have seen or experienced in other schools? In your opinion, what may be the key factors that help to make it a successful programme?
- Taking into account the viewpoints of participating pupils, teachers and the local community, make a list of the programme's main benefits and/or disadvantages.
- To what extent do you agree that pupils' attainment/achievement/progress in PSHEE should be assessed? What problems, if any, might occur and what methods would you suggest as appropriate to use in this context?

If you were managing this PSHEE programme, how might you change it?

The teaching of PSHEE can seem quite different from other curriculum subjects, with its own discrete lessons and curriculum guidance. In fact, as evidenced by the school providing the case study, all subjects can and do contribute to pupils' personal and social education as well as to their preparation for adult and working life. Moreover, in all subjects, pupils need to learn to cooperate in groups, to manage time effectively and make effective connections between their cognitive and emotional or 'affective' development. Therefore, schools should aim to develop strong links between their overall curriculum and PSHEE. In terms of content, they need to take into consideration the learning demands made on pupils at different stages of their school life – for example, timing units on managing transition or preparing for work experience when they will be most useful. The most effective schools will also explore the effectiveness of learning processes and styles across the curriculum. For example, they may use lessons to support pupils in reflecting on their own approaches or attitudes to learning, allowing time for identifying barriers to pupil achievement and developing cross-curricular and integrated approaches to addressing and removing these. Finally, they may aspire to become an 'affective school' – that is, one which has developed strong structures for supporting pupils' acquisition of 'emotional literacy' or an understanding of how emotions affect our decisions and actions (Lang, 1999).

Task 18.3

Draw up a list of key themes and topics that you feel would create a relevant and balanced PSHEE curriculum for pupils in Year 9. Reflect on what influenced your choice and consider the impact of the following factors on these pupils: academic and emotional development; physical development; the impact of social experiences outside school; and issues they may be dealing with in terms of money management and career aspirations.

Ask some teachers and pupils to do the same and compare their ideas with yours.

18.5 Teaching PSHEE

A key challenge for many teachers regarding PSHEE relates to pedagogy. The saying, 'I have never let my schooling interfere with my education', sometimes attributed to Mark Twain (1835–1910), though more likely a paraphrase of Grant Allen (1848–1899), reflects a time when 'schooling' consisted of teachers – expert in particular subjects – teaching facts to passive learners. However, PSHEE teachers are rarely 'experts', even though they may be in other areas of the curriculum. Moreover, they are not only tasked with exploring vital concepts, facts and issues but must also provide their pupils with opportunities for developing essential skills, attributes and strategies, whilst encouraging them to reflect on and make decisions about their attitudes, values and beliefs (PSHE Association, 2017). Critically, these are not just things to learn, like facts – they have to be internalized, and this is more likely to be possible as a result of active experience than through passive assimilation. It is equally clear that teaching pupils to work collaboratively and to make effective contributions to group work demands teaching methods that are based on collaborative and group-based planning.

The difficulties are even more deep-rooted though. The outcomes of teaching history or mathematics are frequently clear in terms of pupils' understanding and ability to put into practice what has been taught. The outcomes of teaching a session on HIV/AIDS are more difficult to assess: pupils' understanding of the biology and epidemiology of HIV could be assessed but, in PSHEE, the concern is more likely to be with pupils' ability to make informed decisions about their behaviour some years after the teaching session. More complex still, in many PSHEE sessions, teachers find themselves dealing with pupils' experiences of life situations with which they are personally unfamiliar and may lack confidence – particularly in light of the complex family and personal circumstances of many young people. Finally, the content of PSHEE differs from much of the conventional academic curriculum in some important respects. First, it is frequently process-based – that is, the content of the curriculum is also its medium: concerns with group work, with learning how to learn and with personal decision-making are both the vehicle and the purpose of the curriculum. Second, it is highly learner-dependent in ways that the content of English or science is not. Third, it is sensitive and potentially controversial in many respects – obvious in the case of developing pupils' capacities to make appropriate decisions about their sexual behaviour, but less so in relation to healthy eating or career choices, where there may be tension between teachers' values and those of pupils, parents or powerful social groups. Fourth, it may involve areas that are not touched upon elsewhere in the curriculum, such as coping with stress or cyber-bullying. The responsibility falls upon the PSHEE teacher to deliver, creating considerable challenges unless they are able to call upon the expertise of other subject teachers or external support agencies.

PSHEE lessons are likely to feature specific techniques, including role-play, trust exercises, questioning, discussions and debates, project work, competitions and imaginative use of the internet. Ofsted (2013a) noted that, where PSHEE was taught effectively, teachers made use of different stimuli to aid discussion, such as case studies, scenarios and visual images with thought-provoking messages. In addition, resources and workshops or presentations devised by external agencies may be used (although assessing the integrity of such resources is vital and may also pose a problem for teachers). Although these techniques are used in most subjects, they are likely to feature more strongly in PSHEE because of the focus on values issues and, in particular, on what has been called 'values-clarification' – namely, that the intended outcome of exploring issues through these activities is not a class agreement on a best course of action, but a clearer sense of what is at stake. It follows that in PSHEE, perhaps more so than anywhere else in the curriculum, a teacher's role may be to ask pupils to clarify their thinking and refine ideas rather than to correct misconceptions and errors. In PSHEE, it is a teacher's responsibility to allow diversity of views and to protect dissent. In PSHEE, exploring the debate may be more important than reaching a particular outcome.

18.6 PSHEE pedagogies

According to Ekwall and Shanker (1988), people generally recall:

- 10% of what they read;
- 20% of what they hear;
- 30% of what they see;
- 50% of what they both see and hear;
- 70% of what they say;
- 90% of what they simultaneously say and do.

Arguably, pedagogies applied to the teaching of PSHEE need to be particularly mindful of these findings, given that pupils are required to recall not just facts but experiences, feelings and emotions.

Question Time

Perhaps more often than in other subjects, PSHEE requires participants to be pro-active in setting the agenda for their lesson. 'Question Time' is a useful activity in this respect: a range of visual stimuli/resources relating to the lesson topic are scattered around the classroom, and pupils take a few minutes to visit each item and devise a question about each one. In a circle, they then ask their questions to stimulate discussion.

Centre of the Universe

This is a technique used to involve the whole class in discussion. Arrange chairs in a circle and in the middle mark out a circle representing the Centre of the Universe. A volunteer stands in the centre and is invited to make a comment about a particular subject – for example, that Birmingham is the centre of the universe because Birmingham City Football Club plays there. Anyone agreeing will stand as close to them as they feel their strength of agreement to be. If they totally agree, they will stand in the Centre of the Universe with the original volunteer. Those disagreeing remain seated. Either the original pupil or someone else in the Centre of the Universe then makes another statement about the subject, and so on. This helps to establish how class members feel about a specific topic.

Thought showering

This can be undertaken as a whole-class activity or with smaller groups who then pool their results. It involves making a list of related ideas without thinking carefully about what springs to mind. Everything that participants suggest is recorded without discussion. No ideas are rejected. A thought-showering exercise should be spontaneous and brief. Some advantages of the technique include:

- everybody is equal and has a contribution to make;
- all ideas are accepted;
- it is a quick way of gaining a lot of information;
- it can help a group leader to assess the level of understanding;
- it is cooperative and open-minded;
- it can help with problem-solving;
- it helps develop self-confidence.

Ranking

There are various methods of ranking, which basically entails listing a series of statements, facts or images according to the demands of the task. For example, ranking a set of opinions from agreement to disagreement or a series of photographs from the most to the least stereotypical image. It is important to provide each statement or picture on a separate card so that they can be manoeuvred during discussion. Items can be ranked in order, or 'diamond ranked' in an activity sometimes known as a 'Diamond Nine'. The aim is to arrange nine different cards into a diamond formation with the highest priority card at the top and the rest placed in descending order of importance. This is useful with, for example, value statements where it may not be possible to create a strict hierarchy. A variation, known as 'Twos and Fours', involves giving pairs of pupils a set of six statements/points. Their task is to decide which four are the most important and discard two. Pupils then form groups of four and have to agree on the four most important statements out of eight. This process is repeated in groups of eight, after which each group reports on their choices, followed by a whole-class discussion.

Values continuum

Individuals consider where they stand on particular issues and rank themselves physically, in a line. This can also be done using statements on pieces of paper but the act of taking a 'standpoint' – for instance, 'Strongly agree' through to 'Strongly disagree' – may be more thought-provoking. Having established their relative viewpoints, pupils can form structured discussion groups.

Role-play

Role-play allows pupils to explore a situation (through the feelings and attitudes they might experience) by assuming the persona of a participant in that situation. Role-play means presenting a set of attitudes rather than any physical change or characterization. It is a way in which teachers can give pupils quick access to a topic or generate more concern for an issue. This can take place in small groups, possibly followed by a reporting-back session. It can also be an excellent medium for whole-group activities where the outcome need not be anticipated in advance. Role-play can help individuals share emotions or concerns they feel unable to express normally, since it allows them to say how they feel whilst distancing themselves from these emotions by placing themselves in a fictional situation.

Circle time

Although there is no definitive PSHEE pedagogy, it is nonetheless true that PSHEE has been particularly influenced by the use of circle time. Participants work in a circle, usually seated on chairs, with the teacher acting as a facilitator. Activities might start with a round where pupils pass an object and take it in turns to complete a statement such as 'I feel happy when . . .' or 'Something I find upsetting is . . .', or make comments on a particular theme. Ground rules normally include: 'only one person talks'; 'everyone else listens'; or 'no negative statements about other individuals are allowed'. From this basis, a wide range of activities, pair work, games, and small and larger group discussions can be developed. The process is normally seen as democratic and unthreatening, with no participant having to speak if they do not wish to do so. However, in practice, there may be considerable varia-tions in what teachers perceive the outcomes to be, ranging from development of speaking and listening skills, through improved behaviour, to increased self-esteem and emotional maturity. One important aspect of circle time is that pupils regularly need to change places (which is much easier to organize if pupils are sitting on chairs) so that everyone is sitting next to someone other than the person they chose to sit next to. In this way, pupils can get to know and work with a much wider group of classmates.

Debates

These can be formal affairs governed by the rules and regulations of debating, or more active sessions, such as 'verbal boxing'. Here, desks are organized in the shape of a boxing ring and pupils are divided into two groups, taking up position outside either side of the 'boxing ring'. The two groups hold diametrically opposing views on a particular issue and will send one representative into the boxing ring to argue their point of view in turn. As each contestant exhausts their argument, they tag another team member to continue. As the debate progresses, pupils may change sides if their views alter. The verbal boxing match ends when either all pupils adopt the same point of view or a pre-defined deadline is met. To encourage participation by all, introduce rules limiting the number of times a pupil can be tagged.

Task 18.4

Think about the range of teaching strategies outlined in the preceding section and any other active learning techniques you know to be effective.

Using one strategy, or a combination of strategies, plan a 30-minute lesson for pupils in Year 10 on a topic relevant to SRE that is also designed to promote pupils' critical thinking skills. Include a starter activity, active involvement, and a conclusion that protects divergence of views and pupils' self-esteem.

18.7 Conclusion

Delivering PSHEE is one of a school's most crucial responsibilities in which teachers are required to work directly with pupils on issues that raise complex moral and values standpoints. They need to do so in ways that are structured and professional so that values can be clarified, and principles protected. PSHEE is not just something teachers teach to other people; if it is given the commitment it deserves, it can affect and possibly change teachers as much as pupils. For many new teachers, this makes PSHEE a challenging prospect. However, it also offers the opportunity to work directly with young people, to gain an insight into their opinions and to better understand the issues they see as affecting their lives. As a result, engagement with both the content matter of PSHEE and, perhaps just as importantly, the pedagogic approaches with which it is associated, has the potential to contribute strongly to teachers' own personal and professional development at any stage of their career.

Recommendations for further reading

Dobson, E., Beckmann, N. and Forrest, S. (2017) Educator–student communication in sex and relationship education: a comparison of teacher and peer-led interventions, *Pastoral Care in Education*, 35 (4): 267–283.

McWhirter, J., Boddington, N. and Barksfield, J. (2017) *Understanding Personal, Social, Health and Economic Education in Secondary Schools.* Los Angeles, CA: Sage.

Radford, M. (2002) Educating the emotions: interior and exterior realities, *Pastoral Care in Education*, 20 (2): 24–29.

Tew, M., Potter, H. and Read, M. (2007) *Circles, PSHE and Citizenship: Assessing the Value of Circle Time in Secondary School.* London: Sage.

Webliography

PSHE Association: https://www.pshe-association.org.uk/ – national policy guidance, CPD and resources.

Young Citizens, Doing SMSC Guide: http://doingsmsc.org.uk/ – social, moral, spiritual and cultural development; British values; and Prevent.

Sex Education Forum: http://sexeducationforum.org.uk/ – SSRE/RSE national policy guidance, CPD and resources.

Anti-Bullying Campaign: http://www.antibullyingpro.com – Anti-Bullying Ambassadors Programme.

Mentor-ADEPSIS: http://mentor-adepis.org/ – Alcohol and Drug Education and Prevention Information Service.

Enterprise Village: http://www.enterprisevillage.org.uk/ – CPD, resources and guidance.

Economics and Business Education Association: http://www.ebea.org.uk/ – professional subject association.

Association for Citizenship Teaching: https://www.teachingcitizenship.org.uk/ – professional subject association.

19

14–19 curriculum reform

Prue Huddleston

19.1 Introduction

There are currently around 2.4 million young people in England between the ages of 14 and 19 (DfE, 2016b). Not all these young people are in full-time education and, of those who are, the majority (744,000) of 16–19-year-olds attend colleges of further education (AOC, 2016), not school. This may surprise those of you who have spent the years between 14 and 19 in a school, probably studying GCSEs and A-Levels. You may be unaware of the range of programmes available for this age range – general, technical, vocational and occupational – and the range of institutions in which they are delivered. Since the early 1980s, there have been several attempts to reform and restructure the 14–19 curriculum in England in an effort to address some long-standing and interrelated problems. The 14–19 curriculum was dominated by a narrow range of academic qualifications, which were perceived to be insufficiently applied or practical. Furthermore, pupils were encouraged to specialize in a small number of subjects, often in related areas, at an early stage in their education.

Vocational awards, on the other hand, were held in low esteem. This problem was compounded by the fact that vocational qualifications were developed on an *ad hoc* basis by different awarding organizations, leading to a proliferation of awards and no coherent framework to show how these different awards might relate to one another or to academic qualifications. Academic and vocational pathways remained separate, making it difficult for learners to combine elements from each or to change pathways.

Perhaps the most serious consequence of these failings was that too many young people left education or training prematurely because available provision failed to meet their needs and aspirations. Over the years, different reforms have attempted to:

- achieve parity of esteem between academic and vocational qualifications;
- develop a flexible system that allows pupils to combine vocational and academic elements or to switch pathways;
- develop a framework that incorporates the three pathways – general (academic), vocational and occupational – and show how they relate to one another;
- treat 14–19 as a unified phase rather than two separate phases, thereby opening up opportunities for pupils to progress at variable rates or to skip certain qualifications altogether;
- encourage more young people to stay in education and training for longer.

Since 2013, young people have been required to participate in some form of education or training, though not necessarily full-time, until age 17; from 2015, participation was extended to 18. These changes were set out in the Education and Skills Act 2008 and have since been followed by further reforms to 14–19 education and training policy. The most recent of these, the Post-16 Skills Plan (DBIS/DfE, 2016a), building on the recommendations of the Sainsbury Review (DBIS/DfE, 2016b), outlines an ambitious agenda for further reform of education and training for 16–19-year-olds, including qualifications, funding and institutional arrangements.

By the end of this chapter, you should:

- understand the policy debate within 14–19 education;
- be familiar with proposed 14–19 curriculum reforms;
- have an awareness of the range of programmes and qualifications on offer to 14–19 learners.

19.2 Background

The current government, like previous administrations, is committed to significant reform of the education system for 14–19-year-olds – this focus on the 14–19 age range is not new. Since 1981, 61 Secretaries of State have launched seven major reviews, leading to 28 Acts related to the development, organization and structure of vocational and further education and skills training in the United Kingdom. Similarly, within the provision for general education there has been change in terms of curriculum and qualifications reform, school performance and accountability measures, and funding and institutional arrangements.

A number of key policy initiatives illustrate the major changes that have taken place over the past two decades. For instance, Curriculum 2000 (QCA, 1999) introduced the first major reform of A-Levels since their inception in 1951, in an attempt to broaden the post-16 curriculum and raise the status of equivalent vocational programmes. This had a significant impact on post-16 teaching and learning in all subjects with, for example, revised subject content, modular programme design and much greater use of coursework as a means of assessment. In addition, pupils could study AS-Level modules during Year 12 and either exit the subject with an award at that level, or continue in Year 13 to A2, or full A-Level award.

This was designed to allow opportunities for a wider range of subjects to be studied, although in practice this did not happen to any significant extent. This arrangement was popular with universities, since offers could be made on the basis of achievement at AS-Level, at the end of Year 12. The modular programme design allowed assessment to be spread throughout the year, and there was opportunity for candidates to re-sit those modules in which they had been unsuccessful, or where they wished to improve their grade.

This has now been reversed as part of the recent reforms to GCSEs and A-Levels, with the emphasis reverting to synoptic assessment, externally set terminal examinations, limited re-sit opportunities, and a consequent reduction in the amount of coursework permitted, even within those subjects that have a substantial practical or applied learning element. The AS-Level has been de-coupled from A-Level and revised subject content has been introduced for some subjects from 2015, the remainder from 2016. In tandem with reforms to general qualifications, there has been a succession of reforms to vocational qualifications. These will be discussed further in section 19.4.

The story of GCSEs, mainly taken by 14–16-year-olds, is similarly convoluted. Having resulted from a merger of O- (Ordinary-) Level and Certificate of Secondary Education (CSE) examinations in 1987, they became associated with the completion of secondary schooling, marking what has now become an arbitrary – and no longer relevant – end-point for young people's compulsory education. GCSEs have also come within the purview of recent reforms with revised subject content, terminal examinations with limited opportunities for re-sits, a reduction in practical assessment (from 60% to 30% in drama, for example), and even the replacement of alphabetical grades with numerical ones (grades G–A* replaced by grades 1–9). This is more fully explored in Chapter 15.

As yet, this has not addressed the fundamental problem of providing appropriate learning opportunities for all young people within this age range, who will have varying interests and levels of maturity, and differing, or unknown, career intentions at this stage. This suggests that flexibility and choice have to be built into the system in order to allow for the needs and interests of such a diverse group of learners (Acquah and Huddleston, 2014).

In September 2002, a range of applied GCSE courses was introduced in eight subject areas. Work-related learning grew in importance and, in the following years, a large number of pupils in Years 10 and 11 had aspects of the National Curriculum (NC) 'disapplied' to allow them to spend part of their week studying vocational programmes at local further education (FE) colleges. Partly as a consequence of this type of development, different partnerships and collaborations developed between schools, colleges and other agencies. Many schools, particularly in urban areas, developed close links with FE colleges to broaden the curriculum available to their pupils across the full range of 14–19 provision.

Some new types of institution were launched, for example University Technical Colleges (UTCs) and Studio Schools, catering for 14–18-year-olds with a particular interest in technical and practical learning combined with general education (UTC, 2017). However, with the change of government following the 2010 general election, many of these reforms were swept aside, or re-imagined and re-presented, as part of a 'new' series of reforms to address the seemingly intractable challenge of 14–19 education.

You should be aware that general FE colleges and sixth-form colleges can still enrol 14–15-year-olds directly: there are currently 20,000 pupils enrolled (3,000 full-time and 17,000 part-time) (AOC, 2016). Colleges receive funding from the Education and Skills Funding Agency (ESFA), provided they fulfil the necessary conditions. These require colleges to provide programmes that include high-quality vocational qualifications alongside general qualifications within the KS4 curriculum, including English, mathematics and science. Pupils must have access to independent careers guidance and to other provision, for example sex and relationships education as prescribed for all Pupils within the school sector (EFA/ESFA, 2017). Further education teachers may also participate in school-based education, particularly where they can provide specialist technical and vocational skills.

There is growing acceptance that the school system should move away from a focus on age 16, with the completion of GCSEs as a cut-off point, particularly since all young people are required to participate in some form of education and training until their eighteenth birthday (Hodgson and Spours, 2014). Instead, 14–19 provision should become more flexible and responsive to individual pupil needs. A number of alternative, but equal, pathways could then be developed (Hodgson and Spours, 2013).

Diversity of provision was a key feature of previous government policy. Schools specialized in certain areas, such as business and enterprise, sport, languages or technology. Greater diversity could lead to increased use of individualized learning programmes. Pupils could study a variety of programmes in different institutions with different learning outcomes. However, with the introduction of Academies, UTCs, Studio Schools and Career Colleges, this collaboration, while highly desirable, may diminish with institutions seeking to retain learners in their own establishments, and for longer.

Whatever the future brings, there is no doubt that the pattern of provision for 14–19 education has altered significantly since 2000 and, given the Wolf Report (DfE, 2011c), the introduction of 16–19 Study Programmes (DfE, 2017a), the Sainsbury Review (DBIS/DfE, 2016b) and the 16–19 Skills Plan (DBIS/DfE, 2016a), further change is certain. You may wish to ponder why appropriate provision for this age range has been so challenging (Raffe and Spours, 2007; Newton, 2017).

As a consequence of this debate and the various policy initiatives implemented by successive governments, 14–19 education and training is likely to remain a contested and shifting terrain. All the major components of the system will be subject to scrutiny and review, including: qualifications; assessment; funding; progression opportunities and routes; patterns of provision; and the organization of education itself. As you enter the teaching profession, you need to keep abreast of the broader policy debate taking place within 14–19 education and how this is likely to affect your subject and your pupils more generally.

Task 19.1

What are the strengths and weaknesses of existing provision for 14–19 learners? For your subject area, list the changes you would like to see introduced to the 14–19 curriculum.

19.3 14–19: the current policy agenda

The current government has professed a desire to design a 14–19 curriculum and qualifications system that meets the aspirations of all and encourages as many young people as possible to participate in education and training post-16 (DBIS, 2014). Compared with our major competitors, the UK's post-16 staying-on rates have lagged behind; however, since the raising of the participation age (RPA), numbers have increased and a target of 90% has been set for 14–19 participation in education and training. This figure, of course, also includes the target for apprenticeships. Whilst not delivered within secondary schools, it is important that teachers are aware of the opportunities presented by apprenticeships for young people as an important route into further education and training and subsequent labour market entry.

The current government has also affirmed its commitment to apprenticeships as the main route for those not participating in full-time education. Apprenticeships involve a blend of work-based and theoretical learning with off- and on-the-job training elements. Apprentices have employed status and work towards achieving industry-standard qualifications. They are offered at a range of levels from Level 2 (equivalent to five good GCSE passes) through Level 3 (two A-Levels) to degree level. There is a duty on schools to make pupils aware of the possibilities offered by apprenticeships. However, in a competitive environment, with schools wishing to retain pupils, independent careers advice and guidance about apprenticeships has not always been available.

Taken together, these targets for post-16 participation, in whatever form, place a significant demand on the system at Key Stage 4 (KS4) to provide a curriculum that is challenging and engaging, and that allows breadth and flexibility of opportunity sufficient to encourage young people to commit themselves to continued learning. The key drivers for reform continue to be the need to build a system that meets the needs of a diverse range of learners, that permits an appropriate choice of courses and qualifications, and allows flexibility across and between learning pathways, for example schools, colleges and workplaces. Central to the vision is the desire to ensure that programmes of learning lead to clear destinations rather than a 'snakes and ladders' arrangement whereby learners are prevented from pursuing different pathways once they have embarked on a particular route.

At the same time, the government has stated it is committed to ensure that the 'basics' are in place for all young people. Although school standards have improved since the mid-1990s, a substantial number of young people still lack sufficient levels of literacy and numeracy to function adequately in the labour market and in life more generally. As a result, the Wolf Report (DfE, 2011c) recommended that young people not achieving at least a grade C in GCSE English and mathematics by the age of 16 should be supported in re-taking the examination post-16. This is restated in the provisions of the 16–19 Study Programmes (see section 19.5).

There is considerable debate as to the suitability of GCSEs in English and mathematics as indicators of basic functionality. In its Annual Report, the Chief Inspector of Ofsted stated it 'remains unclear' whether GCSE re-sits are the 'best way of ensuring that students have the English and mathematical skills needed for their intended career' (Ofsted, 2016: 79). He concluded:

'For many students, an alternative level 2 qualification may be a more appropriate means of improving their English and mathematics and ensuring that they are ready for work.'
(2016: 79)

This debate concerning appropriate qualifications for those not achieving GCSE mathematics and English still has some way to run. You may wish to consider what you regard as adequate in terms of mathematics and English 'functionality' for young people facing career choices at age 16–19 and beyond.

Although Curriculum 2000 was intended to broaden the range of academic and vocational qualifications that could be accessed by young people post-16, in reality this did not happen to any significant extent. Young people tended to take additional qualifications within the same subject group and continued to pursue a vocational or academic pathway, rather than a mixed diet. In addition, a number of 'perverse incentives' (DfE, 2011c) were said to have encouraged schools to enter pupils for large numbers of qualifications, irrespective of their currency in the labour market or for progression opportunities, so that the schools could gain performance table points.

The development of a 14–19 continuum of learning, rather than a system punctuated by a clear end-point at 16, as in the present arrangements, opens up the possibility for increased flexibility in the place, pace and progression of learning. It has been argued that 16 is an arbitrary end-point for many young people (Newton, 2017). For instance, it might be appropriate for some pupils to skip GCSEs in certain subjects and progress immediately to A-Level study. Alternatively, significant numbers might benefit from rather more extended programmes that allow them to reach the 'Holy Grail' of five A*–C (now 4–9) GCSE grades, or their equivalent, in three rather than two years (Huddleston, 2002; Newton, 2017). Many of these pupils choose to continue their studies in FE colleges, often as a result of poor prior learning experiences. The courses that they select are often vocational in orientation.

Task 19.2

What would you suggest as a minimum broad curriculum entitlement for young people embarking on a vocational qualification at 14?

Should vocational qualifications be delivered in specialist establishments with industry-standard equipment by vocational experts, or can they be delivered within the context of a large secondary school?

19.4 The qualifications landscape

If you are starting to teach in a large comprehensive school, you might be struck by the range of programmes offered to 14–19-year-olds. From your own educational experience, you may be far more familiar with programmes leading to qualifications such as GCSEs and A-Levels. However, many schools prepare pupils for a range of qualifications that can be described as general (for example, GCSEs and A-Levels), vocational or vocationally related (for example, BTECs and OCR Nationals), or those that contribute to broader aspects of personal development (for example, functional skills, skills for working life, enterprise awards, ASDAN and Certificates of Personal Effectiveness).

A particular feature of English education reform policy has been the conflation of notions of curriculum reform with qualification and assessment reform. They are not the same, but in policy terms every reform within 14–19 education and training has been expressed in terms of qualification and assessment reform (Oates, 2014). The effect has been to subject schools and colleges to endless 'top-down' introductions of revised qualifications, and nowhere has this been more apparent than in the range of qualifications for post-16 pupils, particularly vocational qualifications.

The sometimes bewildering array of qualifications, their relative status and equivalence, has caused wide-scale debate for decades, focusing attention on what type of curriculum offering and qualifications should be available for 14–19-year-olds within the maintained schools sector. In addition, you should be aware that your school will not be the only institution offering programmes for 14–19-year-olds within your locality. There will be other schools, sixth-form colleges, FE colleges, UTCs and training providers offering qualifications to learners. This quasi-market in education, including the qualifications and institutions available, has had several perverse effects in terms of learner choice, accessibility to informed advice and guidance, duplication of provision and employer understanding, leading to inevitable confusion amongst learners, their parents and carers.

In England, the Department for Education (DfE) has overall responsibility for education, apprenticeships and skills, including determining qualifications for 14–19-year-olds that count towards school and college performance tables (Section 96 Qualifications). This is an important consideration for schools when determining which qualifications to offer and to which learners. The recent debate concerning the EBacc measure (see Chapter 15 for a fuller discussion) has thrown this into sharp focus. Schools are awarded performance points in terms of pupil achievement of GCSEs, in particular the so-called EBacc subjects: English language/literature, mathematics, science, history or geography and a modern foreign language. This has led to a greater emphasis on entering pupils for qualifications in EBacc subjects and a reduction of candidates entered for creative subjects, including music, drama, art and design (Edge Foundation, 2016; Warwick Commission, 2016).

This shifting policy environment requires a qualification landscape that allows young people and other stakeholders, including employers, to navigate in order to understand what a particular qualification means in terms of its degree of difficulty, size, level and expected learning outcomes. While it is invidious to compare different types of qualifications, for example, practical with academic, the education system has long been in the habit of doing so and it is inevitable that the practice will continue, at least in the minds of most stakeholders.

As you begin your career, you may find it challenging to familiarize yourself with the range of qualifications on offer in your school and what they represent in terms of level of difficulty, time taken to achieve and their equivalence to the qualifications with which you are more familiar. The best way to keep up to date is to review regularly the government website: www.gov.uk/what-different-qualification-levels-mean/list-of-qualification-levels [accessed 6 September 2018] as well as the websites of awarding organizations that provide information for teachers on all qualifications offered. Of course, it is important that you check with school staff which qualifications are offered in your department and that you are working from the latest specifications.

As a rough rule of thumb, in England and Northern Ireland (in Scotland and Wales, levels are expressed somewhat differently) there are nine qualification levels from Entry Level to Level 8 (expressed in ascending degree of difficulty and the complexity of skills and knowledge associated with them). A-Levels are Level 3 qualifications, GCSEs grades A*–C/9–4 are Level 2, and GCSEs grades D–G/3–1 are Level 1. Entry Level qualifications, which are also subdivided into Levels 1, 2 and 3, are designed for those pupils not yet ready to embark on full Levels 1 or 2 qualifications, or who may have special educational needs. Vocational qualifications also indicate level, for example BTEC Nationals (Level 3) and OCR Employability Skills (Level 1 award).

Every regulated qualification is expressed in terms of level, size – that is, the number of guided learning hours (GLHs) required to deliver it – and the total qualification time (TQT) – that is, the time in which it is expected that the qualification should be achieved (GLHs + non-GLHs). You will appreciate the complexity in attempting to corral all qualifications into a comprehensible overarching framework when different types of qualifications serve different purposes and attract diverse learners. This has been attempted in the past, with varying degrees of success, chiefly because 'comparisons are odious' and often result in winners and losers in terms of what have come to be regarded as 'high-stakes' qualifications.

The DfE annually publishes lists of approved technical and vocational qualifications for 14–16-year-olds and for 16–18-year-olds for recognition in school and college performance tables. These can be viewed at: https://www.gov.uk/courses-qualifications [accessed 13 June 2018]. Currently, the only technical and vocational qualifications recognized in performance tables are:

- Technical Awards for 14–16-year-olds (Level 2)
- Technical Certificates for 16–19-year-olds (Level 2)

- Tech levels for 16–19-year-olds (Level 3)
- Applied General Qualifications (Level 3)

The picture that emerges of the 14–19 landscape is one that is characterized by a range of provision in terms of qualifications and providers. In schools, the provision is dominated by the general route, GCSEs and A-Levels, although increasingly schools have offered vocational and technical qualifications with, or separate from, the general route, for example BTECs and A-Levels, or BTECs in place of GCSEs. Programmes at Entry Level and Level 1 account for a smaller proportion of learners but are well established. FE colleges predominately offer technical, vocational or occupational qualifications to this age group, although the total number of A-Level candidates in colleges exceeds that of schools (taking into account adult learners as well). For training providers, the main programme on offer is apprenticeships, which include vocational and occupational qualifications. Training providers also offer provision at Level 1 and Entry Level that aims to prepare young people for employment.

A range of factors has influenced this pattern of provision, perhaps most importantly the need for providers to generate qualification outcomes for all young people; after all, these are the metrics by which institutions are judged through performance tables and ultimately through the funding that they receive. In many cases, this broadening of the curriculum offer has been prompted by Ofsted inspections and by area inspections with the aim of improving the chances of young people to gain a qualification, or at least units towards a qualification, to ensure that the system is inclusive and that all learners can access provision suited to their needs and abilities.

What emerges from this, albeit brief, overview is a 14–19 landscape characterized by a heterogeneous group of young people, and a complex and fragmented system of qualifications delivered by a diverse range of institutions and providers. Perhaps most significantly, it is a landscape dominated by a particular view of the world, a world preoccupied with academic qualifications, with an end-point of entry to higher education, although this accounts for less than 50% of the cohort.

Such a world has tended to under-value those qualifications that are not designed for entry to higher education, but could do so, and that are equally important in terms of achieving mass participation to age 19, contributing to developing the high-level skills much lauded by employers.

19.5 Review of vocational education – the Wolf Report

In 2010, the Coalition government commissioned Professor Alison Wolf to undertake an independent review into vocational education specifically focusing on:

> how vocational education for 14- to 19-year-olds can be improved in order to promote successful progression into the labour market and into higher level education and training routes. It provides practical recommendations to help inform future policy direction, taking into account current financial constraints.
>
> (DfE, 2011c: 19)

From earlier sections in this chapter, you will have realized that the provision of high-quality vocational education has been a long-standing challenge. The Wolf Report suggested that while much good-quality provision existed, there was still work to be done to provide young people with good-quality vocational programmes allowing access to the labour market or to further and higher education. Her specific criticisms highlighted:

- a lack of high-quality vocational opportunities for 16–17-year-olds, which results in young people moving in and out of short-term programmes and employment, unable either to progress or to find suitable longer-term employment;
- a large number of low-level vocational qualifications that do not allow progression and that hold little value in the labour market;
- low levels of achievement in English and mathematics (the benchmark considered as GCSE A*–C) among this cohort.

Wolf's Report concluded with 27 recommendations, all of which were subsequently accepted by government and formed the rationale for ongoing reforms contained within the provisions of 16–19 Study Programmes (DBIS, 2014; DfE, 2017a) and the 16–19 Skills Plan (DBIS/DfE, 2016a). These recommendations focus upon a number of 'organizing principles' (DfE, 2011c):

- Young people should not be tracked into 'dead end' routes that fail to allow progression either to further education and training at a higher level, or into the labour market.
- The centrality of high-quality independent information, advice and guidance for young people and their parents/carers about what is available and where it might lead.
- The need to simplify the existing system and thus reduce the proliferation of qualifications and awards.

You should look at Wolf's recommendations, and the government's response, in more detail. Space does not permit a full discussion of all the recommendations, but some clear messages can be distilled that will have a bearing on your work as a teacher. For example, pupils will no longer be able to build up large numbers of qualifications to achieve a higher points score for the school's performance tables; key indicators must be drawn from a common core curriculum including English and mathematics. Emphasis must be placed upon encouraging those in the lowest quintile of achievement at KS4 to move towards Level 2 qualifications as soon after 16 as practically possible.

Those pursuing vocational qualifications full-time post-16 should have the opportunity to access programmes that are broadly based, allow adequate contact time, include rigorous assessment, and include wider learning 'non-qualification' opportunities (often referred to as 'enrichment'). Work experience post-16 is seen as making a positive contribution to young people's learning and preparation for the labour market. Pupils who have not achieved English and mathematics GCSE A*–C by the age of 16 should be required to include these subjects in any further course that they follow.

Drawing on Wolf's recommendations, and as part of the continued reform of 16–19 full-time education, the DfE (2015b) set out guidance for schools concerning the provision that should be offered to all learners whether following a general or vocational route, described as 16–19 Study Programmes. The guiding principles state that every learner should pursue a programme of study tailored to their prior attainment at 16 and future higher education or career intentions. Each programme should contain a substantial qualification (either general or vocational) to provide sufficient 'stretch and rigour' and allow progression to the next stage of education, training or employment. Those who have not achieved a GCSE grade A*–C in mathematics and English should be required to continue to work towards these qualifications, or other approved qualifications at the same level (see section 19.3 for a consideration of the suitability of this proposal). All pupils should have access to a high-quality work experience placement; in the case of vocational qualifications, this should be aligned to the context and content of their course. Finally, all young people should have the opportunity for 'enrichment' activities that allow for the development of wider 'generic' skills, such as 'confidence', 'interpersonal skills' and 'employability' skills. What these are and how they may be developed is a matter of contention.

Task 19.3

Bearing in mind the Wolf Review and the provisions set out within 16–19 Study Programmes, together with your own observation in school:

- What do you understand as 'high-quality core education that equips (young people) to progress, whether immediately or later, to a very wide range of further study, training and employment'?
- What should such a core education include?
- At what age should young people decide to specialize?
- What do you understand the difference to be, if any, between taking a qualification and undertaking a programme of study?
- Why do you think the provision of education and training for the 14–19 age group has proved such a challenge?
- What are the barriers to the full implementation of such reforms? What are the drivers for reform?

19.6 Conclusion

As a teacher, you can be certain that the profession you have entered will change rapidly as your career unfolds. This is especially likely for those of you who spend most of your time teaching young people aged 14–19.

The drivers for reform are multiple, interrelated and complex. They reflect wider changes at a societal and, increasingly, global level. The reforms are being driven by the twin agendas of high standards and inclusion. These include the economic imperative to develop a highly qualified, skilled and flexible workforce to maintain the country's competitiveness in increasingly global markets, and the need to ensure that opportunities are available for all, irrespective of the route they choose to follow. Earlier attempts to reform 14–19 education have resulted in a range of schemes and interventions, the majority of which failed to fulfil their early promise and did not achieve the hoped-for parity of esteem between different pathways.

A key obstacle has been a market-, funding- and qualification-led reform process. Another has been a sectoral approach that has separated off various forms of provision, some of them overlapping, including school-, FE-, higher education- and work-based learning. Although current reforms speak of the need for collaboration and cooperation between institutions, providers, government agencies and employers, and of the importance of a demand-led approach to provision, without impartial information, advice and guidance, it is difficult for learners to make informed choices.

The provision of high-quality information, advice and guidance will be crucial to the successful achievement of the aims set out in the 16–19 Skills Plan. What providers offer their learners will also be influenced by what competitor providers offer. Much remains to be done to put in place the recommendations outlined in the Wolf Report and the subsequent reforms that it set in train. The extent to which a genuine ladder of opportunity is offered to every young person, rather than a series of hurdles to weed people out of education and training, remains to be seen.

Recommendations for further reading

Department for Business Innovation and Skills (DBIS) (2014) *Getting the Job Done: The Government's Reform Plan for Vocational Qualifications*. London: DBIS.

Department for Education (DfE) (2011c) *Review of Vocational Education (The Wolf Report)*. London: DfE.

Department for Education (DfE) (2015) *16–19 Study Programmes. Departmental Advice for Senior Leadership Teams, Curriculum Planners, Teachers, Trainers and Co-ordinators on the Planning and Delivery of 16–19 Study Programmes*. London: DfE.

Department for Education (DfE) (2017a) *16–19 Study Programmes: Planning and Delivery of 16–19 Study Programmes*. London: DfE.

Webliography

Department for Education, 2018 Performance Tables: Technical and Vocational Qualifications: https://www.gov.uk/government/publications/2018-performance-tables-technical-and-vocational-qualifications

University Technical Colleges (UTCs): https://www.utcolleges.org/

PART 4

Making Schools Work for All: *Every Child Matters*, Safeguarding and the Inclusion Agenda

20

Does every child matter? Education, social care and the emerging safeguarding agenda

Steve James

20.1 Introduction

Victoria Climbié was 8 years old when she died. She had been sent by her parents, in West Africa, to be looked after by her great aunt, who lived in the London Borough of Haringey. In 2001, after months of physical and mental abuse, Victoria was murdered by her great aunt and her great aunt's lover. The government established an inquiry into the circumstances of Victoria's death under the chairmanship of Lord Laming, a former chief inspector of social services. Laming's report, published in January 2003, was devastating: he concluded that at every stage child protection arrangements had failed Victoria. Professionals were not sufficiently informed about what was happening to her; those who had information had not shared what they knew; when they shared information, they did not realize its significance. In one dreadful conclusion, he observed:

> 'Sadly, many of those from social services who gave evidence seemed to spend a lot of time and energy devising ways of limiting access to services, and adopting mechanisms designed to reduce service demand.'
>
> (DoH, 2003: para 1.52)

Lord Laming's report called for a fundamental reconfiguration of care for children, integrating child protection with health, education and children's services more generally. The government's response was swift. On 28 January 2003, the Health Secretary, Alan Milburn, outlined legislative plans for the biggest reform of child welfare services in England for 30 years, including the establishment of Children's Trusts in all 150 local authorities. Children's Trusts would aim to improve services for children through coordinated management of education, health and social services, establishing better integration of and access to services and greater strategic coherence. Less than six months later, the government went further, appointing, for the first time, a Minister for Children with overall responsibility for children's welfare and well-being. Nationally, the administration of children's services was brought under the control of a single ministry – the Department for Education and Skills (DfES) – and, in autumn 2003, the DfES published a wide-ranging Green Paper under the title *Every Child Matters*. It outlined an ambitious vision for the reform of children's services:

> 'The key is to ensure children receive services at the first onset of problems, and to prevent any children slipping through the net.'
>
> (DfES, 2003a: 8)

Central to the reform agenda were aspirations that child policy should be framed around all children, so that no child is missed, and that children's well-being should be at the core of the planning, commissioning and delivery of services. *Every Child Matters* set in place two underlying concepts to deliver the government's vision: first, children's services should be reconfigured around the *needs of the child*, rather than around the way teachers, social workers, paediatricians or health visitors worked and were trained; second, these reconfigured children's services should be organized to deliver *five outcomes* for children. These five outcomes – equally weighted in *Every Child Matters*, and covering children's education, health and well-being – should form shared objectives for all children's professionals. The resulting programme was described as the most ambitious cross-government agenda of change for children anywhere in the world, and it transformed the professional world of schools and teachers (House of Commons Education and Skills Committees, 2005).

It was clear from the moment of its publication that *Every Child Matters* commanded widespread professional support and commitment. The inspirational vision at its core – a reconfiguration of children's services around children's needs and the construction of arrangements that allowed all children to thrive – spoke powerfully to the motivation of all those who worked with children. What was also clear was the sheer scale of the reform programme needed to address children's needs. Children's services – schools, hospitals, community paediatrics and social services – provide for the needs of almost 9 million children in England (DfE, 2018b). Of these 9 million, the number of children in need is almost 400,000 with issues including domestic violence, mental health, emotional abuse and – the most significant of all – drug and alcohol abuse (DfE, 2017g). In 2017, the number of children in England subject to a child protection plan was 51,080 (DfE, 2017g). Meeting the needs of all children involves the management of a large and complex workforce, including teachers, special needs coordinators, social workers, nurses, health visitors, doctors, psychologists, police officers and family support workers, each group with a different professional culture, training, accountability framework and set of preoccupations. The challenge is enormous.

By the end of this chapter, you should:

- have a general understanding of the principles of your role in ensuring every child does matter;
- have considered the implications of the broader safeguarding agenda for everyone working with children.

20.2 Child protection

It is fair to say that *Every Child Matters* was the turning point in how those working with children viewed their role in child protection. The issues raised by the Victoria Climbié case are still regularly used in safeguarding training delivered across schools and nurseries in the UK. There is a clear determination in the UK education system that we can never afford to let anything like that tragedy happen again. Yet, of course, no system is fool-proof. What has emerged since 2003 is a year-on-year adaptation to child protection procedures in school, in the realization that to protect all children there needs to be a much broader and flexible focus. Indeed, since around 2010, the reference to Child Protection Officers in school has been replaced with the broader term, 'Safeguarding Lead'. When teachers or those working with children hear 'child protection', there is often an assumption that this just refers to one of the four categories of abuse (emotional, physical, sexual and neglect). However, the definition of safeguarding is much broader. We will explore this later.

It is important to remember that with the Children Act 1989, there was already written legislation in place about how we all had a responsibility to protect all children. Yet, as of 2003 with the Climbié case, the lack of communication exposed in the subsequent Serious Case Review highlighted that those working with Victoria had failed to communicate adequately enough to prevent a tragedy. This came less than a year after the failure of the system to prevent the deaths of Holly Wells and Jessica Chapman, who were murdered by Ian Huntley, a school caretaker who worked in a secondary school where one local authority failed to pass on vital information to another authority about Huntley. Likewise, the era of 'whistleblowing' (encouraging school staff to share their concerns regarding child protection without fear of reproach) had not yet been embedded. Huntley regularly talked about his attitude towards underage sex in the staffroom, but colleagues in that school did not report their concerns or feel confident in doing so.

The key challenge for schools and those working in education was an absence of a culture or legal framework encouraging transparency. Staff were often reluctant to report things for fear of being perceived as 'overreacting'. Subsequent cases and legislation have, thankfully, strived to ensure this is no longer the case. However, as recently as 2012 we saw the tragic case of Daniel Pelka. He was killed by his mother and her partner. The mother convinced the school that Daniel was under medical care for his eating difficulties. The school consequently failed to follow basic procedures. Daniel had unexplained bruising on his face and staff noticed his weight loss and how hungry he seemed. But, due to the absence of a culture of transparency, the concerns of staff members were not written down and shared. Tragically, Daniel eventually died. What we must take away from this terrible case is the value of sharing our concerns over child protection and safeguarding. We cannot be sure, but a culture of transparency, among other changes, may have helped prevent this tragic loss. Our role, working in education, is now more than ever to ensure we are confident to share. Child protection is no longer the role of a sole person sitting in an office in a school. It is everyone's responsibility.

Subsequent legislation in the form of *Keeping Children Safe in Education* (2015, updated almost annually since this date) aimed to address some of these inadequacies. Centralized information sharing became the key priority and way forward. All local authorities now have a multi-agency safeguarding hub (often termed the 'MASH') to ensure that concerns are centrally monitored and acted upon. The government (DfE, 2016g) have set out specific forms of maltreatment or abuse, which often overlap, of which schools and teachers need to be aware:

- Physical abuse
- Emotional abuse
- Sexual abuse
- Neglect

20.3 Developing the children's workforce

Taking these principles together, it is easy to see just how big a challenge *Every Child Matters* posed for children's professionals. Its bold vision of coherent children's services arrangements integrating the work of teachers, social workers and health professionals around a common framework for assessment and action, involving children actively at all stages in their interaction with professionals is compelling – but the challenge should not be underestimated. We have already seen that the sheer number of children involved is enormous – nearly half a million in contact with social services in any one week. To add to this complexity, many children present profound and complex needs, for instance the multiply-disabled adolescent on the autistim spectrum; the speech- and hearing-impaired girl suffering emotional neglect; the sibling children of a drug-abusing mother who has been arrested on serious charges; or the teenager with severe mental health difficulties from an earlier history of abuse. Added to this, the children's workforce is itself huge and diverse, with, as you are likely aware, a number of different staff and associated professionals working within the schools sector.

Every Child Matters attempted to bring coherence to this diverse workforce. Nonetheless, there are demanding challenges. Particular difficulties relate to a common assessment and information framework. The detailed information needed by, say, a community paediatrician to diagnose difficulties and support a case for action is different from the detailed information needed by a school Special Educational Needs and Disabilities Coordinator (SENDCo), and different again from the information needed by a family support worker. A common assessment framework (CAF) that tries to meet the needs of all groups might not, in the end, meet the needs of any one of them. There are particular difficulties – often powerfully articulated by parents – about confidentiality and access to such information: although most professionals will subscribe to the idea that information sharing is essential, in practice there might be strong arguments why some information should remain confidential to the family and the professional group meeting the child's needs. As a result, there are difficult decisions to be made about what is recorded, by whom and for what purpose, and complex decisions about where information should be stored and accessed, and who has 'lead' professional responsibility for maintaining the information base. Subsequently, the notion of a common assessment framework approach has been replaced with an Early Help Assessment (EHA). Since 2015, a team of professionals now work on a particular child, ensuring a lead professional coordinates the interventions put in place to support a child identified as being at risk and guarantees that there is adequate oversight of the child when concerns have been raised through the different agencies who are able to identify children at risk. Likewise, the brief of the EHA ensures that a broad church of professionals is involved, as it is important to remember that concerns about a child's welfare can come through a variety of routes, including education, the NHS, police, social services and any other professional working with families.

Task 20.1

Consider 10 warning signs that you, as a classroom teacher, might use in your day-to-day contact with children to identify a child as being at risk of safeguarding-related issues. Are there any groups of pupils who you think might be at greater risk of safeguarding-related issues than others? Why?

20.4 Safeguarding: everybody's business

Every Child Matters still provides the basis for current policy, which is why the first part of this chapter considers the implications of this seminal document. However, policy continues to evolve, and you need to be aware of changes in your school following developments to the statutory guidance (see, for example, DfE, 2016g). For instance, the term 'child protection' has now become almost obsolete, as the government realized that the risks to children and young people are much more than exclusively those surrounding *abuse*. The rise in external threats (from online sources, in particular) has ensured that a much more encompassing term is needed to ensure that those working with children are aware of the risks; hence the term 'safeguarding' is now the key term with which those working in education should become familiar. Ofsted can now place a school or nursery into a Grade 4 category ('Inadequate') within minutes of visiting a school if safeguarding procedures are not robust.

Every school is required to have a Designated Safeguarding Lead (and Deputy or Deputies) who must be a member of the school's leadership team. Since the Daniel Pelka case, it is expected that no one professional has sole responsibility for sharing information to ensure there is always a 'fail safe', which was sadly lacking in Pelka's case. This subtle change ensured that no school could trivialize the role of child protection and safeguarding, by ensuring it was held by a senior leader in schools. Most schools now have a safeguarding policy comprising at least 25 pages of information (DfE, 2016g). Training for safeguarding professionals in schools (and nurseries) must now be refreshed every two years to ensure that schools are constantly up to date:

> 'Governing bodies and proprietors should ensure that all staff members undergo safeguarding and child protection training at induction. The training should be regularly updated.'

> (DfE, 2016g: 17, para. 64)

It is important to remember that, whilst a Designated Safeguarding Lead is the key person in a school centralizing information gathering and sharing, the person who is most likely to spot child abuse, child radicalization or a child at risk of sexual exploitation, to name but three areas of vulnerability, is the teacher or teaching assistant working day-to-day with children. Spotting changes in behaviour is now central to the duty of staff to ensure warning signs are detected early.

In fact, children themselves could pose a threat to others rather than them always being the victim. The rise of the perceived threat associated with terrorism and the prospect of children becoming radicalized, with some disturbing cases highlighted over the last 10 years, have added to the broader definition of safeguarding.

Two recent high-profile cases of child extremism were seen in the East Midlands. In one case, a young man (subsequently convicted as the youngest person ever charged with terrorism charges and imprisoned) had become withdrawn in his school. Perceived bullying by others and a negative attitude towards him by some staff led him to develop a 'kill list'. When police were alerted by an online comment (discovered initially by the FBI in the US), they visited his house to find draft plans on how to make a pipe bomb for attacking those at school on his list. He had become obsessed at the same time with extremist views. A similar case, just a few miles away, led police to discover a bedroom of a 15-year-old boy adorned with neo-Nazi memorabilia.

The cases here highlight just how the safeguarding agenda over the last 10 years has become much more than being limited to child protection and *Every Child Matters*. The

Prevent Duty of 2015 places a requirement on those working with children and young people to be alert to the potential for radicalization in working together to prevent home-grown terrorist activity, highlighted even further by the events of 2017 around the UK (for example, the terrorism incidents in Manchester and London). Of course, in its broadest sense, where the *Every Child Matters* theme is adhered to, the cases of child terrorism are classic examples of children who slipped through the net and could be cited as examples where the early warning signs of a child not enjoying and achieving were not picked up on.

Task 20.2

Consider how you might identify radicalization of a pupil in a classroom environment. What might be the warning signs?

How would a history teacher differentiate between an interest in historical events and an obsession with neo-Nazi material?

20.5 How did *Every Child Matters* change the work of schools?

It may be tempting to see *Every Child Matters* as being largely about 'complex needs', about special needs or special schools. It may be tempting to believe that its implementation relates to the work of highly-skilled professionals in social work or child health, or that it is chiefly about the challenging issues of child protection and intervention. It may then be tempting to see it as being of limited direct relevance to classroom teaching and learning. *These suppositions are wrong.* It is certainly the case that many children with particularly complex, multiple needs will need the intensive support of specialist professionals, and that many may be educated outside mainstream schools. It would obviously be unwise, and almost certainly counterproductive or dangerous, for any teacher – however well-meaning – to believe that uninformed intervention in case work with a child who is receiving support from social services for complex needs could be justified solely on the grounds of wanting to 'do good'. However, *Every Child Matters* is of huge relevance to classroom teachers. There are a number of reasons for this. The first two are to do with issues of underlying principle. *Every Child Matters* outlines a coherent vision for all children based around the five interlocking outcomes – every child should:

1.   enjoy and achieve;
2.   make a positive contribution;
3.   be safe;
4.   be healthy; and
5.   enjoy economic well-being.

The Green Paper was not written to suggest that only children in difficulty should achieve these five outcomes – but that *every* child should. In the striking words of one children's services professional, this is a reminder that the 'quality of what we offer to the minority in difficulty needs to be judged by the standards we apply to the many' (Dessent, 2006: 18).

Every Child Matters has strong, direct messages for teachers and schools: teachers have a responsibility not just to ensure that children achieve, but that they enjoy and achieve – children should *enjoy* their schooling. Schools need to think hard about how they help children to stay safe: this means how they promote safety not simply in the classroom, but also in the corridor, the playground and beyond this, on pupils' way to and from school. The recent requirement to promote 'fundamental British values' in school would now come under this wider remit, though there is much debate on what constitutes fundamental British values. The government (DfE, 2014b) provides the following list:

- democracy;
- the rule of law;
- individual liberty; and
- mutual respect for and tolerance of those with different faiths and beliefs and for those without faith.

Schools need to consider how in the curriculum they are preparing children to enjoy economic well-being and to be healthy. Finally, they need to consider how far their internal systems and structures provide opportunities and models for young people to make a positive contribution – to the school through participation in decision-making or to the community more generally. The boldness of the *Every Child Matters* vision is a compelling one precisely because it is an aspiration for *all* children.

Task 20.3

Consider how you might promote one of the named fundamental British values in your subject or phase specialism.

The second issue of principle relates to how schools help children to achieve the five outcomes. In the preceding discussion, a distinction was drawn between what we might now call 'universal' and 'targeted' services. Schools, of course, are the universal service *par excellence*: almost every child goes to school, and schools have historically been used by other services that aspire to universality to try to ensure full population coverage – you can probably remember queuing in a school hall to receive vaccinations. Schools were used for this purpose *because* they allowed health workers to reach almost all children. One of the major preoccupations for schools has always been to maximize children's cognitive attainment in tests and examinations, a preoccupation that has intensified since the mid-1980s as targets for pupil achievement have been extended to all schools (Abbott *et al.*, 2013b). Increasingly, schools have realized that the barriers to learning – and the barriers, therefore, to attainment – do not necessarily lie within the school. Whilst it is imperative that teachers plan properly, teach well, meet individual needs in the classroom and make use of assessment to support learning, the barriers to learning for many pupils lie outside the school. They may be to do with pupils' material circumstances at home where child poverty is a major issue. The difficulties may be to do with the consequences of family breakdown, with pupils' mental health, with their emotional well-being, and so on. Schools alone cannot overcome the barriers to learning for children. All schools – and thus all teachers – need to be able to work in partnership with external agencies.

Level 1: Diversionary
Here the focus is before problems can be seen – thus, prevention strategies are likely to focus on whole populations

Children at Level 1 are likely to be in school and the subject of monitoring by class teachers, teaching assistants and learning support

Level 2: Early Prevention
This implies that problems are already beginning to manifest themselves and action is needed to prevent them becoming serious or worse

Children at Level 2 will also be in school, with some supplementary support commissioned from outside the school

Level 3: Intensive Prevention/Intervention
Intensive prevention would focus on where there are multiple, complex and long-standing difficulties that will require a customization of services to meet the needs of the individual concerned

Children at Level 3 may not be in school. However, children may move between Levels 2 and 3 at various points in their school career

Level 4: Restorative Prevention
Restorative prevention focuses on reducing the impact of an intrusive intervention. This is the level of provision that would apply to, for example, those permanently excluded from school or in youth offender institutions and/or those receiving assistance within the child protection framework

Children at Level 4 will not be in school, although, again, there may be long-term aspirations to reintegrate

---

Table 20.1 Tiered model of provision according to acuteness of need

Source: Based on Hardiker *et al.* (1991).

One of the most influential frameworks for thinking about the ways in which schools and other agencies can work together to meet children's needs was developed by Hardiker *et al.* (1991) and adopted by the Children and Young People's Unit (CYPU) within the DfES in its early thinking around intervention and prevention (CYPU, 2000). Hardiker and colleagues outlined a tiered model of provision according to the acuteness of need (see Table 20.1). You may be familiar with a previous version of this model – 'School Action' or 'School Action Plus' – when thinking about special educational needs. The overall intention of *Every Child Matters* is to reduce the need for interventions at Levels 3 and 4 by strengthening the focus and effectiveness of preventative interventions at Levels 1 and 2; in other words, to support schools in dealing with the behavioural and learning manifestations of problems before they escalate out of control. The Hardiker/CYPU framework helps to set *Every Child Matters* into a reasonably clear framework for action, but it is also a reminder that a significant number of children will need additional support and intervention at various stages of their school career and for different purposes; for example, a self-harming 15-year-old needing support from Child and Adolescent Mental Health Services (CAMHS) to respond to serious emotional issues, or a 14-year-old who has become involved in petty theft after serious domestic turmoil needing support from a Youth Offending Team, or even a radicalized teen-ager needing help under the Prevent Duty to help them integrate back into society after a conviction. *Every Child Matters* and subsequent legislation has been about developing a framework to provide these young people with effective support from a variety of agencies.

20.6 The changing role of schools – and what next?

Beyond these issues of principle, the significance of *Every Child Matters* and the safeguarding agenda in schools has been enhanced by a series of policy and practice developments since 2003. One of the most significant was the decision by Ofsted in 2005 to require schools to report on their work across the five *Every Child Matters* outcomes; however, subsequently, the priority of safeguarding has taken some precedence over this (see, for example, DfE, 2016g). Schools are now required to evidence their wider work to support the whole child through their PSHE curriculum, promoting spiritual, moral, social and cultural (SMSC) aspects (see Chapters 18 and 14 for more information on these). Whilst *Every Child Matters* remains at the heart of much of the legislation in education, its profile as an agenda and focus area has been overshadowed by much bigger policy developments that have come to the fore since. However, it does remain important to trace back all of the current safeguarding priorities to the notion that, if every child mattered, the tragedy of Victoria Climbié may not have taken place, and recent policy is clear about this:

> Safeguarding and promoting the welfare of children is **everyone's** responsibility. **Everyone** who comes into contact with children and their families and carers has a role to play in safeguarding children. In order to fulfil this responsibility effectively, all professionals should make sure their approach is child-centred. This means that they should consider, at all times, what is in the **best interests** of the child.
>
> (DfE, 2016g: 4, para. 2; emphasis in original)

At this stage it is worth considering what children have said they need from an effective safeguarding system:

- 'vigilance: to have adults notice when things are troubling them
- understanding and action: to understand what is happening; to be heard and understood; and to have that understanding acted upon
- stability: to be able to develop an ongoing stable relationship of trust with those helping them
- respect: to be treated with the expectation that they are competent rather than not
- information and engagement: to be informed about and involved in procedures, decisions, concerns and plans
- explanation: to be informed of the outcome of assessments and decisions and reasons when their views have not met with a positive response
- support: to be provided with support in their own right as well as a member of their family
- advocacy: to be provided with advocacy to assist them in putting forward their views
- protection: to be protected against all forms of abuse and discrimination and the right to special protection and help if a refugee.'

(DfE, 2018b: 10)

Task 20.4

Consider the *Every Child Matters* outcome 'enjoy and achieve'. Think about:

(i)   the ways in which you can help children *both* to achieve *and* to enjoy; and
(ii) the ways in which you might embed children's participation in your planning for the outcome.

A significant development emerging from the *Every Child Matters* agenda has also been the rapid pace of workforce development in schools. Originally conceived as a set of devices to allow teachers to focus on their core responsibilities for teaching and learning, workforce development has led schools to remodel their workforces, in some cases extensively so. Many schools now have a non-teaching staff group that is as large as the teaching staff (Middlewood and Abbott, 2017). The most obvious developments have been in the areas of teaching assistants and learning mentors. Both groups typically work with individual pupils or small groups, to remove barriers to achievement – barriers that may be cognitive, behavioural or emotional – and to allow pupils to maximize their learning in school. Inevitably, this involves such adults in dealing with what Hardiker would label 'Level 1' activity, perhaps involving liaison with a teacher or with parents but, again, very much in the spirit of the assessment and integrated solution that underlies *Every Child Matters*. Some schools have gone further, appointing family support staff, or liaison officers who have a specific brief to work with families and other agencies to broker solutions at Levels 2 or 3 for individual learners. These procedures seek to keep the child in school and address early and emerging difficulties. Many of these schools report quantifiable indicators of success in the form of reduced exclusions and lower absence rates, as well as a less quantifiable sense that behaviour has improved, and that the small minority of young people who absorb vast amounts of school time and effort in responding to their learning difficulties and emotional and behavioural needs are more effectively supported (DfE, 2018b). It is important to remember that it can be these non-teaching professionals who have the closest contact with children and are therefore well-placed to spot changes in a child that are the first indicators of concerns.

20.7 Conclusion

Every Child Matters grew out of a horrific murder and a catastrophic failure of children's support services. It put in place a bold vision for a holistic children's service with the child at the centre and a shared focus on children's success, broadly conceived. It saw child protection as one strand in the way in which society provides for the welfare of all, and established the principle that the welfare of the vulnerable minority is indivisible from the welfare of the many. It has spawned a huge programme of change and development affecting everyone who works with children. This programme is far from complete. The evidence we have is that the vision commands almost universal support from those who work with children. In the process of implementation, *Every Child Matters* appeared to be doing something else too. It changed our sense of what outcomes we should focus on. It changed the way teachers work with others, broadening the commitment to collaborative and interprofessional working. However, there is a danger, because of local authority funding challenges, that some Level 3 interventions are referred back to schools, meaning schools may increasingly need to start to ensure they have a broader range of professionals in school (for example, counsellors, a school nurse and behaviour professionals) to ensure that children's needs are adequately met. As a result, it may be changing, in fundamental ways, the way we think about the purpose of schools in their work with children, young people and the wider community.

Recommendations for further reading

Department for Education (DfE) (2016) *Keeping Children Safe in Education*. London: DfE.
Department for Education (DfE) (2018) *Working Together to Safeguard Children*. London: DfE.
Department for Education and Skills (DfES) (2003) *Every Child Matters*. London: DfES.
Home Office (2015) *Prevent Duty Guidance*. London: Home Office.
Horner, N. and Krawczyk, S. (2006) *Social Work in Education and Children's Services*. Exeter: Learning Matters (esp. chapters 2 and 5).
Lindon, J. and Webb, J. (2016) *Safeguarding and Child Protection*, 5th edn. London: Hodder Education.
Nicolas, J. (2015) *Practical Guide to Child Protection*. London: Jessica Kingsley.

21

Special educational needs and inclusive schooling

Brian Everest and David Middlewood

21.1 Introduction

Special educational needs (SEN) is an educational term used to describe a difficulty or difficulties in learning that is or are considered more than that which most children and young people experience. So, although some people may feel that in the course of their learning at school they have experienced difficulties in understanding certain concepts and even subject matter, this would not be seen as a SEN unless it was significant, probably affected learning in other areas, and had a profoundly negative impact on the learning experiences and opportunities available to the person in question.

Ofsted (2017) states that approximately one in seven pupils in England and Wales (14.4%) are considered to have SEN. This means that, unless a teacher teaches only high-ability sets in a mainstream school, there is every chance that teacher will have a pupil with some kind of SEN at some time in their classes. Even those circumstances are not exclusive of SEN because there is always the possibility that a teacher may come across an extremely bright pupil with some autistic tendencies (for example, Asperger syndrome) who will need learning materials to be presented in such a way as to ensure effective learning can take place. (For details of teaching more able, gifted and talented [MAGT] pupils, see Chapter 15.) This chapter focuses on those pupils as defined in the opening paragraph as having SEN.

It is important to make clear at the outset that most of what is good practice and effective teaching with pupils with SEN is just the same as for all other pupils. Thus, a new teacher need not be overwhelmed by the thought of having to teach a pupil with SEN in the class in a way that is quite different from everyone else in the class, or be worried that they have not had specialized training. Having knowledge of what the needs are of any pupil is the key, and then, with the support of the school special educational needs coordinator (SENCo) and very often a teaching assistant (TA), the teacher can proceed with confidence.

By the end of this chapter, you should:

- have gained an understanding of the history of SEN since 1944 and the terminology used to describe it;
- understand what is meant by SEN and the legislative framework within which it exists today;

- be aware of the identification of and provision for a pupil with SEN in the classroom;
- have gained an understanding of current multi-professional practices used to meet a pupil's SEN through the use of Education, Health and Care (EHC) plans.

21.2 SEN: history and terminology

The history of SEN in the UK from the 1940s to the present day can be summarized as a steady movement towards inclusion. The Education Act 1944 made provision for children with SEN either in mainstream school or in special schools, and all types of disability were to be recognized. Children were diagnosed medically and then assigned to what was deemed the appropriate provision. The emphasis was on the disability and the treatment it needed. Only with the Education Act 1970 did the notion of some children being unsuitable for education provision end. The Warnock Report (DES, 1978) led to the Education Act 1981, which prioritized the child's educational needs and focused on how to meet them. This Act also gave more rights to parents, encouraged more pupils with SEN to be educated in mainstream schools, and introduced the concept of 'statementing' as a means of identifying and meeting educational needs.

Terminology also changed following the introduction of the phrase 'special educational needs'. For example, pupils labelled 'educationally subnormal (mild)' became pupils with a 'moderate learning difficulty' (MLD), and 'educationally subnormal (severe)' became pupils with a 'severe learning difficulty' (SLD). 'Maladjusted' children changed to children with 'emotional and behavioural difficulties' (EBD). The focus changed from treating a disability to meeting a child's SEN.

21.3 The 2001 SEN Code of Practice

The 2001 SEN Code of Practice developed the definition of SEN further. Its provisions included:

> 'Children must not be regarded as having a learning difficulty solely because the language or form of language of their home is different from the language in which they will be taught.'

> (DfES, 2001: 1:3)

The 2001 SEN Code outlined twelve categories of need under four headings, as shown in Table 21.1. It also set out five principles:

1. children with SEN should have their needs met;
2. these needs will usually be met in mainstream schools;
3. the views of children should be sought and taken into account;
4. parents have a vital role to play in supporting their children's education; and
5. children with SEN should be offered access to a broad and balanced curriculum.

To ensure these principles were met, the 2001 Code formalized the use of Individual Education Plans (IEPs), which all learners provided with support were required to have. Those pupils with statements also had to have an 'Annual Review' of their statement. This involved

Headings

	Cognition and Learning Needs	Behavioural, Emotional and Social Needs	Communication and Interaction Needs	Sensory and/or Physical Needs
Categories	• specific learning difficulties (SpLD) • moderate learning difficulties (MLD) • severe learning difficulties (SLD) • profound and multiple learning difficulties (PMLD)	• behavioural, emotional and social difficulties (BESD)	• speech, language and communication needs (SLCN) • autistic spectrum disorder (ASD)	• visual impairment (VI) • hearing impairment (HI) • multi-sensory impairment (MSI) • physical disability (PD) • pupils with medical needs are usually included in the sensory and physical needs section

Table 21.1 Categories of SEN

Source: Adapted from the 2001 SEN Code of Practice (DfES, 2001).

a meeting with all those involved with the education of the pupil, which often became a multidisciplinary meeting including a school representative, parents, social worker, health professional and other professionals from support agencies. At Year 9, these meetings also involved the Careers Service as plans were put in place for the educational future of the pupil both in school and afterwards.

Ensuring the requirements of the 2001 Code were met became the responsibility of a teacher designated the school's SENCo. In many schools, especially secondary schools, the SENCo leads a department that specializes in provision for pupils with SEN, sometimes known as the Learning Support Department. Thus, the SENCo may be also known as Head of Learning Support.

21.4 The role of the SENCo

According to the 2001 Code, the SENCo should have responsibility for:

- 'ensuring liaison with parents and other professionals in respect of children with [SEN]
- advising and supporting other practitioners in the setting
- ensuring that appropriate Individual Education Plans are in place
- ensuring that relevant background information about individual children with [SEN] is collected, recorded and updated

The [SENCo] should take the lead in further assessment of the child's particular strengths and weaknesses; in planning future support for the child in discussion with colleagues; and in monitoring and subsequently reviewing the action taken.'

(DfES, 2001, 4:15–4:16)

In mainstream schools, the key responsibilities of the SENCo may include:

- 'overseeing the day-to-day operation of the school's SEN policy
- liaising with and advising fellow teachers
- managing the SEN team of teachers and learning support assistants
- coordinating provision for pupils with [SEN]
- overseeing the records on all pupils with [SEN]
- liaising with parents of pupils with [SEN]
- contributing to the in-service training of staff
- liaising with external agencies including the LEA's support and educational psychology services, the Connexions PA, health and social services and voluntary bodies.'

(DfES, 2001, 6:35)

21.5 The new teacher

For a new teacher in a mainstream school encountering a pupil with SEN, the school's SENCo will almost certainly be their first point of reference. It is also quite possible that the SENCo will seek out a particular new teacher who the SENCo knows has a pupil with SEN in one of their classes, to inform that teacher of the pupil's IEP and any immediately relevant targets that may influence the teacher's planning or teaching. This may require the teacher to plan differently for this pupil, to provide differentiated resources and learning materials for that pupil, to plan for a teaching assistant to deliver specific programmes to the pupil, or to use specialized equipment the teacher has not been aware of before. The teacher will also need to be aware that the SENCo will need to monitor the progress of the pupil so as to check on the effectiveness of the interventions provided. This information will be used to inform school managers whether the interventions are worthwhile and to keep parents informed. Along with the teacher, the classroom assistant is the crucial person in supporting pupils with SEN in class. As a new teacher, establishing a good and professional relationship with the assistant(s) is vital for all those involved, especially the pupil. (This relationship is explored further in Chapter 7.)

21.6 Pupils with SEN in secondary schools

It is worth noting the following from the publication *Special Educational Needs in England* (DfE, 2017b):

- Overall, the number of pupils with some form or level of SEN but without statements or EHC plans was 34.4% in state-funded secondary schools. The number *with* a statement or plan was 22.2%.

- Summer-born pupils are more likely to be identified as having SEN than pupils born in the autumn. At the ages of 11 and 16, September-born pupils are about half as likely as August-born pupils to be identified as having SEN (12% versus 22%).

- Pupils with SEN are more than twice as likely to be living in poverty (when defined as eligible for free school meals) as pupils without SEN. In 2017, in secondary schools, the figures were 26.6% for pupils with SEN and almost 12% for pupils without SEN.

- In the age range 12–17 years, most of the SEN pupils without a statement have MLD and, of those with a statement or plan, 26% will be on the autistim spectrum. Note that there are twice as many boys as girls in this last category.

Task 21.1

Study the above statistics about pupils with SEN in secondary schools. Make a note as to where you think the information might be relevant to any individual pupils in your class.

Read the following case study, reflect on it and consider your answer before reading the comments.

Case Study 21.1

In your class, George has fallen behind in his work. He appears listless and uninterested in learning and only wants to play football or go out with his mates. He rarely completes homework and only usually does so in an after-school detention. However, George does not always attend detention.

Sometimes he withdraws into himself and at other times he can become loud and angry. The SENCo tells you she has allocated a teaching assistant to help George keep up with his work, more as a carrot, as the stick has not worked.

How might you plan for the use of the assistant? For example, think how you are going to present the assistant to George.

COMMENTARY: Unless the presence of the assistant is explained carefully to George, he is likely to resent them and not cooperate. Thus, George needs to be told of the potential benefits (to himself) of having an assistant there. These could include no more detentions, more time with his mates and also more educational success (he may not appear to care about this one, but inside he probably does). As he is way behind with his work, a short period of withdrawal on a one-to-one basis will provide the opportunity to catch up. Obviously, the assistant needs to be fully briefed and find something they like in George, so they can build a relationship.

21.7 Class-based support

At an early stage, a pupil identified as having SEN will undergo some form of assessment to identify more precisely what those needs are. In the classroom, the teacher will need to know the details of the pupil's SEN so as to find out how best to organize their learning so that the pupil can make good progress.

In this kind of assessment, the teacher's appraisal is used to inform the direction of future learning. It is a formative assessment process, with the intention of providing valuable information to support the education of the pupil. Following the assessment, a teacher can begin to plan for that pupil's learning and consider what resource needs are appropriate. This could be in terms of requesting specialist equipment, additional staff support at certain times or in certain lessons, or access arrangements to classrooms. Some elements of support may already be in place, as provided by the SENCo, and may require training on the part of the teacher to learn how to use a resource or a plan for a support assistant to deliver a specific programme.

Once an intervention plan has been put in place, it will need to be monitored to decide if the intervention is working; the plan will need to be checked regularly and decisions made regarding its effectiveness. How regularly and by whom are matters for the SENCo, the teacher and the pupil, though it may include other staff (for example, staff who teach the same pupil and senior staff). (Issues of progress and what is defined as progress are discussed in Chapter 15.)

For secondary pupils, one factor to be recognized is whether progress for pupils with SEN:

- 'is likely to lead to appropriate accreditation;
- is likely to lead to participation in further education, training and/or employment.'

(DfES, 2001: 6:49)

The outcome of the monitoring of the intervention plan will then inform the future planning for that pupil. If progress has been considered good, the plan may change to result in less intervention or a change of emphasis requiring similar levels of intervention. If the outcome shows that progress has not been good, the reasons will need to be examined and changes made to the plan.

The essential aim of the *assessment–delivery–monitoring–feedback/assessment* process is to promote both the pupil's understanding of what and how they learn, but also what and how the teacher teaches. This can then inform the best ways for the teacher to plan and deliver learning and for the pupil to benefit from it.

Classroom teaching

As noted earlier, teaching pupils with SEN need not be so different from teaching other pupils in terms of how a teacher manages their classroom. Planning is clearly crucial for all pupils. The classroom needs to be an environment where learning is encouraged, and mistakes are allowed as part of the learning process. Good teaching uses feedback from pupils to provide prior knowledge, which is invaluable to a teacher in steering the direction of the lesson either making recap necessary or moving forward more quickly. It is also important to check on whether learning has taken place in a lesson by using questioning at the end of a lesson. Such questioning needs to take into account the language skills of the pupil with SEN and key words may need to be displayed in the classroom. (For the key principles in assessment for learning, see Chapter 9.)

21.8 Personal learning of the pupil with SEN

We suggest that there are four key principles of personalized learning:

1. Respect: we undertake to listen to you and to speak up for you when you want us to.
2. Self-determination: we will enable you to make choices about your life.
3. Inclusion: we will enable you to take your place in the community.
4. Fostering relationships: we will enable you to be with different groups of people and to choose your friends.

Task 21.2

Consider the above four principles of personalized learning. Make a careful note in each case of what a particular application might be for the teacher in the way the classroom is managed or organized.

These are, of course, equally applicable to all pupils and show how the principles and purposes of assessment and planning have converged over the decades to enable pupils with SEN to be educated in whatever environment is considered best for them.

21.10 School-based support

Teachers operate within the policies, practices and ethos of the whole school community. Attitudes and values of all those within the school community (staff–staff, staff–pupil, pupil–pupil) and beyond provide a good indication of what is important to that school community. The support provided will endeavour to develop systems in which the needs of all pupils are understood, and their learning planned accordingly, and that caters for the range of aptitudes, interests and abilities of all the pupils by providing opportunities for each pupil to succeed.

The Training and Development Agency for Schools (2009) produced a useful checklist of conditions it considered necessary for a school to successfully incorporate pupils with SEN into its school community, something it calls 'making reasonable adjustments' (from the Disability Discrimination Act 1995):

- A 'can-do' attitude from all staff as the attitude of staff is fundamental to achieving successful outcomes for disabled pupils.
- A proactive approach to identifying barriers and finding practical solutions.
- Strong collaborative relationships with pupils and parents/carers (see Chapter 7 for discussion of teacher/parent relationships). Pupils can also be the best judges of what is effective. They can be good advocates for what has worked well for them.
- A meaningful voice for pupils (see Chapter 3 for discussion of pupil voice).
- A positive approach to managing behaviour – many schools use peer support and mentoring schemes to help develop a positive approach to challenging behaviour.
- Effective staff training and development.
- The use of expertise from outside the school.
- Building disability into resourcing arrangements (see Case Study 21.2 as an example of this).
- A sensitive approach to meeting the disability-specific needs of pupils (see Case Study 21.3).
- Critical review and evaluation.
- Regular reviews at a pupil-, departmental- and school-level help ensure that progress is monitored; successes and failures are shared and inform the next steps; and the views of pupils and their parents/carers are sought and incorporated into the 'reasonable adjustments' that the school makes.
- Availability of role models and positive images of disability. Where schools use a range of opportunities to provide disabled role models, both children and adults, this can boost the self-esteem of disabled pupils and have a positive effect for all pupils. This can be supported by positive images of disabled children and adults in pictures, books and the range of materials used in schools.

All of these factors play an important part in defining the ethos of a school and the incorporation of them linked to effective classroom practice goes some way towards the 'inclusive' school.

Read Case Study 21.2, reflect on it and consider your answers before reading the comments.

Case Study 21.2

Debbie is a wheelchair-bound pupil who can manage her electric wheelchair independently. However, she also has SEN in cognition and learning, recognized as MLD. She has motor coordination difficulties and cannot hold a pen or pencil easily, although she can press the knobs and pull the levers of her wheelchair. What might you discuss with the SENCo about her SEN as you see them?

COMMENTARY: Debbie needs specialist equipment such as a large keyboard laptop or tablet. She needs appropriate space in the classroom, so she feels she has an environment for learning success. Discuss this with her and the other pupils affected by it, preferably together. In the discussion, place her needs in the context of everyone having their needs taken account of. If issues arise that have whole-school implications, refer them to the relevant person.

Now read Case Study 21.3. Reflect on what is involved and think about your response before reading the comments.

Case Study 21.3

At a parents' evening, you are approached by the parents of Noel, a 14-year-old boy with Asperger syndrome who has recently joined your class. They tell you that he seems to have no understanding of personal hygiene, or how it impacts on others (you had noticed!). His parents wash him every morning because he will not do it himself. They ask for advice and help.

COMMENTARY: This is definitely one to discuss with the SENCo and others! In school, this can be the subject of any social skills lessons, where one can stress that the way a clean person looks is more socially advantageous than the way a dirty person appears. Different levels of cleanliness can be discussed. Noel's parents ought to be fully involved so that a practical strategy emerges that helps him to learn the task of washing by rote, using a list of words or pictures. If he is one who thrives on rigid routine, he will adapt to this. As a class teacher, you can play your part by complimenting him on his appearance as it improves and using the key words that have become part of his routine.

21.11 A note on the 2014 SEND Code of Practice

The 2014 SEND Code of Practice did not change the definitions of SEN, but it did place much more emphasis on the child and the rights of the family.

The key changes included clarifying that the age range covered is 0–25 years; that involvement of children and young people in decisions about their education is crucial; and that aspirations should be as high as is reasonable. Any teacher will note that this last point is, of course, as true of any pupil in a class, whether they have specifically identified special learning needs or not. After all, in terms of teaching and learning, every individual has special needs for their own learning (Nasen, 2015).

A new concept entitled the 'Local Offer' was included in this Code of Practice, setting out what must be offered and available to those with SEN and their parents. The EHC plan also replaced the Statement of Special Educational Needs. It includes:

Section A: The views, interests and aspirations of the child/young person and their parents.
Section B: The child or young person's SEN.
Section C: The child or young person's health needs which are related to their SEN.
Section D: The child or young person's social care needs that are related to their SEN or to a disability.
Section E: The outcomes sought for the child or the young person including outcomes for adult life. The EHC plan should also identify the arrangements for the setting of shorter term targets, including the name and type of the school or other placement to be attended by the child or young person.

The Code also intended to put children and families right at the heart of the process and to speed up the assessment process so that a decision could be made more quickly – in 20 weeks instead of 26 weeks.

21.12 Conclusion

It seems a long time ago that children with SEN or disabilities were not educated in any type of school, let alone mainstream schools. The changes in social and political attitudes over the decades have meant that such children are no longer 'brushed under the carpet' or put out of view. The focus is now on meeting their needs in the most appropriate setting. This will usually be their local mainstream school, and many pupils who, some years ago, would have attended a special school, will now attend a mainstream school. (The SEN of those pupils that do attend special schools are now more complex, with pupils often exhibiting several and complex special needs. Also, with advances in medical science, there are now more life-limited pupils attending special schools than was previously the case.)

The chances of a new teacher in their first year of teaching in a mainstream secondary school having in class at least one pupil with SEN are extremely high and therefore any new teacher needs to be prepared for this if they are to perform their job successfully.

Recommendations for further reading

Department for Children, Schools and Families (DCSF) (2008) *The Assessment for Learning Strategy*. Available at: dera.ioe.ac.uk/8161 [accessed 6 October 2017].

Department for Education (DfE) (2012) *Supporting Young People with Learning Difficulties to Participate and Progress: Incorporating Guidance on Learning Difficulty Assessments*. London: DfE. Available at: dera.ioe.ac.uk/id/eprint/705 [accessed 30 September 2017].

Department for Education and Skills (DfES) (2001) *Special Educational Needs (SEN) Code of Practice*. London: DfE. Available at: www.gov.uk/government/publications/special-educational-needs-sen-code-of-practice [accessed 10 October 2017].

Department of Education and Science (DES) (1978) *Special Educational Needs (The Warnock Report)*. London: DES. Available at: http://www.educationengland.org.uk/documents/warnock/warnock 1978.html [accessed 14 June 2008].

Education Act (1981) (c. 60). London: HMSO. Available at: legislation.gov.uk/ukpga/1981/60/contents [accessed 11 November 2017].

Gillard, D. (2011) *Education in England: A History*. Available at: http://educationengland.org.uk/history/timeline.html [accessed 8 September 2017].

Nasen (2015) *The SEND Code of Practice: 0–25 Years*. Tamworth: Nasen. Available at: http://www.nasen.org.uk/utilities/download.29628CBA-F6C6-4F3E-87EE43D23B1F757E.html [accessed 14 June 2018].

Office for Standards in Education (Ofsted) (2010) *The Special Educational Needs and Disability Review*. London: Ofsted. Available at: www.gov.uk/government/publications/special-educational-needs-and-disability-review [accessed 30 October 2017].

Training and Development Agency for Schools (TDA) (2010) *PGCE Session 1 Statutory Requirements, Handout 1: Types of Need from SEN Code of Practice 2001*. Available at: dera.ioe.ac.uk/13818/ [accessed 17 October 2017].

22

Schooling, ethnicity and English as an additional language

Robert Sharples, Judith Hanks and Jean Conteh

22.1 Introduction

Ethnicity, multilingualism and English as an additional language (EAL) have often been treated as synonymous in the school system. In a way, this is understandable, because many of the languages spoken in the UK first arrived with migration from other countries, but it is important to make the distinction. Ethnicity and multilingualism are terms that describe *people and communities*; they allow us to talk about groups (such as Black Caribbean pupils or Polish speakers) and they form part of our broader vocabulary for talking about identity. These terms change over time, both in our everyday usage and in formal policy (most recently, when the 2016/17 school census introduced 'Arab' as a new category). 'EAL' is different: the term is contested (Bracken *et al.*, 2017: 6–9) but it broadly denotes a specialism for teachers and the young people with whom these specialists work. If we use the terms as synonyms, we risk putting very different people into a generic category ('ethnic or linguistic minority') and losing sight of the specialist knowledge and skills that are needed to support young people who are learning English alongside the curriculum.

This chapter focuses on that distinction, using it to draw out the specialist knowledge that new teachers need to make a difference with multilingual children. Treating EAL and ethnicity separately allows us to think more critically about the experiences of young people in the education system, to consider the role of language and learning more clearly, and to see how the pressures of the National Curriculum and other policy initiatives have shaped our responses to both (see Chapter 19 for more on the curriculum). The chapter accordingly begins with an overview of the history, showing how 'ethnicity' and 'EAL' have been intertwined in education policy and have only recently begun to receive separate attention.

By the end of this chapter, you should:

- know the relevant legislation, understand the relevant national data and be able to apply both to your school;
- be more aware of the factors that can marginalize ethnic minority and multilingual children;
- be familiar with strategies for supporting EAL pupils;
- know where to turn for further support as you develop in your teaching career.

22.2 A brief history

Although the UK has a long history of inward migration, attention began to focus on multi-lingual and multi-ethnic classrooms only with the arrival of young people from the 'New Commonwealth' of newly (re-) independent countries. There was then – as now – no national approach to majority-language education in schools, but teachers were encouraged to model Standard English norms through their own speech (Ministry of Education, 1963). This initial policy response was based around the assumption that these young people would settle in the UK for the long term (Tomlinson, 2008: ch. 1) and that the goal was to help them become 'invisible', 'truly integrated member[s] of the school community . . . as soon as possible' (Derrick, 1977: 16). Specific funding was allocated to support this integration into the mainstream through Section 11 of the Local Government Act 1966 (and so these early specialist staff were often known as 'Section 11 teachers'). Provision was limited and was often organized through 'language centres' that isolated young migrants from the mainstream and often presented English in a 'de-contextualised way [that] did not prepare pupils for curriculum content' (Graf, 2011: 3).

A second phase – the 1970s to the 1990s – can be seen as a reflection of a country coming to terms with broader issues of diversity, equality and mobility. The language centres established in the previous decade came under greater scrutiny as a number of government reports found that they isolated migrant learners from mainstream classes and did not offer sufficient preparation for academic success (for example, DES, 1971, 1972). The Bullock Report (DES, 1975) was particularly significant because it made a clear argument for multilingualism as part of the mainstream school. A changing political climate also contributed to the increased emphasis on mainstream provision: where previously migrant children had been seen as a 'threat to "standards" and the quality of education in schools', an increasing awareness of racial discrimination meant that the risk of legal challenges to language centres posed the greater threat (see Leung, 2016: 160–162). The Race Relations Act 1976 allowed for legal challenges on grounds of racism and the Rampton Report (DES, 1981) introduced the notion of institutional racism. The Swann Report (DES, 1985) built on Rampton's findings and implied that the use of separate language centres was discriminatory. The Calderdale Report (Commission for Racial Equality, 1986) found that Calderdale local authority's policy of providing separate English-language tuition could not be justified on educational grounds and amounted to indirect racial discrimination. By 1993, when the Local Government (Amendment) Act widened Section 11 funding to all ethnic-minority pupils, issues of diversity, equality and discrimination were firmly part of the discourse around multilingual classrooms.

The most recent phase – from the late 1990s to today – can be seen as a period in which global migration flows began to shift, leading to increasing diversity in the classroom (see Appadurai, 1990 and Bauman, 2007 on global mobility; Blackledge and Creese, 2010 on mobility and multilingual classrooms; and Arnot et al., 2014 and Strand et al., 2015 on their presentation of these trends in EAL data). Pupils are increasingly likely to arrive or leave mid-year and may bring with them experience of learning in several different education systems and languages. New technologies mean that young people can stay in closer touch with family and events far away and may see their time in the UK as part of a broader migration trajectory. These changes should be seen in the context of an education system that is struggling to adapt to the increasing mobility of its pupils.

Reforms to the education system since 2010 have led to increasing fragmentation at national level and increasing isolation at school level. Changes to initial teacher education (ITE) have significantly increased the role of schools and multi-academy trusts in training teachers, while the role of universities and local authorities has been reduced. One advantage of the former system was a relatively effective network of EAL provision, with expertise shared between schools, local authorities and universities. In a 'school-led' system (see Gilbert *et al.*, 2013), schools are expected to provide that level of expertise themselves, of which few can. As a result, very few schools now have access to an EAL specialist and there has been a substantial reduction in the support available from local authorities and in the number of specialist ITE and postgraduate courses available to EAL teachers. This loss of professional expertise comes at an important time: schools are increasingly responsible for identifying gaps in attainment and provision (see Chapter 15) but rarely have the capacity to do so alone. The current systems of data collection and management make it very challenging for schools to identify gaps in attainment or to hold schools to account for their EAL provision. Young people are increasingly mobile, classrooms are increasingly multilingual, and sustained partnerships between schools, universities and local authorities are needed if we are to equip them for a changing world.

22.3 EAL and ethnicity in educational data

The current 'school-led' system places great responsibility on teachers to understand educational data. It is important, therefore, to have a clear sense of how the data are produced, of what they can tell us and (crucially) what they cannot.

In 2017, 20.6% of primary and 16.2% of secondary pupils in England used English as an additional language (over 1.3 million pupils in total). The proportion of ethnic minority children is different: 32.1% of primary and 29.1% of secondary pupils (note that these figures relate to state-funded schools only) (DfE, 2017e). The data support an important observation: there are many ethnic minority pupils in England for whom English is *not* an additional language. The two categories overlap, but it is important to keep them distinct to avoid making broad (and often inaccurate) assumptions about 'ethnic and linguistic minority' pupils.

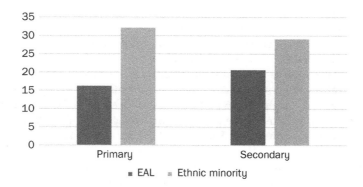

Figure 22.1 Percentage of EAL and ethnic minority pupils in English schools

Source: DfE (2017b).

A more accurate account of EAL would consider at least five different profiles of EAL learner. The following are adapted from Conteh (2012): the first two address the learner's proficiency in English and the latter three relate to their experience of the education system:

- Advanced bilingual learners
- New-to-English children
- Asylum-seekers and refugees
- Isolated learners
- Sojourners

The vast majority of learners with EAL in the UK are advanced bilingual learners. Typically, these young people are born in the UK and are categorized as EAL because they have exposure to another language in the home. They are also likely to be bi-literate (Datta, 2007), meaning that they read and write using more than one language, and may use these other languages for religious purposes (see Lytra *et al.*, 2016) or in a complementary school (see Blackledge and Creese, 2010). Bringing these languages and literacies into the mainstream classroom can yield great results. Other advanced bilingual learners arrive later in their school careers, but with a high level of proficiency in English and (usually) having been in formal education in another country. In either situation, the challenge is to help learners to transfer the skills they already have in one language to their academic learning in English.

Task 22.1

Think of the different dimensions of EAL learners' experiences (for example, whether they have attended school before, or what roots they may have in the local community). How might their needs differ from other pupils in the school?

Support for new-to-English learners should be planned carefully, as their level of English is a poor guide to their broader abilities. Some will progress at a much faster rate than others, and some will have been high achievers in other school systems. At all stages of English proficiency, learners need to encounter curriculum language in the context of real learning; withdrawal from classes risks creating a negative cycle in which more support makes it more difficult for them to re-join the mainstream. EAL learners need to gain experience using both general academic vocabulary and the specific genres and language patterns used in each subject (see section 22.5 on Pauline Gibbons and her work on academic literacy and EAL; see also Lea and Street, 2006 for an application of the 'academic literacies' model to compulsory education, and Andrews, 2009 for a discussion of the knowledge base for EAL).

The three other groupings of EAL learners could overlap with either of the first two. In each case, it is important to understand the experiences that each young person brings to the classroom. Young asylum-seekers and refugees, for example, are more likely to have had their schooling disrupted and to have experienced a range of educational settings – formal and informal – as a result. They may be withdrawn to begin with and settle in only after a period of time has passed, or they may appear to make quick progress and then fall back (see Mallows, 2012 for a broad overview of teaching migrants and refugees, and Sharples, 2017 for a study of one learner in a UK secondary school). Regardless of the trajectory, which can vary significantly between individuals, it is important to maintain high expectations of the young person and to place them in more advanced groups if there is any doubt about their ability.

Task 22.2

- What factors contribute to a learner being 'isolated'?
- What can individual schools do to make a more supportive, challenging and welcoming environment for isolated learners?

Case Study 22.1

Read the following description of one young person's experiences and then answer the questions that follow.

Hayat is an Eritrean pupil at a Somerset secondary school. He arrived in the UK some six months ago, following a year-long migration with his family through the Sudan, Libya, Italy and France. There are very few other Eritrean families in the area: Hayat is the only young person from East Africa at his school, and the only one who does not have secure legal status in the country (his application for asylum is still being decided). His primary language is Tigrigna but there are no other speakers of that language in the area; the school is having difficulty identifying translators and there are few English classes in the area for his parents.

- How might Hayat's experiences differ from pupils who grew up in bilingual homes in the UK? What about his needs (as seen by him, his family and the school)?
- How could the school make sure that Hayat is included in the mainstream curriculum as soon as possible ?
- What information would the teachers need (from Hayat or elsewhere) to stretch Hayat in learning English and his curriculum subjects? Likewise, what information would they need to support him?

COMMENTARY: Schools have a particularly important role to play with isolated learners (see, for example, Murakami, 2008; Grieve and Haining, 2011). There is a lot they can do to make such pupils feel more welcome by learning more about the young person's language, culture and experiences and making them a visible part of school life. Sojourners join the school for a limited time: their parents are often professionals posted to the UK or studying in a local university. They may attend a complementary school to keep up with the curriculum from their home country, so that they can move back into that education system when they return.

22.4 Theory and practice

Effective EAL provision involves more than just 'teaching English'. It means drawing on a body of knowledge about language, language learning, pedagogy and young people and using it to help pupils develop the linguistic and cognitive skills they need for academic success. This section outlines some of the key principles of that specialist knowledge.

Connecting home and school: funds of knowledge

An important starting point is to recognize that much learning happens outside school, and that teachers can draw on those experiences in the classroom. Children might develop literacy skills, for example, through religious practice (Gregory et al., 2013; Lytra et al., 2016), through interactions with grandparents (Kenner et al., 2007) or through learning a heritage language (Blackledge and Creese, 2010). In such settings, learning often revolves around children being respected and active participants alongside adults, building funds of knowledge (Gonzalez et al., 2005) that encompass skills and cultural knowledge. These 'contrast so sharply with typical classroom practices' (Moll et al., 1992: 133) because they are flexible, adaptive and involve a number of people across a number of settings. Secondary schooling typically involves an authoritative adult who plans and delivers programmes of study but does not participate alongside the young people. Complementary schools, faith and family settings often involve adults and young people collaborating to complete tasks, whether those are to prepare a meal or to learn how to perform worship.

Task 22.3

Find out more about the additional learning that the children in your class are doing. This might include learning in complementary schools, places of worship or extended families. Apart from the children and parents, who else might be good to ask in this effort?

There are practical ways to draw on EAL learners' funds of knowledge in the classroom. One approach is to make links to local complementary schools and to make the connections between the different classrooms explicit. There are between 3,000 and 5,000 such schools in the UK (NRCSE, 2017) and they generally teach a combination of heritage languages and cultures, usually in the evenings or at weekends. They are attended by both monolingual and multilingual children and often staffed by parents and members of the community, sometimes on the premises of mainstream schools and sometimes in community halls or private homes. These schools 'complement' mainstream schools and they are spaces where young people are able to use their other languages for learning. Another way to use the learners' funds of knowledge in the classroom is to use them for meaningful academic tasks: using first languages to make notes during experiments in science, for example, or using literary texts in different languages (perhaps with translations made by pupils) for formal analysis in English literature. A fuller discussion of classroom strategies using funds of knowledge is given in section 22.5.

Balancing linguistic and cognitive challenges

Classroom activities also need to balance linguistic and cognitive challenges – that is, they need to be pitched at the right linguistic level, so that they build on the learner's academic language skills, and they need to stretch the learner's understanding of curriculum content. In this section, we introduce a set of linked theories developed by Jim Cummins, one of the best-known theorists of bilingual education. They offer a powerful explanation of why first and second language learning are always linked, and why academic language proficiency needs time to develop.

It used to be believed that a bilingual person had two or more language systems at their disposal, and that they had to be kept separate in order to prevent the first language 'interfering' with the language being taught (hence, for example, strict English-only policies in the classroom). Cummins (2001) observed the ways that bilingual children used their languages in oracy as well as literacy. He recognized that these languages were not kept separate, but that bilinguals drew on them both to communicate effectively. He concluded that instead of having a separate proficiency for each language, all human beings have a 'common underlying proficiency' (CUP) for language. This can be imagined as a reservoir of knowledge and skill that informs communication in all languages, and it is often represented using the famous 'iceberg diagram' (Figure 22.2). What appear to be separate languages are better understood as different surface presentations of the bilingual person's deeper language proficiency.

The CUP suggests that the bilingual person's languages depend on each other (called linguistic interdependence) and separating them artificially will delay the development of them both. This has important implications: it is often assumed that the most effective way to support EAL learners is through immersion or by maximizing their 'time-on-task' in English lessons, but the interdependence hypothesis suggests that the opposite is true. EAL

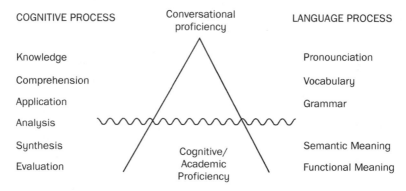

Figure 22.2 Surface and deeper levels of language proficiency
Source: Cummins (1984).

learners need to use all their languages in challenging, curriculum-based learning if they are to develop the strong English skills they need for academic study. (This has important implications for literacy [see Chapter 16], as Cummins and Early [2011] set out in their book on 'identity texts'.) Learners use the full range of their linguistic and cultural resources to communicate in their wider lives, and it is important to make sure that classroom literacy tasks are designed to welcome and reflect those experiences. This might mean going beyond the linear development of print-based writing skills: multilingual learners are likely to have communicative skills in advance of their English language literacy. They may be 'biliterate' (Datta, 2007) and have access to print literacy skills in other languages, or they may have experience of developing and articulating ideas in ways that are unfamiliar to those of us educated in the UK system. One way to look at this is to see the learners' identities becoming 'sedimented' (Rowsell and Pahl, 2007) in the texts they produce. This shifts the emphasis from a 'deficit', where learners are described by what they cannot do, to a view of English language literacy as a process of transfer and development. This is especially important for learners who are new to formal education, or to the UK system. When they join the classroom, they bring with them deep funds of knowledge, including established ways of developing ideas and communicating them. By making these an explicit and valued part of classroom activities, teachers can use them as a base for further literacy development (see section 22.5 for practical classroom strategies).

Cummins (1979, 2001) proposed two terms to describe the types of activities learners might encounter in the classroom. The first describes the sort of everyday English learners might focus on in transition or withdrawal EAL programmes. These are part of their basic interpersonal communication skills (BICS). He described the more challenging, curriculum-based academic skills as cognitive academic language proficiency (CALP). It is important to note how 'cognitive', 'academic' and 'language' are brought together here: language and thinking are inseparable and are best learned in the context of subject learning. Withdrawal or transition lessons often focus on the BICS (also known as 'survival' or 'conversational' English), but the lack of cognitive challenge and of academic context can hold pupils back from making progress.

The teacher's role in this can be understood in terms of context and cognitive demand. This is illustrated in Figure 22.3. The two axes can be thought of as continua, encouraging the teacher to gradually reduce the amount of contextual support given in the classroom while also increasing the cognitive challenge of the learning activities. In other words, the teacher's task is to move learners from quadrant A (high context but low demand) towards quadrant C (high demand and low context). Quadrant A includes, for example, giving instructions for a task, matching exercises or retelling sequences of events. These rely primarily on non-linguistic cues, and the items to be explained, matched or retold give a great deal of context for the task. Quadrant B activities involve more challenging tasks, such as generalizing from a set of examples, comparing and contrasting, or summarizing, but are still supported by the context. Quadrant C activities are cognitively challenging but are less reliant on the context of the task. They often make greater use of linguistic cues, such as arguing a case from a series of written extracts (common in history), interpreting results (common in science) or analysing a text (common in English). Quadrant D activities should be avoided: no learning occurs where there is low challenge and low contextual support.

EAL learners are not a homogenous group. The progression that learners demonstrate will be strongly influenced by their prior experiences, their existing literacy skills and the quality of support offered in school. For example, learners with limited English proficiency

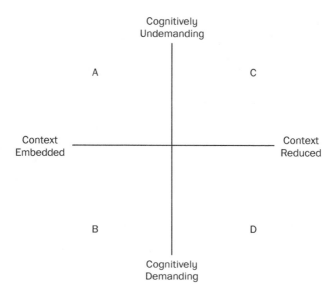

Figure 22.3 The Cummins quadrants
Source: Cummins (1984).

but with a strong track record of achievement in another school system will need a minimal 'survival' or 'conversational' English programme (typically involving Quadrant A activities) and should move quickly to work that is curriculum-based and cognitively challenging but where the context is made explicit (Quadrant B). As the young person's proficiency in English grows, the teacher can begin to shift the work towards more linguistically demanding – and less context-embedded – activities (Quadrant C). Advanced bilingual learners, including those arriving from other countries during secondary schooling, are unlikely to benefit from 'Quadrant A' activities. The challenge with these pupils is often to develop the language and literacy skills without reducing the cognitive challenge (that is, moving from Quadrant B to Quadrant C; no learning can occur in Quadrant D, where there is low contextual support and low demand). Different learner profiles, including isolated learners, refugees and sojourners, will need different patterns of support. The goal with all EAL provision, though, is to move learners towards linguistically and cognitively challenging, curriculum-focused study.

So far, this chapter has argued that we need to look critically at educational data, because it groups EAL and ethnic minority pupils into such broad categories that it is difficult to see the important distinctions within them. It has outlined two key hypotheses that can support teachers to have high expectations and to turn them into classroom practice, before highlighting the range of experiences and ways of learning that young people can bring into the classroom. The final sections of this chapter suggest ways to draw on those funds of knowledge in the classroom, and where to look for further support.

22.5 EAL in the classroom

Section 22.4 provided a practical discussion of key theories that underpin effective EAL pedagogy, and the advice in this section about teaching and learning leads directly from this. Currently, most of the published guidance for EAL teaching is for primary settings, but secondary schools are increasingly gaining attention. In this brief section, we refer to key texts that provide practical examples from secondary classrooms.

It has become something of a cliché to say that good practice for all pupils is good practice for EAL learners. There is some truth in this, but it can perhaps lead to the misconception that strategies to meet the distinctive needs of EAL learners can be tagged on to the primary business of mainstream classrooms or addressed outside them. Turning the statement around and claiming that good EAL practice is also good mainstream practice may offer a better way of thinking about how EAL issues can be placed at the centre of discussions about pedagogy. In this light, we propose four broad 'principles for practice' to underpin pedagogy for EAL learners and suggest that they can equally underpin pedagogy for all:

1. Recognize and value the knowledge that pupils bring to the classroom from their families and communities.
2. Provide opportunities for pupils to use their funds of knowledge as positive resources for learning.
3. Plan for progression: scaffold, rather than support.
4. Promote the development of academic language across the whole curriculum.

In what follows, each principle is briefly explained, and further reading is indicated that will help teachers to think about how to put them into practice in their own classrooms.

Principle 1: Recognize and value the knowledge that pupils bring to the classroom from their families and communities

This links with the Funds of Knowledge philosophy (Gonzalez *et al.*, 2005) and focuses on ethos and attitude. Research shows that pupils learn better when their identities are recognized and valued in their classrooms (Cummins, 2001). As a teacher, it is crucial to understand that you need to think of your pupils as competent rather than deficient, trust that they are doing the best they can and affirm their efforts as much as possible. You need to interpret positively what they say and develop conversations with them that extend thinking and promote learning. This can be difficult: it is much easier to identify with pupils with whom you share cultural and language experiences. Cummins and Early (2011) present a powerful set of case studies written mostly by teachers that explore the concept of 'identity texts'. In one of them, with pupils aged 13–14 years, Lisa Leoni (p. 48) lays out her 'instructional philosophy' in which 'identity affirmation and expansion' is central. In Conteh (2015: 145–147), Ruse and Sadler offer another perspective on pupil identity in secondary settings, discussing exit interviews conducted with Year 11 pupils (15–16-year-olds). These elicit and value learner voice, while also informing the development of teachers' practices in the school.

Principle 2: Provide opportunities for pupils to use their funds of knowledge as positive resources for learning

The second principle is also aligned with the Funds of Knowledge philosophy. It is about planning for specific kinds of learning that allow pupils to activate the learning they do in

the home and community. The main 'fund of knowledge' that multilingual pupils bring to the classroom is, of course, *language*. Allowing pupils to use their home languages for their learning is an essential element of this approach. This is not about teaching home languages but constructing 'safe spaces' for pupils to learn (Conteh and Brock, 2010). Chapter 8 in Conteh (2015) sets out the arguments for using home languages and cultures in learning, and a case study by Wood (pp. 198–200) provides an example in a secondary science context. Creese (2005) discusses ways that two teachers, or a teacher and a bilingual assistant, can work together in multilingual secondary classrooms to provide rich affordances for learning using home languages and other funds of knowledge. She develops practical principles on teacher collaboration (chapter 6) and partnership teaching (chapter 7).

Principle 3: Plan for progression: scaffold, rather than support

The explanation of the Cummins Quadrants above illustrates the importance of planning for progression, which entails constructing a strong scaffold for learning (see 'Balancing linguistic and cognitive challenges' on page 283). Too often, 'scaffold' and 'support' are seen as synonymous – but they are very different. Support is about helping someone in trouble to get by, usually making up for some kind of deficit; scaffolding is about building strong foundations so that the building will last. Myhill *et al.* (2005) provide an excellent discussion of scaffolding through talk in primary classrooms. Their book offers some very helpful general principles that can be taken into secondary classrooms, and chapter 4 of Conteh (2015) discusses joint planning for collaborative talk in secondary classrooms to develop effective scaffolds for learning.

Principle 4: Promote the development of academic language across the whole curriculum

Teachers of EAL pupils are not just responsible for teaching English, they also have to ensure that their pupils make progress across the whole curriculum. (For more on literacy and language across the curriculum, see Chapter 16.) Language learning and content learning need to go hand in hand, and the development of 'academic language' is essential in order to nurture that progress. As many scholars have pointed out, literacy is central to the whole process of learning and achievement, and Gibbons' (2009) book contains a wealth of ideas to help teachers plan relevant and challenging activities that will develop their pupils' academic literacy and contribute to their academic achievement in all areas of the curriculum.

22.6 Conclusion

This chapter began with a brief history of how EAL and ethnicity have been treated in UK education policy. It recognized that this is a time of instability, both globally and in the way that the UK education system is structured. The former means that patterns of migration are changing, introducing new challenges for schools to adapt to; the latter means that many teachers are working with less support from local authority- and university-based specialists. Teachers increasingly need to:

* seek out new sources of advice, particularly through subject associations such as NALDIC (UK-wide), SATEAL (in Scotland) and EALAW (in Wales);

- be critical of the data presented to them; and
- rely on peer networks for professional development.

What has not changed, though, are the fundamentals of teaching and learning EAL. The middle sections of this chapter introduced a series of concepts that help us to think more deeply about what young people bring to the classroom, and about the teacher's role in helping them translate that learning to the UK school curriculum. The first of these concepts was 'Funds of Knowledge' (Gonzalez *et al.*, 2005), an approach that recognizes both skills and knowledge built up in non-school settings (including faith learning, family storytelling and complementary schooling). The second concept was the balance between linguistic and cognitive challenge: EAL pupils need more than just language tuition if they are to succeed in mastering the curriculum. Higher-order thinking skills are inseparable from the language used to express them, and young multilinguals can develop both more successfully if the full range of their languages is used for classroom learning.

The final section of the chapter suggested four broad 'principles for practice' to underpin pedagogy for EAL learners. They focused on recognizing and valuing the knowledge that pupils bring to the classroom; on providing opportunities for young people to use those funds of knowledge for learning; on planning for progression; and on promoting the development of academic language across the whole curriculum. These are starting points: there is a rich literature and there are well-established pedagogies for EAL that can be used for further research and professional development.

Recommendations for further reading

Bracken, S., Driver, C. and Kadi-Hanifi, K. (2017) *Teaching English as an Additional Language in Secondary Schools: Theory and Practice*. Abingdon: Routledge.

Conteh, J. (2015) *The EAL Teaching Book: Promoting Success for Multilingual Learners in Primary and Secondary Schools*, 2nd edn. London: Learning Matters.

Conteh, J. and Brock, A. (2010) 'Safe spaces'? Sites of bilingualism for young learners in home, school and community, *International Journal of Bilingual Education and Bilingualism*, 14 (3): 347–360.

Creese, A. (2005) *Teacher Collaboration and Talk in Multilingual Classrooms*. Clevedon: Multilingual Matters.

Cummins, J. (2001) *Negotiating Identities: Education for Empowerment in a Diverse Society*, 2nd edn. Ontario, CA: California Association for Bilingual Education.

Cummins, J. and Early, M. (eds.) (2011) *Identity Texts: The Collaborative Creation of Power in Multilingual Schools*. London: Trentham Books.

Department for Education and Science (DfES) (2003) *Aiming High: Raising the Achievement of Minority Ethnic Pupils*, DfES/0183/2003. Available at: https://www.education.gov.uk/consultations/downloadableDocs/213_1.pdf [accessed 22 September 2017].

Gibbons, P. (2009) *English Learners, Academic Literacy and Thinking: Learning in the Challenge Zone*. Portsmouth, NH: Heinemann.

Gonzalez, N., Moll, L.C. and Amanti, C. (eds.) (2005) *Funds of Knowledge: Theorizing Practices in Households, Communities and Classrooms*. New York: Routledge.

Webliography

The *EAL Journal*: https://naldic.org.uk/publications/eal-journal and http://ealjournal.org – this is an important source of professional knowledge and support. It is written by and for practitioners and is published termly by NALDIC (the subject association for EAL).

NALDIC: http://naldic.org.uk – the UK-wide subject association for EAL.

SATEAL: http://www.sateal.org.uk – the Scottish Association for Teaching EAL.

EALAW: http://www.ealaw.org.uk – the EAL Association of Wales.

The EAL Nexus: https://ealresources.bell-foundation.org.uk – free resources produced by practising teachers.

23

Schooling and gender

Jenni Ingram, Victoria Elliott and Kate Shilvock

23.1 Introduction

Any reader of the national press could not fail to be aware of the discussions around the difference in attainment of girls and boys. Each summer, when GCSE and A-Level results are announced, attention is paid to these differences in relative performance.

A generation ago, there was national concern about the relative underachievement of girls. Research published in the 1970s suggested that girls were marginalized in the classroom, resulting in their low representation in higher education. Measures were taken to address girls' perception of themselves as achievers, to increase girls' interest in traditionally 'male' subjects such as maths and science, and to ensure equal opportunities within, and access to, the school curriculum. In addition, schools began to adopt teaching strategies designed to suit girls' 'learning styles' and examination boards adapted assessment methods to shift the emphasis from terminal examinations towards the inclusion of more continuous assessment. This included coursework at GCSE for many subjects. At the same time, changes in society resulted in more women entering the workforce and changes in law resulted in greater equality of access to some jobs that had hitherto remained male preserves.

In the late 1980s and the 1990s, the government of the day focused on raising standards of achievement by making schools more explicitly accountable. This saw the introduction of a National Curriculum (NC) in many subjects (see Chapter 13 for more information on the NC). This prescribed what should be studied and obliged girls to continue with science subjects, which previously many had dropped at Key Stage 4 (KS4). Against this background, girls have steadily improved their performance in areas of the curriculum once thought to be 'male' preserves, matching boys' performance in maths and science at GCSE for the first time in 1995. By 2001, girls outperformed boys at GCSE in all subjects except physics (Ofsted, 2003). As a result of these changes, attention shifted to boys' underachievement. In 2017, girls continued to outperform boys in all but four subjects: boys continue to outperform girls in mathematics, physics, economics and statistics. There has also been a shift in policy priorities – there is no longer a focus on boys' or girls' underachievement but rather a focus on achievement for all pupils irrespective of gender, ethnicity or social class.

In terms of the publication of data around gender differences in achievement, more recently attention has shifted from a focus on the proportion of pupils achieving a 'passing' grade, to the proportion of pupils achieving the highest possible grades. Internationally, whilst girls often outperform boys when considering average levels of attainment or passing grades, the reverse is often the case for the very highest grades (although there are also more boys than girls gaining the lowest grades). However, GCSE results in 2017 indicated that girls are also outperforming boys at the very highest grades with the exception of mathematics, economics, statistics and physics. Across all GCSE subjects, 16.3% of boys achieved a grade A/7 or above compared with 23.6% of girls in 2017. Notably, in English, 9% of boys achieved a grade 7 or above compared with 18.5% of girls, whereas in mathematics the respective figures are 16.3% of boys and 14.8% of girls. In 2017, 60% of the pupils who achieved the highest possible grade across English, English literature and mathematics were girls. For English, 1.3% of boys and 2.2% of girls achieved a grade 9, in English literature the results were 1.9% of boys and 3.2% of girls, whilst in mathematics 4.0% of boys and 3.5% of girls achieved the highest possible grade (JCQ, 2017). Similarly, at the highest grade at A-Level, an A*, females perform better than males (7.3% versus 7.0%), though this gap is smaller than it has been in previous years. This picture is reversed when you look at the proportion of pupils achieving an A* or A. It is this latter figure that was reported widely in the press, perhaps because it was 'the first time in at least seven years' where boys achieved more A* and A grades together than girls. Girls outperform boys at GCSE not just in absolute terms but also in terms of progress from KS2 to KS4 (Sammons *et al.*, 2014).

It remains the case, however, that women earn less than men at all levels, even when comparing men and women who have the same qualifications and work in the same industries. In 2017, although there was only one all-male board in the FTSE 100, only six FTSE 100 CEOs were women. And whilst in the UK there have been two female prime ministers, at the time of writing the US is yet to have a female president. Less than 5% of the prison population in England is female.

By the end of this chapter, you should:

- begin to reflect on the debate surrounding academic achievement and gender;
- know about current patterns of achievement and choice for boys and girls;
- understand the possible factors that might influence gender differences in achievement;
- understand other aspects of education surrounding issues of gender, such as LGBT pupils and well-being;
- have reflected upon the implications for your practice as a classroom teacher.

23.2 The global picture

The UK is not alone in its concern about boys' achievement. International comparisons of achievement in reading, science and mathematics, such as the Programme for International Student Assessment (PISA), report on the larger variation in boys' achievement compared with that of girls, with larger numbers of boys achieving the highest levels of performance and experiencing the lowest levels of achievement. In the 2012 study, 14% of boys and 9% of girls did not attain the baseline level in any of the three subjects surveyed (OECD, 2015: 3). A large number of boys in particular struggle to achieve even basic skills within the assessments. Similar to the examination results in the UK, internationally girls outperform boys in reading and boys outperform girls in mathematics. However, there are differences between countries in these international comparisons, which may help us to understand why these differences occur. The 2015 PISA study focused on science performance and this found that in Finland more girls than boys were identified as top performers, and in Hong Kong and

Singapore the results of boys and girls were similar at these highest levels of performance (OECD, 2016). It is noticeable that in the UK, the variation in performance in reading, mathematics and science is similar across boys and girls in contrast to the other countries that participated in the study.

However, the 2015 PISA study showed large gender differences in pupils' attitudes towards science-related careers. For example, in Germany, Hungary and Sweden, the highest performing boys in science were significantly more likely than the highest performing girls in science to expect a career that would require further training in science (OECD, 2016). The OECD report suggests that gender stereotypes about work in science-related occupations is a possible cause for these differences, arguing that schools need to counter these stereotypes. Interestingly, these gender differences were not apparent in the data for England: 28% of girls and 27% of boys aspired to have a STEM (science, technology, engineering, maths) career by the age of 30. Yet, if we look at what these careers might be, there still exists a clear difference between the genders: 21% of girls were interested in a career as a health professional compared with only 7% of boys, whereas 16% of boys were interested in a career as a scientist or engineer versus only 6% of girls.

Task 23.1

When you are in school, look at attainment data analysed by gender to identify trends in achievement over recent years. Are there particular issues in particular subjects or between particular Key Stages for your school?

23.3 Patterns of achievement

Differences in achievement are evident very early in a child's schooling. Assessment data of children aged 5 in England show that, whilst 74.3% of girls achieved the expected standards in maths and literacy, only 58.6% of boys did so. This also indicates that there are differences in the skills with which children begin school. Whilst social class is a better predictor of literacy attainment at all ages, a gender gap remains within all social class groups (Moss and Washbrook, 2016). This is not true for maths attainment, where the gender gap is insignificant across social classes from age 7 onwards.

A large longitudinal study that traced pupils from ages 3 to 16 found gender differences from the very beginning. Boys tended to have lower scores in the home learning environment at age 3. This study looked at both children's attainment in national assessments and social behaviours. At KS1, girls not only scored more highly in reading, but they also had higher scores in self-regulation and positive social behaviour. Boys were also rated by their teachers as having higher levels of anti-social behaviour at the end of KS1 (Sylva et al., 2004). These differences continued into KS2, where girls were rated more highly on self-regulation and pro-social behaviour than boys, whereas boys were rated by teachers as displaying more hyperactive and anti-social behaviour than girls (Sylva et al., 2008).

It should also be noted that differences in achievement by gender are not as pronounced as differences associated with ethnic origin, month of birth or social class. For instance, an analysis of attainment gaps over time shows that the social class attainment gap at KS4 was two and a half to three times as wide as the gender gap between 2003 and 2013 (Strand, 2015). Being summer-born has a greater effect than being female.

23.4 Implications for young people's futures

Differences in achievements can lead to differences in the opportunities that young people have when they leave school. In this section, we explore the gender differences within employment and higher education and the potential consequences of the gender differences in attainment at GCSE and A-Level.

The gender gap for those entering higher education is widening. In 2014/15, 53% of women began a university degree compared with 43% of men. If we consider pupils' aspirations to go on to university, this gap is similar with 47% of girls aged 15 indicating that they intend to complete a university degree versus 37% of boys. This gender disparity is especially apparent when we look at those from disadvantaged backgrounds where women were 51% more likely to enter higher education than men within this group. Men are also more likely to drop out of their degree (8% of men versus 6% of women) and are less likely than women to get a good degree (73% of women achieve a 2:1 or above compared with 69% of men) (Hillman and Robinson, 2016).

However, there are also noticeable differences in gender disparities depending upon the subject area and nature of the degree. For postgraduate research degrees, men outnumber women, but the reverse is true for postgraduate taught degrees. Only 15% of undergraduates and 26% of postgraduates studying computer science are women.

Gender differences in employment have been persistent over time. Young men, for example, dominate manual and skilled trades, and young women dominate jobs in personal services and sales. At the end of 2015, 200,000 men between the ages of 18 and 24 were considered to be economically inactive compared with 360,000 women. Women tend to work in occupations with lower pay and fewer prospects. Also, women who go straight into employment after school tend to do jobs that are paid less than men with similar qualifications. For those who have gone to university, men continue to earn higher salaries than women even when matched by higher education institution and subject area. However, men are more likely to be made redundant and are less likely to be re-employed than women. Also, despite changes to the law that enable fathers to share parental leave with mothers, so far only 1% of the men eligible have taken up this opportunity.

As mentioned at the beginning of this chapter, many high-profile positions in industry, education and politics are dominated by men. In 2017, the majority of chief executive officers (CEOs) and board members of FTSE 100 companies were men; only six FTSE 100 CEOs were women. Whilst in the UK, at the time of writing, we have a female prime minister, only four cabinet ministers are female. In 2016, the University of Oxford appointed its first ever female vice-chancellor, Professor Louise Richardson.

As also noted earlier, less than 5% of the prison population is female, with poor educational backgrounds often given as an explanation – for example, more than half of all prisoners have no qualifications compared with just 15% of the general population. Furthermore, around 25% of prisoners have learning difficulties. Less than a third of police officers and the judiciary are women compared with two-thirds of those working in the Ministry of Justice and Crown Prosecution Service.

23.5 Reasons for differences in attainment

It is difficult to isolate any one reason or area that could be responsible for differences in attainment between girls and boys, and there is a lot of debate around the roles of nature and nurture. Potential influential factors that have been investigated by researchers include assessment procedures, such as the role of coursework, pupils' attitudes and aspirations, teacher expectations, teachers' responses to pupil behaviour, and school, family or societal culture.

Historically, some attempts at explaining the gender gap have focused on biological factors, the argument being that there are biological differences between boys and girls that can affect their learning. Recent research has found that there is no such thing as a female or male brain; instead, we are each a unique mix of features previously thought to be either male or female (Joel *et al.*, 2015). There is some evidence that female brains mature more quickly than male brains during adolescence, suggesting that female brains may be working more efficiently than male brains (Storr, 2015). However, in terms of biology and physiology, boys and girls are more similar than they are different, and gender is generally a poor predictor of most kinds of behaviours (Joel *et al.*, 2015).

Another explanation is that gender differences stem from differences in pupils attitudes towards learning and their behaviour. For example, in the 2012 PISA survey, girls reported less self-confidence than boys in their ability to solve mathematics or science problems and were more likely to express strong feelings of anxiety towards mathematics. When the attainment of girls and boys with similar levels of reported self-confidence and anxiety was taken into account, there was no longer a gender gap. Boys also reported less time spent doing homework and were less likely to read for pleasure (OECD, 2015). From a very young age, children identify brilliance as a male trait. When a group of 6- and 7-year-olds was given the opportunity to play two very similar games, one that was described as being for 'really, really smart' children and the other for children who 'try really, really hard' both boys and girls were interested in the 'hard' game, but girls were less interested in the game for 'smart' children than boys (Bian *et al.*, 2017). This bias is also evident in teachers who have been found to attribute good grades in maths to hard work for girls but to natural ability for boys (Fennema *et al.*, 1990).

Other explanations focus more on social factors. Younger and Warrington (2005) point to the importance for boys of conforming to group norms, which are often in conflict with the expectations of the school. There is a narrower range of behaviour acceptable to the peer group for boys than for girls. Vantieghem and colleagues (2014) point out that the educational gender gap is most prevalent in Anglo-Saxon countries, which also tend to have greater levels of gender inequality on a wider level in society (which is interesting, given that males and females end up on different sides of those inequalities).

Further explanations originate from the different ways in which children are treated, depending on their gender. In the UK, there is currently a campaign to challenge the gendered marketing of toys. Yet research has shown that toy preferences are highly gendered, with boys' toys and resources concentrating on technology and action and girls' toys and resources focusing on care and stereotypically 'feminine' interests (Francis, 2010). Gender preferences for toys only show up after children are aware of their own gender, with younger children showing no preference. However, different toys enable children to develop different skills, such as spatial awareness and social skills. The Institution of Engineering and Technology (IET) found that toys with a STEM focus were three times more likely to be targeted at boys than girls and 89% of toys targeted at girls were pink (IET, 2016). Research into how gender features in children's books also shows that the majority have a male central character.

Vantieghem and colleagues (2014) summarize the research as saying that boys suffer more from demotivation, disruptive behaviour, overestimation of their own abilities and lack of self-discipline, which would then all contribute to the gender gap in school performance. Masculinity theory, which has been used to try to explain the gender gap, would suggest that things like being the class clown or 'having a laugh' in lessons – both things that are identified with being masculine – both detract from paying attention to the lesson that's happening, and produce more negative interactions with teachers, because they have to sanction this behaviour. Similarly, the more positive masculine stereotypes, such as achieving highly at sport, are not necessarily compatible with high levels of attendance and sitting quietly in class. The flipside of masculinity theory says that schools are feminized environments, particularly in certain subjects such as languages and English, and in their required behaviours, such as compliance, sitting quietly and listening.

One clear illustration of this mechanism (boys minimizing their 'feminine' high attainment in order to maintain their masculinity) is how the classroom behaviour of British high-achieving boys changes remarkably when they get older. At first, all through primary school, their classroom behaviour resembles most closely that of high-achieving girls: being enthusiastic, providing answers and having positive interactions with the teacher (Jones and Myhill, 2004). By age 14, however, this behaviour changes dramatically. High-achieving boys are the least likely to answer questions in class, even less likely than low-achieving boys. Researchers attribute this change to the emerging male culture, in which being seen as hard-working or enthusiastic about school is not 'cool' (Vantieghem *et al.*, 2014).

This is a rather simplistic view, however. There are other masculine identities, such as 'nerd' or 'geek' (Lyng, 2009), which are compatible with doing well at school. On the other hand, the 'lad' behaviour was mostly closely associated with a working-class background, and it is white working-class boys who underachieve the most.

Task 23.2

The following are some commonly expressed views about the differences between boys' and girls' aptitudes and preferences:

- Boys are loud and demanding in the classroom and get more attention from teachers.
- Boys don't like writing.
- Girls prefer to work in groups.
- Girls find it difficult to think logically.
- Boys find it difficult to express themselves.
- Girls do not perform well under pressure of timed exams.
- Boys prefer physical activity to academic work.
- Boys are competitive.
- Girls underestimate their abilities.

Consider your reaction to each of these. Note your responses for later reference.

23.6 Groupings

A quick perusal of the league tables published following GCSE results shows that single-sex schools are highly placed. Many of these schools have a selective intake and a history and tradition of achievement. Research shows that it is difficult to separate the effects of single-sex teaching from other factors. The picture that emerges is very mixed and the proportion of pupils in single-sex schools is relatively small, so results should be treated with caution.

There is some evidence that girls' schools have a positive effect in encouraging girls to study subjects considered to be 'masculine' and in challenging stereotypical views, and girls in single-sex comprehensives achieve more highly than those in mixed-sex comprehensives. Boys in single-sex grammar schools perform better than those in mixed-sex grammar schools. Boys of low attainment perform better in single-sex comprehensives, but for boys of middle or higher attainment whether the school is single- or mixed-sex does not appear to make a significant difference. The school's size, pupils' social class, prior attainment levels, history and tradition of achievement may all impact upon achievement: league tables are far too crude to give a picture that schools could use to make decisions. In addition, one needs to be aware that schools are concerned to develop pupils' social skills in addition to their academic skills and there are disadvantages in single-sex schooling. Consider, for example, the consequence of having the views of only one sex represented in discussion, or drama, and there is often a negative behavioural effect on all-boys' low-attaining groups.

Some mixed schools have experimented with single-sex teaching, often in a few subject areas such as English and science. Single-sex teaching in a subject that sets by ability may avoid the problem of sets that are dominated by one sex. Many schools find that in English, higher-ability sets are predominantly female, while in maths, higher-ability sets are predominantly male. Such a situation can have negative effects on the self-esteem of boys and girls and lead to reinforcement of the idea that subjects are 'male' or 'female'. Younger and Warrington (2005) reported an evaluation of examples of single-sex grouping in three mixed comprehensive schools. The effects on pupils' achievements, on the whole, appeared to be positive, but it was very difficult to isolate the effect of the intervention. Nevertheless, their work provided strong evidence that pupils felt more relaxed about contributing to lessons without the pressure of having members of the opposite sex in the class and that they felt better able to concentrate. They concluded that the success of single-sex grouping depended on the teacher developing a relationship with the class that provided a basis for collaborative effort.

Sukhanandan et al. (2000) found that when teachers adapted their teaching for single-sex groups, boys responded well to fast-paced, highly structured lessons. However, many teachers did not adapt their teaching style for the all-girl groups and there was little effect on girls' achievement.

Task 23.3

What has been your experience, if any, of single-sex teaching? Reflect upon the classroom situation and the advantages and disadvantages of the grouping adopted.

> If you have no experience of single-sex teaching, consider your own schooldays and the way the two sexes behaved and learnt in the classroom. What differences can you discern? What is your experience of the distribution of the sexes in ability sets and what impact did this have on the classroom environment?

23.7 Teaching and learning

Many schools are focusing their attention on a whole-school approach to raising the quality of teaching and learning, with a consequent effect for all pupils but particularly for those who are under-achieving, many of whom will be boys. Contributions from boys in lessons are prominent, both physically and verbally, and they often have more experience than girls of having their contributions evaluated by a teacher. Boys also show greater adaptability to approaches to learning that require memorizing facts, rules and procedures. They appear willing to sacrifice deep understanding in exchange for fast answers. Girls, on the other hand, do better on sustained, open-ended tasks, related to real-life situations and that require pupils to think for themselves (Beaman *et al.*, 2006).

There have been suggestions that boys are more likely to prefer more kinaesthetic, active, fast-paced and competitive teaching and learning styles. However, the picture is complex. In the interim report of their four-year research project, referred to earlier in this chapter, Younger and Warrington (2003) found little overall difference in the styles of learning favoured by boys and girls. They reported that girls are more likely than boys to have a good grasp of effective learning strategies (2003: 5).

23.8 Assessment

Chapters 9, 10 and 15 have considered a range of issues relating to assessment. However, it is widely believed that terminal examinations favour boys, emphasizing short-burst effort, whereas continuous assessment and coursework, which demand reflection and sustained effort over a considerable length of time, favour girls. With the removal of coursework from all GCSE examinations and most A-Level examinations, the gap between the sexes has not decreased. Differences may reflect the type of questions asked. For example, questions that demand discussion and reflection and require high-level language skills favour girls, whereas multiple-choice questions and ones that do not require written English favour boys. It has also been shown that boys believe that a last-minute burst of revision will suffice, whereas girls work more conscientiously over a longer period. Encouraging self-assessment may help boys to develop a more realistic assessment of their learning and potential.

There is also some research showing that teachers' assessments of pupils can vary according to gender. For example, teachers were less likely to judge boys as above average in reading, and more likely to judge them as above average in maths, than they should have done, when compared with standardized test scores (Campbell, 2015).

23.9 Literacy

Chapter 16 described in detail how literacy is an area to which many schools are paying particular attention to raise standards. Young people entering secondary school face heavy new demands on their literacy skills. Reading competence is particularly important.

The quantity of reading they are expected to do increases while the time devoted to teaching literacy skills decreases. Most pupils will already be aware of their difficulties with literacy and the effect of this on their achievement, and many of these will be boys. When a pupil whose literacy skills are insufficient begins secondary school, the demands on their ability to read and write can be overwhelming and decrease motivation. Many pupils fail to make progress in Year 7 and teachers note that demotivation and the resultant disaffection often begins in Year 8 (Barber, 1994).

23.10 Special educational needs

Special educational needs (SEN) have consistently been identified as more prevalent in boys than girls (see Chapter 17). In January 2017, 14.6% of boys were identified as needing SEN support compared with 8.1% of girls, and 4% of boys have an education, health and care (EHC) plan compared with 1.6% of girls (DfE, 2017b). Within this, autistim spectrum condition was the most prevalent primary type of need for boys that had an EHC plan (31.1% of boys with an EHC plan).

23.11 Well-being and behaviour

The Children's Worlds study, an international comparison of well-being in 15 countries, found that children in England ranked 14th out of 15 for life satisfaction; English children tended to not like going to school (compared with children in other countries in the survey) and reported poor relationships with teachers (Pople *et al.*, 2015). This is also seen in the PISA data: on average, in the UK pupils are significantly less satisfied with life than the OECD average (6.98 versus 7.31), and girls are significantly less satisfied than boys (OECD, 2015). When asked if they agreed with the statement 'even if I am very well prepared for a test, I feel anxious', 20% more 15-year-old girls than boys agreed, and on average the UK pupils were much more anxious about school work overall (OECD, 2015).

The regular survey of children's well-being carried out by The Children's Society since 2009 also found that a gender gap has opened up in recent years, with girls becoming increasingly unhappy with their appearance and with their lives in general, while boys' levels of satisfaction have remained stable (The Children's Society, 2016). More than a third of girls (34%) in 2016 were dissatisfied with the way they looked, compared with 20% of boys. The gender gaps in body image were not seen in other countries in the Children's Worlds study (Pople *et al.*, 2015).

Research has shown that teachers treat boys more negatively than girls, though female teachers are fairer in the way they treat the different gender groups (Myhill and Jones, 2006). Boys are over three times more likely to be permanently excluded and almost three times more likely to receive a fixed period exclusion than girls (DfE, 2016e). Younger boys were also more likely to be unhappy with their schoolwork and to have problems with behaviour or conditions such as ADHD than girls; as pupils got older, girls became more likely than boys to have emotional problems and to experience conditions such as depression. The authors of the report by The Children's Society suggested this might explain why boys were more likely than girls at age 10 to have mental health issues, but the situation was reversed by the time children became 14 (The Children's Society, 2016).

Ten per cent of children and young people aged between 5 and 16 have a clinically diagnosable mental health problem and, in any given year, 20% of adolescents may experience a mental health problem. Exams are a significant trigger for mental illness in young people and rates of depression and anxiety have been rising among teenage girls in England (Lessof *et al.*, 2016).

23.12 LGBT young people in school

Sexualities equality has been growing in importance over recent years as more and more pupils identify as lesbian, gay, bisexual or transgender (LGBT). In many schools, heteronormativity, the 'organisational structures in schools that support heterosexuality as normal and anything else as deviant' (Donelson and Rogers, 2004: 128), is embedded in the culture and everyday routines of the school. Homophobia is one example of a behaviour that normalizes heterosexuality, and anti-bullying initiatives have often focused in particular on combating homophobic bullying (for example, DCSF, 2007). More recently, there has been a shift towards schools proactively incorporating discussions and curriculum materials around sexuality and gender within their teaching (see, for example, the *No Outsiders* project reported in DePalma and Atkinson, 2009). A key challenge facing schools today is how to create and maintain schools as a safe environment for LGBT and non-binary pupils.

In 2017, nearly half of all LGBT pupils experienced homophobic bullying in school (Bradlow *et al.*, 2017) and LGBT young people who experience high levels of rejection, including homophobic bullying, are likely to experience mental health problems, which may well continue into adulthood (Rivers, 2000). Furthermore, fewer than a third of LGBT pupils who experience bullying said that teachers intervened when they were present during the bullying. Many of these pupils say they don't have an adult at school they can talk to about being LGBT and many also reported that they don't have an adult at home they can talk to. Whilst some of these figures have been decreasing over the last few years, homophobic, biphobic and transphobic bullying is still common in UK secondary schools.

The majority of homophobic bullying goes unreported, and pupils report that this is because they don't find it easy to talk to teachers either about the bullying or their sexuality. Some schools have set up LGBT groups for their pupils, and young people in these groups are more likely to report that they feel that they are part of the school and have an adult they believe they can talk to. Many trans pupils also report that they are not able to be known by their preferred name in school.

Many schools support pupils to wear clothing or uniforms in line with their gender identity but many trans pupils talk about issues around not being able to use the changing rooms or toilets in which they feel comfortable. In the classroom, seating plans are sometimes based on gender, such as boy–girl seating or group work with two girls and two boys placed in a group, but where does a trans or non-binary pupil fit into this? Similarly, sports teams are often delineated by gender.

Task 23.4

When you are in school, look at the school policies related to SEN, behaviour and sexualities. Are there particular aspects of these policies aimed at specific genders or gender identifications?

23.13 Conclusion

In this chapter, you have learnt about the patterns of attainment shown by boys and girls and examined some of the reasons for the differences. Research evidence for the nature of gender differences within education has also been outlined. You have considered broader issues associated with gender that teachers and schools need to consider. Schools that have set out to raise the standards achieved by all pupils and tackle under-achievement in general are most successful in narrowing the gender gap. Schools also need to consider the broader role of education, such as pupils' well-being.

Recommendations for further reading

Bian, L., Leslie, S.-J. and Cimpian, A. (2017) Gender stereotypes about intellectual ability emerge early and influence children's interests, *Science*, 355 (6323): 389–391.

Bradlow, J., Bartram, F. and Guasp, A. (2017) *School Report: The Experiences of Lesbian, Gay, Bi and Trans Young People in Britain's Schools in 2017*. London: Stonewall. Available at: https://www.stonewall.org.uk/sites/default/files/the_school_report_2017.pdf.

Bramley, T., Vidal Rodeiro, C.L. and Vitello, S. (2015) *Gender Differences in GCSE*. Cambridge Assessment Research Report. Cambridge: Cambridge Assessment. Available at: http://www.cambridgeassessment.org.uk/Images/gender-differences-in-gcse.pdf.

Department for Children Schools and Families (DCSF) (2009) *Gender and Education – Mythbusters. Addressing Gender and Achievement: Myths and Realities*. Nottingham: DCSF. Available at: http://dera.ioe.ac.uk/9095/1/00599-2009BKT-EN.pdf.

24

Supporting disadvantaged children to raise their attainment

David Middlewood

24.1 Introduction

Every child has their own individual context and personal situation or circumstances. In this sense, they all have their own specific learning needs, which are affected by factors such as age, ability or disability, gender and domestic circumstances. Several of these factors have been discussed elsewhere in this book (for example, Chapter 23 explores gender disparities, Chapter 14 looks at spiritual development and religion, and Chapter 20 investigates safeguarding concerns). Some children have a particular set of circumstances beyond their control that can have a significant effect on their progress and attainment at school. These are those who face extreme deprivation, often described as 'disadvantaged' children.

By the end of this chapter, you should:

- be aware of the factors involved in deprivation and disadvantage;
- understand the link between deprivation and levels of school pupil attainment;
- know how to identify disadvantaged children and be aware of the sensitivities involved;
- know about some of the practices and interventions that can support these children in raising their attainment;
- be able to consider what interventions you might use to support disadvantaged children in your professional experience.

24.2 Deprivation and disadvantage

In many countries across the world, both developing and developed, one encounters schools operating in what are often called 'challenging circumstances' (Harris and Chapman, 2002). In the developing world, these circumstances can typically include periods of drought, local ethnic warring groups, parents who cannot or do not pay the required fees, and widespread use of unqualified staff (Abaya, 2016). Other circumstances that are replicated in developed countries, although often in less extreme forms, include significant poverty in the local area, high levels of unemployment, low levels of formal qualifications in the local adult population, poor quality housing, neighbourhoods with high levels of crime, substance misuse and drug-taking, gang cultures and general anti-social behaviour. Thus, households in communities such as these will often have poor diet, insufficient income for warm clothing in winter, poor prospects of employment, above average numbers of teenage pregnancies, lack of privacy within the home and an above average reliance on state benefits, all of which pose a challenge to children's education.

Schools that are located in such areas in developed countries may be at risk of high staff turnover; poor facilities for staff, children and visitors; a lack of resources; declining pupil numbers; weak support from regional authorities; and, mostly in rural areas, geographical isolation (Clarke *et al.*, 2005). Children from such communities and schools are more likely than others to move into low-income employment (Blanden *et al.*, 2008). Additionally, lower skilled workers are more likely to be employed in hazardous occupations with an increased risk of workplace accidents (Feinstein and Sabates, 2006). Furthermore, whilst at school, children's exclusion from extra-curricular activities such as music lessons, school trips and arts activities lessens their opportunities to learn and perhaps gain better paid employment. Governments, in the UK and elsewhere, have become increasingly aware of the huge costs to national productivity and economic growth that such deprivation causes, as well as the disproportionate cost to public services. Various initiatives in England and Wales have therefore tried to offset such disadvantages in the environmental context of the children concerned through focusing on raising the levels of educational attainment at school, by increasing the number of classroom assistants (Nelson and O'Beirne, 2014), for example, or through peer mentoring (Sutton Trust, 2014).

24.3 The link between deprivation and attainment

As far as the link between deprivation and attainment was concerned, the Department for Education was unequivocal in 2015 that children from disadvantaged backgrounds were far less likely to get good GCSE results than their more advantaged counterparts (DfE, 2015e). Of course, this is a universal situation. As noted by Bloom (2012: 3):

> 'Whether in Tokyo or Finland, Britain or Bulgaria, from Venezuela to Morocco, the picture is clear that children from affluent homes out-perform those from poorer homes.'

Although this problem is faced around the world, each country has to tackle this divide by beginning with its own particular contextual problems. For many years in the UK, the best indicator of deprivation for children in school was their eligibility for free school meals (FSM). In England and Wales, a detailed analysis of statistics for 2009 showed that only 55% of pupils eligible for FSM met the expected levels at Key Stage 2 (KS2) compared with 75% of those not eligible for FSM. By KS4, the gap had widened so that in 2011, only 33% of pupils in the most deprived areas were achieving five or more GCSEs including maths or English, compared with 72% in the least deprived areas (DfE, 2011b). Furthermore, the longer a pupil had been eligible for FSM, the poorer their educational outcomes were likely to be (DfE, 2010a).

Of course, eligibility for FSM was not an infallible way of measuring deprivation. Some parents whose children were eligible did not apply for FSM, and over a period of a child's school life some pupils would move in and out of eligibility as home circumstances fluctuated, for example between unemployment and periods of work that might make a parent eligible or otherwise depending on the amount of time worked. Also, those pupils who fell marginally just outside the threshold of qualification for FSM could have similar disadvantages to those just within the threshold. Thus, the picture is more complex.

It is worth noting that the problem of low school attainment by those from deprived or disadvantaged contexts was not simply an educational issue but one for society at large. Such low attainers were likely to earn considerably less in their adult working life (Blanden *et al.*, 2008), more likely to have a poor diet and to smoke tobacco products – and thereby poorer health. This perpetuated the cycle of deprivation.

Additional factors such as attendance and behaviour could also be affected by deprivation, which in turn had an impact on school attainment. Children claiming FSM had three times more unauthorized absences from school, three times the number of permanent exclusions from school and four times the number of fixed-term exclusions from secondary school (DCSF, 2009b).

Demographics of children eligible for FSM (Sobel, 2018) showed that the ethnic groups most eligible were Irish Heritage Travellers, Gypsy Roma, Black African, White and Black Caribbean, Pakistani and Bangladeshi children. Black African and Black Caribbean pupils were more likely to live in areas of high deprivation. Of all groups, White British students had the greatest attainment difference between children eligible and not eligible for FSM. Gender differences did not appear to be significant, although female FSM pupils did better than male FSM pupils. (See Chapter 23 for more on gender.) From 2006 to 2011, the rate of improvement in attainment for White male and female groups was lower than for other ethnic groups (Sobel, 2018).

Against this background, action was deemed necessary. The government of 2011 responded by introducing the Pupil Premium for children of low-income families, eligible for FSM or who had been 'looked after' continuously for more than six months.

Task 24.1

Research your school statistics, then answer the following:

- How many children on the school roll are in receipt of Pupil Premium funding support? What percentage is this of the school population as a whole?
- How are these children identified generally, if at all?
- What proportion is male/female?
- What proportions are from specific groups, such as by ethnicity or disability?
- Do you know – or are you able to find out – which pupils are in receipt of Pupil Premium support in each of the classes you teach or in your form?

REMEMBER! This may be confidential information in your school, so ensure that you treat these data as such, but it is important for you to have an overall picture of the situation in your school. Make sure you know who is the specific senior person in the school responsible for Pupil Premium policy implementation (if there is a single person). You also need to be certain who is responsible overall for data management. These are two key roles and may or may not be carried out by the same person.

24.4 The Pupil Premium

Of course, resources such as the Pupil Premium will only help raise pupil attainment if they are effectively used in schools, both by the leaders of the school through their implementation and approach and by the teachers and support staff through the way they act in the classrooms. Clearly, it is important for all staff to be fully aware as to which children should be focused on. If the school policy is for every Pupil Premium learner to be known by each member of staff, you may want to follow the practice in many of the secondary schools that have been outstanding in raising attainment for disadvantaged pupils – that of having a seating plan for easy identification of such pupils.

Task 24.2

This task focuses on spotting characteristics and patterns.

- Keep careful records of attendance. Have you noticed any patterns of absence for particular pupils? For example, is there someone who tends to be absent on a Monday or a Friday? Is there someone who is regularly absent for three or four days at a time?
- Keep a careful check on lateness, especially at the start of the day and at the beginning of the afternoon session. Are there some pupils who tend to be late on a regular basis?
- Are there pupils who regularly fail to hand in homework?
- Do you have pupils in your class or form who have an above-average number of school sanctions, such as detentions? Are there any who have been excluded from school on more than one occasion?
- Are there pupils who are persistently without items of basic school equipment, such as pens or a PE kit?
- Have you noticed any pupils who appear excessively tired, especially at the beginning of the school day?
- Are there any pupils who seem to be malnourished?

You are not expected to be an expert in all of these things, especially the final two, but a discreet inquiry or comment to another relevant member of staff can sometimes turn out to be a first step in setting a support process in place. It is better to err on the side of caution than ignore any possible signs.

Schools are allowed to use the funding from the Pupil Premium as they deem necessary, but they are required to publish information on how it has been used, and this is subject to scrutiny by the Ofsted inspection service. Various research, such as that by the Sutton Trust (2013), Nelson and O'Beirne (2014) and Abbott *et al.* (2015), has been carried out into the use and relative effectiveness of the Pupil Premium, and inevitably practices have become refined over the years since it began. For example, initially most schools – both primary and

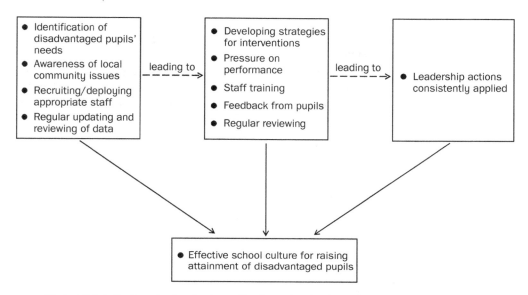

Figure 24.1 Factors in developing effective school culture for raising attainment of disadvantaged pupils

secondary – invested most of the funding in employing additional staff, including teaching assistants and other support staff. Since then, research has found that schools have focused much more on specific strategies and interventions, and many schools have in fact reduced the number of additional assistants (DfE, 2015e). There is a clearer picture emerging of the various practices and strategies that are seen to be effective and widely used in schools. It should be stressed that each school is a unique institution with its own culture and should therefore develop strategies with its own pupils in mind (Abbott *et al.*, 2015). In fact, Abbott and colleagues carried out several pieces of research, across a range of contexts, and found that all but a very small number of schools adopted a strategy of using the Pupil Premium funding for *all* disadvantaged pupils, whether they were on the official list or not (2015: 180). This overcomes the problems mentioned earlier about FSM, where some children narrowly missed out and others were in and out of the system according to changing circumstances.

Schools that have been very successful in raising the attainment of disadvantaged pupils have developed particular cultures with certain features, and the overall strategy of these schools is shown in Figure 24.1. The features of successful school cultures include the following:

- A total commitment to ensuring that every pupil achieves, in so far as possible, the highest attainment possible. This is often reflected in a 'no blame' culture where everyone in the school takes responsibility for the whole of the positive achievements and the falling short. It is not a school where people are encouraged to say, 'Well, it's not my fault!'

- In some schools, this is known as a 'no excuses' culture. However dysfunctional and extreme the circumstances of an individual child or young person are, with the many barriers to learning these appear to create, the schools allow no excuses for that child not being able to achieve the maximum of what they are capable of – as long as they are given the required support.

- These schools are all focused on and relentless in their collection and use of data concerning pupil progress. All schools have huge amounts of data, but it is the use of that data that is significant. Such schools make extensive use of charts and graphic illustration – found in many staff offices – and are able to pinpoint every pupil's current performance and progress. In some school offices, these are accompanied by individual photographs, so that the children are never mere numbers! Reviews of progress take place in every school at regular intervals so that an overall picture of progress can be gained and interventions put in place where required, either for whole groups or for individuals.

- Pupils believe that their individual opinions matter in such schools. Whatever the circumstances or ability of a young person, they need to know that someone believes in them. In some dysfunctional environments, children and young people have no one to speak for them, but these schools provide this. In the past, depending on the school intake, certain pupils, generally middle-class ones, tended to dominate particular activities. These schools, without reducing opportunities for those children, ensure that *all* have an equal place and an opportunity to succeed. A deputy head interviewed by Abbott and colleagues (2014: 9) expressed it well:

'It is not a question of everyone being equal; human beings are not equal, but they all can have equal human value, or rather what they can do is shown to be equally valued. They can all make a contribution to the school and to society. After all, if we only valued professional contributions to society, how would all the other things get done?'

In most such schools, ensuring pupils are listened to is formalized through a commitment to 'pupil voice' or 'student voice', as described and discussed in Chapter 3. This development is seen by many as crucial for education in the UK, and many secondary schools have clear systems in place. The Nordic countries, for example, among the most successful in terms of pupil achievement, see this development as 'one of the ways in which the next generation of citizens are introduced to democracy' (Mortimore, 2013: 232). It can be argued it is a recognition of the changing relationships between adults and children where instead of adults speaking for children, 'Children and young people are more likely to speak on their own behalf' (Middlewood and Abbott, 2015: 41). Such schools find pupil voice a powerful way of supporting all children, including disadvantaged ones, in making their views known and listened to.

The cultures of such high-achieving schools can be described as follows:

- The role modelling of all school staff is critical in these cultures. It is not reasonable to expect children and young people to behave in a certain way if they see adults behaving otherwise. Disadvantaged children often have plenty of poor examples of adults behaving badly outside of school, and it is crucial that everyone at school shares the same values in the way they go about life.

- A strong feature of such cultures is trying to ensure the children and young people feel safe and secure at school. Young people from difficult circumstances, including some very extreme cases such as abusive or neglectful homes, are in particular need for anxieties to be alleviated. Some of these young people may be under great stress when they come to school. Schools should therefore try to make the school environment a place where pupils can find their true selves, and then, as they gain confidence in who they are, they can begin to realize what they might achieve. Such schools are strong on child protection and safeguarding procedures (see Chapter 20) and train staff to be alert for signs of problems. In secondary schools, such problems can be hidden by such adolescent behaviour as aggression and surliness.

- Such cultures recognize and celebrate success and achievement. These schools realize that the most disadvantaged children have rarely or never received praise or recognition for accomplishment, and thus have devised systems of reward for effort and achievement that are appropriate and relevant to particular age groups. A culture of celebrating success ensures that all adults are included, and the achievements of teachers, assistants, administrative staff, lunchtime supervisors and technicians are noted and recognized in an appropriate way.

- These schools offer opportunities for *all* children and young people to experience things outside of their normal life and school routines. This is achieved mostly by external visits to places that some learners would never go, and by in-school events such as artists or writers in residence and special one-off occasions where timetables are suspended to enable a focus on important and enjoyable experiences.

It is important to remember that such features of a school's culture are realized through activities throughout the school, in classrooms most of all but also in corridors, social areas and playing fields. Your own classroom therefore should reflect as many of the best features of your own school's culture as possible in order to support these pupils.

Task 24.3

To what extent do you try to celebrate the success of individuals in your classes or, when appropriate, the whole class? Remember that people are different – some like public praise, while others would be embarrassed by this and much prefer a quiet word!

How do you try to ensure that your own conduct in the way you manage learners displays the same characteristics as the way you ask them to behave? What happens when you fall short of this, and how do you address this?

Do you take any steps to try to ensure that your classroom is one where learners can feel safe and secure? Are there further steps that you might be able to take?

How effective do you think you are in showing that you value the opinions of all learners in your classes, even when you strongly disagree with their views? Do you have any semi-formal systems in place to try to ensure everyone's views are respected?

Some of these things are very difficult to achieve and, as a new teacher, you are unlikely to succeed in them all. It is important to begin thinking about them, however, as soon as possible, so that you can develop strategies as you gain experience. You should strive to become a teacher with a set of values to which you are committed and try to encapsulate these in your classroom. In the meantime, there are specific practices and strategies that have been found to be successful in schools, raising the attainment of disadvantaged pupils, and these, along with the commitment of staff, help to develop effective cultures.

24.5 Specific strategies and interventions

Target setting

Setting targets for learners is a widely recognized and used technique for enabling learners to be 'stretched' and to achieve ever higher levels of attainment. In the school, subject departments may set targets for levels of achievement for specific groups after discussion with senior staff. However, individual pupil targets are generally seen as the most important and effective. Such targets need to be both high in aspiration and realistic. For disadvantaged pupils, this can mean targets gradually being raised as they grow in confidence. This target-setting can often become a powerful tool for motivation for these pupils, especially underachieving ones. Even if hard evidence is not easy to obtain for this claim, as motivation is partly an emotional thing, the belief of staff and learners in this may be a useful factor in the process. The use of the SMART targets is therefore strongly recommended here.

Ensuring returning absentees are properly catered for

The following case study is typical of what happens to pupils from disadvantaged contexts who have poor attendance records.

Case Study 24.1

Dale is a pupil in the first term of Year 10 at an urban school. His attendance record has been well below average throughout his primary and secondary schooling. His school has embarked on a drive to raise its overall attendance performance through various strategies and it has successfully increased its rate from 89.7% to 92.4%. Dale returned to school after a month-long absence. He had neither a pen nor basic equipment with him. In two of his classes on the first day, he was told that he could not be given anything but a very low grade or no grade at all as he had not completed sufficient work. He was told to attend after-school classes to catch up on his work. He did attend these on that day and appeared to do the work. The next day, however, he was again absent and the school's usual procedures for trying to get him back to school began all over again.

COMMENTARY: This example illustrates that, whilst increasing attendance records for the whole school may be laudable, it is often ineffective for pupils like Dale unless the experience of being in school is one that makes them feel it is worthwhile. Dale clearly felt there was no value in attending school as he would inevitably get further behind. The teachers concerned were correct in saying what they did about his grades but were there things that might have been done differently to get Dale to attend school? Here are some points for consideration:

- Attendance at school is not an end in itself. Sitting all day in classes doing nothing may be recorded as being present but is not something to be desired by either the staff or the pupil!
- Without a positive experience to make someone feel it is worth coming to school, absence will recur.
- A 'reward' for coming to school may only last for a while and may not be enough to encourage regular attendance

What do you think you might have done as Dale's teacher or tutor that might have encouraged him to attend the next day?

Stressing good presentation of work

This may seem a very simple thing to focus on but research by Abbott and colleagues (2013b, 2014) has shown that helping disadvantaged pupils in this area can have valuable effects. Pupils who already lack confidence in their ability to achieve can benefit from a relatively brief but intensive focus on the way to present submitted work. This appears to be because:

- it is something they can do by working to a set formula;
- it shows them how to improve their marks/grades by simply following this procedure;
- it shows them that in one area they can be as good as anyone else;
- it boosts their confidence as to how their work will be received and assessed in the future.

Thus, for example, someone who has been absent from school for a while can learn something that, although limited, is valuable. It means they may go home more satisfied with a sense of achievement. Note that there may be a relevant link here to Case Study 24.1, depending on the individual pupil. There is also scope for the teacher to discuss *why* presentation is important and, of course, an opportunity to praise the individual concerned.

Providing effective feedback

Everyone (both teachers and pupils) needs effective feedback to know how they are progressing and how they can do even better in the future. It is therefore an entitlement for learners of all levels and abilities. The two main kinds of feedback are written feedback on work submitted and oral feedback on all work carried out or attempted. For the individual teacher, it may be best to do whatever is felt optimal for the individual pupil. For this to happen, you need to establish clear principles for what constitutes effective feedback, including the following:

- Mention positives first – find something positive to say first, whatever the overall quality of the work.
- Focus on what can be acted upon – there is no point in talking about things that cannot be changed.

- Focus on the work, not the person's character or personality.
- Avoid using jargon.
- Ensure you have specific evidence for what is said – give specific examples and do not talk in general terms.
- Avoid making comparisons with other pupils' work.
- Do not overload with too many criticisms and/or tasks for improvement next time. It is better to focus on one or two specifics at a time. This is why we mentioned above that a focus on good presentation can be a valuable starting point for some pupils.

Once the framework of principles is established, you can attend to the specific feedback on an individual's work, knowing what you do about what kind of feedback is appropriate for them. Remember that the key purpose of feedback is to ensure that pupils can learn and improve. Some pupils learn better when gently prompted by a question from the teacher in the feedback, others prefer and react better to more direct statements. However, effective feedback always involves an element of being clear about what to do better next time. (Refer back to the sections on feedback in Chapter 9.)

Using mentoring, including peer mentoring

Schools that are successful at raising the attainment of disadvantaged pupils tend to use some form of mentoring. This can include mentoring according to topic such as in literacy, numeracy or another curriculum subject; examination techniques; helping to catch up on course work; computer and/or library skills; study techniques including those related to homework and revision; even social skills.

Mentoring can be carried out by an additional staff member employed for that purpose, a teacher willing to use their spare time, an assistant or other member of the school support staff, specific learning mentors or peer mentors. Peer mentoring has been found to be very effective in many cases. If carefully managed and dealt with in a sensitive manner, some schools find that some disadvantaged pupils react well to working with pupils of the same age, especially if they have an understanding or experience of deprivation themselves. In all cases, schools provide training for peer mentors, just as they do for all other kinds of mentors.

Early intervention on literacy and/or numeracy

This is only mentioned briefly here because Chapters 16 and 17 deal with this subject in detail. The more successful secondary schools find that a significant focus in the first two years on literacy and/or numeracy problems helps immensely in raising attainment levels for pupils in receipt of the Pupil Premium in Years 10 and 11. This may involve you making referrals to small groups that support pupils with literacy or numeracy problems.

Referring pupils to specific school groups for extra support

Your school will probably have in place a number of small groups that help support those pupils who are disadvantaged and falling behind with their work for various reasons.

These may be through withdrawal from normal lessons or extra classes at lunchtime or after school. These may be taken by staff members who are available and willing and, more likely, by additional staff funded by Pupil Premium money. Examples of these are reading recovery groups, targeted teaching, IT for those without PCs at home, children with English as an additional language and homework 'clubs'. It is the duty of every teacher, as a result of their careful monitoring of each individual pupil, to refer the needs of a particular learner to the appropriate member of staff, so that the pupil can get that extra support.

In thinking about extra support, it can be easy to forget that a deprived or disadvantaged pupil may have especially high ability! (Differentiation between different abilities was examined in Chapter 6.) One of the specific groups may be one for more able, gifted and talented (MAGT) pupils. (See Chapter 15 for more on MAGT pupils.) If you believe that a Pupil Premium learner in your class has high ability or a special talent in something, make sure you mention this to the person with responsibility for MAGT pupils. There may be specific provision available for them. Examples can be in any area of the curriculum, but Pupil Premium funding has been used successfully to pay for extra classes or community provision (where it is not available in school) in activities such as dance, playing a musical instrument, drama, athletics, gymnastics, art and ceramics, maths and swimming.

24.5 Conclusion

As a newly qualified teacher (NQT), you are almost certain to encounter pupils who are from deprived or disadvantaged circumstances, which can adversely affect their likely levels of attainment at school in a significant way. This is likely to place them at a severe disadvantage for much if not the whole of their working lives – and maybe longer. You may work in a school where the vast majority of the pupils are in this situation. Regardless, the duty of the school and its staff is to every single individual. As suggested in this chapter, you need to:

- know the overall numbers of disadvantaged pupils and their proportion in relation to the pupil population as a whole – this can affect the school's policy in this area;
- be able to identify which are the disadvantaged pupils, especially those who are in your classes;
- treat this knowledge in confidence and with sensitivity;
- be aware of the kinds of interventions that have been found to be effective in helping pupils raise their attainment and try to select those that seem most appropriate to the individuals you know;
- be aware of the various strategies that the school has in place to help these pupils and especially be clear about the support groups and mechanisms to which you may be able to refer them.

The professional rewards for helping a deprived pupil achieve a level of attainment that, without support, they might never have achieved are among the most satisfying encountered by teachers.

Recommendations for further reading

Abbott, I., Middlewood, D. and Robinson, S. (2015) It's not just about value for money: a case study of values-led implementation of the Pupil Premium in outstanding schools, *Management in Education*, 29 (4): 178–184.

Borough School Partnership (2015) *Pupil Premium Best Practice Case Study: Clearview High School*. London: Clearview High School.

Office for Standards in Education (Ofsted) (2012) *The Pupil Premium: How Schools are Using the Pupil Premium Funding to Raise Achievement for Disadvantaged Pupils*. London: Ofsted.

25

Pastoral care and the role of the tutor

Cheryl Cane

25.1 Introduction

Many teachers are drawn to a secondary school career because of their passion for a particular subject and a desire to support young people in developing a love for learning through that subject. However, as Marland suggested, in his seminal text about pastoral care in schools: 'The school *is* its pastoral organization' (1974: 11). And, if the 'pastoral task' is to support the total welfare of the pupil and assist them in their 'search for identity in a changing world' (Best, 2014: 183), then any division between pastoral and subject needs would seem fragmented and artificial.

It would appear, then, that however a teacher might come to be involved in pastoral care, they are likely to discover that it is one of the most important aspects of their role, putting them at the centre of any school's 'entire mission' (Best, 2014: 183). Pastoral care has been described as underpinning 'a whole-school atmosphere in which relationships are centrally important' (Purdy, 2013: 2). Schools today are as likely to promote 'excellent provision for pastoral care' as they are 'outstanding examination results', and yet there is also confusion about the nature and status of pastoral care. There seems to be a 'lack of recent guidance on this role and . . . lack of recognition of the importance by schools themselves or by government' (2013: 19).

Alternatively, it could be claimed that the recent absence of distinct guidance and recognition of pastoral issues could indicate an acceptance of pastoral care as indistinguishable from other aspects of learning and education. Indeed, the Teachers' Standards (DfE, 2011a) make no distinction between the academic and pastoral elements of a teacher's role and yet there are clear pastoral dimensions to each standard. Whatever your personal views on the current status of pastoral care in schools, it is the case that pastoral care will be an important aspect of your professional role as a teacher.

By the end of this chapter, you should:

- understand the nature of pastoral care and the way it has developed;
- be aware of the relationship between pastoral care, subject teaching and other related areas;
- understand the different dimensions and possibilities for your potential role as a form tutor;
- have thought critically and reflectively about pastoral care.

25.2 The nature of pastoral care

A fixed definition of pastoral care, as distinct from education or learning, can be a 'diffuse and elusive concept' (Purdy, 2013: 9). Much of what can be said about striving for effective pastoral care is also what can be said about effective schools, education and learning in general. However, as Best highlights (after Marland, 1974), pastoral care 'must be planned and institutionalized in systems which begin with the needs and lives of the pupils' (Best, 2014: 183). Without such planning, there is the risk that provision might be inconsistent and that, if not 'recognized', pastoral care cannot be evaluated and improved (Rosenblatt, 2002: 21). Perhaps, then, whilst acknowledging that pastoral care is a vital aspect of learning and education in general, it is also useful to recognize some specific descriptions of pastoral care in action.

Task 25.1

Read and consider the following descriptions of pastoral care. *Pastoral care is*:

- 'providing support for the emerging adolescent identity and looking after the total welfare of the pupil' (Marland, 1974);
- 'more than a device for providing emotional first aid . . . [It is] a carefully planned integration of the pastoral and curricular aspects of the school' (Hamblin, 1978: 1);
- 'that part of the curriculum that caters for the "social/emotional" aspects of the pupil, as opposed to their "cognitive" needs' (Power, 1991: 193);
- 'the heart of the work of a secondary school . . . enabling a child to become a student and develop fully as a person' (Marland and Rogers, 2004: 1);
- 'providing the appropriate emotional support alongside learning support' (Weare, 2004, cited in Schofield, 2007: 31);
- 'the vision of education as a moral endeavor, one that is aimed at human development in its widest sense' (Wortley and Harrison, 2008: 241);
- 'concerned with the welfare of the person as an individual. That is, there is an implicit recognition that each person is unique and that care . . . should thus recognise individual and not merely communal need' (Carroll, 2010: 147).

Consider these descriptions. Are there particular aspects that seem important? Can you find further descriptions from other sources or from your own experience? Do you notice particular differences that might suggest emphasis on certain aspects? What aspects of a teacher's daily activity might fit under the description of 'providing pastoral care'?

A regularly cited survey of the types of pastoral activities in which teachers engage included: reactive activity responding to individual need; proactive activity that anticipates 'critical incidents' for pupils; developing a specific pastoral curriculum; promoting a supportive environment with an ethos of mutual care and concern; and management and administration (Best, 1999). While these aspects remain relevant today and are likely to relate to some of the suggestions you made for Task 25.1, Wortley and Harrison point out that they do not take account of support for 'students' academic progress and achievement' (2008: 250). This highlights an important point about the context surrounding pastoral care. Best's (1999) survey reflects a particular time in the development of pastoral care and may well respond to a context where separate systems were commonly in place for monitoring pastoral and academic progress. It seems important, then, to consider the origins and organization of pastoral care over time to understand the different influences that emerge.

25.3 The origins and organization of pastoral care

Marland wrote of the importance of 'looking back', particularly at the 'enduring purpose of pastoral care' (2002: 2). He noted that it was common to see the 'cyclic sequence of today's fashionable thinking actually unknowingly re-visiting past ideas' (2002: 3). Whilst Purdy considers the etymological roots of 'pastoral', most other descriptions of pastoral education in schools tend to date back to 'the church's role in the nineteenth century in founding church schools and instilling Christian values of care' (2013: 9). Lang (2007) described the beginnings of pastoral care in England in the public schools of the first half of the nineteenth century. Using examples of 'reforming headmasters of whom Thomas Arnold of Rugby School is the best known' (2007: 316), Lang recounted Arnold's ideals (from Rugby's re-establishment in 1828) of religious, moral and 'gentlemanly' conduct alongside intellectual ability. Thus, almost 200 years ago, we find a perception of education that goes beyond the academic to encompass morality and principled behaviour. By the middle of the nineteenth century, these perceptions had been developed further to include consideration of how pastoral organization might respond to these needs. In 1861, the Clarendon Commission collected examples from prestigious public schools of the day. They found that, at Eton, each pupil had a tutor 'whose connection with him remains unbroken during his whole stay in the school and whose duty it is to bestow that attention on him and undertake that responsibility for him that cannot be expected of the class teacher' (cited in Lang, 2007: 316). Such a system was designed to provide each pupil with a link to an adult responsible for their overall welfare in school, but it also offered a structure for referring discipline issues. The relationship between pastoral care, support for welfare and well-being, and the notion of control and discipline can thus be traced back to at least the nineteenth century.

The early development of comprehensive schooling, from the late 1940s, created fresh challenges for pastoral care, particularly regarding the size and organization of schools. Comprehensive schools tended to be much larger than previous schools and required new systems to ensure that each 'individual pupil is made to feel that he belongs . . . and in which careful supervision of progress of the individual is the responsibility of someone who has under his care a manageable number of pupils' (Chinn, Director of Education for Coventry, 1949: cited in Marland, 2002: 5). As a result, Coventry comprehensive schools were established using house systems much like those of the public schools. Power (1991) suggested a 'house' system was also an appropriate fit because it encapsulated the 'comprehensive spirit'. This organization of pupils by means other than the 'academic' promoted a sense of 'inclusion' rather than selection (Power, 1991: 197).

Marland highlighted that the 'pastoral aspect appeared thin throughout the fifties' (2002: 4) but, with the further expansion of comprehensive schools in the mid-1960s, many schools were operating a house system. The 'house' would have a head and tutorial team working within it on a permanent basis. The house system offered some key advantages in being able to introduce collaborative activities and competitions between houses, pupils from different years could support others at critical points, siblings could join the same house and, most importantly, caring for a smaller 'home' group of pupils within a larger school meant that pupils could feel a greater sense of belonging and value. It is important also to understand that the house system, originating from public boarding schools, had originally been created to offer a sense of home where parents and carers were entirely absent for long periods of the pupils' academic year. That meant that there was a particular emotional investment and desire for the public-school house system to 'mean a very great deal' (Chetwynd, 1960: cited in Marland, 2002: 6), whereas for some day-schools, concerns were raised that the concept of houses 'tended to be a weak, artificial imitation . . . a convenient channel through which to collect conduct marks' (ibid.).

The 1970s saw a decline of the house system partly as a result of the mistaken assumption that a house system could take care *by itself* of all guidance in the social and educational domains (Benn and Chitty, 1996: 230). There was also often a separation between what the house masters and the teachers knew (Marland, 2002: 7). One of the aspects that had been less developed was that of the form tutor, and that particular role enjoyed new attention as schools moved away from house systems to year group or 'horizontal' systems. The arguments for horizontal year group systems were partly administrative, but also pastoral. If all the pupils in a pastoral grouping were at the same stage, both administrative and personal issues were likely to be similar. Hamblin (1978) presented the idea of 'critical incidents' and suggested that a priority for pastoral care was to support pupils at key points in their development. It allowed for Heads of Year and tutor teams to become specialists in particular aspects of development such as transition from primary to secondary education or choosing options for Key Stage 4 or 5 (KS4 or KS5) study.

The horizontal organization seems to have enjoyed popularity through the 1980s and 1990s, but the aspect of tutor specialism and the annual shift to a new tutor could be said to have disrupted the continuity of care and could have also contributed to a widening distance between pastoral and academic support. In some settings, the subject specialists in their subject departments were seen as responsible for academic subject development, whilst the tutor teams were seen as responsible for all other aspects of a pupil's development.

It is unsurprising, then, that given the importance of finding pastoral and academic unity, the millennium brought further changes and a renewed interest in both academic tutoring and the house system for some schools. Initiatives such as the specialist school movement meant that some schools adopted a particular specialism that was reflected in all aspects of their work. Many schools have retained their specialism, and this can be reflected in the names of their pastoral houses: theatre names in a performing arts specialist setting or inspirational leaders' names in a leadership specialist setting. Workforce remodelling in recent years also created a 'blurring of boundaries between previously distinct roles' (Edmond and Price, 2009: 302): these changes have resulted in a wide range of new or revised roles within pastoral care, including 'associate professional' roles such as learning mentors, school counsellors, parent support advisors alongside, in some settings, non-teaching pastoral leaders who can be 'on-call' throughout the school day.

Most schools today operate pastoral systems that are horizontal, vertical or a combination thereof. Some schools organize their tutoring of pupils by year group but within a house system. Many schools have retained the full vertical arrangement throughout their houses with all tutor groups made up of mixed ages. For some schools, traditional form groups have been abandoned in favour of small mentor groups led by all staff (teaching and non-teaching). The move from large tutor groups towards small mentor or personal tutor groups could be said to promote a greater focus on the individuals within each group. The allocation of pastoral time within the school day has also increased in many settings possibly in response to 'the increased prominence of wellbeing indicators used in Ofsted inspections' (Symonds and Hagell, 2011: 299 and Ofsted, 2015). It is important, then, to consider the use of allocated pastoral time and to consider relationships between this and other aspects of the curriculum.

Relationships between pastoral care, subject teaching and other aspects of the curriculum

Pastoral care is at the heart of any school. It interconnects with the work of subject departments and the school as a whole and it relies on support from subject departments and senior management to work effectively. Effective pastoral care relies on curriculum systems that display awareness of the *affective* dimension within each subject. Affective education is not confined to pastoral care, and all curriculum subjects, whether explicitly or implicitly, have an affective dimension. All curriculum areas impact on pupils' understanding of the world and can influence their developing sense of 'being' and 'belonging'. Whether it is through the choice of curriculum content, the way that learning takes place or the pupils' perceptions of how they are treated, every experience within school plays a part in their developing sense of identity and morality.

Alongside the affective dimension of subject teaching, there are specific areas of the curriculum where pupils will learn about citizenship, personal, social, health and economic education (PSHE), religious education, or sex and relationships education (DfE, 2014a). For many schools, some aspects of these areas are led by form tutors in designated form periods. In some settings, there might also be contributions from visiting, or in-house, specialist teams, but it is usually important for form tutors to offer further follow-up sessions for consolidation. It is also commonplace for schools to incorporate 'learning' and 'leadership' into the pastoral programme with pupils learning how to manage key aspects of their own development. Some settings provide further enhancements with contributions such as mindfulness. The school's understanding of the nature of affective education can influence the relationship between the pastoral and other manifestations of affective education within school.

25.5 The role of form tutor

Many student teachers experience the role of form tutor through observation or participation. Marland has described the form tutor as providing daily 'first-level pastoral and academic care to each pupil in their group' (2002: 7). He also charted what he observed to be the extremes of tutor effectiveness, providing a useful continuum from tutor subordinate to tutor ascendant (2002: 10). He used this terminology to indicate national movement, describing the rise and fall of tutor importance over time. The chart is also helpful in considering individual tutors and their value in particular settings. For example, the tutor ascendant is the vision for the most effective form tutoring. It describes an individual who is obliged to have full access to relevant information, is a vital part of the tutee's induction, is first contact for subject teachers, plays a major advisory role in educational decisions, is consulted by senior staff and feels primary responsibility for tutees in their care (Marland, 2002).

At the other end of the scale, the tutor subordinate is not given relevant information regarding their form group, is not consulted or involved in decision-making and is basically reduced to a mere 'register checker'. Arguably, in these current, technologically advanced times where the use of biometric data and finger print scanning means that even register checking can occur without tutor intervention, then a subordinate tutor might even find their role lacking any purpose other than being the designated adult in the room. It is clear from these descriptions that a form tutor's role and effectiveness can be influenced by the context in which they are operating and the general school ethos and values. It would be useful, then, to consider your own vision for tutoring and to think about the atmosphere and support you will want your pupils to experience regardless of any particular local limitations or difficulties.

Task 25.2 Personal vision for pastoral care

Imagine yourself as a form tutor. How will you present yourself? What will your pupils experience and how will they feel supported? How will you attend to emotional and mental well-being? How will you offer all pupils a sense of belonging?

The term 'unconditional positive regard' (Lodge, 2002: 36) is a helpful description for the atmosphere to be promoted within a tutor group. A key feature is ensuring that all members are treated positively and understand their responsibility in treating others positively. Consider how you might promote such an atmosphere.

Here are some useful suggestions from experienced form tutors who took part in Lodge's (2002) study 'Tutors Talking' that could be used as a starting point:

- Be fair, open and honest
- Be positive and constructive
- Value all as worthwhile individuals
- Provide guidance rather than control
- Be non-judgemental
- Establish trust
- Avoid favouritism or a perception of 'dislike' for any individual

Consider practical strategies that you could use. For example, to ensure that you listen to and value everyone's opinion, you could use a Voice Box. This is a simple postal box (in real terms or could be created virtually through technology) where all individuals are asked to deposit anonymous comments about a particular situation, an aspect of school, or the form and content of tutor sessions. It is a simple device that ensures that everyone's voice is heard and, although you might expect that pupils would be able to discuss many issues openly, the Voice Box can help to uncover unexpected issues or to give voice to the concerns that many have but in which they think they are alone.

What other strategies might you employ with your tutor group and why?

There are many aspects to a form tutor's multi-dimensional role. Marland and Rogers have described the tutor as 'the integrative centre for the school's efforts in personal development, from attendance to welfare, study skills to behaviour' (2004: 1). Important aspects of pastoral support were explored by Schofield (2007) in a small study based on the perceptions of post-16 pupils and their form tutors. The study found agreement between form tutors and pupils that (a) offering emotional support, (b) monitoring academic progress and (c) supporting academic progress were three of the most important aspects. Other aspects included: monitoring attendance, negotiating with other teachers or adults, and dealing with discipline. Thus, Schofield found that, while advocacy, accountability and administration were important parts of the tutor role, support and monitoring of academic progress were considered the most important aspects. The primary focus on academic progress and support might be particularly relevant because of the academic stage of the pupils involved in the study, but there is an expectation that this will feature strongly at all stages.

As a form tutor, you are likely to be involved in scrutinizing performance data, setting and reviewing targets with pupils, and helping pupils to understand and develop their own learning. A form tutor can bring together information from across the curriculum and, alongside subject specialists, ask questions when a pupil is not attaining at a level that might be expected of them. Support for academic progress is also reliant on the relationship and atmosphere that have been created. Pupils need to feel genuine engagement, from the tutor, with their own development, rather than this being seen as an administrative exercise. The focus on pride in achievement and pride in school is important to foster and is also featured as a grade descriptor for outstanding personal development, behaviour and welfare provision in the common inspection framework (Ofsted, 2015).

Building positive learning relationships with pupils and their parents or carers will also be important. It is an expectation for the form tutor to hold conversations regarding pupil progress across the curriculum. In some settings, these conversations have removed the need for any direct subject contact for parents or carers. These longer 'overview' conversations have, in some settings, replaced the traditional curriculum evenings where parents meet with many subject teachers for just a few minutes. Some schools set one or two whole days aside in the year when an individual tutor undertakes parent and tutee discussions. Alternatively, for some schools, tutees are withdrawn from classes for individual interviews. Such approaches provide an opportunity to develop your tutor role to the full. Though a key task of the interviews is likely to be target-setting and review, it is also an opportunity to gain a fuller understanding of your tutees' general well-being and to strengthen relationships. If you are in a school that does not provide time for working with pupils individually, it is still important to find time for these discussions in order to identify pupils who are in particular need of support.

As a form tutor, you will be responsible for recording and monitoring attendance and punctuality. School attendance is a legal issue, as parents or carers are legally responsible for ensuring that their children attend school. It is also an important factor in how schools are judged externally. High attendance rates can be used as indicators that pupils value their education (Ofsted, 2015). Schools usually have strict procedures for recording and following up absence and you need to make sure that you understand and follow these procedures. Even where biometric registration processes are in place, the follow-up procedures for persistent lateness or absence still need to be more of a personal contact. It is likely that the form tutor will be the one to probe emerging patterns of absence and to liaise with the network of support in the school to deal quickly and effectively with any issues.

The form tutor has to maintain a difficult balance because they are often the central person to enforce school rules on matters like dress, equipment and completion of homework. They may be working with their tutor group to educate young people about prevention of bullying, staying safe, keeping healthy and being respectful, which may also include, in some instances, needing to step in firmly to challenge inappropriate attitudes, stereotypes and derogatory language. Blending roles needs skill and sensitivity but a central theme to come back to is that of *care*. As form tutor, it is your place to challenge, guide and instruct *because* you care. The form tutor wants the best for their pupils, even though this will involve some challenging moments, much like a positive parental or carer role.

This sense of care is also evident with the form tutor as advocate. There are circumstances in which pupils benefit from the support of an adult who knows them well and can speak on their behalf, particularly with other teachers or sometimes with family members. Pupils who come to you for help will need to have their concerns recognized and not dismissed – they need to be listened to. They may also need reassurance or space to deal with anger. In these types of situations, always be aware of your responsibilities for safeguarding and child protection and take care not to promise confidentiality (see Chapter 20 for more information on safeguarding). What you can commit to is *partnership* – you can be there for them as a listener, as an adviser and as a member of a wider support network. Make it clear to them that they are not alone.

Task 25.3

Use your contact with form tutors in school to consider the individual support that a form tutor might be called upon to provide. The examples below are based on real events but there are many other types of situations that a tutor might encounter. Consider ways that you might respond to such situations yourself but also ask other tutors about the types of issues that they are currently dealing with. Because each situation is individual and will require an individual response, learning from real examples can be helpful.

Safe practice note: Conversations need to be handled sensitively and your day-to-day practical research as a teacher needs to uphold the highest ethical standards. Be careful with any note-taking and ensure that information is treated professionally. Check with your own training mentor in school about the information that you are able to collect and how this should be handled. If you are keeping notes, then do so in such a way that information is anonymized and/or coded so that no individual or school setting could be identified if the notes were accidentally misplaced.

Consider what you might do if a member of your form group:

- achieves highly in a number of curriculum areas, has recently received a 'Head's award' for progress and yet seems to be on a downward spiral in one particular curriculum area receiving numerous detentions and reports of low-level disruptive behaviour;

- struggles with basic literacy and, even though they receive additional support in school, you are concerned about whether the support is effective;
- recently suffered a bereavement of a close family member and is struggling to remain in school;
- expresses some worrying views and possible support for acts of terrorism;
- has identified themselves as transgender and is going through the process of transitioning (see Equality Act 2010);
- displays difficulty with body image and staff have raised concerns about the pupil's drastic weight loss, but you are also aware that the pupil's parent or carer is a medical professional;
- seems unable to maintain lasting friendships and appears more comfortable staying with you at breaks and lunch times;
- seems to have an unhealthy relationship with social media or electronic gaming.

The form tutor role places high demands on teachers. You need to know your pupils well enough to offer them advice and support and to notice when they have difficulties. It also demands that pupils know you well enough to trust you and to rely on your guidance. Many of the activities that tutor groups and tutors undertake can support the development of trust and mutual respect. Getting to know your form through wider activities can bring an added dimension to your role. Working collaboratively on community projects, charity collections, organizing an assembly or planning a tutor group outing can create a real sense of family and can have a significant impact on relationships.

25.6 Conclusion

The intention of this chapter has been to provide a thoughtful starting point for your pastoral role in school. This role is central to the work of secondary schools, particularly in terms of the contribution it makes to supporting the personal, academic and social progress of pupils. Schools vary enormously in terms of the time and resources they allocate to pastoral care, the importance they attach to it and their interpretation of what it entails. This chapter recognizes that pastoral care is an important part of any teacher's role. The Teachers' Standards promote the creation of safe and stimulating environments with an atmosphere of mutual respect, the promotion of positive attitudes, values, behaviours and relationships, and a concern for welfare (DfE, 2011a), amongst many other aspects that can be seen to encompass both the academic and the pastoral domain. To return to where this chapter began, with Best's reminder about pastoral care 'facilitating the adolescent's search for identity in a changing world' (2014: 183), secondary school can be an exciting, challenging time for a young person, but it can be equally intimidating. Pupils are searching for a sense of individual identity whilst attempting to 'fit in'. They are striving to make sense of their changing world and their changing bodies whilst also trying to challenge themselves and find a sense of achievement and meaning in their lives. Their teachers, and particularly their form tutor, can have a significant impact on the experience of pupils as they journey through difficult years. Whether your setting is an academy, a specialist college, a free school, a faith school or a grammar school, the concept of pastoral care and the role of the tutor remains central. Marland (2002) reminded us of the importance of revisiting the past and I do so again here to reiterate an important phrase that has resonated through pastoral care and remains significant to the form tutor role today:

> 'The tutor is the heart of the school, the specialist whose specialism is bringing everything together, whose subject is the pupil herself.'
>
> (Marland and Rogers, 1997: 17)

When we consider our contribution to pastoral care in school, we need to view this not as an addition to our subject teaching role, but as being at the heart of our role.

Recommendations for further reading

Best, R. (2014) Forty years of pastoral care: an appraisal of Michael Marland's seminal book and its significance for pastoral care in schools, *Pastoral Care in Education*, 32 (3): 173–185.
Purdy, N. (2013) *Pastoral Care 11–16: A Critical Introduction*. London: Bloomsbury.
Rosenblatt, M. (2002) Effective tutoring and school improvement, *Pastoral Care in Education*, 20 (4): 21–26.

26

Government policy

Ian Abbott

26.1 Introduction

Task 26.1

Before you read this chapter, list five recent education issues that have been in the news. Why do you think education is so important to the government?

As a student teacher, you should be aware that the present government, elected in 2017, and the previous Coalition government, formed in 2010, have devoted a great deal of time and effort to a major reform of the education system. Even if you attended secondary school as a pupil fairly recently, you will have noticed a great deal of change when you went back into school as a student teacher. Teachers are always complaining about the amount and pace of change they have to deal with. You've probably heard teachers make comments such as: 'Why did they have to change that?' or 'Not another government initiative!'

Alongside the reform of the National Health Service (NHS), education has been at the forefront of the government's domestic policy agenda. Of course, Brexit has dominated government time since the referendum result, when the decision was taken to leave the European Union. However, every part of the education system, ranging from nursery education to adult education, has been subject to scrutiny and change. The secondary sector has been at the forefront of these changes, with policy shifts in areas such as inspection, management, curriculum content, teaching methods, and assessment. The pace of change has been so rapid that many teachers have felt unable to accommodate each initiative before the next arrived. Given this rate of change, there is a danger that a chapter about government initiatives will become dated very quickly, as policy continues to be developed and implemented. However, it is important that you are aware of some of the most important changes and have an understanding of the reasons for the government's emphasis on education. Therefore, we need to analyse the reasons for the government's approach to education, to use some recent policy initiatives as exemplars of government strategy, and to consider whether the policies have been successful.

By the end of this chapter, you should:

* understand the rationale for the recent reform of the education system;
* begin to develop an awareness of overall government policy for secondary education;
* understand the specific pattern of reform;
* have an awareness of the impact of recent reforms on secondary teachers' lives.

26.2 What's the problem with our education system?

According to the government, the simple answer to this question has to be standards, which have been considered too low in this country. Whilst arguing that considerable progress has been made, the government argues that the education system has considerable room for improvement and has consistently failed to perform to its potential, especially in meeting the needs of the most disadvantaged members of society. The White Paper, *Educational Excellence Everywhere* (DfE, 2016d), sets out how the government aims to set high expectations and develop a world-leading curriculum and numerous policies have since been introduced to raise standards for individual pupils and for schools (DfE, 2016d). So, why has the government placed this emphasis on standards?

Most commentators would agree that access to education is a basic human right, and it is clearly important in a civilized democracy that opportunities for a high-quality education are made available to all young people. While the government accepts this argument, it also believes that education has a key role in dealing with a range of social and economic issues. Reducing social exclusion is a key factor in this range of issues, and the economic consequences of globalization and the technological developments of the last decade have increased the need for the UK to have a highly educated and skilled workforce. To compete with other industrialized and developing nations, the UK must have well-educated and adaptable workers who are able to respond to the demands of the twenty-first century. The economic argument for improving school standards can be viewed as straightforward:

1.   In a global economy, the UK must be able to compete effectively with other countries.
2.   Given the UK is not able to compete solely on the basis of cost, because of the emergence of low-cost economies, it must focus on ideas, innovation and high-skill sectors (the so-called 'knowledge economy').
3.   To enable the UK to compete, standards in its schools have to be high and rising at least as fast as those of its competitors.
4.   The government has a responsibility to ensure that standards in schools and colleges continue to rise and to develop strategies and systems that produce skilled and motivated young people.
5.   To maintain the UK's economic competitiveness, this will involve major changes in the education system.
6.   A successful education system will produce young people who are able to make a positive contribution to the economic well-being of the country.
7.   A flexible and skilled workforce will enable the UK to compete successfully in a global economy (Abbott *et al.*, 2013b).

The government places a strong emphasis on the importance of international comparisons. Many of the most recent policy initiatives have been 'borrowed' from other countries where they have been considered to be successful. The education systems and the teaching methods from the Scandinavian countries, Singapore and Shanghai are often cited as exemplars of good practice. One of the biggest policy initiatives, the establishment of Free Schools, is based on the Charter Schools in the USA.

While there are obvious advantages to looking at other successful school systems, there are also some potential problems. It is important to remember that what is successful in one country might not be easily transferred to another. There will be cultural, social and economic differences that make it difficult to implement particular policies. International comparisons are useful but have to be treated with some caution, and it is essential to recognize the particular features of the English domestic education system.

However, the government has instigated fundamental reform of the education system, and it has introduced a range of specific policies to raise standards. You might disagree with the policies, but it is difficult to disagree with the government's drive to raise standards in education. Earlier in this book, you will have read about strategies to raise standards in areas such as literacy and numeracy, to reduce truancy and to combat social exclusion. Particular focus has been placed on raising the attainment levels of pupils from the poorest sectors of the community. Targets have been set for pupils and schools, and performance indicators are used to gauge the success of policy. The results of these have been published in an attempt to drive up standards across the board. Probably the best examples of this are the annual publication of league tables for schools and the regular Ofsted inspection process. If you are undertaking a school placement, or are looking for a teaching job, you will almost certainly have consulted the school Ofsted report and looked at the various measures of school performance that are publicly available. An army of inspectors and statisticians is employed to collect these data. All of this effort will clearly result in better information and should enable clear identification of problem areas. As a consequence, remedial action can be taken to address particular issues, such as the recent emphasis on raising standards in some of the most disadvantaged coastal towns in England (Middlewood and Abbott, 2018). The collection and the publication of data by the government is a valuable means of evaluating particular policy initiatives. However, what we need to do now is to consider in broad terms what policies have been implemented and how they are likely to impact on you as a new secondary school teacher.

26.3 Government policies

The early part of the twenty-first century was characterized by an unprecedented increase in the resources made available to schools. There was to be massive capital expenditure on education with a £45 billion building programme to rebuild or renew every one of England's 3,500 secondary schools over a 15-year period (Partnerships for Schools, 2007). The composition and overall size of the workforce increased with significantly more teachers and the recruitment of large numbers of teaching assistants.

Since the onset of the global financial crisis, however, the growth in resources devoted to education has stalled. Austerity hit education hard with reduced funding, restrictions on public sector pay and cuts to capital investment. All sectors of education are still affected by the cuts in funding, but the major impact fell on capital expenditure, 16–19 education and early years' provision. Spending on schools has received some protection but most schools have seen real cuts in revenue. The recent reforms to school funding, 'Fairer Funding', are an attempt to offset some of the impact of cuts in government expenditure. However, many head teachers have been very vocal in voicing their concerns about a funding shortfall and the impact this might have on staffing, capital provision and curriculum choice. This is a major change to the earlier part of the century, which was a period of unprecedented growth. The cuts in education funding are predicted to be the largest for over 50 years.

Against a background of reduced resources, the government aims to develop a radical new school system that is supported by improved choice and access for all. While teachers are central to the drive to improve education standards, other aspects of the system are also being reformed:

- the curriculum, assessment and qualifications;
- school funding;
- behaviour policies;
- school improvement policies;
- school leadership; and
- the school system.

There will be ongoing reform of the National Curriculum (NC) and greater emphasis on academic standards. Vocational programmes will be strengthened to ensure progression to further education and employment routes. The emphasis will be on high-quality and rigorous qualifications. Schools will be encouraged to offer a broad range of academic subjects and the implications for these developments were considered earlier in the book (see, for example, Chapters 10, 13 and 19).

Task 26.2

What have been the major curriculum reforms in your subject area? What is the likely impact of curriculum reform on your subject area?

At the time of writing, it is too early to judge the impact of the reforms that are being implemented, but as you begin your teaching career you will be affected by the many reforms taking place. In particular, you are likely to find yourself working in different types of schools that are structured and controlled in a variety of ways. A central part of the reform process is the belief that schools can make a significant difference to raising standards and this can be achieved by giving greater independence to individual schools. The government has placed a strong emphasis on school autonomy, which will seek to enable schools to be part of a self-improving school system.

Given this belief that school autonomy will lead to a stronger education system, the government is attempting to introduce a new schools system based around different types of school. These include:

- Academies;
- Maintained Schools: Community/Foundation;
- Technical Academies, University Technical Colleges (UTCs) and Studio Schools;
- Voluntary and Faith Schools;

- Free Schools;
- Trust Schools;
- Teaching Schools; and
- Specialist Schools.

As a consequence of these policies, we have seen a significant number of new schools being opened, especially Free Schools.

However, the major area of expansion in the system proposed by the previous Coalition government and continued by the current government is the number of schools becoming Academies. It is highly likely that at least one of your school placements or your first job will be in an Academy school. Originally, Academies were a New Labour policy initiative and the first Academy schools opened in 2003. Initially, they were designed to deal with the problems facing a number of failing schools in inner cities (Gorard, 2009). In effect, Academies were new schools that provided the opportunity for a fresh start and a break from past failures (Abbott *et al.*, 2013b). Academies were freed from many regulations, removed from local authority control and sponsored by an external organization that brought fresh ideas and enthusiasm. Initially, evidence of the success of Academies was mixed but there were some notable success stories with some schools being transformed into highly successful institutions. Successive governments have aimed to build on the successes of the Academy programme and the eventual aim is that every school in England should become an Academy. In 2010, the first stage of this process enabled outstanding schools rated as 'outstanding' to become Academies and these schools would provide leadership and inspiration for the wider education system. At the other end of the spectrum, the weakest schools would also convert to Academy status with the support of an outstanding school or a strong sponsor to provide the stimulus for change. The sponsor plays a significant role in the operation of an Academy and can provide a range of common services and approaches to leadership and professional development. A number of sponsors such as Absolute Return for Kids (ARK), a UK education charity, are associated with a range of schools and provide a common approach across all their Academy schools. This process has occurred in a number of different countries, with the development of networks or chains of schools operating under the control of one group or sponsor. In England, this has been primarily through the creation of Multi-Academy Trusts (MATs), whereby individual Academies or Free Schools lose their own legal identity and become part of a wider grouping under the control of a sponsoring organization who will set up a MAT board. The amount of delegation to individual schools will differ between individual boards, but the MAT board has ultimate control over all decisions. Within some MATS, individual schools may have almost total autonomy, but in other cases there may be significant central control across a wide range of areas, including teaching methods, discipline policy and even school uniform.

Task 26.3

Given the potential loss of independence, consider the reasons why a school might become part of a MAT.

The ultimate aim of the current government is that Academy status will be the norm for all state schools, with schools enjoying direct funding and full independence from central and local bureaucracy. In practice, this is likely to be difficult to achieve, and political and financial factors may put a stop to this process. However, the move to greater school autonomy through the establishment of Academies and other types of new school organization is designed to have a positive impact on standards and to improve the overall quality of teaching and learning. As part of a package of policy measures, it is designed to encourage the development of a quasi-market in education aimed at promoting choice and competition.

Another type of school in which you may find yourself during your training programme or with which you may working as part of your professional development is a Teaching School (Middlewood and Abbott, 2018). Teaching Schools have been established to work with other schools in their area and to provide a lead to other schools in the Teaching School Alliance. More specifically, the Teaching Schools have six main areas of responsibility, often referred to as 'the Big Six':

- school-led initial teacher training;
- continuing professional development;
- school-to-school support;
- identifying and developing leadership potential;
- specialist leaders of education; and
- research and development.

The identification of six major areas of activity has placed some pressure on the Teaching Schools in terms of delivery and reach. However, it is clear that the individual teacher is at the heart of each of the big six. The intention is to raise the overall quality of teaching and learning in schools through the activities instigated and developed by the Teaching School, which can then cascade throughout the Teaching School Alliance. Again, this is an example of schools taking responsibility for school improvement and for raising the performance of the system as a whole.

According to the government, allowing different types of school to open will encourage innovation and lead to rising standards of pupil achievement (DfE, 2016d). For example, parents, teachers, charities and interested groups are able to open a Free School if there is evidence of parental demand in a particular locality. Another example of an alternative type of school is the University Technical Colleges (UTCs), which are established by a partnership of universities, colleges and businesses. University Technical Colleges will

Task 26.4

Do you agree with the argument that giving schools greater autonomy will lead to improvements in the education system? Find out the status of the school where you are training or working.

offer a combination of technical and academic education and are designed to raise overall standards in vocational education.

There is a strong desire on the part of the government to provide the highest educational opportunities for all children. Against a background of cuts in public expenditure, additional funding has been made available through the introduction of the Pupil Premium, which provides additional money to pupils from deprived backgrounds and to existing expenditure on schools (for more detail, see Chapter 24). The intention is to raise educational standards among the poorest sections of society and to reduce the attainment gap between rich and poor pupils. The drive to improve the performance of the poorest group of school pupils is a significant part of government policy and is reflected in a number of initiatives. For example, the number of teachers training through the Teach First route has increased significantly: from 2002 to 2018, 10,000 teachers have trained through this route (Teach First, 2017: 4). Teach First is a charity that aims to address educational disadvantage and inequality due to socioeconomic differences by transforming exceptional graduates into effective, inspirational teachers and leaders in all fields. They work in disadvantaged, typically inner-city schools in challenging circumstances with a high level of poverty and/or under-achievement. Another example of policy in this area is the drive by the government to encourage more children from disadvantaged backgrounds to aspire to a university education and, in particular, to study at Russell Group universities. If you train or teach in a school in a disadvantaged area, you will soon become aware of the range of initiatives that are designed to encourage and support your pupils to apply to university.

26.4 Impact of government policies

The government has placed a great deal of emphasis on the drive to raise standards in schools and to improve the education system. It is important to remember that the notion of educational standards is open to more than one interpretation – an ambiguity that complicates any attempt to measure educational standards. Moreover, statistics are ambiguous and different groups will put a different emphasis on the same data. You need to be aware that there are conflicting agendas and messages in the daily output of government statistics and information relating to education. Clearly, political factors will have a bearing on education policy, which is increasingly driven by central government.

For you, as a beginning teacher, the significance of any government initiative is the impact it has on your school and your classroom teaching. Policies will directly impact on you in your subject area as you are compelled by the government to adopt particular approaches, introduce new subject content or alter your assessment procedures. In a wider school context, government initiatives will directly affect the amount of resource available, staffing levels, your conditions of service and, of course, your salary. If you are training or working in a specialist school or in an Academy, there is a strong likelihood that you will have greater access to additional resources and more specialized equipment. If, however, you find yourself teaching in a rural school, you might have significantly fewer resources to deal with similar issues. Despite this, the key significance of all education initiatives is the impact they have on the individual school pupil and, for you, your ability to operate effectively as a classroom teacher.

Task 26.5

During your school placement, find out what new initiatives the school has been involved in over the past two years. How were these initiatives evaluated and how successful have they been in improving standards?

26.5 Conclusion

There is general agreement on the importance of education for the individual and for the wider community. All political parties recognize the need to improve educational standards and to create a more educated workforce to enable the creation of:

- a fair and just society that gives equal opportunities to all regardless of background;
- a safe society that enables young people to make a positive contribution; and
- a prosperous society that contributes to economic well-being for all.

There is no general agreement, however, about how these objectives can be achieved. In political terms, education remains a key battleground between the main parties. All governments will be keen to be seen to be improving education and it is very easy to confuse *change* with *improvement*. Many teachers claim, with some justification, that the one constant in their working life is change. Whether they can be unambiguously viewed as improvements, changes in policy are set to continue and you will be heavily involved as you start your teaching career. The policy debate taking place in Parliament and in the media might seem far removed from your day-to-day responsibilities as a classroom teacher and the issues of dealing with your Year 9 group on a Friday afternoon; however, you cannot close your classroom door and ignore the latest policy initiatives. Ultimately, policy initiatives filter down to the classroom and affect the way you teach, what you teach and how you assess pupil work. You will be in the best position to make the changes effective in a positive way if you have taken the time to understand where they are coming from and why.

It is rather early to judge the success or failure of many recent government policies. The pace of change continues at a rapid rate and you will need to keep up to date with current developments. At times, this can be daunting given the sheer volume of legislation and the demands placed on you as you begin your teaching career. Often, education policies are not properly evaluated, and a new initiative replaces one that has not had time to be properly reviewed and assessed. In addition, education policies often take a great deal of time to produce results and numerous questions about ongoing government reform remain unanswered. For instance:

- Even if standards are improving, are they rising at a fast enough rate or in the right areas?
- Should the emphasis be on developing skills for employment or on more general education?

- How important is the study of academic subjects?
- Are the changes being suggested for the secondary curriculum right?
- Should the government develop a radical new school system?
- Is the pace of change right?
- Is the level of funding appropriate?
- What role can technology play?
- Is the level of support sufficient?

At times, you will find it difficult to keep up with the pace of change and at times you may become resistant to further change. Some of these changes will seem more desirable to you than others. More than ever, teachers, through their schools, professional associations, subject associations and research networks, have the chance to influence the policies that impact on their work at local, regional and national levels. As a new teacher, you may just want to focus on teaching your subject. However, as you move through the system, you are likely to develop stronger views about policy changes and how they impact on you, your teaching, your school and, most importantly, your pupils. It is important that you are aware of the direction of policy and the changes that are taking place. This can often be helped by a sense of what has happened in the past and how policy has been developed.

Do not underestimate the power of teachers and their importance in the system. Head teachers, through their leadership role, have a clear part to play in any school system that places an emphasis on self-improvement. However, teachers are also being placed at the forefront of the current policy reforms and, in this sense as well as others, the future of teaching is in your hands.

Recommendations for further reading

Abbott, I., Rathbone, M. and Whitehead, P. (2013) *Education Policy*. London: Sage.

Benn, M. (2011) *School Wars: The Battle for Britain's Education*. London: Verso.

Department for Education (DfE) (2016) *Educational Excellence Everywhere*. London: DfE. Available at: https://www.gov.uk/government/publications/educational-excellence-everywhere.

Gorard, S. (2009) What are Academies the answer to?, *Journal of Education Policy*, 24 (1): 101–113.

Middlewood, D. and Abbott, I. (2018) *Collaborative School Leadership: Managing a Group of Schools*. London: Bloomsbury.

Bibliography

Abaya, J. (2016) School leadership challenges along Kenya's Borabu-Sotik border, *Educational Management Administration and Leadership*, 44 (5): 757–774.

Abbott, I., Middlewood, D. and Robinson, S. (2013a) *Report on Effective Use of Pupil Premium in an Urban Authority*. Coventry: University of Warwick.

Abbott, I., Rathbone, M. and Whitehead, P. (2013b) *Education Policy*. London: Sage.

Abbott, I., Middlewood, D. and Robinson, S. (2014) Prospecting for support in a wild environment: investigating a school-to-school support system, *School Leadership and Management*, 34 (5): 439–453.

Abbott, I., Middlewood, D. and Robinson, S. (2015) It's not just about value for money: a case study of values-led implementation of the Pupil Premium in outstanding schools, *Management in Education*, 29 (4): 178–184.

Academies Act (2010) London: HMSO. Available at: https://www.legislation.gov.uk/ukpga/2010/32/contents [accessed 1 March 2018].

Acquah, D. and Huddleston, P. (2014) Challenges and opportunities for vocational education and training in the light of Raising the Participation Age, *Research in Post-Compulsory Education*, 19 (1): 1–17.

Adey, P. and Shayer, M. (2002) Cognitive acceleration comes of age, in M. Shayer and P. Adey (eds.) *Learning Intelligence: Cognitive Acceleration Across the Curriculum 5–15*. Buckingham: Open University Press.

Ainley, J. (2008) Task design based on Purpose and Utility, Topic Study Group 34: Research and Development in Task Design and Analysis, *Eleventh International Congress on Mathematics Education*, Monterrey, Mexico.

Alexander, R. (2005) *Towards Dialogic Teaching: Rethinking Classroom Talk*, 2nd edn. Cambridge: Dialogos.

Anderson, R.C. and Klofstad, C.A. (2012) Preference for leaders with masculine voices holds in the case of feminine leadership roles, *PLoS One*, 7 (12): e51216.

Andrews, R. (2009) *Review of Research in English as an Additional Language (EAL)*. London: Training and Development Agency for Schools.

Appadurai, A. (1990) Disjuncture and difference in the global cultural economy, *Theory, Culture and Society*, 7 (2): 295–310.

Apter, A.J., Cheng, J., Small, D., Bennett, I.M., Albert, C., Fein, D.G. *et al.* (2006) Asthma numeracy skill and health literacy, *Journal of Asthma*, 43 (9): 705–710.

AQA Education (2014) *GCSE English Literature: Specification Assessment Objective 3*. Available at: https://filestore.aqa.org.uk/resources/english/specifications/AQA-8702-SP-2015.PDF.

Arlin, M. (1984) Time, equality, and mastery learning, *Review of Educational Research*, 54 (1): 65–86.

Armstrong, V., Barnes, S., Sutherland, R., Curran, S., Mills, S. and Thompson, I. (2005) Collaborative research methodology for investigating teaching and learning: the use of interactive whiteboard technology, *Educational Review*, 57 (4): 457–469.

Arnot, M., Schneider, C., Evans, M., Liu, Y., Welply, O. and Davies-Tutt, D. (2014) *School Approaches to the Education of EAL Students: Language Development, Social Integration and Achievement*. London: The Bell Foundation.

Askew, S. and Lodge, C. (2000) Gifts, ping-pong, and loops – linking feedback and learning, in S. Askew (ed.) *Feedback for Learning*. London: RoutledgeFalmer.

Assessment Reform Group (2002) *Assessment for Learning: 10 Principles*. Cambridge: University of Cambridge School of Education. Available at: http://www.hkeaa.edu.hk/DocLibrary/SBA/HKDSE/Eng_DVD/doc/Afl_principles.pdf [accessed 1 April 2017].

Association of Colleges (AOC) (2016) *College Key Facts 2016/17*. Available at: https://www.aoc.co.uk/about-colleges/research-and-stats/key-further-education-statistics [accessed 22 April 2018].

Ayers, H., Clarke, D. and Murray, A. (2000) *Perspectives on Behaviour: A Practical Guide to Effective Interventions for Teachers*, 2nd edn. London: David Fulton.

Bandura, A. (1985) *Social Foundations of Thought and Action*. Englewood Cliffs, NJ: Prentice-Hall.

Barber, M. (1994) *Young People and Their Attitudes to School*. Keele: Keele University.

Barnes, D., Britton, J. and Rosen, H. (eds.) (1969) *Language, the Learner and the School*. Harmondsworth: Penguin.

Basford, J.M. and Dann, R. (2017) Assessment for learning, in J. Moyles, J. Georgeson and J. Payler (eds.) *Beginning Teaching, Beginning Learning*, 5th edn. London: Open University Press.

Bauman, Z. (2007) *Liquid Times: Living in an Age of Uncertainty*. Cambridge: Polity Press.

Beaman, R., Wheldall, K. and Kemp, C. (2006) Differential teacher attention to boys and girls in the classroom, *Educational Review*, 58 (3): 339–366.

Bell, M., Cordingley, P. and Goodchild, L. (2010) *Map of Research Reviews. QCA Building the Evidence Base Project: September 2007–March 2011*. Coventry: Centre for the Use of Research and Evidence in Education. Available at: http://dera.ioe.ac.uk/1208/1/CUREE_Map_of_research_reviews_FINAL.pdf [accessed May 2017].

Benn, C. and Chitty, C. (1996) *Thirty Years On: Is Comprehensive Education Alive and Well or Struggling to Survive?* London: David Fulton.

Bennett, R.E. (2011) Formative assessment: a critical review, *Assessment in Education: Principles, Policy and Practice*, 18 (1): 5–25.

Bergmann, J. and Sams, A. (2012) *Flip Your Classroom: Reach Every Student in Every Class Every Day*. Washington, DC: International Society for Technology in Education.

Best, R. (1999) The impact of a decade of educational change on pastoral care and PSE: a survey of teacher perceptions, *Pastoral Care in Education*, 17 (2): 3–13.

Best, R. (2014) Forty years of pastoral care: an appraisal of Michael Marland's seminal book and its significance for pastoral care in schools, *Pastoral Care in Education*, 32 (3): 173–185.

Bian, L., Leslie, S.-J. and Cimpian, A. (2017) Gender stereotypes about intellectual ability emerge early and influence children's interests, *Science*, 355 (6323): 389–391.

Biesta, G. (2017) *The Rediscovery of Teaching*. Abingdon: Routledge.

Bigger, S. (1999) Spiritual, moral, social and cultural education, in S. Bigger and E. Brown (eds.) *Spiritual, Moral, Social and Cultural Education: Exploring Values in the Curriculum*. London: David Fulton.

Birkinshaw, S. (2015) 'Spiritual friends': an investigation of children's spirituality in the context of British urban secondary education, *British Journal of Religious Education*, 37 (1): 83–102.

Black, P. (2015) Formative assessment – an optimistic but incomplete vision, *Assessment in Education: Principles, Policy and Practice*, 22 (1): 161–177.

Black, P. and Wiliam, D. (1998a) Assessment and classroom learning, *Assessment in Education: Principles, Policy and Practice*, 5 (1): 7–74.

Black, P. and Wiliam, D. (1998b) Inside the black box: raising standards through classroom assessment, *Phi Delta Kappan*, 80 (2): 139–148.

Black, P., Harrison, C., Lee, C., Marshall, B. and Wiliam, D. (2004) Working inside the black box: assessment for learning in the classroom, *Phi Delta Kappan*, 86 (1): 1–21.

Blackledge, A. and Creese, A. (2010) *Multilingualism*. London: Continuum.

Blanden, J., Hansen, K. and Machin, S. (2008) *The GDP cost of the lost earning potential of adults who grew up in poverty*. Birmingham: Joseph Rowntree Foundation. Available at: https://www.jrf.org. uk/report/gdp-cost-lost-earning-potential-adults-who-grew-poverty [accessed 23 December 2017].

Blatchford, P., Russell, A., Basset, P., Brown, P. and Martin, C. (2007) The role and effects of teaching assistants in English primary schools (Years 4 to 6) 2000–2003, *British Educational Research Journal*, 33 (1): 5–26.

Bloom, B.S. (1968) Learning for mastery, *Evaluation Comment*, 1 (2). Available at: https://files.eric. ed.gov/fulltext/ED053419.pdf.

Bloom, B.S., Ebgelhart, M., Furst, E., Hill, W. and Krathwohl, D. (1956) *Taxonomy of Educational Objectives*. New York: Longmans Green.

Bloom, L. (2012) Disadvantages and educational progress, Talk to SEN Conference, Leeds, Conference Pamphlet (unpublished).

Blum, L. (1980) *Friendship, Altruism, and Morality*. Boston, MA: Routledge & Kegan Paul.

Board of Education (1921) *The Teaching of English in England (The Newbolt Report)*. London: HMSO.

Bowring-Carr, C. and West-Burnham, J. (1997) *Effective Learning in Schools*. London: Pitman.

Bracken, S., Driver, C. and Kadi-Hanifi, K. (2017) *Teaching English as an Additional Language in Secondary Schools: Theory and Practice*. Abingdon: Routledge.

Bradlow, J., Bartram, F. and Guasp, A. (2017) *School Report: The Experiences of Lesbian, Gay, Bi and Trans Young People in Britain's Schools in 2017*. London: Stonewall. Available at: https://www. stonewall.org.uk/sites/default/files/the_school_report_2017.pdf [accessed 3 February 2018].

Bradshaw, P. and Younie, S. (2017) *Debates in ICT and Computing*. London: Routledge.

Brighton, C.M., Hertberg, H.L., Moon, T.R., Tomlinson, C.A. and Callahan, C.M. (2005) *The Feasibility of High-end Learning in a Diverse Middle School*, Research Monograph #05210. Storrs, CT: National Research Center on the Gifted and Talented. Available at: https://files.eric.ed.gov/ fulltext/ED505377.pdf.

Broadfoot. P.M., Daugherty, J., Harlen, W., James, M. and Stobart, G. (2002) *Assessment for Learning: 10 Principles*. Cambridge: University of Cambridge School of Education.

Bromfield, C. (2005) PGCE secondary trainee teachers and effective behaviour management: an evaluation and commentary, *Support for Learning*, 21 (4): 188–193.

Brooks, V. (2012) Learning to teach and learning about teaching, in V. Brooks, I. Abbott and P. Huddleston (eds.) *Preparing to Teach in Secondary Schools*. Maidenhead: Open University Press.

Brown, P.C., Roediger, H.L., III and McDaniel, M.A. (2014) *Make it Stick: The Science of Successful Learning*. Cambridge, MA: The Belknap Press.

Burnitt, M. and Gunter, H. (2013) Primary school councils: organisation, composition, and headteacher perceptions, *Management in Education*, 27 (2): 56–62.

Bush, T. and Middlewood, D. (2013) *Leading and Managing People in Education*, 3rd edn. London: Sage.

Byron, T. (2010) *Do We Have Safer Children in a Digital World? Review of Progress since the 2008 Byron Review*. Nottingham: DCSF Publications.

Campbell, T. (2015) Stereotyped at seven? Biases in teacher judgement of pupils' ability and attainment, *Journal of Social Policy*, 44 (3): 517–547.

Carroll, M. (2010) The practice of pastoral care of teachers: a summary analysis of published outlines, *Pastoral Care in Education*, 28 (2): 145–154.

Cassen, R., Feinstein, L. and Graham, P. (2009) Educational outcomes: adversity and resilience, *Social Policy and Society*, 8 (1): 73–85.

Cavanaugh, K., Huizinga, M., Wallston, K.A., Gebretsadik, T., Shintani, A., Davis, D. *et al.* (2008) Association of numeracy and diabetes control, *Annals of Internal Medicine*, 148 (10): 737–746.

Cazden, C.B. (2001) *Classroom Discourse: The Language of Teaching and Learning*, 2nd edn. Portsmouth, NH: Heinemann.

Central Advisory Council for Education (CACE) (1959) *15 to 18: A Report of the Central Advisory Council for Education (The Crowther Report)*. London: HMSO.

Child Exploitation and Online Protection Agency (CEOP) (2014) *Think U Know*. London: CEOP. Available at: https://www.thinkuknow.co.uk/11_13/need-advice/ [accessed 10 August 2016].

Children and Young People's Unit (CYPU) (2000) *Children's Fund Guidance*. London: DfES.

Children's Society (2016) *The Good Childhood Report 2016*. London: The Children's Society.

Chitty, C. (2002) *Understanding Schools and Society*. London: Routledge.

Clark, C. and Formby, S. (2013) *Young people's views on literacy and employment*. London: National Literacy Trust. Available at: https://files.eric.ed.gov/fulltext/ED560636.pdf.

Clarke, P., Reynolds, D. and Harris, A. (2005) Challenging the challenged, in P. Clarke (ed.) *Improving Schools in Difficulty*. London: Continuum.

Coleman, P. (1998) *Parent, Student and Teacher Collaboration: The Power of 3*. London: Paul Chapman.

Commission for Racial Equality (CRE) (1986) *Teaching English as a Second Language: Report of a formal investigation by the Commission for Racial Equality into the Teaching of English as a Second Language in Calderdale Local Education Authority*. London: CRE.

Confederation for British Industry (CBI) (2011) *Building for Growth*. Available at: www.cbi.org.uk/media-centre/news-articles/2011/05/building-for-growth [accessed 5 June 2017].

Confederation of British Industry (CBI) (2012) *Employers' Views on Youth Literacy and Employability*. London: National Literacy Trust.

Conteh, J. (2012) *Teaching Bilingual and EAL Learners in Primary Schools*. Exeter: Learning Matters.

Conteh, J. (2015) *The EAL Teaching Book: Promoting Success for Multilingual Learners in Primary and Secondary Schools*, 2nd edn. Exeter: Learning Matters.

Conteh, J. and Brock, A. (2010) 'Safe spaces'? Sites of bilingualism for young learners in home, school and community, *International Journal of Bilingual Education and Bilingualism*, 14 (3): 347–360.

Cope, B. and Kalantzis, M. (eds.) (2000) *Multiliteracies: Literacy Learning and the Design of Social Futures*. London: Routledge.

Creese, A. (2005) *Teacher Collaboration and Talk in Multilingual Classrooms*. Clevedon: Multilingual Matters.

Cummins, J. (1979) Cognitive/academic language proficiency, linguistic interdependence, the optimum age question and some other matters, *Working Papers on Bilingualism*, 19: 121–129.

Cummins, J. (1984) *Bilingualism and Special Education: Issues in Assessment and Pedagogy*. Bristol: Multilingual Matters.

Cummins, J. (2001) *Negotiating Identities: Education for Empowerment in a Diverse Society*, 2nd edn. Ontario, CA: California Association for Bilingual Education.

Cummins, J. and Early, M. (eds.) (2011) *Identity Texts: The Collaborative Creation of Power in Multilingual Schools*. London: Trentham Books.

Dann, R. (2002) *Promoting Assessment as Learning: Improving the Learning Process*. London: Psychology Press.

Dann, R. (2014) Assessment as Learning: blurring the boundaries of assessment and learning for theory, policy and practice, *Assessment in Education: Principles, Policy and Practice*, 21 (2): 149–166.

Dann, R. (2016) Developing the foundations for dialogic feedback in order to better understand the 'learning gap' from a pupil's perceptive, *London Review of Education*, 13 (3): 5–20.

Dann, R. (2018) *Developing Feedback for Pupil Learning*. London: Routledge.

Datta, M. (ed.) (2007) *Bilinguality and Literacy*. London: Continuum.

Dawkins, R. (1989) *The Selfish Gene*. Oxford: Oxford University Press.

Deaney, R., Ruthven, K. and Hennessy, S. (2003) Pupil perspectives on the contribution of information and communication technology to teaching and learning in the secondary school, *Research Papers in Education*, 18 (2): 141–165.

Dekker, S., Lee, N.C., Howard-Jones, P. and Jolles, J. (2012) Neuromyths in education: prevalence and predictors of misconceptions among teachers, *Frontiers in Psychology*, 2012 (3): 429.

DePalma, R. and Atkinson, E. (2009) 'No Outsiders': moving beyond a discourse of tolerance to challenge heteronormativity in primary schools, *British Educational Research Journal*, 35 (6): 837–855.

Department for Business Innovation and Skills (DBIS) (2014) *Getting the Job Done: The Government's Reform Plan for Vocational Qualifications*. London: DBIS.

Department for Business Innovation and Skills and Department for Education (DBIS/DfE) (2016a) *Post-16 Skills Plan*, Cm 9280. London: DfE. Available at: https://www.gov.uk/government/publications/post-16-skills-plan-and-independent-report-on-technical-education [accessed 1 March 2018].

Department for Business Innovation and Skills and Department for Education (DBIS/DfE) (2016b) *Report of the Independent Panel on Technical Education (The Sainsbury Review)*. London: DfE.

Department for Children, Schools and Families (DCSF) (2007) *Homophobic Bullying: Safe to Learn*. London: DCSF. Available at: http://www.educationengland.org.uk/documents/pdfs/2007-dcsf-homophobic-bullying.pdf [accessed 21 August 2017].

Department for Children Schools and Families (DCSF) (2009a) *Learning Behaviour: Lessons Learned – A Review of Behaviour Standards and Practices in Our Schools*, DCSF-00453-2009. Nottingham: DCSF.

Department for Children, Schools and Families (DCSF) (2009b) *Deprivation and Education: The Evidence on Pupils in England*. London: DCSF.

Department for Children Schools and Families (DCSF) (2010) *Smoking Out Underachievement*. Nottingham: DCSF.

Department for Education (DfE) (2010a) *School Funding Consultation: Introducing a Pupil Premium*. London: DfE. Available at: https://assets.publishing.service.gov.uk/government/uploads/system/uploads/attachment_data/file/175429/CM-7980.pdf.

Department for Education (DfE) (2010b) *The Importance of Teaching (The Schools White Paper 2010)*, Cm 7980. London: TSO. Available at: http://www.education.gov.uk/publications/standard/publicationdetail/page1/CM%207980 [accessed 30 October 2017].

Department for Education (DfE) (2011a) *Teachers' Standards: Guidance for School Leaders, School Staff and Governing Bodies*. London: HMSO. Available at: https://assets.publishing.service.gov.uk/government/uploads/system/uploads/attachment_data/file/665520/Teachers__Standards.pdf.

Department for Education (DfE) (2011b) *Education of Disadvantaged Children*. London: DfE. Available at: https://www.gov.uk/government/policies/education-of-disadvantaged-children [accessed 4 August 2017].

Department for Education (DfE) (2011c) *Review of Vocational Education (The Wolf Report)*. London: DfE. Available at: https://www.gov.uk/government/publications/review-of-vocational-education-the-wolf-report [accessed 20 August 2017].

Department for Education (DfE) (2013a) *National Curriculum in England: Citizenship Programmes of Study for Key Stages 3 and 4*. London: DfE. Available at https://www.gov.uk/government/publications/national-curriculum-in-england-citizenship-programmes-of-study/national-curriculum-in-england-citizenship-programmes-of-study-for-key-stages-3-and-4 [accessed 13 June 2017].

Department for Education (DfE) (2013b) *Reform of the National Curriculum in England*. London: DfE.

Department for Education (DfE) (2013c) *The National Curriculum in England: Framework Document*. London: DfE. Available at: http://www.educationengland.org.uk/documents/pdfs/2013-nc-framework.pdf [accessed April 2017].

Department for Education (DfE) (2014a) *The National Curriculum for Secondary Education*. London: DfE.

Department for Education (DfE) (2014b) *Promoting Fundamental British Values as Part of SMSC in Schools: Departmental advice for maintained schools*. London: DfE. Available at: https://www.gov.uk/government/uploads/system/uploads/attachment_data/file/380595/SMSC_Guidance_Maintained_Schools.pdf [accessed 4 March 2018].

Department for Education (DfE) (2014c) *The National Curriculum in England: Framework for Key Stages 1 to 4*. London: DfE. Available at: https://www.gov.uk/government/publications/national-curriculum-in-england-framework-for-key-stages-1-to-4 [accessed 5 March 2018].

Department for Education (DfE) (2015a) *Final Report of the Commission on Assessment Without Levels (J. McIntosh, Chair)*. London: DfE. Available at: https://www.gov.uk/government/publications/commission-on-assessment-without-levels-final-report [accessed 6 November 2017].

Department for Education (DfE) (2015b) *16–19 Study Programmes. Departmental Advice for Senior Leadership Teams, Curriculum Planners, Teachers, Trainers and Co-ordinators on the Planning and Delivery of 16–19 Study Programmes*. London: DfE.

Department for Education (DfE) (2015c) *Citizenship Programmes of Study: Key Stages 1 and 2*. London: DfE. Available at: https://www.gov.uk/government/publications/citizenship-programmes-of-study-for-key-stages-1-and-2 [accessed 17 October 2017].

Department for Education (DfE) (2015d) *Reading: The Next Steps – Supporting Higher Standards in Schools*. London: DfES. Available at: https://www.gov.uk/government/publications/reading-supporting-higher-standards-in-schools [accessed 2 February 2018].

Department for Education (DfE) (2015e) *Effective Ways to Support Disadvantaged Pupils' Achievement*. London: DfE.

Department for Education (DfE) (2016a) *Eliminating Unnecessary Workload Around Marking*. London: DfE. Available at: https://assets.publishing.service.gov.uk/government/uploads/system/uploads/attachment_data/file/511256/Eliminating-unnecessary-workload-around-marking.pdf [accessed 12 April 2017].

Department for Education (DfE) (2016b) *Statistical First Release 20_2016*. London: DfE.

Department for Education (DfE) (2016c) *The Link between Absence and Attainment at KS2 and KS4: 2013/14 Academic Year*. London: DfE. Available at: https://assets.publishing.service.gov.uk/government/uploads/system/uploads/attachment_data/file/509679/The-link-between-absence-and-attainment-at-KS2-and-KS4-2013-to-2014-academic-year.pdf.

Department for Education (DfE) (2016d) *Educational Excellence Everywhere*. London: DfE. Available at: https://www.gov.uk/government/publications/educational-excellence-everywhere [accessed 4 April 2018].

Department for Education (DfE) (2016e) *The Permanent and Fixed Period Exclusions in England: 2014 to 2015*, SFR 26/2016. London: DfE. Available at: https://www.gov.uk/government/statistics/permanent-and-fixed-period-exclusions-in-england-2014-to-2015 [accessed 20 February 2018].

Department for Education (DfE) (2016f) *Behaviour and Discipline in Schools: Advice for Headteachers and School Staff*. London: DfE. Available at: http://dera.ioe.ac.uk/25117/.

Department for Education (DfE) (2016g) *Keeping Children Safe in Education*. London: DfE. Available at: https://www.gov.uk/government/publications/keeping-children-safe-in-education--2 [accessed 3 January 2018].

Department for Education (DfE) (2017a) *16–19 Study Programmes: Planning and Delivery of 16–19 Study Programmes*. London: DfE.

Department for Education (DfE) (2017b) *Special Educational Needs in England: January 2017*, SFR37/2017. London: DfE. Available at: https://www.gov.uk/government/statistics/special-educational-needs-in-england-january-2017 [accessed 22 January 2018].

Department for Education (DfE) (2017c) *Progress 8 and Attainment 8: Guide for Maintained Secondary Schools, Academies and Free Schools*, DFE-00075-2015. London: DfE. Available at: https://radicaled.files.wordpress.com/2017/07/progress-8.pdf.

Department for Education (DfE) (2017d) *GCSE New Grading Scale: Factsheets*. London: DfE. Available at: https://www.gov.uk/government/publications/gcse-new-grading-scale-factsheets [accessed 3 April 2018].

Department for Education (DfE) (2017e) *Schools, Pupils and their Characteristics: January 2017*. London: DfE. Available at: https://www.gov.uk/government/statistics/schools-pupils-and-their-characteristics-january-2017 [last accessed 29 August 2017].

Department for Education (DfE) (2017f) *Creating a Culture: How School Leaders can Optimise Behaviour (The Bennett Review)*, DFE 00059-2017. London: DfE. Available at: https://www.gov.uk/government/publications/behaviour-in-schools [accessed 4 May 2018].

Department for Education (DfE) (2017g) *Characteristics of Children in Need: 2016 to 2017, England.* London: DfE. Available at: https://www.gov.uk/government/statistics/characteristics-of-children-in-need-2016-to-2017 [accessed 4 May 2018].

Department for Education (DfE) (2018a) *School and College Performance Tables: Statements of Intent.* Available at: https://www.gov.uk/government/publications/school-and-college-performance-tables-statements-of-intent [accessed 30 August 2018].

Department for Education (DfE) (2018b) *Working Together to Safeguard Children.* London: DfE. Available at: https://www.gov.uk/government/publications/working-together-to-safeguard-children--2 [accessed 1 September 2018].

Department for Education and Employment (DfEE) (1997a) *Excellence in Schools (White Paper),* Cm 3681. London: HMSO.

Department for Education and Employment (DfEE) (1997b) *Excellence for All Children: Meeting Special Educational Needs.* London: DfEE.

Department for Education and Employment (DfEE) (1999) *The National Numeracy Strategy.* London: DfEE. Available at: http://www.satspapers.org/Resources/maths%20resources/oldstrategy/introduction.pdf [accessed 22 March 2017].

Department for Education and Employment (DfEE) (2001) *Schools Building on Success: Raising Standards, Promoting Diversity, Achieving Results.* London: DfEE. Available at: https://www.gov.uk/government/publications/schools-building-on-success-raising-standards-promoting-diversity-achieving-results [accessed 15 May 2017].

Department for Education and Skills (DfES) (2001) *Special Educational Needs (SEN) Code of Practice.* London: DfES Publications. Available at: www.gov.uk/government/publications/special-educational-needs-sen-code-of-practice [accessed 10 October 2017].

Department for Education and Skills (DfES) (2002) *Effective Lessons in Science: Notes for Tutors.* London: DfES Publications.

Department for Education and Skills (DfES) (2003a) *Every Child Matters.* London: TSO. Available at: https://www.gov.uk/government/publications/every-child-matters [accessed 15 May 2017].

Department for Education and Skills (DfES) (2003b) *Effective Teaching and Learning in Science.* London: DfES.

Department for Education and Skills (DfES) (2004) *A National Conversation about Personalised Learning.* Nottingham: DfES Publications.

Department for Education and Skills (DfES) (2005a) *Higher Standards, Better Schools for All.* London: TSO.

Department for Education and Skills (DfES) (2005b) *Social and Emotional Aspects of Learning (SEAL): Improving Behaviour, Improving Learning.* London: DfES.

Department for Education and Skills (DfES) (2005c) *Learning Behaviour (The Steer Report).* London: DfES.

Department for Education and Skills (DfES) (2006) Personalised Learning website.

Department for Education and Skills (DfES) (2007) *2020 Vision: Report of the Teaching and Learning in 2020 Review Group (The Gilbert Review).* London: DfES Publications.

Department of Education and Science (DES) (1971) *The Education of Immigrants: Education Survey 13.* London: HMSO.

Department of Education and Science (DES) (1972) *The Continuing Needs of Immigrants: Education Survey 14.* London: HMSO.

Department of Education and Science (DES) (1975) *A Language for Life (The Bullock Report).* London: HMSO.

Department of Education and Science (DES) (1978) *Special Educational Needs (The Warnock Report).* London: DES. Available at: http://www.educationengland.org.uk/documents/warnock/warnock1978.html [accessed 14 June 2008].

Department of Education and Science (DES) (1981) *West Indian Children in Our Schools (The Rampton Report),* Cmnd. 8273. London: HMSO.

Department of Education and Science (DES) (1982) *Mathematics Counts (The Cockcroft Report)*. London: HMSO.

Department of Education and Science (DES) (1985) *Education for All (The Swann Report)*. London: HMSO.

Department of Education and Science (DES) (1989) *Discipline in Schools (The Elton Report)*. London: HMSO.

Department of Health (DoH) (2003) *The Victoria Climbié Inquiry (The Laming Report)*, Cm 5730. London: TSO. Available at: https://www.gov.uk/government/publications/the-victoria-climbie-inquiry-report-of-an-inquiry-by-lord-laming [accessed 6 June 2017].

Derrick, J. (1977) *Language Needs of Minority Group Children: Learners of English as a Second Language*. Slough: NFER.

Desforges, C. and Abouchaar, A. (2003) *The Impact of Parental Involvement, Parental Support and Family Education on Pupil Achievement and Adjustment: A Literature Review*, DfES Research Report #433. London: DfES.

Dessent, T. (2006) Will Mrs Thatcher have her way? Future options for children's services, in B. Norwich (ed.) *Taking Stock: Integrated Children's Services, Improvement and Inclusion*, SEN Policy Options Group, Policy Paper #1, 6th series. Available at: http://www.nasen.org.uk [accessed 8 June 2017].

Document Summary Service (2017) *Professional Responsibilities and Statutory Frameworks for Teachers and Others in Schools: The Bristol Guide*. Bristol: University of Bristol Graduate School of Education.

Donaldson-Feilder, E., Yarker, J. and Lewis, R. (2011) *Preventing Stress in Organisations*. Chichester: Wiley-Blackwell.

Donelson, R. and Rogers, T. (2004) Negotiating a research protocol for studying school-based gay and lesbian issues, *Theory into Practice*, 43 (2): 128–135.

Dubin, R. (1964) *Self Concepts and Training Potential*. London: Pan Books.

Dunne, E. and Bennett, N. (1997) Mentoring processes in school-based training, *British Educational Research Journal*, 23 (2): 225–238.

Edge Foundation (2016) *14–19 Education: A New Baccalaureate*. London: The Edge Foundation.

Edmond, N. and Price, M. (2009) Workforce re-modelling and pastoral care in schools: a diversification of roles or a de-professionalisation of functions?, *Pastoral Care in Education*, 27 (4): 301–311.

Education Act (2002) (c. 32). London: HMSO. Available at: https://www.legislation.gov.uk/ukpga/2002/32/contents [accessed 23 June 2017].

Education Endowment Foundation (EEF) (2018) *Teaching and Learning Toolkit*. Available at: https://educationendowmentfoundation.org.uk/public/files/Toolkit/complete/EEF-Teaching-Learning-Toolkit-July-2018.pdf [accessed 1 September 2018].

Education Funding Agency (EFA) (2016) *Funding Guidance for Young People 2016 to 2017*, EFA-00102-2016. London: EFA. Available at: https://www.gov.uk/government/publications/advice-funding-regulations-for-post-16-provision [accessed April 2017].

Education Funding Agency/Education and Skills Funding Agency (EFA/ESFA) (2017) *Guidance: Full-time enrolment of 14- to 16-year-olds in further education and sixth-form colleges*. Available at: www.gov.uk/guidance/full-time-enrolment-of-14-to-16-year-olds-in-further-education-and-sixth-form-colleges [accessed 21 August 2017].

Education Reform Act (1988) (c. 40). London: HMSO. Available at: http://www.legislation.gov.uk/ukpga/1988/40/contents [accessed 8 May 2017].

Education and Skills Act (2008) (c. 25). London: HMSO. Available at: https://www.legislation.gov.uk/ukpga/2008/25/contents [accessed 8 May 2017].

Ekwall, E.E. and Shanker, J.L. (1988) *Diagnosis and Remediation of the Disabled Reader*, 3rd edn. Boston, MA: Allyn & Bacon.

Elliott, J. (1997) *The Curriculum Experiment: Meeting the Challenge of Social Change*. Buckingham: Open University Press.

Ellis, S. and Tod, J. (2009) *Behaviour for Learning: Proactive Approaches to Behaviour Management*. London: Routledge.

Ellis, V., Butler, R. and Simpson, D. (2002) Planning for learning, in V. Ellis (ed.) *Learning and Teaching in Secondary Schools*. Exeter: Learning Matters.

Emira, M. (2011) I am more than just a TA!, *Management in Education*, 25 (4): 163–174.

Equality Act (2010) (c. 15). London: HMSO. Available at: https://www.legislation.gov.uk/ukpga/2010/15/contents [accessed 2 August 2017].

Feinstein, L. and Sabates, R. (2006) *The Prevalence of Multiple Deprivation for Children in the UK*. Manchester: Centre for Research on the Wider Benefits of Learning.

Fennema, E., Peterson, P.L., Carpenter, T.P. and Lubinski, C.A. (1990) Teachers' attributions and beliefs about girls, boys, and mathematics, *Educational Studies in Mathematics*, 21 (1): 55–69.

Fielding, M. (2006) Leadership, student engagement and the necessity of person-centred education, *International Journal of Leadership in Education*, 9 (4): 299–313.

Flutter, J. and Rudduck, J. (2004) *Consulting Pupils: What's in It for Schools?* London: Routledge.

Flynn, J.R. (1994) IQ gains over time, in R.J. Sternberg (ed.) *Encyclopaedia of Human Intelligence*. New York: Macmillan.

Fones, D. (2001) Blocking them in to free them to act, *English in Education*, 36 (3): 21–31.

Francis, B. (2010) Gender, toys and learning, *Oxford Review of Education*, 36 (3): 325–344.

Fredricks, J., Blumenfeld, P.C. and Paris, A.H. (2004) School engagement: potential of the concept, state of the evidence, *Review of Educational Research*, 74 (1): 59–109.

Fullan, M. (2001) *The New Meaning of Educational Change*, 3rd edn. London: RoutledgeFalmer.

Furlong, J. and Maynard, T. (1995) *Mentoring Student Teachers: The Growth of Professional Knowledge*. London: Routledge.

Gardner, H. (1983) *Frames of Mind*. New York: Basic Books.

Gardner, H. (1993) *Multiple Intelligences: The Theory in Practice*. New York: Basic Books.

Gardner, H. (2003) *Multiple intelligences after 20 years*, Presentation to the Annual Meeting of the American Educational Research Association, Chicago, IL, April.

Gibbons, P. (2009) *English Learners, Academic Literacy and Thinking: Learning in the Challenge Zone*. Portsmouth, NH: Heinemann.

Gilbert, C., Husbands, C., Wigdortz, B. and Francis, B. (2013) *Unleashing Greatness: Getting the Best from an Academised System*. London: The Academies Commission. Available at: https://www.thersa.org/discover/publications-and-articles/reports/unleashing-greatness-getting-the-best-from-an-academised-system [accessed 30 August 2017].

Gilbert, J.K. (2008) Visualization: an emergent field of practice and enquiry in science education, in J.K. Gilbert, M. Reiner and M. Nakhleh (eds.) *Visualization: Theory and Practice in Science Education*. New York: Springer.

Gipps, C. (1994) *Beyond Testing: Towards a Theory of Educational Assessment*. London: Falmer Press.

Goldstein, H. and Moss, G. (2014) Knowledge and numbers in education, *Comparative Education*, 50 (3): 259–265.

Goleman, D. (1996) *Emotional Intelligence: Why It Can Matter More than IQ*. London: Bloomsbury.

Gonzalez, N., Moll, L.C. and Amanti, C. (eds.) (2005) *Funds of Knowledge: Theorizing Practices in Households, Communities and Classrooms*. New York: Routledge.

Gorard, S. (2009) What are Academies the answer to?, *Journal of Education Policy*, 24 (1): 101–113.

Gould, J. (1983) *The Mismeasure of Man*. New York: W.W. Norton.

Graf, M. (2011) *Including and Supporting Learners of English as an Additional Language*. London: Continuum.

Graham, D. (1993) *A Lesson for All of Us? Making the National Curriculum*. London: Routledge.

Gregory, E., Choudhury, H., Ilankuberan, A., Kwapong, A. and Woodham, M. (2013) Practice, performance and perfection: learning sacred texts in four faith communities in London, *International Journal of the Sociology of Language*, 220: 27–48.

Grieve, A.M. and Haining, I. (2011) Inclusive practice? Supporting isolated bilingual learners in a mainstream school, *International Journal of Inclusive Education*, 15 (7): 763–774.

Guppy, P. and Hughes, M. (1999) *The Development of Independent Reading: Reading Support Explained*. Buckingham: Open University Press.

Guskey, T.R. (2009) Mastery learning, in T.L. Good (ed.) *21st Century Education: A Reference Handbook*, Vol. I. Thousand Oaks, CA: Sage.

Hardiker, P., Exton, K. and Barker, M. (1991) *Policies and Practices in Preventive Child Care*. Aldershot: Avebury.

Haydn, T. (2007) *Managing Pupil Behaviour: Key Issues in Teaching and Learning*. London: Routledge.

Hamblin, D. (1978) *The Teacher and Pastoral Care*. Oxford: Blackwell.

Hammond, M. (2014) Introducing ICT in schools in England: rationale and consequences, *British Journal of Educational Technology*, 45 (2): 191–201.

Hammond, M., Reynolds, L. and Ingram, J. (2011) How and why do student teachers use ICT?, *Journal of Computer Assisted Learning*, 27 (3): 191–203.

Hardy, I. (2015) Data, numbers and accountability: the complexity, nature and effects of data use in schools, *British Journal of Education Studies*, 63 (4): 467–486.

Harford, S. (2017) Myth-busting – one of the keys to reducing workload, *The Teacher*, January/February.

Hargreaves, A. and Shirley, D. (2012) *The Global Fourth Way: The Quest for Educational Excellence*. Thousand Oaks, CA: Corwin.

Harlen, W. (2005) Teachers' summative practices and assessment for learning – tensions and synergies, *Curriculum Journal*, 16 (2): 207–223.

Harris, A. and Chapman, C. (2002) Leadership in schools facing challenging circumstances, *Management in Education*, 16 (1): 10–13.

Hartshorne, M. (2011) *Speech, Language and Communication in Secondary Aged Pupils*. I CAN Talk Series, Issue #10. London: I CAN.

Hattie, J. (2012) *Visible Learning for Teachers: Maximizing Impact on Learning*. New York: Routledge.

Hattie, J. and Timperley, H. (2007) The power of feedback, *Review of Educational Research*, 77 (1): 81–112.

Haydn, T. (2007) *Managing Pupil Behaviour: Key Issues in Teaching and Learning*. London: Routledge.

Haydon, G. (1997) *Teaching About Values: A New Approach*. London: Cassell.

Hayes, S.G. and Clay, J. (2007) *Progression from Key Stage 2 to 4: Understanding the context and nature of performance and underperformance between the ages 11–16*, Paper presented at the British Educational Research Association Annual Conference, Institute of Education, University of London, 5–8 September. Available at: http://www.leeds.ac.uk/educol/documents/167840.htm [accessed 4 April 2017].

Hayes, S.G., Shaw, H., McGrath, G. and Bonel, F. (2009) *Using RAISEonline as a research tool to analyse the link between attainment, social class and ethnicity*, Paper presented at the British Educational Research Association Annual Conference, University of Manchester, 2–5 September. Available at: http://www.leeds.ac.uk/educol/documents/184218.pdf [accessed 13 April 2017].

Hertberg-Davis, H. (2009) Myth 7: Differentiation in the regular classroom is equivalent to gifted programs and is sufficient – classroom teachers have the time, the skill, and the will to differentiate adequately, *Gifted Child Quarterly*, 53 (4), 251–253.

Hilgard, E. (1995) *Theories of Learning*. New York: Appleton.

Hillman, N. and Robinson, N. (2016) *Boys to Men: The underachievement of young men in higher education – and how to start tackling it*, HEPI Report #84. Oxford: Higher Education Policy Institute.

Hirsch, E.D. (1996) *The Schools We Need and Why We Don't Have Them*. New York: Anchor Books.

HM Government (2017) *Building Our Industrial Strategy (Green Paper)*, January 2017. London: HM Government. Available at: https://www.gov.uk/government/consultations/building-our-industrial-strategy [accessed April 2017].

Hodgson, A. and Spours, K. (2013) Tackling the crisis facing young people: building 'high opportunity progression eco-systems', *Oxford Review of Education*, 39 (2): 211–228.

Hodgson, A. and Spours, K. (2014) Middle attainers and 14–19 progression in England: half-served by New Labour and now overlooked by the Coalition?, *British Educational Research Journal*, 40 (3): 467–482.

Hoggart, R. (1998) Critical literacy and creative reading, in B. Cox (ed.) *Literacy is Not Enough*. Manchester: Manchester University Press.

Holland Junior School (2018) *What is mastery?* Available at: http://www.holland.surrey.sch.uk/_files/8F80E3ED73182A92720D93E3A5BE54E9.pdf [accessed 3 August 2018].

Honey, P. (1988) *Improving Your People Skills*. London: Institute of Personnel Management.

Honey, P. and Mumford, A. (1989) *Manual of Learning Styles*. Maidenhead: Honey Publications.

House of Commons Education Committee (2015) *Life Lessons: PSHE and SRE in Schools*, HC 145. London: TSO. Available at: https://publications.parliament.uk/pa/cm201415/cmselect/cmeduc/145/145.pdf.

House of Commons Education and Health Committees (2017) *Children and Young People's Mental Health: The Role of Education*, HC 849. London: TSO. Available at: https://publications.parliament.uk/pa/cm201617/cmselect/cmhealth/849/849.pdf.

House of Commons Education and Skills Committees (2005) *Every Child Matters* (Ninth Report of Session 2004–5). London: TSO.

Howe, M.J.A. (1997) *IQ in Question: The Truth about Intelligence*. London: Sage.

Huddleston, P. (2002) Uncertain destinies: student recruitment and retention on GVVQ intermediate programmes, *SKOPE Research Paper*, 37 (Winter).

Independent Teacher Workload Review Group (2016) *Eliminating Unnecessary Workload around Planning and Teaching Resources*. London: DfE.

Institute of Engineering and Technology (IET) (2016) *Parents, retailers and search engines urged to 're-think the pink' next Christmas*, Press release, 6 December. Available at: https://www.theiet.org/policy/media/press-releases/20161206.cfm [accessed 10 July 2018].

Ishikawa, T. and Kastens, K.A. (2005) Why some students have trouble with maps and other spatial representations, *Journal of Geoscience Education*, 53 (2): 184–197.

Jerrim, J. and Choi, Á. (2014) The mathematics skills of school children: how does England compare to the high-performing East Asian jurisdictions?, *Journal of Education Policy*, 29 (3): 349–376.

Joel, D., Berman, Z., Tavor, I., Wexler, N., Gaber, O., Stein, Y. *et al.* (2015) Sex beyond the genitalia: the human brain mosaic, *Proceedings of the National Academy of Sciences USA*, 112 (50): 15468–15473.

Joint Council for Qualifications (JCQ) (2017) *GCSE (Full Course) Results Summer 2017*. Available at: https://www.jcq.org.uk/examination-results/gcses/2017/gcse-full-course-results-summer-2017/gcse-full-course-results-summer-2017 [accessed 29 August 2017].

Jones, J. (2005) *Management Skills in Schools*. London: Paul Chapman.

Jones, S. and Myhill, D. (2004) 'Troublesome boys' and 'compliant girls': gender identity and perceptions of achievement and underachievement, *British Journal of Sociology of Education*, 25 (5): 547–561.

Karaali, G., Villafane Hernandez, E.H. and Taylor, J.A. (2016) What's in a name? A critical review of definitions of quantitative literacy, numeracy, and quantitative reasoning, *Numeracy*, 9 (1): Art. 2.

Kaufman, D. and Moss, D. (2010) A new look at pre-service teachers' conceptions of classroom management and organization: uncovering complexity and dissonance, *The Teacher Educator*, 45 (2): 118–136.

Keddie, A. (2016) Children of the market: performativity, neoliberal responsibilisation and the construction of student identities, *Oxford Review of Education*, 42 (1): 108–122.

Kenner, C., Ruby, M., Jessel, J., Gregory, E. and Arju, T. (2007) Intergenerational learning between children and grandparents in East London, *Journal of Early Childhood Research*, 5 (3): 219–243.

Kerr, K. and West, M. (eds.) (2010) *Social Inequality: Can Schools Narrow the Gap?*, Insights #2 Publication. London: BERA.

Kirschner, P., Sweller, J. and Clark, R. (2006) Why minimal guidance during instruction does not work: an analysis of the failure of constructivist, discovery, problem-based, experiential, and inquiry-based teaching, *Educational Psychologist*, 41 (2): 75–86.

Klein, P.D. (1997) Multiplying the problems of intelligence by eight: a critique of Gardner's theory, *Canadian Journal of Education*, 22 (4): 377–394.

Klishis, M.J., Hursh, D.C. and Klishis, L.A. (1980) Individualized spelling: an application and evaluation of PSI in the elementary school, *Journal of Personalized Instruction*, 4 (3): 148–156.

Kluger, A.N. and DeNisi, A. (1996) Feedback interventions: towards the understanding of a double-edged sword, *Current Directions in Psychological Science*, 7 (3): 67–72.

Kress, G. (2003) *Literacy in the New Media Age*. New York: Routledge.

Kuczera, M., Field, S. and Windisch, H.C. (2016) *Building Skills for All: A Review of England*. Paris: OECD Publishing.

Kulik, J.A., Jaksa, P. and Kulik, C.-I.C. (1978) Research on component features of Keller's Personalized System of Instruction, *Journal of Personalized Instruction*, 3 (1): 2–14.

Lang, P. (1999) Counselling, counselling skills and encouraging pupils to talk: clarifying and addressing confusion, *British Journal of Guidance and Counselling*, 27 (1): 23–33.

Lang, P. (2007) Pastoral care and the role of the tutor, in V. Brooks, I. Abbott and L. Bills (eds.) *Preparing to Teach in Secondary Schools*. Maidenhead: Open University Press.

Lea, M.R. and Street, B.V. (2006) The 'academic literacies' model: theory and applications, *Theory into Practice*, 45 (4): 368–377.

Leask, M. and Pachler, N. (2014) *Learning to Teach Using ICT in the Secondary School: A Companion to School Experience*. London: Routledge.

Lessof, C., Ross, A., Brind, R., Bell, E. and Newton, S. (2016) *Longitudinal Study of Young People in England Cohort 2: Health and Wellbeing at Wave 2*, Research report. London: DfE. Available at: https://assets.publishing.service.gov.uk/government/uploads/system/uploads/attachment_data/file/599871/LSYPE2_w2-research_report.pdf.

Leung, C. (2016) English as an additional language – a genealogy of language-in-education policies and reflections on research trajectories, *Language and Education*, 30 (2): 158–174.

Lewis, M. and Wray, D. (1998) *Writing Across the Curriculum*. Reading: Reading Language Information Centre.

Lewis, M. and Wray, D. (eds.) (2000) *Literacy in the Secondary School*. London: David Fulton.

Lingard, B. (2010) Policy borrowing, policy learning: testing times in Australian schooling, *Critical Studies in Education*, 51 (2): 129–147.

Local Government Act (1966) (c. 42). London: HMSO. Available at: https://www.legislation.gov.uk/ukpga/1966/42/contents [accessed 2 July 2017].

Local Government (Amendment) Act (1993) (c. 27). London: HMSO. Available at: http://www.legislation.gov.uk/ukpga/1993/27/pdfs/ukpga_19930027_en.pdf [accessed 15 August 2017].

Lodge, C. (2002) Tutors talking, *Pastoral Care in Education*, 20 (4): 35–37.

Louden, M.R. (2010) The conscience clause in religious education and collective worship: conscientious objection or curriculum choice?, *British Journal of Religious Education*, 26 (3): 273–284.

Lyng, S. (2009) Is there more to 'antischoolishness' than masculinity? On multiple student styles, gender, and educational self-exclusion in secondary school, *Men and Masculinities*, 11 (4): 462–487.

Lynn, R. and Mikk, J. (2009) Sex differences in reading achievement, *Trames: A Journal of the Humanities and Social Sciences*, 13 (1): 1–12.

Lytra, V., Volk, D. and Gregory, E. (eds.) (2016) *Navigating Languages, Literacies and Identities: Religion in Young Lives*. Abingdon: Routledge.

Macdonald, A. (2009) *Independent Review of the Proposal to Make Personal, Social, Health and Economic Education Statutory*. London: DCSF.

Macey, E. (2013) *Employers' Views on Youth Literacy and Employability*. London: National Literacy Trust.

Macrae, S. and Quintrell, M. (2001) Managing effective classrooms, in J. Dillon and M. Maguire (eds.) *Becoming a Teacher: Issues in Secondary Teaching*. Buckingham: Open University Press.

Male, T. and Burden, K. (2014) Access denied? Twenty-first-century technology in schools, *Technology, Pedagogy and Education*, 23 (4): 423–437.

Mallows, D. (2012) *Innovations in English Language Teaching for Migrants and Refugees*. London: British Council.

Marden, S., Thomas, P.W., Sheppard, Z.A., Knott, J., Lueddeke, J. and Kerr, D. (2012) Poor numeracy skills are associated with glycaemic control in Type 1 diabetes, *Diabetic Medicine*, 29 (5): 662–669.

Marland, M. (1974) *Pastoral Care*. London: Heinemann.

Marland, M. (2002) From 'form teacher' to 'tutor': the development from the fifties to the seventies, *Pastoral Care in Education*, 20 (4): 3–11.

Marland, M. and Rogers, R. (1997) *Art of the Tutor: Developing your Role in the Secondary School*. London: David Fulton.

Marland, M. and Rogers, R. (2004) *How to be a Successful Form Tutor*. London: Continuum.

Marzano, R.J. (2009) Setting the record straight on 'high yield' strategies, *Phi Delta Kappan*, 91 (1): 30–37.

McGuinness, C. (1998) *From Thinking Skills to Thinking Classrooms*. London: DfEE.

McIntyre, D., Pedder, D. and Rudduck, J. (2005) Pupil voice: comfortable and uncomfortable learnings for teachers, *Research Papers in Education*, 20 (2): 149–168.

McNally, J., I'Anson, J., Whewell, C. and Wilson, G. (2005) 'They think swearing is OK': first lessons in behaviour management, *Journal of Education for Teaching*, 31 (3): 169–185.

McWilliam, N. (1998) *What's in a Word?* London: Trentham Books.

Middlewood, D. and Abbott, I. (2015) *Improving Professional Learning through In-House Inquiry*. London: Bloomsbury.

Middlewood, D. and Abbott, I. (2017) *Managing Staff for Improved Performance*. London: Bloomsbury.

Middlewood, D. and Abbott, I. (2018) *Collaborative School Leadership: Managing a Group of Schools*. London: Bloomsbury.

Midgley, P., Beskeen, L., Egginton, N., Davies, E., Pascoe, L., Badley, R. *et al.* (1999) *Promoting Students' Spiritual, Moral, Social and Cultural Development through Specific Teaching and Learning Strategies across the Curriculum*. London: Teacher Training Agency.

Ministry of Education (1963) *English for Immigrants*. London: HMSO.

Mishra, P. and Koehler, M.J. (2006) Technological pedagogical content knowledge: a framework for teacher knowledge, *Teachers College Record*, 108 (6): 1017–1054.

Molfese, V.J., Molfese, P.J., Molfese, D.L., Rudasill, K.M., Armstrong, A. and Starkey, G. (2010) Executive function skill of 6 to 8 year olds: brain and behavioral evidence and implications for school achievement, *Contemporary Educational Psychology*, 35 (2): 116–125.

Moll, L. (1992) Literacy research in community and classrooms: a sociocultural approach, in R. Beach, J. Green, M. Kamil and T. Shanahan (eds.) *Multidisciplinary Perspectives on Literacy Research*. Urbana, IL: National Council of Teachers of English.

Moll, L.C., Amanti, C., Neff, D. and Gonzalez, N. (1992) Funds of knowledge for teaching: using a qualitative approach to connect homes and classrooms, *Theory into Practice*, 31 (2): 132–141.

Morgan, H. (1996) An analysis of Gardner's theory of multiple intelligences, *Roeper Review*, 18 (4): 263–269.

Morley, L. (2000) The micropolitics of gender in a learning society, *Higher Education in Europe*, 25 (2): 229–235.

Mortimore, P. (2013) *Education Under Siege*. Bristol: Policy Press.

Moss, G. and Washbrook, L. (2016) *Understanding the Gender Gap in Literacy and Language Development*, Bristol Working Papers in Education #01/2016. Available at: https://www.bristol.ac.uk/

media-library/sites/education/documents/bristol-working-papers-in-education/Understanding%20
the%20Gender%20Gap%20working%20paper.pdf [accessed 3 June 2018].

Muijs, R.D. (1997) *Self, School and Media: A Longitudinal Study of Media Use, Self-Concept, School Achievement and Peer Relations among Primary School Children.* Leuven: Catholic University of Leuven.

Muijs, R.D. (2004) *Doing Quantitative Research in Education.* London: Sage.

Muijs, D. and Reynolds, D. (2003) Student background and teacher effects on achievement and attainment in mathematics, *Educational Review and Evaluation,* 9 (1): 289–313.

Muijs, D. and Reynolds, D. (2010) *Effective Teaching: Evidence and Practice.* London: Sage.

Murakami, C. (2008) 'Everybody is just fumbling along': an investigation of views regarding EAL training and support provisions in a rural area, *Language and Education,* 22 (4): 265–282.

Myhill, D. and Jones, S. (2006) 'She doesn't shout at no girls': pupils' perceptions of gender equity in the classroom, *Cambridge Journal of Education,* 36 (1): 99–113.

Myhill, D.A., Jones, S. and Hopper, R. (2005) *Talking, Listening, Learning: Effective Talk in the Primary Classroom.* Maidenhead: Open University Press.

Nasen (2015) *The SEND Code of Practice: 0–25 Years.* Tamworth: Nasen. Available at: http://www. nasen.org.uk/utilities/download.29628CBA-F6C6-4F3E-87EE43D23B1F757E.html [accessed 14 June 2018].

National Advisory Committee on Creative and Cultural Education (NACCCE) (1999) *All Our Futures: Creativity, Culture and Education.* London: DfEE.

National Institute of Adult Continuing Education (NIACE) (2011) *Numeracy Counts. Final Report of the NIACE Committee on Inquiry on Adult Numeracy Learning.* Leicester: NIACE. Available at: http://www.learningandwork.org.uk.gridhosted.co.uk/wp-content/uploads/2017/01/Numeracy-Counts.pdf [accessed 14 October 2017].

National Literacy Forum (2015) *Vision for Literacy 2025.* London: National Literacy Trust.

National Numeracy (2015) *Numeracy for Health.* Lewes: National Numeracy. Available at: https://www. nationalnumeracy.org.uk/sites/default/files/numeracy_for_health_full.pdf [accessed April 2017].

National Resource Centre for Supplementary Education (NRCSE) (2017) *Supplementary Education.* London: NRCSE. Available at: https://www.supplementaryeducation.org.uk/supplementary-education-the-nrc/ [last accessed 31 August 2017].

Neill, S. and Caswell, C. (1993) *Body Language for Competent Teachers.* London: Routledge.

Nelson, J. and O'Beirne, C. (2014) *Using Evidence in the Classroom: What Works and Why?* Slough: NFER.

Newton, O. (2017) *Our Plan for 14–19 Education: Coherent, Unified, Holistic.* London: Edge Foundation.

Norman, K. (ed.) (1992) *Thinking Voices: The Work of the National Oracy Project.* London: Hodder & Stoughton.

Oates, T. (2010) *Could Do Better: Using International Comparisons to Refine the National Curriculum in England.* Cambridge: Cambridge Assessment.

Oates, T. (2014) The 'qualifications sledgehammer': why assessment-led reform has dominated the education landscape, in G.H. Sahlgren (ed.) *Tests Worth Teaching to Incentivising Quality in Qualifications and Accountability.* Wimbledon: The Centre for Market Reform of Education.

O'Donohue, W. and Ferguson, K.E. (2001) *The Psychology of B.F. Skinner.* Thousand Oaks, CA: Sage.

OECD (2012) *Literacy, Numeracy and Problem Solving in Technology-rich Environments: Framework for the OECD Survey of Adult Skills.* Paris: OECD Publishing. Available at: http://www.oecd. org/skills/piaac/PIAAC%20Framework%202012–%20Revised%2028oct2013_ebook.pdf [accessed 7 July 2017].

OECD (2013) *PISA 2012 Assessment and Analytical Framework: Mathematics, Reading, Science, Problem Solving and Financial Literacy.* Paris: OECD Publishing. Available at: https://www.oecd. org/pisa/pisaproducts/PISA%202012%20framework%20e-book_final.pdf [accessed 7 July 2017].

OECD (2015) *The ABC of Gender Equality in Education: Aptitude, Behaviour, Confidence.* Paris: OECD Publishing. Available at: https://www.oecd.org/pisa/keyfindings/pisa-2012-results-gender-eng.pdf [accessed 3 March 2018].

OECD (2016) *PISA 2015 Results (Volume I): Excellence and Equity in Education*. Paris: OECD Publishing. Available at: http://www.oecd.org/publications/pisa-2015-results-volume-i-9789264266490-en.htm [accessed 3 March 2018].

Office for Standards in Education (Ofsted) (1994) *Spiritual, Moral, Social and Cultural Education: A Discussion Paper*. London: Ofsted.

Office for Standards in Education (Ofsted) (2002) *Inspecting Spiritual, Moral, Social and Cultural Education: Guidance for Inspectors*. London: Ofsted.

Office for Standards in Education (Ofsted) (2003) *Boys' Achievement in Secondary Schools*. London: HMSO.

Office for Standards in Education (Ofsted) (2004) *Promoting and Evaluating Pupils' Spiritual, Moral, Social and Cultural Development*. London: Ofsted.

Office for Standards in Education (Ofsted) (2005) *The Secondary National Strategy: An Evaluation of the Fifth Year*, HMI 2612. London: Ofsted. Available at: http://dera.ioe.ac.uk/5649/1/The%20Secondary%20National%20Strategy_An%20evaluation%20of%20the%20fifth%20year%20%28PDF%20format%29.pdf.

Office for Standards in Education (Ofsted) (2010) *Personal, Social, Health and Economic Education in Schools*. London: Ofsted. Available at: http://dera.ioe.ac.uk/id/eprint/1129.

Office for Standards in Education (Ofsted) (2011) *Removing Barriers to Literacy*. London: Ofsted. Available at: https://www.gov.uk/government/publications/removing-barriers-to-literacy [accessed 22 April 2017].

Office for Standards in Education (Ofsted) (2013a) *Not Yet Good Enough: Personal, Social, Health and Economic Education in Schools*. London: Ofsted. Available at: https://assets.publishing.service.gov.uk/government/uploads/system/uploads/attachment_data/file/413178/Not_yet_good_enough_personal__social__health_and_economic_education_in_schools.pdf [accessed 28 May 2017].

Office for Standards in Education (Ofsted) (2013b) *Improving Literacy in Secondary Schools: A Shared Responsibility (Report Summary)*. London: Ofsted. Available at: https://www.gov.uk/government/publications/improving-literacy-in-secondary-schools-a-shared-responsibility [accessed 30 June 2017].

Office for Standards in Education (Ofsted) (2015) *Common Inspection Framework: Education, Skills and Early Years*. London: Ofsted. Available at: https://www.gov.uk/government/publications/common-inspection-framework-education-skills-and-early-years-from-september-2015 [accessed 3 March 2017].

Office for Standards in Education (Ofsted) (2016) *The Annual Report of Her Majesty's Chief Inspector of Education, Children's Services and Skills 2015/16*. London: Ofsted. Available at: https://www.gov.uk/government/publications/ofsted-annual-report-201516-education-early-years-and-skills [accessed 4 August 2018].

Office for Standards in Education (Ofsted) (2017) *Education of Children with Special Needs in Schools*. London: Ofsted.

Office for Standards in Education (Ofsted) (2018a) *Ofsted Inspections: Myths*, Guidance. London: Ofsted. Available at: https://www.gov.uk/government/publications/school-inspection-handbook-from-september-2015/ofsted-inspections-mythbusting.

Office for Standards in Education (Ofsted) (2018b) *School Inspection Handbook*. London: Ofsted. Available at: https://www.gov.uk/government/publications/school-inspection-handbook-from-september-2015.

Office of Qualifications and Examinations Regulation (Ofqual) (2017) *Qualifications Reform: Resources for Teachers*. Coventry: Ofqual. Available at: https://www.gov.uk/government/publications/qualifications-reform-resources-for-teachers [accessed 31 July 2018].

Owens, J.A., Belon, K. and Moss, P. (2010) Impact of delaying school start time on adolescent sleep, mood, and behavior, *Archives of Pediatrics and Adolescent Medicine*, 164 (7): 608–614.

Parameshwaran, M. and Thomson, D. (2015) The impact of accountability reforms on the Key Stage 4 curriculum: how have changes to school and college Performance Tables affected pupil access to qualifications and subjects in secondary schools in England?, *London Review of Education*, 13 (2): 157–173.

Partnerships for Schools (2007) *Partnerships for Schools*. Available online at: www.p4s.org.uk/ [accessed 6 May 2017].

Pearcy, M. (2016) A Wordle to the wise: using 'word clouds' meaningfully in the classroom, *Social Studies Research and Practice*, 11 (2): 96–110.

Peters, E. (2008) Numeracy and the perception and communication of risk, *Annals of the New York Academy of Sciences*, 1128 (1): 1–7.

Peterson, A., Lexmond, J., Hallgarted, J. and Kerr, D. (2014) *Schools with Soul: A New Approach to Spiritual, Moral, Social and Cultural Development*. London: RSA Action and Research Centre. Available at: https://www.thersa.org/globalassets/pdfs/reports/schools-with-soul-report.pdf [accessed 13 August 2017].

Piaget, J. (2001) *The Child's Conception of Physical Causality*. New Brunswick, NJ: Transaction Publishers.

Plant, K. (1975) *Managing Change and Making it Stick*. London: Fontana.

Pople, L., Rees, G., Main, G. and Bradshaw, J. (2015) *The Good Childhood Report 2015*. London: The Children's Society.

Porter, L. (2000) *Behaviour in Schools: Theory and Practice for Teachers*. Buckingham: Open University Press.

Power, S. (1991) 'Pastoral care' as curriculum discourse: a study in the reformation of 'academic' schooling, *International Studies in Sociology of Education*, 1 (1/2): 193–208.

Pring, R. (1984) Personal and social education in the primary school, in P. Lang (ed.) *Thinking about Personal and Social Education in the Primary School*. Oxford: Blackwell.

Pro Bono Economics (2014) *Cost of Outcomes Associated with Low Levels of Adult Numeracy in the UK*. London: Pro Bono Economics. Available at: http://www.probonoeconomics.com/resources/ high-cost-low-adult-numeracy [accessed April 2017].

PSHE Association (2017) *PSHE Education Programmes of Study: Key Stages 1–5*. London: PSHE Association. Available at: https://www.pshe-association.org.uk/curriculum-and-resources/resources/ programme-study-pshe-education-key-stages-1–5.

Purdy, N. (2013) *Pastoral Care 11–16: A Critical Introduction*. London: Bloomsbury.

Qualifications and Curriculum Authority (QCA) (1999) *Qualifications 16–19: A Guide to the Changes Resulting from the Qualifying for Success Consultation*. London: QCA.

Race Relations Act (1976) (c. 74). London: HMSO. Available at: http://www.legislation.gov.uk/ ukpga/1976/74/pdfs/ukpga_19760074_en.pdf [accessed 3 April 2017].

Raffe, D. and Spours, K. (eds.) (2007) *Policy Making and Policy Learning in 14–19 Education*, Bedford Way Papers. London: Institute of Education.

Reiss, M. and White, J. (2013) *An Aims-based Curriculum: The Significance of Human Flourishing for Schools*, Bedford Way Papers. London: IOE Press.

Reyna, V.F., Nelson, W.L., Han, P.K. and Dieckmann, N.F. (2009) How numeracy influences risk comprehension and medical decision making, *Psychological Bulletin*, 135 (6): 943–973.

Rivers, I. (2000) Social exclusion, absenteeism and sexual minority youth, *Support for Learning*, 15 (1): 13–18.

Rodd, J. (2002) *Learning to Learn in Schools*. Crediton: Campaign for Learning.

Roehrig, A.D., Turner, J.E., Grove, C.M., Schneider, N. and Liu, Z. (2009) Degree of alignment between beginning teachers' practices and beliefs about effective classroom practices, *The Teacher Educator*, 44: 164–187.

Roffey, S. (2011) *The New Teacher's Survival Guide to Behaviour*, 2nd edn. London: Sage.

Rogers, B. (2015) *Classroom Behaviour: A Practical Guide to Effective Teaching, Behaviour Management and Colleague Support*, 4th edn. London: Paul Chapman.

Rosas, C. and West, M. (2009) Teachers' beliefs about classroom management: pre-service and in-service teachers' beliefs about classroom management, *International Journal of Applied Educational Studies*, 5 (1): 55–61.

Rosenblatt, M. (2002) Effective tutoring and school improvement, *Pastoral Care in Education*, 20 (4): 21–26.

Rosenshine, B. (2009) Systematic instruction, in T.L. Good (ed.), *21st Century Education: A Reference Handbook*, Vol. I. Thousand Oaks, CA: Sage.

Rowsell, J. and Pahl, K. (2007) Sedimented identities in texts: instances of practice, *Reading Research Quarterly*, 42 (3): 388–404.

Sadler, D.R. (1989) Formative assessment and the design of instructional systems, *Instructional Science*, 18 (2): 119–144.

Sage, R. (2006) Communicating with students who have learning and behaviour difficulties: a continuing professional development programme, *Emotional and Behavioural Difficulties*, 10 (4): 281–297.

Sammons, P., Sylva, K., Melhuish, E.C., Siraj, I., Taggart, B., Toth, K. *et al.* (2014) *Influences on Students' GCSE Attainment and Progress at Age 16: Effective Pre-school, Primary and Secondary Education Project (EPPSE)*. London: DfE. Available at: http://dera.ioe.ac.uk/20875/1/RR352_-_Influences_on_Students_GCSE_Attainment_and_Progress_at_Age_16.pdf.

Sampson, G. (1921) *English for the English*. Cambridge: Cambridge University Press.

Schofield, T. (2007) Student and tutor perceptions of the role of the tutor in a sixth form college, *Pastoral Care in Education*, 25 (1): 26–32.

Schools Curriculum and Assessment Authority (SCAA) (1995) *Spiritual and Moral Development*. London: SCAA.

Schools Curriculum and Assessment Authority (SCAA) (1997) *Consultation on Values in Education and the Community*. London: SCAA.

Scriven, M. (1967) The methodology of evaluation, in R.W. Tyler, R.M. Gagne and M. Scriven (eds.) *Perspectives of Curriculum Evaluation*. AERA Monograph Series on Evaluation Vol. 1. Washington, DC: American Educational Research Association.

Sebba, J., Brown, N., Steward, S., Galton, M. and James, M. (2007) *An Investigation of Personalised Learning Approaches Used by Schools*. Nottingham: DfES Publications.

Selwyn, N. (2017) *Education and Technology: Key Issues and Debates*, 2nd edn. London: Bloomsbury.

Sharples, R. (2017) Local practice, translocal students: conflicting identities in the multilingual classroom, *Language and Education*, 31 (2): 169–183.

Shaw, M. (2003) Brighouse blessing for rebellious crisp-eaters, *Times Educational Supplement*, 21 February.

Skinner, B.F. (1974) *About Behaviorism*. New York: Random House.

Slavin, R.E. (1987) Mastery learning reconsidered, *Review of Educational Research*, 57 (2): 175–213.

Smyth, J. (2006) Educational leadership that fosters student voice, *International Journal of Leadership in Education*, 9 (4): 279–284.

Sobel, D. (2018) *Narrowing the Attainment Gap*. London: Bloomsbury.

Sousa, D. (1998) Brain research can help principals reform secondary schools, *NASSP Bulletin*, 82 (598): 21–28.

Spielman, A. (2017) Keynote speech delivered to the Association of School and College Leaders (ASCL) Annual Conference, Birmingham, 10–11 March.

Standards and Testing Agency (STA) (2015) *2015 Key Stage 2 Assessment and Reporting Arrangements (ARA)*. London: STA.

Standards and Testing Agency (STA) (2016) *National Curriculum Assessments at Key Stage 2 in England, 2016 (Interim)*. London: DfE. Available at: https://assets.publishing.service.gov.uk/government/uploads/system/uploads/attachment_data/file/534573/SFR30_2016_text.pdf.

Storr, K. (2015) Science explains why women are faster to mature than men, *Mic*, 24 February.

Strand, S. (2006) Comparing the predictive ability of reasoning tests and national end of Key Stage 2 tests: which tests are the 'best'?, *British Educational Research Journal*, 32 (2): 209–225.

Strand, S. (2015) *Ethnicity, Deprivation and Educational Achievement at Age 16 in England: Trends Over Time*. London: DfE.

Strand, S., Malmberg, L. and Hall, J. (2015) *English as an Additional Language (EAL) and Educational Achievement in England: An Analysis of the National Pupil Database*. Oxford: University of Oxford.

Subramaniam, K. (2010) Integrating writing frames into inquiry-based instruction, *Science Educator*, 19 (2): 31–34.

Sukhanandan, L., Lee, B. and Kelleher, S. (2000) *An Investigation into Gender Differences in Achievement*. Slough: NFER.

Sutton Trust (2013) *Effective Strategies for Implementing Pupil Premium in Schools*. Birmingham: Sutton Trust.

Sutton Trust (2014) *How Schools Use Pupil Premium*. Birmingham: Sutton Trust.

Sylva, K., Melhuish, E.C., Sammons, P., Siraj, I. and Taggart, B. (2004) *The Effective Provision of Pre-School Education (EPPE) Project: Technical Paper 12 – The Final Report: Effective Pre-School Education*. London: DfES.

Sylva, K., Melhuish, E.C., Sammons, P., Siraj, I. and Taggart, B. (2008) *Final Report from the Primary Phase: Pre-school, School and Family Influences on Children's Development during Key Stage 2 (7–11)*, Research Report #61. Nottingham: DCSF.

Symonds, J.E. and Hagall, A. (2011) Adolescents and the organization of their school time: a review of changes over recent decades in England, *Educational Review*, 63 (3): 291–312.

Tanner, D. (2013) Race to the top and leave the children behind, *Journal of Curriculum Studies*, 45 (1): 4–15.

Teach First (2017) *Our Work and Its Impact*. London: Teach First. Available at: https://www.teachfirst.org.uk/sites/default/files/2017-09/teach_first_impact_report.pdf [accessed 3 June 2018].

TES (2009) *TES AfL Toolkit*. Available at: https://www.tes.com/teaching-resource/assessment-for-learning-toolkit-6020165 [accessed 11 April 2017; last updated February 2018].

Thomson, P. (2009) Consulting secondary pupils about their learning, *Oxford Review of Education*, 32 (6): 671–687.

Tomlinson, C.A. (2014) *The Differentiated Classroom: Responding to the Needs of All Learners*, 2nd edn. Alexandria, VA: ASCD.

Tomlinson, S. (2008) *Race and Education: Policy and Politics in Britain*. Maidenhead: Open University Press.

Training and Development Agency for Schools (TDA) (2009) *Annual Report 2009*. London: TDA.

Tyler, K. and Jones, B.D. (2002) Teachers' responses to the ecosystemic approach to changing chronic problem behaviour in schools, *Pastoral Care in Education*, 20 (2): 30–39.

Unsworth, L. (2001) *Teaching Multiliteracies Across the Curriculum*. Maidenhead: Open University Press.

UTC (2017) *A Guide to University Technical Colleges*. London: Baker Dearing Educational Trust.

Vacher, H. (2014) Looking at the multiple meanings of numeracy, quantitative literacy, and quantitative reasoning, *Numeracy*, 7 (2): Art. 1.

Vantieghem, W., Vermeersch, H. and Van Houtte, M. (2014) Why 'gender' disappeared from the gender gap: (re-)introducing gender identity theory to educational gender gap research, *Social Psychology of Education*, 17 (3): 357–381.

Visser, B.A., Ashton, M.C. and Vernon, P.A. (2006) Beyond g: putting multiple intelligences theory to the test, *Intelligence*, 34 (4): 487–502.

Vygotsky, L.S. (1978) *Mind and Society: The Development of Higher Psychological Processes* (edited by M. Cole, V. John-Steiner, S. Scribner and E. Souberman). Cambridge, MA: Harvard University Press.

Vygotsky, L.S. (1986) *Thought and Language*. Cambridge, MA: MIT Press.

Warwick Commission (2016) *Enriching Britain: Culture, Creativity and Growth. The 2015 Report of the Warwick Commission on the Future of Cultural Value*. Coventry: University of Warwick.

Waterhouse, L. (2006) Multiple intelligences, the Mozart effect, and emotional intelligence: a critical review, *Educational Psychologist*, 41 (4): 207–225.

Watkins, C. and Wagner, P. (2000) *Improving School Behaviour*. London: Paul Chapman.

Watkins, C., Carnell, E. and Lodge, C. (2007) *Effective Learning in Classrooms*. London: Paul Chapman.

Wells, G. (1999) *Dialogic Inquiry: Towards a Sociocultural Practice and Theory of Education*. Cambridge: Cambridge University Press.

Wertsch, J. and Tulviste, P. (1992) L.S. Vygotsky and contemporary developmental psychology, *Developmental Psychology*, 28 (4): 548–557.

White, J. (1998) *Do Howard Gardner's Multiple Intelligences Add Up?* London: Institute of Education.

Whitty, G. and Wisby, J. (2007) Whose voice? An exploration of the current policy interest in pupil involvement in school decision-making, *International Studies in Sociology of Education*, 17 (3): 303–319.

Wiggins, G. and McTighe, J. (2005) *Understanding by Design*. Alexandria, VA: Association for Supervision and Curriculum Development.

Wiliam, D. (2011) *Embedded Formative Assessment*. Bloomington, IN: Solution Tree Press.

Wiliam, D. (2016) *Leadership for Teacher Learning*. West Palm Beach, FL: Learning Sciences International.

Willingham, D. (2004) Reframing the mind, *Education Next*, 4 (3).

Willingham, D. (2008) When and how neuroscience applies to education, *Phi Delta Kappan*, 89 (6): 421–423.

Wintersgill, B. (2002) *Spiritual development – what do teenagers think it is?* Unpublished MA Field Study, University of Warwick.

Wolfe, S. and Alexander, R.J. (2008) *Argumentation and Dialogic Teaching: Alternative Pedagogies for a Changing World*. London: Futurelab.

Wortley, A. and Harrison, J. (2008) Pastoral care and tutorial roles, in S. Dymoke and J. Harrison (eds.) *Reflective Teaching and Learning: A Guide to Professional Issues for Beginning Secondary Teachers*. London: Sage.

Young, M. (2008) *Bringing Knowledge Back In: From Social Constructivism to Social Realism in the Sociology of Education*. London: Routledge.

Young, M. and Lambert, D. (with Roberts, C. and Roberts, M.) (2014) *Knowledge and the Future School: Curriculum and Social Justice*. London: Bloomsbury.

Younger, M. and Warrington, M. (2003) *Raising Boys' Achievement: Interim Report*. London: DfES.

Younger, M. and Warrington, M. (2005) *Raising Boys' Achievement*, DfES Research Report #RR636. London: HMSO.

Younie, S. and Bradshaw, P. (eds.) (2017) *Debates in Computing and ICT Education*. London: Routledge.

Younie, S. and Leask, M. (2013) *Teaching with Technologies: The Essential Guide*. Maidenhead: Open University Press.

Index